AF889879

CONSTITUTIONAL POLITICAL ECONOMY IN A PUBLIC CHOICE PERSPECTIVE

Constitutional Political Economy in a Public Choice Perspective

Edited by

CHARLES K. ROWLEY

Center for Study of Public Choice, George Mason University

Reprinted from *Public Choice*, Volume 90, Nos. 1–4, 1997

Kluwer Academic Publishers

Dordrecht / Boston / London

A C.I.P. Catalogue record for this book is available from the Library of Congress.

ISBN 0-7923-4497-9

Published by Kluwer Academic Publishers,
P.O. Box 17, 3300 AA Dordrecht, The Netherlands.

Kluwer Academic Publishers incorporates
the publishing programmes of
D. Reidel, Martinus Nijhoff, Dr W. Junk and MTP Press.

Sold and distributed in the U.S.A. and Canada
by Kluwer Academic Publishers,
101 Philip Drive, Norwell, MA 02061, U.S.A.

In all other countries, sold and distributed
by Kluwer Academic Publishers Group,
P.O. Box 322, 3300 AH Dordrecht, The Netherlands.

Printed on acid-free paper

All rights reserved

©1997 Kluwer Academic Publishers
No part of the material protected by this copyright notice may be reproduced or
utilized in any form or by any means, electronic or mechanical,
including photocopying, recording or by any information storage and retrieval system,
without written permission from the copyright owner.

CONTENTS

Public Choice **90:** 1–10, 1997.
© 1997 *Kluwer Academic Publishers.*

Introduction: The relevance of public choice for constitutional political economy

CHARLES K. ROWLEY
Department of Economics, George Mason University, Fairfax, VA 22030-4444, U.S.A.

Constitutional political economy is a research program that directs inquiry to the working properties of rules and institutions within which individuals interact and to the processes through which these rules and institutions are chosen or come into being (Buchanan 1990: 1). As such, it has both normative and positive connotations, although arguably the normative emphasis has tended to dominate the early contributions of this relatively young program (Voigt, 1996), which developed initially as an important extension of Paretian welfare economics to determine the logical foundations of constitutional democracy (Buchanan and Tullock, 1962).

The distinction between constitutional political economy and public choice is clearly evident in the two seminal texts that made the case for analyzing political markets from the perspective of rational choice theory. Anthony Downs, in *The Economic Theory of Democracy* (1957), focussed attention almost exclusively on a positive analysis of the behavior of legislatures modelled on the British parliamentary system, which allocates supreme authority to parliament and imposes minimal constraints on that authority. By investing political markets with the self-seeking impulses central to rational choice theory. Downs was able to define a testable theory, rich in insight, which has formed the basis for a vast, empirical literature which has come to dominate the public choice research program. It may not be strictly true that 'it is all in Downs' but surely a great deal of the public choice literature links to ideas that germinated from his book.

James M. Buchanan and Gordon Tullock, in *The Calculus of Consent* (1962), focussed attention explicitly on the nature of the state, viewing collective action as the action of individuals when they choose to accomplish purposes collectively rather than individually and the government as nothing more than the set of processes, the machine, which allows such collective action to take place. Carefully deploying a methodological individualist rational choice theory, the authors relied upon the rule of unanimity to provide a weak ethical criterion for 'betterness' in constitutional design. On all other possible changes in the constraints on human behavior, they noted that nothing could be said without the introduction of much stronger, and more questionable, ethical precepts. An imposed constitution that embodies the coerced agreement of some members of the group was not something examined in *The Calculus of Consent.*

Buchanan and Tullock skillfully developed an economic theory of constitutions based on the principle of unanimity and driven by the veil of uncertainty behind which individuals must negotiate rules that are expected to be long-lived. Once again, this approach has been widely accepted by scholars working in the field of normative constitutional political economy, although competing unanimity viewpoints, notably by John Rawls (1971) and Robert Nozick (1974), also have played a role. Perhaps because of the explicitly normative basis of *The Calculus of Consent*, positive analysis has been slow to develop, although as Voigt (1996), evidences, it is far from non-existent.

Given that constitutional political economy has developed primarily along normative lines and that public choice has developed primarily along positive lines, the reader may ask why such a separation should not be maintained, why indeed such a division should not be reinforced by journal specialization. In my view, such a division would be disastrous for both research programs, potentially as damaging as the separation of classical political economy into political science and economics which allowed both disciplines to unmoor themselves from reality. To understand this judgement it is helpful to reflect on the constitutional premise in its broad rather than in its narrow conception.

A constitution can be thought of as the set of rules that define a community's political institutions (Mueller, 1996: 43). By this definition all communities (assuming that communities are not defined in the state of nature) are endowed with constitutions whether or not they are democracies. Whether or not such constitutions are based on anything approaching the principle of unanimity, whether they are written or unwritten, whether or not they are durable or effective, must depend on the particular circumstances of the community in question.

Certainly, it cannot be assumed that written constitutions necessarily are more durable or more effective than unwritten constitutions (the United Kingdom is a clear counter-example). Nor can it be assumed that constitutions created with design and purpose will achieve what their framers anticipated, however broadly represented the community may have been.

In such circumstances, it is important that public choice should contrive to embrace the study of constitutional political economy in all its forms, positive as well as normative. Political markets function under the shadow of written or unwritten constitutions and, inevitably, are affected by them to a greater or lesser degree.

It is important, therefore, not only to explore the properties of 'good' constitutions (as Mueller, 1996, does in considerable detail) but also to analyze the implications for political market behavior of constitutions that in no sense reflect the unanimity principle but which nevertheless exist and exert an influence upon 'politics as usual'. To omit to do so is to imply that legislatures are supremely sovereign, which they rarely if ever are. To ignore the role of constitutional constraints as a mechanism for preserving good government in a rationally self-seeking legislative environment predictably is to condemn public choice as the most dismal of all dismal sciences and to do so unjustifiably.

This *Special Issue of Public Choice* is dedicated to the unification of constitutional political economy and public choice into a single comprehensive research program focussed on choices between rules, on choices subject to rules that define any community's political institutions and on the manner in which such institutions impact on collective decision-making. Such a unification was signalled in *The Calculus of Consent* (Buchanan and Tullock, 1962) but because its normative message dominated its positive message the marriage was never truly consummated.

Stefan Voigt sets the scene for the volume with his far-reaching, well-researched survey of positive constitutional economics. He cites early work by McCormick and Tollison (1981: 126) as questioning the relevance of normative theory by doubting whether such analysis will make a perceptible difference in the character of prevailing institutions, yet recognizing that the normative approach to constitutional analysis is much better developed in the literature than the positive approach. Voigt's survey of the subsequent literature is less than optimistic that a robust positive theory of constitutions has emerged over the subsequent fifteen years.

Rather, there seem to be diverging approaches that differ not only in their assumptions or their conceptions of constitutions but also in their research agenda. In such circumstances, most of the available knowledge is theoretical rather than empirical, and is often based on plausibility rather than on stringent models. He remains (somewhat) optimistic, however, that a more comprehensive, testable theory can emerge and locates the new institutional economics as a likely source of such a consolidation.

Peter Ordeshook neatly bridges the gap between normative and positive analyses in his thoughtful discussion of constitutions for new democracies. His paper clearly illustrates the interaction between constitutional political economy and public choice even at the constitutional moment: 'The delegates in Philadelphia in 1787 might have shuttered their windows and sprinkled straw on the streets outside Independence Hall to muffle the distraction of the external world, but that world, not merely political theory, weighted heavily on their decisions'.

Less concerned with the principle of unanimity and more with the implementation of 'viable' political institutions (viability determined from the perspective of public choice), Ordeshook defines three lessons to be learned from the war of words that surrounds the framing of any constitution. First, those who draft such documents act as if words are of consequence, otherwise contentious negotiation over their content is irrational. Second, the product of these wars need not correspond to any optimal or rational design. Third, the observed failures of constitutional democracy should not be interpreted to mean that constitutions have little of no effect. Rather, failed democracies illustrate the consequences of poor constitutional designs born of the imperatives of myopic self-interest.

With devastating effect, Ordeshook reviews the implications of these lessons for the Russian constitution ratified by direct popular vote in December 1993. He explains every public choice weakness in this doomed constitution by reference to the myopic pressures of 'politics as usual'. (Do not hold your breath for its long-term survival).

Martin Bailey effectively blends both normative and positive constitutional political economy with public choice in his radical plan for a new constitution for a future country. He draws upon recent experience with current constitutions, corporate charters and private arbitration procedures as well as upon recent contributions to constitutional political economy and public choice to show that we can learn from history and from ideas in rethinking constitutions, that the framing of a constitution may not be a lost eighteenth century skill. Bailey's proposed constitution is truly radical and few (if any) public choicers will agree with it in its entirety. However, if we are honest with ourselves, we should admit that he draws fairly consistently from ideas that circulate widely in the public choice literature. His proposal at least tests the practicality of those ideas from the viewpoint of constitutional design.

I find myself comfortable, for example, with his proposal to use random selection procedures in compiling the legislature (although not as he suggests the present method for jury selection which is far from random). I am uncomfortable with his proposal to force legislators to serve or with his toying with the idea of sequestering legislators with their families when the legislature is in session. If his proposal lies well over towards constructivist rationalism, well so do many others that are much more explicitly cloaked than his in the language of methodological individualism. If his proposal is Hobbesian rather than Lockeian in its downplaying of individual rights in favor of order and efficiency, well he is not alone among constitutional political economists in that prejudice. If he draws heavily from the literature on corporate charters, well the East India Company performed fairly well in establishing efficiency and order in India before the British government played any formal role; a lot better in these respects, one might add, than parliamentary democracy since Indian independence was granted in 1948.

James Buchanan's paper returns to a topic that has been an important concern to him since 1954, namely the inability of modern representative government under conditions of democracy to balance the budget. His paper provides a powerful response to the various criticisms that have been raised against the proposed United States amendment to require budget balance. Buchanan counters objections based on the loss of fiscal flexibility by reference to the political inefficacy of attempted budgetary manipulation. He counters objections based on enforcement problems by reference to observed respect for other constitutional rules. He emphasizes throughout the paper the *symbolic* significance of a constitutional rule for budget balance.

Prior to the Keynesian epoch, the symbolic status of budget balance, as an ideal, was in itself sufficient to limit violation of the implicitly accepted rule in political reality. Approval of a constitutional amendment would reaffirm the symbol for government fiscal responsibility. As Buchanan correctly surmises, 'to violate a moral norm is one thing, and especially as one decision maker in a large group. To violate a moral norm that also involves breaking a constitutional law is quite another.'

In order to build flexibility into a constitution designed to live forever, the American Founding Fathers wrote two alternative amendment procedures (*Article V*) into the 1787 constitution. The states convention route has never been successfully deployed (it is not a dead letter since threat of its use has galvanized Congress into deploying the congressional route). Twenty seven amendments have been made through the congressional route. Of these, only one, the 18th Amendment, passed in 1919, has been repealed in its entirety (by the 21st Amendment in 1933). Moreover, the 21st Amendment is the only Amendment to be ratified using the votes of state convention delegates.

It is particularly appropriate, therefore, that *Munger and Schaller's* paper should explore why *Prohibition* was first imposed and then abolished in such a relatively short time-span in the absence of any wholesale change in preferences of citizens. It is noteworthy that the authors are able to explain the reversal so convincingly in terms of the interest group theory of politics. The authors' conclusion that the most powerful force in the Repeal movement may well have been the desire of New Deal reformers to finance their programs sits well with a growing body of case study literature that focusses attention on '*cherchez l'argent*' as the key to understanding significant public policy reversals.

The United States Constitution specifies term limits for presidents (a maximum of two four year terms) and for federal judges (life subject to good behavior). It provides no term limits for members of Congress, leaving time served to the judgement of the electorate. Growing dissatisfaction with congressional performance since 1980 has given rise to an increasing electoral interest in the imposition of term limits through a constitutional amendment. This electoral interest has been tempered, however, by uncertainty concerning the likely impact of term limits on such important issues as the level of campaign expenditures, the closeness of races, the number of candidates running for office and whether candidates run unopposed.

The paper by *Daniel and Lott* which evaluates the impact of term limits on electoral competitiveness on the basis of California's legislative experience in the light of the successful 1990 term limit initiative, therefore, is timely and extremely well executed. The paper analyses California state assembly and senate races between 1976 and 1994 by reference to cutting edge public choice theory. The authors demonstrate conclusively that California's legislative term limits have dramatically reduced campaign expenditures, have resulted in more incumbents being defeated, closer races, more candidates running and fewer single candidate races. In terms of the vitality of the democratic process, these are encouraging results for those who seek to impose term limits on Congress, presumably through the states convention route.

Perhaps because the 1787 Constitution was written at a time when the federal government was not expected to intrude significantly on the United States economy, there is no overt economic constitution designed to contain the appetite for growth that is such a feature of post-1936 United States legislative experience. Surely if the Founding Fathers had been blessed with omniscience they would have written the balanced budget requirement into the original parchment.

Even a decade after the publication of Adam Smith's *The Wealth of Nations* (1776), however, it is by no means clear that they would have written a unilateral free trade article into the Constitution. The tariff, from the outset, was viewed as a (the ?) major source of revenue for the newly-emergent republic, a revenue source that threatened the propertied classes who wrote the constitution far less than would an income tax or a property tax. Even if comparative advantage theory had been enunciated, a little self-interest might be expected from notables who feared that private property might be turned into a commons by a property-less majority armed with the authority of a direct federal income tax.

Willem Thorbecke's paper applies the public choice approach in analyzing why the comparative advantage theory of international trade is not reflected in United States trade policy even some eighty years after the 16th Amendment successfully paved the way for the income tax which quickly dominated the tariff as a federal revenue source (and made a commons of private property). Using a narrative approach, Thorbecke demonstrates that politicians respond to the demands of special interests both by forcing open foreign markets and by closing domestic markets. They do so at a high cost both to individual liberty and to the wealth of the nation. He shares with Milton and Rose Friedman (1979) the view that a unilateral free trade amendment to the Constitution is politically impossible, despite counter-arguments see (Rowley, Thorbecke, and Wagner, 1995). Instead, he reviews a range of more modest reforms designed to restore a badly-battered multilateral bargaining approach as the fulcrum of trade liberalization initiatives.

Between 1781 and 1789, the American states were bound together in a 'league of friendship' established by the Articles of Confederation which created a Continental Congress to provide for common interests, notably defense. Although the Articles of Confederation included cost sharing provisions, enforcement provisions were weak, if not non-existent, and many of the separate states frequently failed to pay their way, adding to the burdens of those prepared to honor their commitments. Such loss of revenues raised serious problems for Congress in responding to British non-compliance with the 1783 Anglo-American peace treaty and to the Spanish blockade of the Mississippi River between 1784–1787. Ultimately, it led to the collapse of the Continental Congress and to the Philadelphia Convention.

Dougherty and Cain argue in their paper that the breakdown of the Continental Congress, and with it the American Confederation, was a predictable consequence of the Articles of Association which were fatally flawed from the perspective of public choice. Instead of providing institutions which alleviated problems of collective action among the states, the Articles adopted a system of requisitions where incentives to free-ride were unconstrained. This failure of constitutional design exacerbated both short and long term non-co-operation among the confederated states. Dougherty and Cain illustrate in some detail the extent of such non-co-operation within the American Confederation and note that similar problems of incentive incompatibility threaten more recent confederations such as those of the Commonwealth of Independent states and of the Baltic Assembly.

Razzolini and Shughart return in their paper to the balanced budget debate earlier addressed by James Buchanan. They present an empirical public choice analysis, based on performance in the fifty United States states plus the District of Columbia over the period 1967 through 1992, that challenges one important argument in favor of a balanced budget constitutional amendment. Specifically, they test a hypothesis advanced by Milton and Rose Friedman (1979) that current spending and current taxes, not deficits and debt are the root of government's harmful effects on the economy, proxied by the annual growth rate of state per capita income.

Their evidence indicates that growth rates in income per capita are higher in states with smaller public sectors and that, while both deficits and taxes reduce the rate of income growth in the typical state, the negative impact of taxes is considerably larger at the margin. They conclude that a small public sector whose expenditures are financed in part by running a budget deficit appears to be the best way of fostering economic growth.

Such a judgement, even if correct, begs the question as to how such a solution is to be achieved and how it is to be sustained. If the economic constitution is more appropriately focussed on procedures than on specific interventions, the balanced budget route still may be the better way to proceed, allowing public choice pressures to constrain the taxing appetite of government and thus to control the size of public expenditure. Furthermore, per capita economic growth is not the only issue at stake in the deficit debate as Buchanan's paper clearly demonstrates.

Jean-Luc Migué's paper focusses attention, from a public choice perspective, on a distinguishing feature of federal systems of government, once constitutional limits break down. In such circumstances, two or more levels of government compete for the same voters in the supply of similar services in a given territory. Viewing votes as inputs in the production of political outputs, the situation can be viewed as an arrangement where two suppliers compete for a common pool of resources. Migué argues, in such circumstances, that it is in the interest of both suppliers to seek to gain the votes by implementing the program first. To the extent that they are equally adept at supplying political output, the political profit may be dissipated by such competition, with consequences of oversupply and a wasteful expansion of the public sector that lower the wealth of the state or province.

Migué cleverly shows that there are two forces typically operating in a federalist system. An expansionist force is rooted in the common pool problem that he identifies. A restrictionist force is rooted in the mobility of resources among decentralized entities. This may explain the mixed empirical record on the contribution of federalism to containing the growth of government. The relevance of Migué's argument for the situation of the Province of Quebec in Canada is briefly discussed.

In an ambitious and far-ranging paper, *Dennis Mueller* makes use of a public choice approach developed in his recently published book, *Constitutional Democracy* (Mueller, 1996), to evaluate the structure and procedures of the European Community from the perspective of constitutional political economy. He views the Maastricht Treaty, like its predecessors signed in Rome and Paris, as a form of constitution for Europe, albeit a constitution sanctified in ways quite dissimilar from the United States Constitution. Herein lies a serious problem, he argues, for those who would like to see a federalist Europe evolve from the Maastricht Treaty.

Although Jean Monnet's original vision for Europe was for it to become a federation, the steps by which it has now moved (if at all) toward that goal have been a series of treatises and more informal agreements among representatives of the several governments. Thus, the decision making process by which integration has advanced has taken the confederate form. Not surprisingly, the end product resembles much more closely the confederate than the federal model. The bulk of power lies with the Council of Ministers in Brussels, not with the European Parliament in Strasburg.

Dennis Mueller's paper sets out the relevant issues that determine whether or not the union should take a federalist or a confederate form, defines the processes that ought to lead to some resolution of the issue and the voting and citizenship implications. Although Mueller does not disclose his hand in this paper, I suspect that he is more favorably inclined to federalism than I am. In any event, the paper sets out clear criteria in terms of which many economists (although not all classical liberals) will be happy to make their choice.

The paper by *Jurgen Backhaus* continues the debate over the nature of European union, post-Maastricht, by focussing upon the constitutional implications of the principle of subsidiarity re-affirmed in that treaty for the evolution of ecologically based taxation in the European Community. The principle of subsidiarity is an organizing principle applicable to all areas of European Community policy. It requires that any policy should be carried out at the lowest functional echelon capable of effecting such policy. Evidently, its role is to decentralize decision-making throughout the Community, inevitably invading the particular hierarchies of decision-making developed by individual nation states.

Backhaus outlines the history of the subsidiarity principle within the European Community and shows how it can be adapted to help in defining relevant organizational units for the implementation of ecological policy. He recognizes that central authorities are often reluctant to enter into consultations with the governments of independent nations at lower levels. But he emphasizes that this is precisely what the principle of subsidiarity implies for the European Community. He makes an interesting case for deploying a Henry George 'single tax constitution' as the basis for an ecological policy for the European Community compatible with the principle of subsidiarity.

For twelve centuries after the fall of Rome there was no growth in *per capita* output in the West. In the latter half of the eighteenth century two major events occurred: the Industrial Revolution and the rise and spread of democratic capitalism as evidenced in free markets, private property, the rule of law and representative government. From 1820 to 1980 real *per capita* growth in the West averaged 1.6 percent per annum. The living standard of the West increased thirteen-fold. Yet, with the exception of certain Asian nations (the Pacific Rim Tigers) economic growth in the Third World has been low despite significant rates of *per capita* capital formation.

Gerald Scully's thesis in the closing paper of this volume is that capital formation and technical change are the main engines of economic growth. However, not all nations are equally adept at transforming increases in capital and technology into increases in output. Some countries are blessed with rules that are wealth-promoting and others are not. The poor economic performance of many Third World nations, especially in Africa, is the consequence of adverse economic, legal and political institutions, not of any shortage of capital accumulation and technology transfer. On the basis of empirical analysis based on all nations with at least ten years of data, excluding the communist countries and the Middle East oil-exporting nations. Scully is tempted to conclude that a modern standard of living is quite impossible to achieve without free institutions.

I find this to be a suitably invigorating note on which to close a volume that attempts to make the case for a constitutional political economy that is grounded in consistent, hard-nosed public choice analysis. Effective institutional design is simply not feasible unless the designers build their structures to withstand rational choice pressures from the political market place. If mean, sensual man is here to stay, then let us, in our better moments, incorporate that knowledge into the institutions that must govern his behavior. That rightly, was the thinking that governed negotiations in Philadelphia in 1787, not some silly notion of an 'original position' in which the participants negotiate behind a 'veil of ignorance'; from which perspective the blind inevitably would lead the blind.

References

Buchanan, J.M. (1990) The domain of constitutional economics. *Constitutional Political Economy* 1 (1): 1–19.

Buchanan, J.M. and Tullock, G. (1962). *The calculus of consent.* Ann Arbor: University of Michigan Press.

Downs, A. (1957). *An economic theory of democracy.* New York: Harper and Row.

Friedman, M. and Friedman, R. (1979). *Free to choose: A personal statement.* New York: Harcourt Brace Jovanovich.

McCormick, R.E. and Tollison, R.D. (1981). *Politicians, legislation and the economy.* Boston: Martinus Nijhoff Publishing.

Mueller, D.C. (1996). *Constitutional democracy.* New York: Oxford University Press.

Nozick, R. (1974). *Anarchy, state and utopia.* New York: Basic Books.

Rawls, J. (1971). *A theory of justice.* Cambridge: Belknap Press.

Rowley, C.K., Thorbecke, W. and Wagner, R.E. (1995). *Trade protection in the United States.* Aldershot: Edward Elgar Publishing.

Voigt, S. (1996). Positive constitutional economics: A survey. *Public Choice* this volume.

Public Choice **90:** 11–53, 1997.

© 1997 *Kluwer Academic Publishers.*

Positive constitutional economics: A survey

STEFAN VOIGT
*Max-Planck-Institute for Research into Economic Systems, D-07743 Jena, Germany**

Abstract. The author distinguishes between normative and positive constitutional economics. Taking the observation that the normative branch of the new discipline is much better developed than its positive counterpart as a starting point, the available positive literature is surveyed nevertheless. The available evidence is arranged into four categories: (1) Constitutional rules and the procedures bringing them about, (2) constitutional rules as the result of preferences and restrictions, (3) constitutional rules channeling constitutional change, and (4) the economic effects of constitutional rules. Additionally, various concepts of the constitution are presented, the tools suited for a positive theory of constitutional economics discussed, and precursors as well as related research programs shortly described.

1. Introduction

Constitutional economics is a relatively young strand of research whose adherents are concerned with the choice of rules as constraints to human behavior as opposed to the choice within these rules. Neoclassical theory has primarily focused on this latter aspect, thus taking the institutional environment as given. As soon as institutions are perceived as allocationally or distributionally relevant and as subject to deliberate modification, however, it seems to make sense to analyze the choice of rules from an economic perspective.

James M. Buchanan as the most prominent proponent of the new research program has always insisted on its having two components: a positive and a normative one (e.g., 1990a: 17). His *capo lavoro, The Limits of Liberty* (1975), clearly belongs to the normative strand as well as John Rawls' *A Theory of Justice* (1971). As early as 1981, two public choice-scientists questioned the relevance of normative theory: "..., it is extremely doubtful whether such analysis will make a perceptible difference in the character of prevailing institutions. Normative theory is useful in helping us clarify our norms, but is is another question whether such analysis will impact on the pattern of real institutional development" (McCormick and Tollison, 1981: 126). They

* The author would like to thank Dennis C. Mueller and Manfred E. Streit for helpful comments and suggestions and Antje Hagen for improving his English.

clearly preferred a positive approach enabling one to predict developments in the real world. They were rather critical, however, in their evaluation of the state of the art of positive theory: "There is thus a sharp contrast in the two approaches to constitutional-institutional analysis. It is also fair to say, however, that at this point in time the normative approach to constitutional analysis is much better developed in the literature than the positive approach." This was written a decade and a half ago and is taken here as a reason to survey the literature that has since appeared. A first look does not lead us to be very optimistic. In 1993, one could still write that a positive theory of constitutions was necessary now (Weingast, 1993: 288), thus implying its non-existence.

The choice among constraints – the subject matter of constitutional economics – can take place on different levels. On the individual level, it has been analyzed as the economics of self-management or "egonomics" (Heiner, 1983; Schelling, 1984; Thaler and Shefrin, 1981). In the economic theory of clubs (Buchanan, 1965) one can conceptualize the rules according to which the club-members structure their interactions as its constitution (e.g., a firm's constitution as analyzed by Gifford, 1991; and Vanberg, 1992). Further still, the all-inclusive club that we call society is also structured by a constitution. The constitution of the state is the classical area of inquiry and will also be the main focus of this survey.

Prima facie, analyzing the ways in which societies choose among constraints, i.e. create constitutions, might appear to be a dull exercise, since constitutions are often perceived as invariable and static. This impression is false: between 1974 and 1987, about half of the then some 160 constitutions of this world were entirely rewritten (Goldwin and Kaufman, 1988: vii). Additionally, the transformation of Central and Eastern Europe including the dissolution of the Soviet Union has increased the number of new constitutions substantially. But even if constitutions were not written or modified often, they could still be the subject of the economist's interests as long as one has reasons to suspect constitutions to be allocationally or distributionally relevant.

What is the state of the art of constitutional economics, then? It seems to be premature to talk of *the* theory of constitutional economics. Rather, there seem to be diverging approaches that differ not only in their assumptions or their conceptions of constitutions but also in their research agenda. In the last decade, there have been edited volumes as well as conferences on the topic. In 1990, the journal *Constitutional Political Economy* first appeared. Although more than a decade has passed since McCormick's and Tollison's dictum, positive constitutional economics is still in its infancy. This paper is therefore not only a survey but also a – subjective – research program (for an early survey, cf. Blankart, 1985). Authors that do not think of themselves as constitutional economists might be incorporated as long as their research interests conform to the program demarcated here.

I will proceed as follows: the next section will be devoted to the various precursors of constitutional economics. Section 3 contains a description of the research program, whereas Section 4 focuses on the tools of constitutional economics. The following section elaborates on the economics of constitutional economics, the sixth part on the behavioral assumptions. Section 7 concentrates on different conceptions of the constitutio and Section 8 finally constitutes the central part of the survey in which the positive knowledge generated so far is presented. In the concluding section, some open questions will be named.

2. Precursors and related disciplines

Before describing the research program of constitutional economics in the next section of this survey, it seems useful to pay tribute to some of the new discipline's precursors. Since reinventing the wheel anew is a waste of resources, knowing one's precursors can help to economize. In some sense, many of the great social and political philosophers of passed centuries can be considered as precursors. Buchanan is, however, rather restrictive in paying tribute because many of the social philosophers (1) did not sufficiently distinguish between political and moral analysis, (2) did not assign individual interest and rational choice its proper place, (3) did not sufficiently recognize the distinction between "total" and "marginal" explanations of the political constitution, (4) did not elaborate on the private action vs. collective action dichotomy. There are, of course, exceptions of which he names Spinoza and Hume (with regard to problem 1), Hume again, Althusius, Wolff and Fouillée (2), and Humboldt (4) (Buchanan and Tullock, 1962, appendix 1). In other writings, Buchanan (1987: 585) refers explicitly to Adam Smith who used the same methodology in his research as constitutional economics, namely comparative institutional analysis (Buchanan 1987: 585).

It is somewhat astonishing that mention of Alexander Hamilton, John Jay, James Madison and their *Federalist Papers* is only made in passing. The whole concept of constitutionalism was developed in the wake of the movement towards an independent America and the creation of a federal state (Hayek, 1960: Ch. 12). Although it is important to keep theoretical reasoning and historical development apart, they do certainly influence each other. In recent years, the Federalist Papers have increasingly been recognized not only as a political manifesto but also as a theory of the constitution whose central assumption is almost identical with that made in economics.[1]

Such an interpretation is, however, not universally accepted (Sunstein, 1987: 118: "In recent years, there have been many efforts to understand the Framers as thoroughgoing modernist skeptics – indeed as forerunners of Chicago-school economists – ... Such efforts are badly off the mark; they read into the period of the framing something that simply was not there."). For the specific concept of the constitution that Buchanan has developed, Swedish economist Knut Wicksell and his *Finanztheoretische Untersuchungen* (1896) have turned to be an important precursor. It was Wicksell who elaborated upon unanimity in collective choice settings as a necessary and sufficient criterion for Pareto-superior moves, a recognition that was later to become the cornerstone of Buchanan's constitutional economics.

In 1913, *An Economic Interpretation of the Constitution of the United States* by Charles Beard appeared. Beard claims that the Founding Fathers were not motivated by some conception of the common good but simply by their own economic interests. Beard could thus be viewed as a direct precursor of public choice analysis. Nevertheless, many modern public choice scholars almost seem to be embarrassed to have someone like Beard in their family tree (Buchanan and Tullock, e.g., put the "economic" in Beard's title between inverted commas; 1962: 25). There are, however, some exceptions, notably the papers by McGuire and Ohsfeldt (1986, 1989a, b). The reason for the embarrassment of some public choice scholars is probably not so much the imputed Marxian basis of Beard's argument (which can be questioned if not refuted, cf. McDonald, 1986: xii ff.) or the inaccuracy in dealing with data, but an inconsistency in the behavioral model of modern public choice analysis (on this, cf. Section 6).

Germany's economic constitution is largely based upon the reflections of the Freiburg School of Law and Economics or Ordo-Liberalism (cf. Streit, 1992, 1995 for an overview). American scholars of constitutional economics have usually not recognized this German school as a precursor. Papers comparing the two approaches have stressed the common features of the research programs and their (common) foundation in classical political economy (Leipold, 1990; and Vanberg, 1988 respectively). Additionally, both schools perceive institutions as a matter of deliberate choice. Whereas constitutional economics focuses on adequately restraining Levathian, Ordo-Liberalism puts more emphasis on a strong state securing a competitive order – and making the state rent-seeking proof. Here, Ordo-Liberalism remains much closer to the benevolent dictator-assumption of orthodox theory. Concerning the applicability of the models, Ordo-theory seems to have a certain advantage over constitutional economics as the revival of Eucken's constitutive and regulative principles (Eucken, 1952/1990: 254–304) with regard to constitution-making in Central and Eastern Europe shows.

Constitutional economics does not only have precursors but also related disciplines which focus on similar research objects. Buchanan (1987: 586) names six: (1) Public Choice, (2) Economics of Property Rights, (3) Law and Economics, (4) Political Economy of Regulation, (5) the New Institutional Economics, and (6) the New Economic History. Buchanan himself is obviously not only a pioneer of constitutional economics but also of public choice. *The Calculus of Consent* can be identified as the starting point of constitutional economics emerging out of public choice. In its introduction, Buchanan and Tullock (1962: 7) envisage the new discipline for the first time: "The attainment of consent is a costly process, however, and a recognition of this simple fact points directly toward an 'economic' theory of constitutions." This book contains substantial positive analysis and can thus be said to be the starting point of positive constitutional economics. Buchanan and Tullock even planned to give it the subtitle "An Economic Theory of Political Constitutions" but were afraid that this could be misinterpreted due to its resemblance to Marxian parlance (p. 13).

Dennis Mueller (1989: 1) defines public choice as "the application of economics to political science." Economics is thus thought of as a certain method of analysis which has traditionally been applied to a certain research object (market decision-making) but whose application can be extended to other research objects (political, i.e., non-market decision-making). Constitutional economics perfectly fits within this demarcation but is less broad: whereas public choice scholars are interested in the resulting (public) choices within (constitutional) rules, scholars of constitutional economics are primarily interested in analyzing the process that leads to certain constitutional rules. Brennan and Buchanan (1980: 14f.) argue that early public choice-models put too much emphasis on the median-voter determining the actions of politicians. Those models would thus be almost entirely determined by the demand side, leading to a benign neglect of the supply side. They argue that the discretionary powers of politicians would not be adequately restricted by the median voter (i.e., on the process level) but on the level of constitutional rules.

Representatives of Property Rights as surveyed e.g. by Furubotn and Pejovich (1972) and more recently by De Alessi (1980) or Pejovich (1990) are – as constitutional economists – interested in the (economic) effects brought about by alternative sets of property rights. Their central focus is in general on a more concrete level than that of constitutional economics. A typical research topic could, for example, be the analysis of the differential incentives – and effects – brought about by different organizational constitutions such as firms.

Law and Economics or the economic analysis of law seems a natural terrain also for the economic analysis of constitutional law. Somewhat astonishingly, "constitutional law and economics" only emerged very recently: the textbook by Cooter and Ulen (1988) does not contain an entry "constitution." In a more recent paper, Ulen (1992) explains this non-recognition by pointing towards the fact that the tools of modern microeconomics can help to analyze efficiency *given* some initial distribution of rights but nothing on the initial assignment of these rights themselves. Recognizinfg the impossibility theorems à la Arrow and Sen, he wishes to make a point for the safeguarding of individual rights that are "beyond the reach of the notion of economic efficiency and of the routing social choice mechanisms" (Ulen, 1992: 211). From the economist's point of view, this is a rather awkward justification for the new research program since constitutional economists are interested in possibilities of finding sets of rights that bring the potentially conflicting interests of various actors into a balance that most of them can agree to. Richard A. Posner seizes the research object in a different manner: he names no less than eight distinct topics in which economics might be used to study constitutions. These include the economic consequences of requiring supermajorities for some kinds of political change, the economic effects of specific constitutional doctrines and the interpretation of constitutional provisions or doctrines that may have an implicit economic logic (1987). Whereas Posner describes a research program, recent articles by Boudreaux and Pritchard (1993, 1994) can be viewed as first steps in working it off (cf., however, the proceedings on a conference on "Constitutional law and economics" printed in a special edition of the "International Review of Law and Economics," 1992; cf. also the monograph "Constitutional Law and Economics" by Cooter [in print]).

As long as constitutional rules are viewed as a specific kind of institution, the New Institutional Economics can be interpreted as the more inclusive research program. Surveys or textbooks of New Institutional Economics might thus include the economics of constitutions. But they usually do not. Neither the book-length survey by Eggertsson (1990) nor the shorter one by Furubotn and Richter (1991) pays special attention to constitutional rules which is astonishing since a comparison of different kinds of institutional change (constitutional vs. sub-constitutional) almost suggests itself (Eggertsson, 1990, does, however, include a chapter on the theory of the state in which the emergence of states is conceptualized using economic tools).

The New Economic History tries to apply quantitative research to historical phenomena. Its focus remains the explanation of singular phenomena whereas economists in general and constitutional economists in particular are interested in nomological hypotheses. Nevertheless, some of the research done in this program can possibly help to transfer heuristic into historically validated insight (cf. also the section on the tools of constitutional economics in this survey). Finally, a research area not named by Buchanan seems worth mentioning, namely the economic theory of federalism. It could, of course, be supposed to be a sub-discipline of constitutional economics but that would probably not do justice to the independence of this strand of research.

3. The research program

One of the classical questions of political philosophy is: "Quis custodiat ipsos custodes?" Some of the scholars of constitutional economics seem indeed primarily motivated by this question. The state is perceived as Leviathan, and constitutional economics is the science of producing adequate chains. One example for such a rather narrow view is McKenzie (1984: 1) who interprets constitutional economics as an intellectual movement that "...proposes to reconsider the constitutional constraints on the fiscal, monetary, and regulatory powers of the federal government." Scholars not belonging to the public choice tradition have criticized this focus as somewhat narrow since fiscal and monetary regimes often do not belong to the constitution (Elster 1994: 1). It has also been criticized as reducing constitutional economics to the business of political controlling (Priddat, 1993; for an explicit attempt in this direction, cf. Leschke, 1993). Translating this narrow focus into economic dimensions, it can be asked whether constitutions can be designed that are rent-seeking proof (Macey, 1988 can be read as pursuing this research program) or how society's members can optimally control the persons acting on behalf of the state who are their agents. Besides often being at least partially motivated by ideological considerations (McKenzie, 1984: 13: "By way of solid theoretical and empirical work, constitutional economics seeks to reverse the intellectual revolutions brought about by Keynesian economics..."), this narrow research program will not be worked out here in more detail because it is normative theory, interested in something like the "optimal constitution." Coleman (1988a, b) and Hardin (1990) are rather critical on the achievements of normative contractarian constitutional economics.

Instead of this, the focus will be on the research program of positive constitutional economics. In broad terms, the constitutional economist is interested in the study of rules, in their functionality as well as the way by which they are chosen (Buchanan 1991: 4). Since the functionality of a system of (constitutional) rules can only be ascertained when they are supposed to perform a certain function, it is necessary to specify this function (which is, of course, connected with the danger of falling back into normative analysis). For an economist, it seems obvious to analyze the relationship between the constitutional rule-system and the rate of economic growth. Since neither orthodox growth theory nor orthodox development theory pay attention to the constitutional system as a causal factor for growth or development, the research program constitutes a challenge for both of these theories.

The constitutional rule-set can be conceived as the top-layer of a whole hierarchy of institutions, including simple legislation, but also institutions that private actors use to structure their interactions which are not backed at all by the state (Kiwit and Voigt, 1995). Constitutional and sub-constitutional institutions are supposedly closely interdependent: assuming a constitution is respected, it structures the processes by which legislation can be enacted. But it is also conceivable that the values and norms shared by the members of a society – which can be conceptualized as internal institutions – finally lead to a change in constitutional rules, either explicitly by a modification of its content or implicitly, by an interpretation of the courts. All this is part of the ways in which constitutional rules are chosen, and in which they effect economic performance. Put differently, one part of the constitutional economist's research program are the transmission mechanisms between sub-constitutional and constitutional institutional change.

The "double question" posed by Buchanan (how are rules chosen, what is their functionality) is roughly analogous to a dichotomy which will be used in Section 8 to structure the positive knowledge hitherto available (that between the inputs and procedures leading to certain rules on the one hand and the rules producing certain outcomes or patterns on the other). It would, of course, be fascinating to ascertain systematic relationships between certain organizational arrangements and the rate of economic growth. Trying to come up with systematic relationships between, say, federalism and centralism seems *prima facie* very unlikely. On the other hand, constitutional arrangements like an independent central bank are very often supposed to be advantageous to economic growth. One should be able to test hypotheses like these empirically. Posner can be interpreted to ask still broader questions: he proposes to analyze constitutional provisions that might only have an implicit economic logic like the freedom of speech (1987, similarly Elster, 1994 with the demand to analyze economic consequences of non-economic rules). Further, it is of interest to inquire into the conditions which have to be fulfilled so that the constitutions will be obeyed (Davidson, 1984: 61).

Another aspect of the research program is to ask for the existence of patterns in the modification of constitutional rules over time. These can take place either explicitly or implicitly. Such a theory of constitutional interpretation would also have to recognize the possible relevance of values and norms as suggested above.

4. The tools of constitutional economics[2]

Scientists in general are in search of nomological hypotheses of the form "always and everywhere if, then." Producing nomological hypotheses is usually not an end in itself. Economists are interested in prognoses, i.e., in conditional predictions. The focus will now be on possible tools which promise to be helpful in the generation of hypotheses, namely: (1) comparative institutional analysis, (2) (economic) history and (3) laboratory experiments.

Comparative institutional analysis asks how alternative institutional arrangements effect (economic) outcomes. Frey (1990: 445) stresses that comparative institutional analysis consists solely of comparing existing institutions and not unattainable ideas. Comparing the different outcomes that alternative institutional arrangements provoke presupposes the availability of a number of cause-effect-conjectures. If they do not exist, one does not have any clues what outcomes one should look at. The number of comparisons one can make at a single point in time – for example, the present – is severely limited because of the rarity in which "the other circumstances" will at least be similar. Three ways to increase the number of observations almost suggest themselves: (1) One could compare institutional arrangements realized at one single point in the past; for this, one might want to draw on the competence of the economic historian (cf. below). (2) Turning the procedure around, one might enquire into seemingly *identical* institutional arrangements that have nevertheless les to different outcomes. This procedure might help to formulate the "if"-component in a more specific way. (3) It might also be helpful to compare different institutional arrangements realized within one society at different points in time. Of course, more will change than just the realized institutional setting and the *ceteris paribus*-condition will be violated again. But the advantageousness of a certain institutional arrangement might depend on factors that can very well be supposed to be quasi-constant over a certain period of time. The values and norms shared by a vast majority of a society's members might be a case in point. It might therefore be promising to compare, e.g., the different constitutions realized in *nouveau régime* France.

Ascertaining the effects of institutional change with certainty is impossible. It is impossible because it amounts to a comparison of the effects of a realized (unrealized) institutional arrangement with an unrealized (realized) one. Statements concerning the effects of an unrealized institutional arrangement will of necessity always remain hypothetical. Another problem of comparative institutional analysis is that of causality: one might very well be able to discover correlations between certain institutional arrangements and certain patterns. Whether these patterns are, however, primarily caused by those institutional arrangements that a scientist suspects is a wholly different question. Of course, Hume's epistemic point that it is not valid to infer from an invariance observed in the past to a general invariance that will also hold in the future is also relevant here.

The advantage of not committing the "Nirvana"-fallacy of comparing realized with unrealizable institutional arrangements simultaneously constitutes a shortcoming of this tool: if, as Frey (1990: 445) claims, only institutions "as they exist in reality" are compared, institutional change only striven for, i.e., not (yet) realized, cannot be analyzed. In other words: institutional proposals designed by scientists or having emerged from public discussion are not amenable to comparative institutional analysis. Laboratory experiments which will be discussed below might be an adequate tool for a first approximation of the effects that a new institution might probably cause.

If constitutional economists are not satisfied with "hypothetically positive" theory but are interested in empirically tested theory, it might be necessary to turn to history because the number of cases amenable to analysis realized at present is fairly small. Since economists are no experts in interpreting historical events they might turn to (economic) historians for help. *Prima facie*, economic history seems especially apt for analyzing institutional – or constitutional – change. A general theory explaining constitutional change is, of course, a very ambitious endeavor. It might be the role of economic historians to remind constitutional economists not to behave too carelessly in their collection and use of data. In other words: the orientation toward the analysis of singular events enables the economic historian to prevent the constitutional economist from abstracting of too many relevant details and of generalizing too broadly. The validity of some "general law" might be seriously hampered as soon as one realizes the importance of chance.

The last tool to be discussed here are laboratory experiments. Three areas of applicability come to mind, one of which has already been mentioned: (1) procedures that people will use when entering into a constitutional discourse, (2) studying basic principles people can agree on in laboratory settings and (3) testing new institutional arrangements.

It has been argued that the "lived" constitution will not only be determined by the written document but also by judicial interpretation as well as the "constitutional system"[3] which comprises values, norms, attitudes and the like of elites as well as the populace at large. If the constitutional system is indeed a crucial factor for the "real" constitution under which a society lives, it should also be relevant for the formal procedure as well as the substantive rules a group of persons chooses when agreeing on a constitution. Laboratory experiments with groups of different backgrounds, i.e., different values, norms and attitudes that obtain the task of creating a constitutional document almost suggest themselves. I am not aware of any such experiments.

The second area of applicability of laboratory experiments was said to be the study of basic principles that people can agree on. The basic principles would, of course, reflect the value judgments of the participants. These would not only enter into the procedures – as just discussed – but also into the substantive part of the constitution itself. Normative inquiries into constitutional economics often contain "basic principles" that people would agree on under specific circumstances: Rawls, e.g., elaborates two principles, the second being the difference principle that is supposed to be a manifestation of the people's concept of fairness. The deduction of the difference principle is based on precisely specified initial conditions and logically derived therefrom. The derivation itself can therefore claim positive status: "If certain initial conditions are given then people will agree on the difference principle as an expression of their value judgments concerning fairness." If one is able to approximate the initial conditions in a laboratory setting, the hypothesis becomes testable. Rawls' difference principle has indeed been subject to such a test. It was found that people overwhelmingly preferred another principle, namely maximizing the average income with a floor constraint (Frohlich, Oppenheimer and Eavey, 1987).

A third area in which laboratory experiments could be useful is in the testing of new institution settings that are the result of some theoretical reasoning but have never been applied in practice. The non-access of comparative institutional analysis to this category of institutions was identified as a weakness of that approach. Comparative institutional analysis and laboratory experiments therefore complement each other. Testing theoretically useful institutional innovations in the laboratory might enable scientists to make better predictions concerning the consequences of a modified institutional setting. It might draw their attention to hitherto neglected side-effects. Laboratory consequence evaluation therefore stands in the tradition of critical rationalism à la Popper. Since the consequences of a new solution to a problem – in this case a new constitutional rule – can never with certainty be anticipated completely by the human mind, it should be attempted to restrict possible negative side-effects as much as possible. Popper has thus proposed to proceed by trial and error in a piecemeal engineering manner. Laboratory experiments could be conceived as an additional plane of negative side-effect containment: keeping them in the laboratory – and possibly burying some of the hypotheses incorporated in the institutional reform proposals already there – is probably the least costly way of experimenting for society.

The three areas in which laboratory experiments promise to be useful have distinct functions: the first area discussed is simply based on some conjectures. In case there are indeed systematic regularities revealed in the laboratory, this might be the starting point for a new theory. The second area rather consists of the testing of available theory and the last one serves to evaluate new institutional proposals. Some of the arguments in favor of laboratory experiments have already been alluded to: "hypothetically positive" statements like the cited one by Rawls can be put to a "quasi-empirical" test. It seems possible furthermore to contain the negative consequences of some new institutional arrangements by trying them first in the laboratory. There are, however, limits too: it is the general function of rules to enable a society's members to form expectations that have a good chance of turning out to be true. The longer a (consistent) set of rules remains stable over time, the easier it is for the members of a society to form expections. The longevity of a certain rule might thus be an important factor for determining its consequences. It seems difficult to capture these effects within laboratory settings.

5. The economics of constitutional economics

The economist's occupation with constitutional rules leads to a demystification of constitutions. Remains of natural rights conceptions which today manifest themselves in the claim of universally valid human rights are substituted for marginalist calculations in which potentially competing rights are traded off. The economic approach to human behavior (Becker, 1976) does not define economics with regard to its object matter but with regard to its analytical approach. Consequently, all human action becomes amenable to economic analysis and economic imperialism results (McKenzie and Tullock, 1975; Radnitzky and Bernholz, 1987). Two of the disciplines traditionally concerned with the analysis of constitutions, political science and legal science, have long been invaded by economic analysis. Public choice and law and economics, respectively, are the results.

Every society must willy-nilly decide on which actions are to be carried out on the individual level and those to be carried out on the collective one. An individual will opt for collective action, if this promises to lead to an increase in its utility. In order to conceptualize this decision problem, Buchanan and Tullock introduce three cost categories: *External costs* as those costs that the individual expects to bear as a result of the actions of others over which she has no direct control. Secondly, there are *decision-making costs* which the individual expects to incur as a result of her own participation in an organized activity. They only include the estimated costs of participating in decisions when the agreement of two or more individuals is required. The sum of these two cost categories is, thirdly, called the *costs of social interdependency*, or simply *interdependence costs*. For purely private activity, they will be zero. According to Buchanan and Tullock, a rational individual confronted with questions of constitutional choice will opt for their minimization.

After having decided upon the range of collective action, societies have to choodse decision-making rules that are to be used in order to determine the amount of collective action to be had. This choice can be conceptualized using the three cost categories already introduced to delimit the range of collective action. The larger the number of individuals required to take collective action, the lower the external costs an individual can expect to be exposed to. If the number of individuals includes everybody in the community, i.e., the rule of unanimity is chosen, then external costs must by definition be zero. Decision-making costs tend, however, to increase dramatically the larger the number of individuals required to take collective action becomes. With the unanimity rule, each voter has a veto and it becomes rational to misrepresent one's true preferences in order to get compensation. Buchanan and Tullock (1962: 70) claim that "for a given activity the fully rational individual, at the time of constitutional choice, will try to choose that decision-making rule which will *minimize* the present value of the expected costs that he must suffer." That chapter is entitled "A Generalized Economic Theory of Constitutions," and the authors put their main focus on the choice of collective decision-making rules here. The issue of collective action can also be tackled from a different angle, namely that of public goods. They do not only include material goods but also immaterial ones such as rights and the sanctioning in case someone has violated them. Although the private production of institutions is a very old phenomenon, it can be argued that the state has a comparative advantage in sanctioning (Nozick, 1973; North, 1990; Milgrom, North and Weingast, 1990). A constitution contains the rules and procedures for producing public goods. Its analysis can therefore be an economic endeavor.

Buchanan and Tullock try to draw an analogy from economic markets to political markets, the instrument most frequently used being the exchange paradigm according to which two or more parties only enter voluntarily into a contract if they expect to be better off afterwards.[4] What are individuals exchanging in constitution-making? If the reference-system is anarchy in which no collectively enforced rights – and therefore no legal limits to individual action – exist, they exchange reduced possibilities of individual action. Offering a reduction of one's own possibilities to act can be beneficial if all other (n-1) individuals living in the same community promise to do likewise.

If the function of constitutions is seen as reducing the transaction costs of reaching voluntary agreements (North, 1981), economic theory seems a natural tool for analyzing and comparing the effectiveness of various constitutions. Transaction cost theory can also be used for an almost diagonally opposed approach: some scholars see the function of the constitution in augmenting the transaction costs of rent-seeking but warn at the same time that the fact that rent-seeking is not totally eliminated does not allow for the conclusion that the constitution would be ineffective because rent-seeking cannot be eliminated at zero cost (Macey, 1986).

The last argument here advanced in favor of an economic theory of constitutions deals with the question of constitutional change. In case a constitution is enforced, it will most likely enable individuals to form expectations that have a good chance of turning out to be satisfied. They will base their planning (i.e., their savings and investment decisions), on the assumption that today's rules will also be tomorrow's rules. Constitutional changes are therefore costly because they can lower the returns on investment. Additionally, the costs of getting acquainted with the modified rules have to be considered. These costs would have to be weighted with the expected benefits of constitutional change.

6. The behavioral model of constitutional economics

An assumption entirely undisputed in modern economics is methodological individualism. If all the processes and outcomes on the constitutional as well as the sub-constitutional level are the product of human action, they must – in principle – all be explainable by pointing towards individual behavior which brought the *explanandum* about. From this assumption, it follows straightforwardly that the behavioral model focuses only on the behavior of individuals. When Buchanan (1984: 21) claims that "(t)he constitutional perspective embodies a two-stage (or multistage) conceptual model of behavior, whether the acting entity is the person, the voluntary association, or the inclusive collectivity," he supposedly means that there are problems of collective action as elaborated by Olson (1965) and that it makes sense to distinguish between voluntary associations (cf. Buchanan's theory of clubs, 1965) and the state whose representatives are backed by the monopoly to use force (cf. already Buchanan and Tullock, 1962: Ch. 5).

The behavioral model used in constitutional economics should comprise all those actors who are potentially relevant for the creation, modification, and interpretation of the constitution. This set comprises scattered, unorganized individuals, representatives of organized interest-groups, voters, politicians representing the executive and legislative branches as well as those representing only political parties, but also judges as those who will supposedly interpret the constitution.

In economics, the behavior of the actors is usually modelled as the result of their preference-function and the available means to maximize this function.[5] The means component not only includes their monetary resources but also the theoretical, technological and situational information that the actors are supposed to dispose of as well as the capability to process this information (their "rationality"). If these elements are sufficiently specified, one disposes of a behavioral model.

Chapter four of Brennan and Buchanan (1985) contains an ardent defence of the *homo oeconomicus* assumption. The authors aim at convincing their critics that *homo oeconomicus* is not only an adequate behavioral model for market contexts but also for the behavior in non-market ones. Their main argument is concerned with methodological consistency: since it is the same individual that acts in market as well as in non-market settings, it would be inconsistent to operate with two (or more) different behavioral models. This, however, is only an argument for always using the same model but not necessarily for using *homo oeconomicus*.

For their substantive defence they claim that a behavioral model which is based on average behavior overestimates the benefits (produced by altruists) and correspondingly underestimates the costs (produced by egoists). The individuals that are evaluating alternative institutional arrangements would thus be smart if they chose a worst-case scenario. In other words: Brennan and Buchanan explicitly opt for an assumption that is descriptively wrong. The imputed asymmetry would lead the individuals in the constitutional choice-situation to behave risk-averse. Although they might factually very well be risk-neutral, the purported asymmetry would lead them to behave *as if* they were risk-averse.

In the meantime, this ardent defence of *homo oeconomicus* has not only been criticized by others (e.g., Brooks, 1994 or La Manna and Slomp, 1994) but Brennan and Buchanan, writing with different co-authors or on their own, have both somewhat modified their positions: Brennan now explicitly rejects the notion of behavioral neutrality (between market and political behavior, Brennan and Lomasky, 1993: 14 and passim) so central to the 1985 argument. In a contribution to a conference on bounded rationality, Buchanan (1994: 124) describes the standard exercise of utility maximization subject to a budget constraint – indeed *homo oeconomicus* as commonly modelled – as "relatively narrow" in its usefulness. If opportunism is frequently encountered, "preaching becomes more productive." He continues that deficit spending by government will only be stopped after a "shift of moral attitudes" has taken place (pp. 125 and 130). Since this contradicts the approach of constitutional economics, Frey (1994a: 138) even writes of "two Buchanans." The introduction of consciously chosen moral constraints adds even more ambiguity to the *homo oeconomicus* model (for a critique of Buchanan's behavioral model, cf. Voigt, 1994).

Homo oeconomicus as conventionally portrayed comprises a utility function and the rational maximization thereof. Under these assumptions, it is not only irrational to vote in large number settings, but it is equally irrational to acquire information about the working properties of alternative constitutional rules and it is further irrational to participate in a constitutional convention. Scholars of constitutional economics have therefore developed additional arguments that make the participation in constitutional conventions at least plausible. Ackerman (1984: 1020ff.) introduced the notion of "constitutional moments" in which people act altruistically and out of "revolutionary wisdom." This notion is, of course, criticized by public choice scholars, since it is based on a split behavioral model (e.g., Macey, 1988). A different approach to make participation plausible is introduced by Frey (1979: 317) who writes: "... it is relatively easy to bring latent groups to participation in the working out of a constitutional contract with its once-and-for-all character even where they cannot be induced to participate continuously" (cf. also McCormick and Tollison, 1981: 127f.). The argument is based on the assumptions (1) that constitutions comprise a multitude of rules which will have substantial consequences for every actor and 92) that constitutions are made to last, which makes their allocational and distributional effects even more severe. Once the basic constitutional decisions have been made and constitutional change only occurs at the margin, the potential external costs that can be put onto individuals are relatively small so that participation will only be rational for organized interest groups with special stakes. These arguments imply that the rational interest of individuals leads to a public discourse in constitutional matters, a notion that both Ackerman and Frey would normatively endorse. Casual empirical evidence suggests, however, that this is not always the case: the French constitution of 1958 had to be approved by referendum. Participating in a referendum seems to be a relatively cheap way of expressing one's preferences. Yet "... the public was tired of the constitutional debates. In the referendum, the proposal was approved by a little more than a third of the registered voters. Abstentions were about as numerous" (Foyer, 1988: 10). As a consequence of German unity, the necessity for revising the German constitution was discussed and a "constitutional commission" formed. Public interest in its proceedings was practically non-existing.[6] This observation is, of course, in no way an argument against a behavioral model based on rational choice. But it would lead to questioning the argument that constitutional conventions are more or less rent-seeking proof due to the very broad participation in their genesis, an argument explicitly advanced by McCormick and Tollison (1981: 128). Elster (1994: 31) comments on this: "Note that this statement suggests or presupposes that there is a systematic and substantial difference in rent-seeking potential between constitutional matters and matters that are subject to ordinary legislation. To my knowledge, that claim has not been tested."[7]

7. Concepts of the constitution

7.1. The constitution as a social contract

Buchanan has not reinvented social philosophy but has made extensive use of Hobbes and others. The situation out of which the social contract emerges is the "equilibrium of anarchy" in which marginal costs and returns for producing, stealing and protecting goods are equally high. The individuals realize that they could all be better off if they could agree on a disarmament contract which would allow them to reduce the resources used for protecting – and stealing – goods. Since the individuals find themselves in a prisoner's dilemma situation, they all have an incentive to sign a disarmament contract and to break it subsequently. As they all foresee this, they create a protective state to protect the individuals' private spheres. Additionally, they create the productive state which is to provide the society with those (collective) goods whose private production would not be profitable.

The idea that individuals create a state by way of contract is not meant to be a historically correct description but simply a heuristic means. Buchanan (1975: 50ff.) believes it to be helpful not only in explaining existing institutions but also hopes to be able to derive some criteria for their evaluation from it.

7.2. The constitutional contract as principal-agent-relationship

The principal-agent theory developed out of the observation that contracting partners often dispose of differing information. A principal entrusts an agent with a number of tasks but cannot observe the actions of the agent costlessly. Additionally, the agent might have to act in situations too complex to be amenable for a clear-cut evaluation with regard to the respective aim. The agent thus disposes of a certain degree of liberty in her actions that she will use to optimize upon her own – and not the principal's – utility function. The main focus of the principal-agent theory therefore lies on the design of the optimal contract under the assumption of asymmetrically distributed information.

Conceptualizing the members of society as the principals and the government as the agent almost suggests itself. The problem consists of designing a contract – in this case the constitution – in such a way that the agents will be led to maximize the expected utility of the principals while simultaneously maximizing their own. It is therefeore normative theory. The recommendations derived by Anderson and Hill (1986) do not go beyond those already contained in Buchanan's contract model. Merville and Osborne (1990) show that under a number of fairly restrictive assumptions, politicians only have a chance of being reelected if they break the principal-agent contract implying that elections do not function quasi-automatically as a monitoring or enforcement mechanism of the original contract. The hope that one could be able to restrict politicians via an adequately designed contract has been evaluated quite critically by Tullock (1987: 317f.): "The view that the government can be bound by specific provisions is naive. Something must enforce those provisions, and whatever enforces them is itself unbounded."

7.3. The constitutional contract as precommitment-device

Precommitment can be used as an instrument against one's own (short-term) weakness of will. The most famous example for such a use of precommitment stems from antiquity: Ulysses had himself bound against the mast in order not to succumb to the singing of the Sirens. In economic parlance, the problem of *akrasia* is often discussed under the heading of time-inconsistent preferences. Whereas the principal-agent theory contains a modification of traditional theory by taking account of the fact of asymmetrical information, the precommitment-approach contains a modification with regard to the imputed rationality of the actors.

If not only individuals but also entire groups might be subject to time-inconsistent preferences, one could ask whether societies are capable of protecting themselves from those inconsistencies by precommitment devices. This would presuppose that (a) the members of the respective society know their own weaknesses, (b) dispose of the adequate technology for precommitting themselves, (c) a vast majority of the society's members including its politicians are willing to restrain themselves by such mechanisms. From a normative point of view, one could ask why a society at one point in time should be able to tie the society at a later point in time. Since it could be made up of different individuals, one could even question whether one would still be dealing with the same society. Additionally, preferences might also shift (Elster, 1984, discusses the Ulysses-procedure and presents various devices used throughout history; Holmes, 1988, contains a discussion of the moral issues at stake).

7.4. The constitution as the result of cultural evolution

Whereas Buchanan is clearly leading the contract notion of the constitution, Hayek (e.g., 1973, 1976, 1979, 1988) is almost as clearly leading the notion of the constitution as the result of cultural evolution (for a critical evaluation, cf. Voigt, 1992). Buchanan conceptualizes individuals as rational actors who have enough foresight to recognize the advantageousness of rules and therefore implement them, i.e., consciously choose to constrain their possible range of actions. Hayek turns this concept upside down: man only became rational because he followed some rules. The emergence of rules is thus not the result of an explicit process of rational choice but the (unintended) result of human action (but not of human design). He further does not assume the actors to dispose of a comprehensive theoretical knowledge concerning the functioning of rules. Instead, he repeatedly stresses that actors dispose of subjective knowledge that can only partially be communicated and can therefore not be aggregated. Although Hayek shares the assumption of methodological individualism, the relevance of the surrounding group for the individual actors is an important element of his theory. To take the Hobbesian war as a starting point of a theory of the state in his eyes is a worthless endeavor because survival can only be thought of in groups (Hayek, 1988: 12).

The concept of the constitution as the result of social evolution does not rest on *as if*-explanations but in descriptions that claim historical accuracy. Constitutional rules are seen as the result of a trial and error-process. Those constitutional rules that have survived the selection process of evolution must have served the groups whose interactions they regulate better than other, potentially competing rules, which have not survived. A second selection process takes place simultaneously: groups observe each other and those perceived as being more successful are imitated, supposedly implying that their rules will also be imitated. Hayek does not dispose of an explicit measure of the efficiency of a constitution but seems to be willing to derive the adequacy of an existing rule-set from the (relative) capability of a group to grow in size and feed its members.

7.5. The constitution as a bundle of conventions

Some scientists argue that the constitution cannot meaningfully be conceptualized as a contract but that it is rather comparable to social norms which emerge unintendedly and which are accepted by most members of society in a general and unconscious way (e.g., Hardin, 1989; Ordeshook, 1992). Constitution-making can then be thought of as an attempt to (1) hasten the process of the emergence of conventions and (2) to guide it in a certain direction. Hardin (1989: 119) writes: "Establishing a constitution is a massive act of coordination that creates a convention that depends for its maintenance on its self-generating incentives and expectations." Since the concept is developed out of a dissatisfaction with and in explicit distance from the constitution as contract-notion, here are four differences between the two concepts: (1) A contract serves to solve a prisoner's dilemma whereas a constitution serves to solve a coordination game that can, however, include a considerable degree of conflict. (2) In order for a contract to be valid, the explicit consent of the contracting parties is necessary whereas a constitution can be viable without the explicit consent of a majority as long as there is no serious opposition. (3) The enforcement of a contract is usually secured by the availability of external sanctions whereas a constitution is secured by the immense difficulty of establishing an alternative constitution. (4) Contracting parties frequently try to take as many contingencies as possible into consideration, which often gives contracts a static character whereas constitutions are more easily amenable to evolution.

8. Positive constitutional economics

8.1. Preamble

In this section, various approaches towards a positive theory of constitutional economics will be presented, their performance evaluated, and questions for further research sketched. The available theory is structured into four areas: in the first one, (constitutional) rules are analyzed as the outcome of a certain procedure. A procedure, however, is nothing but a certain modus of aggregating inputs and will therefore not bring any rules (outputs) about by itself. This is why a look at possible inputs is taken in the second area where a distinction between individual factors (preferences, restraints) and collective factors (external influence, distribution of resources) is made. These first two areas are a rather static approach towards a positive theory. This is why the third area is dedicated to a more dynamic analysis, namely of asking for the possibilities to explain constitutional change. Two kinds of change will be introduced, namely explicit and implicit constitutional change. For constitutional change to occur, an equilibrium situation must have turned into a disequilibrium one. In this section, the relevance of constitutional rules themselves for structuring constitutional change plays an important role. Whereas the first three areas are concerned with the emergence and modification of constitutional rules, the fourth area focuses on their (economic) effects.

8.2. Constitutional rules and the procedures bringing them about

This subsection deals with hypotheses in which the constitutional rule is a function of the procedure chosen to bring it about. Using comparative institutional analysis, the question would be how different procedures lead to different constitutional rules. Jon Elster's research program concerning constitutional economics puts a strong emphasis on hypotheses of this kind. In his Storrs-lectures, he compares the use of rational discourse as opposed to bargaining strategies in the constitutional conventions that led to the U.S.-constitution as well as to the first constitution of Nouveau Régime France. His scientific interest does not center around possibilities to explain what happened during those conventions but to identify a mechanism (Elster, 1991: 80). In a more recent paper, he has rendered this idea more precisely (Elster, 1993: 194).

Concerning procedures, he asks about the consequences of time-limits for constitutional conventions, about how constitutional conventions that simultaneously serve as legislature allocate their time between the two functions, about which effects the regular information of the public concerning the progress of the constitutional negotiations has[8] and about how certain supermajorities and election rules can determine the outcome of conventions (Elster, 1991: 30). Some of Riker's articles (1983, 1984) can also be interpreted as an encouragement to search for hypotheses of this kind. He calls for an extension of traditional rational choice-theory pointing to the fact that in its traditional form it is incapable of taking into account dynamic and creative processes which structure the decision room of the actors. He diagnoses a deficit in the analysis of processes concerning creative adjustments which he also labels *heresthetics* or the art of political strategy (Riker, 1984: 2). Using rhetoric, one tries to convince others by argument. Using heresthetics, one tries to structure the situation in such a way that others would accept it readily (p. 8). He names several categories of heresthetics: strategic voting (the avoidance of "wasted" votes, the creation of a voting cycle, vote-trading) and the manipulation of the agenda (arranging the sequence of decisions in a certain manner, introducing new voting alternatives) (Riker, 1983: 63f.)

Concerning the state of knowledge of this pat of constitutional economics, Elster (1993: 174) deplores that there is not one single paper describing the process of constitution-making from a general perspective. There is, however, a large number of case studies of which the volume edited by Goldwin and Kaufman (1988) deserves special mention because participants in the constitution making-process from nine countries have depicted their experience within a frame of questions developed by the editors.

8.3. Constitutional rules as the result of preferences and restrictions

Procedures are a modus of aggregating inputs and can therefore never bring a constitutional rule about by themselves. This is why possible inputs are named in this subsection. One can ask whether there are systematic relations between rules on the one hand and individual preferences (the ones towards time and risk included), the values and norms of the actors, their ideologies, the disposable constitutional technologies, the distribution of resources within the society analyzed, the taking into account of existing constitutions of other societies, the influence of external organizations etc. on the other hand. This is a heterogeneous bunch of variables which might be usefully grouped into two categories, namely individual factors such as the preferences and their restrictions on the one hand and collective factors such as the influence of external organizations on the other. At times, a clear-cut assignment of a variable to one of the categories might be difficult; values and norms, e.g., are only held by individuals but owe much of their relevance to the fact that they are shared by large parts of a society. This might be especially relevant in times where a new constitution is worked upon because these are often characterized by great uncertainty (to a certain degree, internal institutions might jump in to fill the gap, a hypothesis that is elaborated in Kiwit and Voigt, 1995). The two categories might be heuristically useful because individual factors can be seen as potentially causing conflicts (as, e.g., ideologies) whereas collective factors are potentially unifying (as, e.g., values and norms). The generation of testable hypotheses in the first category should be more difficult because the evolution of a process of conflict is difficult to predict.

There are, nevertheless, some papers which could be subsumed under the first category. Charles Beard (1913) tried to explain the rules of the U.S.-constitution via the interests of the members of the Philadelphia-convention. Following Beard's lead but using modern econometric techniques, McGuire and Ohsfeldt (1986, 1989a, b) have tried to explain the voting behavior of the Philadelphia-delegates as well as those of the delegates to the 13 state ratifying conventions. They (1989a: 175) write: "The statistical results show that merchants, western landowners, financiers, and large public-securities holders, *ceteris paribus,* supported the new constitution, whereas debtors and slave owners, *ceteris paribus,* opposed the Constitution." The possibility that a hypothetical delegate to a ratifying convention in one of the 13 states which had average values for all other independent variables voted in favor of the constitution increased from 59 to 84% in case he owned private securities, decreased from 62 to 36% in case he was in personal debt, increased from 59 to 72% in case he was pursuing merchant interests, and increased from 58 to 74% in case he had landed interests in the western territories (p. 195f.). Also of interest are the differences between the two phases of the ratifying procedure: whereas for the delegates of the Philadelphia-Convention, the interests of their constituents are a better predictor for their voting behavior than their own interests, the opposite is true for the delegates to the 13 state conventions. An *ad hoc*-hypothesis for this difference could be that the Philadelphia-delegates were more narrowly constrained in their voting behavior than those in the 13 states because the constitution would not have turned into effect if not at least nine of the 13 states had ratified it.

McGuire and Ohsfeldt (1989a) conceptualize the behavior of the representatives to the conventions within the realm of the principal-agent model, i.e., they differentiate between the interests of the representatives and those of their constituents. They further point to the fact that the ratification process can hardly be claimed to have taken place behind a veil of uncertainty à la Buchanan and Tullock and that it seems therefore justified to assign its ratification to the operational as opposed to the constitutional level (p. 184).

I am not aware of other empirically tested hypotheses within the sketched research strategy. There are nevertheless hypotheses based on plausibility. Przeworski (1991: 92), e.g., notes that societies with firmly rooted organic conceptions of the state have a strong tendency to establish a rule of unanimity in their constitutions; this tendency was frequently inspired by Catholicism. In their analysis of the Spanish constitution, Brennan and Pardo (1991: 61) point to the observation that the consent of large parts of the society to a constitution has to be evaluated taking the context out of which it emerged explicitly into account. It might be perfectly rational to opt in favor of a constrained dictatorial regime if the alternative is an unconstrained dictatorial regime.

The limited number of available empirical studies shows that the sketched research strategy has rarely been chosen. Questions that could be elucidated within this strategy concern the existence of systematic relationships between the values and norms shared by the members of a society and the constitutional rules that are the result of a constitutional convention. The question of a possible systematic relationship can also be asked concerning permanent constitutional change: e.g., does a change of values and norms over time have systematic effects on the – explicit or implicit – change of constitutions? In how far can one prove systematic relationships between the internal institutions of a society and its constitution? What is, in this case, the independent, what the dependent variable? What role do the ideologies present in a society play? What is the relevance of external forces such as the allies after World War II in Germany and Japan? To what extent was the Soviet Union able to force the countries of Central and Eastern Europe to copy its own constitution? How viable are constitutions copied from another country in general?

8.4. Constitutional rules channelling constitutional change

This subsection concentrates on constitutional change. The distinction between the first two subsections and this one can also be interpreted as the first two dealing with total constitutional change, whereas this one focuses on marginal change. Here, the constitutional rules that remain unchanged (potentially) constrain the ways in which the rules can be changed. Constitutional rules can channel constitutional change but can hardly be its sole initiator.[9] For constitutional change to occur, some sort of disequilibrium must exist, i.e., one or more of the inputs discussed in the previous subsection must have changed. Mueller (1991: 326) distinguishes three ways of reinterpreting and amending the constitution: (1) a constitutional convention, (2) a referendum and (3) the appointment of agents which could be (a) elected representatives or (b) the judiciary. Mueller thus focuses on the procedures that bring about constitutional change. Whereas the first two procedures involve direct citizen participation, the third procedure is based on some sort of representation. We propose an alternative classification which explicitly separates constitutional change by reinterpretation from change by amendment. The first kind will be called implicit change whereas the second kind is dubbed explicit change. Explicit change occurs when the text of the constitutional document is modified, implicit change can be brought about by all three branches of government: by the executive if it interprets constitutional rules differently over time, by the legislature if it passes laws that would have been considered unconstitutional in some former time and by the judiciary if it lets the executive and the legislature get away with their modified interpretation. This last option promises to be important because it is difficult to conceive of an organization which checks upon the conformity of those who are given the competence to check upon the (constitutional) conformity of legislative action. It is not only possible to separate explicit from implicit constitutional change but also constitutional from unconstitutional change. Whereas the first aspect focuses on its *formality,* the second aspect is concerned with its *legality*. A simple matrix can thus be drawn:

Table 1. Conceptualizing constitutional change

Legality formality	Constitutional	Unconstitutional
explicit	1	3
implicit	2	4

8.4.1. Explicit and constitutional constitutional change

The first step in analyzing explicit constitutional change is an analysis into the possibilities of proposing it. Constitutional change is *inter alia* channelled by the possibility to control the agenda. Denzau (1985: 185) inquires into agenda access, i.e., "the ability to propose changes to the status quo, changes that receive formal consideration by a body empowered to make such changes." He considers constitutional matters as "the carrying out of ordinary political relation by other means]] (p. 188) and asks how different institutions can affect outcomes, i.e., he performs a comparative institutional analysis. The institutions compared are popular referendum (i.e., a constitutional amendment proposed by a legislature must be ratified by the citizens), bicameralism, popular initiative (i.e., any individual willing to incur the costs of getting sufficient signatures has agenda access), and executive veto. The empirical implications on constitutional change proper are straightforward. The relevance of this approach rather lies in its analyzing constitutional change as an alternative to ordinary legislation.

Explicit constitutional change can be sought by interest groups who try to convince legislators to change the constitution. If constitutional change is only sought in a disequilibrium, the interest group seeking change must perceive its own relevance as having changed. Boudreaux and Pritchard (1993) analyze the hitherto 27 amendments of the U.S.-constitution from an economic perspective. They begin with the conjecture that a lobby-group interested in constitutional change principally has two possibilities of seeking its realization: it can either lobby for a simple law or it can lobby for constitutional change. The second option is, however, more expensive. The trivial prediction of rational choice theory is that the group will choose the option with the higher expected utility. In order to be able to make predictions concerning the option chosen, it is therefore necessary to specify the cost- and benefit-categories implied. Boudreaux and Pritchard specify two categories, namely "maintenance costs" on the one hand, and the force and the development of opposition forming against the proposed change over time on the other hand. The "maintenance cost" category is an attempt to add the time-dimension to Olson's *Theory of Collective Action* (1965): Boudreaux and Pritchard do not ask for the possibilities of a latent interest group to overcome the organization-dilemma for the first time but are interested in the question of how the striking power of an organization can change over time. Their argument is directly connected with Olson's: if the number of potential members increases over time, it will also become more difficult to exclude non-members from consuming the public good produced by the group. From this, they derive the hypothesis that groups with high maintenance costs are more likely to demand constitutional change than groups with lower maintenance costs.

The second category introduced by Boudreaux and Pritchard is the force and the development of opposition forming against the proposed change over time. They differentiate between four cases namely (1) a weak opposition today that remains weak tomorrow, (2) a strong opposition today that remains strong tomorrow, (3) a weak opposition today that is, however, expected to become strong tomorrow, (4) a strong opposition today which is expected to loose strength. Boudreaux and Pritchard consider the third case to be the relevant one. It follows that they predict a demand for constitutional change in cases of high maintenance costs and in cases in which today's opposition is weak but expected to be strong in the future. It is possible to interpret the paper by Boudreaux and Pritchard as the starting point for positively oriented research into the process of explicit constitutional change.

8.4.2. Implicit and constitutional constitutional change

It was conjectured above that implicit constitutional change can be brought about by all three branches of government. Twight (1992) claims that the constitution is often factually changed without there being a consensus on this change. Politicians would be able to modify the set of rights of the citizens without a corresponding consensus. Her argument is that a substantial part of political transaction costs[10] would be endogenous and that they are explicitly manipulated by politicians in order to reduce political opposition against diminishing the set of rights. Niskanen (1990) also claims that the effective constitution of the U.S. has massively changed over the last 200 years and that it has been relatively effective in protecting political property rights but has failed in the protection of economic property rights.

By interpreting the constitution, judges can also bring about constitutional change. Regarding the interpretation of the U.S.-constitution by the Supreme Court, Merville and Osborne (1990) have observed that the Court has "occasionally" enforced the constitution but this "in a manner that has struck many observers as capricious and unreliable." This should – according to Merville and Osborne – not be a surprise since the constitution deals with the incentives of judges as inadequately as it deals with those of the legislators. The question of which particular design of constitutional rules enhances the judges' incentives so as to take the intentions of the constitution-makers into consideration has until now not been dealt with extensively. Formulated differently: the arguments in the utility functions of judges have not been subject to investigation. It seems to be a promising research task to enquire into the utility functions as well as the (perceived) constraints of judges in their professional activities. The constitutional changes brought about by judges are themselves based on some rules. It would be equally interesting to enquire in how far statements gained with regard to the common law are also valid for continental law systems.

8.4.3. Unconstitutional constitutional change

Neither Twight nor Niskanen claim that the observable implicit constitutional changes are themselves connected with an infringement of the constitution and could thus be deemed unconstitutional or illegal. In a principal-agent model, Merville and Osborne (1990) ask whether the government conceived of as agent can be induced to respect the contract by which it comes into existence by properly designing this (constitutional) contract. Their conjecture is that political competition – democracy – and the reputation with regard to respecting the limits of the constitution interact perversely and conclude that the agent will only be re-elected if it breaks the constitution. In other words: constitutionalism and democracy are incompatible. Supposing that there are two organized groups in society and the election cannot be won without the votes of at least one of these groups, the authors show that an incumbent who respects the constitutional contract will lose against a challenger who takes the interests of the organized interest-groups – at the expense of the non-organized voters – into account. Of course, one can criticize the assumptions. There are no ideological bounds of the candidates whatsoever because they formulate their platform solely on the prospects of being able to win the election with it. Merville and Osborne (1990: 28) further assume that legislative proposals even if unconstitutional "... can be enacted if enacting them will not cost the agent his job." This assumption not only presupposes a certain acting of the judges but also of the voters and can thus be questioned. This is equally true for the assumption of perfect ignorance: the authors suppose that the members of the two organized groups completely abstain from voting if none of the candidates presents a platform reflecting the preferences of the members of the interest-group.

Davidson (1984) enquires into the conditions under which the constitutional provisions can be expected to be respected and conjectures that politicians are most likely to break those rules whose non-compliance will only imply a small reduction in their future legitimacy. Thus, those rules that are least understood by the citizens will be broken with the highest probability. Both Merville and Osborne as well as Davidson ask about the incentives that politicians have to comply with the constitution if compliance is costly. The possibility of unconstitutional change points to the necessity of adequately specifying the preference function and the constraints of politicians as well as analyzing their incentives for compliance with constitutional rules. The cited studies show that research is at the very beginning: Merville and Osborne's model is hypothetically positive, Davidson's reasoning based on plausibility, i.e., no empirical test is available.

The question whether constitutional rules can really make a difference in constitutional development has recently also been discussed with regard to the question of secession. Sunstein (1991: 647) conjectures that such a right would encourage strategic behavior by certain subgroups whose resources are unrenouncable for the further existence of the state but who do not depend themselves on its further existence. Those groups could draw unreasonably high advantages from their position. He also fears that such a right would produce large destabilizing effects which may disrupt expectations whose existence is indispensable both to economic prosperity and democratic self-determination (p. 651). Whereas a right to secede could produce unwanted political and economic patterns, the renunciation on such a right is equated with the solution of a prisoner's dilemma.

With regard to possible effects of a right to secede, the argument often goes exactly the other way round: the government of a federal union could be restrained effectively by a right to secede established for memberstates of the union: should the utility of being a member become negative this member could credibly threaten its withdrawal. A right to secede would thus be an instrument to constrain government activities on the federal level (e.g., Buchanan, 1990b; Bernholz, 1991). Chen and Ordeshook (1994) start their analysis one step before. They ask whether establishing a right to secede within the constitution will have any relevance on later processes: if a subgroup is determined to part from the state in existence until now, will the non-existence of a right to secede be relevant to the behavior of the actors and the outcome of the game? Chen and Ordeshook conceptualize constitutions as self-enforcing conventions. A constitutional rule is only self-enforcing if it is a Nash-equilibrium. If secession is the only Nash-equilibrium, then it would supposedly be the outcome of the game, no matter if it was a right guaranteed by the constitution or not. The authors name three conditions that must hold for a constitutional right to secession to become relevant: "Put differently, ..., we must establish that there are at least two alternative equilibria, that without some means of coordination, society need not achieve either of these equilibria (...), and that alternative constitutional language can direct society to one or the other of these equilibria" (p .47). They claim that these conditions could hold in cases where a subgroup disposes of credible commitments and if the decision of a sub-group to exit from a state or to remain within it, depends on prior agreement (p. 53).

Young (1994) analyzes the issue of secession using simple game theory with regard to Canada. His central question is why secession is so rarely observed. Hechter (1992) analyzes the dynamics of secession using four archetypal steps. Our positive knowledge concerning the effects of a constitutional right to secede remains rather scarce. I do not know of any systematic empirical test. The non-existence of tested positive knowledge is also relevant to the normative branch of constitutional economics: if the effects of such a right are not known, opting for its implementation will be hard to defend on scientific grounds. Sunstein (1991: 635): "The argument also has general implications for the theory of what does and does not belong in constitutions. This theory remains in a surprisingly primitive state."

8.4.4. *The separation of powers*

The separation of powers can be put to a twofold analysis: the first kind would concentrate on its emergence. Analyzing the separation of powers under the heading "constitutional rules channelling constitutional change" seems justified if the emergence of the separation of powers can be conceptualized as the result of formerly valid constitutional rules. The second kind of analysis would concentrate on the effects that the separation of powers and its many variants bring about. This second kind is the topic of the next subsection into which we will therefore slip while analyzing the separation of powers. First, however, a very controversial hypothesis concerning the emergence of the independent judiciary is presented and discussed.

With their theory of the independent judiciary from an interest-group perspective, Landes and Posner (1975) put the conventional wisdom concerning the separation of powers on its head. According to them, the legislature is not controlled by the judiciary, but legislators have an interest in an "independent" judiciary because its existence makes it more valuable to be a legislator as it can prolong the life-span of the legislative deals that the legislators strike with representatives of interest groups. This increases their value for the interest-groups and simultaneously increases their willingness to pay the legislators. Landes and Posner define a judiciary as independent if it enforces "existing statutes in accordance with the intent of the enacting legislature" (p. 883) and produces stable expectations this way. The legislators have an interest in being able to make credible commitments vis-à-vis the representatives of interest groups. The existence of the independent judiciary enables them to do this by reducing the possibilities of post-contractual opportunism either by themselves or by their successors. According to Landes and Posner, the political branches have various means of imposing costs upon the judiciary ("budgetary harassment, tinkering with the courts' jurisdiction and altering the composition of the judiciary by the creation of many new judgeships" [885]) which – in turn – could maintain its independence best by enforcing the "contracts" that earlier legislatures had struck with interest groups.

A number of scientists mostly originating from the Virginia tradition of public choice have tried to test the hypothesis empirically: Crain and Tollison (1979a) ask whether a modified version of the model can be used to explain the constitutional amendment process of the U.S. state constitutions. The idea is that amending the constitution is a secure way of reducing the probability that legislative deals will be repealed in future periods, which is, however, also more costly to use than ordinary legislative statutes. In states where the judiciary can be expected to enforce the original deals struck by legislators and interest-groups (is "more independent" in Landes' and Posner's terminology), ordinary legislation will suffice. The more independent the judiciary, the less constitutional amendment activity is expected to occur. As a proxy for the degree of judicial independence, Crain and Tollison choose judicial tenure and find it negatively correlated and significant at the 15 percent level with amendment activity at the state level.

A very similar approach is chosen by Anderson, Martin, Shugart II, and Tollison (1990). Here, constitutional activity is operationalized by the change in the length of the state constitution, measured in words. In both tests, the respective authors claim to be able to explain around 50 percent of the variation in constitutional activity across the 50 states. In their concluding remarks, Anderson et al. (1990) claim that the small number of amendments at the federal level would indicate the effectiveness of the judiciary in securing the viability of the deals made between Congress and special interest-groups. Another conclusion reads that "because amendments to constitutions can be explained on the basis of the benefits and costs of constitutional versus statutory change, the origins of constitutions are likely to be understood in those terms as well (p. 99).

In still another test, Anderson, Shugart II and Tollison (1989) inquire into the incentives of judges to remain independent. They hypothesize that the salaries of the judges will be positively correlated with their independence. To grasp this hypothesis, one has to remember that "independence" is interpreted as "enforcing original contracts." The legislature would thus reward judges for positively sanctioning their deals. Anderson et al. find that the overall regressions can explain around 50 percent of the cross-state variation in judicial salaries.

At first sight, this theory seems both realistic and awkward. Apparently, it puts an end to the split model of man often found in constitutional economics: here, the bad (self-interested) legislator that is opposed by the good ("public-oriented") judges who repeal the statutes which diverge too openly from "public interest." The interest group theory of judicial independence can, however, be criticized on various grounds: first of all, the concept of "independence" seems shaky. Landes and Posner (1975: 875) define an independent judiciary as "one that does not make decisions on the basis of the sorts of political factors (...) that would influence and in most cases control the decision were it to be made by a legislative body such as the U.S. Congress." But what are the political factors that control legislative decisions? Later on, judicial independence is simply equated with "enforcing the original intent of legislative deals" which is supposed to produce predictability. Macey (1988) has argued that the positive correlation between "judicial independence" and "judges salaries" reported by Anderson et al. is inconsistent with the theory it purports to defend. If judges are rewarded by the legislature, they are dependent on it. This is why Boudreaux and Pritchard (1994: 7) write about the "dependent independent judiciary." The adherents of the interest-group theory would furthermore have to present arguments why the judiciary should enforce deals made by previous legislatures and not the current one since their salaries depend on the current legislature. Anderson et al.'s (1990) conclusion that the small number of amendments on the federal level indicates the effectiveness of judicial interpretation can, of course, also be interpreted the other way round: because the judiciary will not let special interest amendments pass, they are seldom initiated (cf. also Boudreaux and Pritchard, 1994: 15 who argue that judicial independence makes constitutional provisions more costly for interest groups seeking rents).

If one reads the Landes and Posner article as a hypothesis on the emergence of an independent judiciary, an implicit hypothesis must be that the legislature (probably jointly with the executive) not only dominates the judiciary but also has the power to create it, in other words: also acts as the constitutional convention. Landes and Posner would have to prove that it was not Chief Justice Marshall's ingenious interpretation of the constitution that led to judicial control but that he acted merely as a puppet of legislator interest. This would seem to be a re-interpretation of history hard to defend indeed. The Landes and Posner theory can be read as a theory of constitutional change because it interprets the introduction of the "independent" judiciary as the ingenious invention of the legislature-cum-constitutional convention. We now turn to the effects that various constitutional rules provoke and start with the analysis of the separation of powers.

8.5. The economic effects of constitutional rules

8.5.1. The separation of powers

I am not aware of any study analyzing the separation of powers from the perspective of positive constitutional economics. In a survey-article, Posner (1987) writes that the separation of powers increases the transaction costs of governing. This would hold for welfare-enhancing as well as for redistributive or even exploitative measures: "This makes unclear as a matter of theory whether the separation of powers results in a net improvement in social welfare compared to a system such as England's" (p. 11). The concept of the separation of powers can be classified into the horizontal separation (legislature, executive, judiciary) and the vertical separation (federalism). The structure of the isolated powers can vary to a considerable extent. We begin this part of the survey with papers that focus on different ways to set up the legislature.

The differential effects of unicameral and bicameral legislatures were first analyzed from an economic point of view by Buchanan and Tullock (1962:

Ch. 16). In their analytical frame, that decision-rule is optimal which leads to a minimum of interdependence costs. They conjecture that in comparison with unicameral systems bicameral systems have higher decision costs and continue: "On the other hand, if the basis of representation can be made significantly different in the two houses, the institutions of the bicameral legislature may prove to be an effective means of securing a substantial reduction in the expected external costs of collective action without incurring as much added decision-making costs as a more inclusive rule would involve in a single house" (pp. 235f.). The larger the majority required to reach a certain decision, the lower the external costs connected with that decision because the number of opponents to a decision is negatively correlated with the required majority. On the other hand, it will become increasingly difficult to reach a decision at all because the decision costs are positively correlated with the required majority. One possibility of keeping the external costs down is to require a supermajority (say of 3/4 or 5/6) in the single house system. Supermajorities in a single house system and simple majorities in a two house system can thus be considered as alternatives. Buchanan and Tullock now conjecture that – given identical external costs – the decicion costs would be lower in a bicameral than in a unicameral system.

Miller and Hammond (1989) inquire into the effects of bicameralism and the executive veto – which is sometimes simply considered the third chamber – on stability in the sense of reducing the probability of cycling majorities à la Condorcet or Arrow (1951). They conclude that bicameralism and the executive veto increase stability. The stability-enhancing effect of bicameralism depends on some preference-difference between the two chambers.

Levmore (1992) somewhat changes the focus of the analysis when he conjectures that a bicameral system might be better suited than a corresponding qualified majority in a unicameral system to reduce the power of the agenda setter. Bicameral systems are often interpreted as a break against overly active legislatures. Levmore relates this interpretation to the concept of federalism in a double sense: first, all federations have a bicameral legislature. Second, "(f)ederalism is likely to increase the chance of regulation because federal arrangements nearly always create some overlap in jurisdictional responsibilities so that there are multiple sources of regulation" (Levmore, 1992: 159). According to Levmore, federations tend to produce active legislatures but come systematically along with bicameral systems which tend to reduce legislator activism. Many of the hypotheses advanced by Levmore are mainly based on intuition (e.g., pp. 147f., 156, 160). Robust knowledge concerning the effects of bicameral systems is thus still scarce. Elster (1994: 22) even writes that "(t)he economic analysis of bicameralism (...) or of the separation of powers more generally (...) has not yielded much by the way of robust conclusions."

Concerning the effects of bicameral systems, one could analyze whether the legislative activity in bicameral systems is indeed lower than in unicameral ones, whether this is reflected in government consumption of economic output and whether there are even different growth rates. For a clear-cut comparative analysis of institutions the description of the exact functioning of the institutions to be compared is, however, primordial. One would have to inquire how a mediation committee influences the functioning of a bicameral system and how a presidential veto – which can be interpreted as a "third house" – influences the decision and the external costs. More general inquiries into the (economic) effects of the separation of powers could try to proceed by way of comparative institutional analysis, i.e., by comparing common features of constitutions which do know a separation of powers with those which do not.

A second aspect of the separation of powers can be their vertical separation, i.e., federalism. It has entered into mainstream economics under the heading of "fiscal federalism." Besides incorporating a second – and possibly third – layer of government into their analyses, the representatives of the approach remain within the traditional model, i.e., assume government to be efficiency maximizing. It is then asked on what governmental level public goods will be (optimally) provided taking externalities explicitly into account. This approach need thus not concern us here (examples are Oates, 1972; Gordon, 1983; Breton, 1987; Sinn, 1990).

In his *tour d'horizon* on the constitution as an economic document, Posner (1987: 13f.) claims that federalism would not substantially increase the transaction costs of governing because "... the federal government can always override the states in matters within the scope of its authority." In other words: the common presumption (e.g., held by Anderson and Hill, 1986; Buchanan, 1990) that the competition between the governments on the lower plane(s) that is inherent in federalism could serve as one device to tame Leviathan would be erroneous. Scharpf (1991: 422), likewise, calls the assumed capability of federalism to keep some governmental competences with the lower levels of government its "living lie." On the other hand, there are huge differences in the amount of competences that the top-level of government holds in various federal states. To my knowledge they have not been systematically analyzed from an economic point of view. Weingast (1995) makes a first step into this direction: he is concerned with instruments which can solve the dilemma between the necessity of governments comprising enough power to protect property rights on the one hand and the possibility of using this power to confiscate the wealth of the citizens on the other. In theoretical terms, a credible commitment to limited government is needed which needs to be self-enforcing. Weingast considers "market-preserving federalism" as such a device and describes two historical cases in which it has been the foundation of economic development, namely 18th-century England and the United States between 1787 and the 1930s. He thus describes a nomological hypothesis ("market-preserving federalism will result in faster economic development than constitutional settings not so characterized") which would now have to be tested empirically.

8.5.2. Direct vs. representative democracy

In a paper on the politico-economic lessons to be drawn from the Swiss experiment with institutions of direct democracy, Frey (1994b: 338) observes that "public choice associates 'direct democracy' with various voting rules (...), but the *institutions* of direct democracy as such are neglected." To compare the differential effects of direct-democratic institutions amongst each other and with institutions of representative democracy is a task for constitutional economics. Until now, the comparative analysis has often stopped at comparing direct democracy and representative democracy on a very general level, neglecting the concrete institutions and the possible synthesis of the two whose possibility is proven by reality.

In reality, we also observe that the vast majority of decisions in modern democracies is taken by representative bodies and direct-democratic elements play – at best – only a minor role. Switzerland is a major exception which is why most studies concentrate on it or on the second or third level governments of the U.S.. The *Calculus of Consent* already contains a hypothesis on the vast use of representative as compared with direct voting systems. Buchanan and Tullock (1962) show that assuming different intensities in preferences, log-rolling can be welfare enhancing. With very many people eligible to vote, log-rolling becomes, however, almost impossible (p. 134). A constitutional economist interested in explaining the emergence of certain constitutional arrangements would have to come up with a mechanism linking the welfare enhancing effects of log-rolling and the emergence of representative democracy in order to refrain from committing the functionalist fallacy.

In a number of recent papers, Frey and his various co-authors (e.g. 1994) argue that referenda are a feasible and effective institution for having the preferences of a society's members reflected in the public goods bundle produced by the politicians. Referenda could make politicians' cartels directed against the voter ineffective (p. 338). In 39% of the referenda that took place in Switzerland between 1848 and 1990, the majority among the population was different from the majority in Parliament (p.73) which is interpreted as a proof of the hypothesis of a better reflection of voters preferences via referenda. Pommerehne showed already in 1978 that tax rates are *ceteris paribus* lower when taxpayers decide themselves on the bundle of public goods supplied (for an overview over comparative studies, cf. Pommerehne, 1990). Additionally, taxpayer honesty is positively correlated with voters chances to participate directly in the choice of the bundle of public goods to be supplied (Pommerehne and Frey, 1992). Steunenberg (1992), using basic game theory, compares the effects of ten different institutional arrangements on the level of public expenditure and concludes that different arrangements allow the politicians to varying degrees to manipulate the result according to their own preferences.

In a paper co-authored with Kirchgässner, Frey (1990: 63) speculates that the readiness of voters to incur information costs would, *ceteris paribus*, be higher in democracies with direct-democratic institutions because they participate more directly in the decisions. The authors obviously believe their conjecture to be an advantage of direct-democratic institutions. Supporters of representative democracy would supposedly claim that this was a disadvantage because voters had to incur high information costs. Direct democracy would thus be a decision procedure in which resources were wasted whereas representative democracy would make use of the welfare enhancing principle of the division of labor. Frey and Kirchgässner (1960: 65) further stress that time is scarce and the number of questions that could usefully be decided by referenda was naturally limited in number.

Suppose that it is true that direct-democratic institutions do allow for a better inclusion of voters preferences in deciding on the collective goods bundle and that this was itself a preference shared by the majority of a society's citizens but not by its politicians. One could then ask how the constitution could be changed against the apparent cartel of politicians. One possibility could be to inquire into the history of the introduction of direct-democratic institutions in Switzerland and to check whether and to what degree experiences made could be used today (this entire enterprise being a normative endeavor, however).

8.5.3. Individual rights and economic growth

The conjecture that individual rights and economic growth are correlated is hardly a new one but remains controversial among economists. For thinkers such as Tocqueville (1840/1945), Hayek (1944) or Friedman (1962), individual liberty increased the prospects of economic growth. Przeworski and Limongi (1993: 64) survey the literature that focuses on the relationship between democracy – which is often used as a proxy for individual liberty – and economic growth and conclude that "the simple answer to the question ... is that we do not know whether democracy fosters or hinders economic growth." Bhalla (1994) proposes to search for a relationship not between democracy and growth rates but between political, civil and economic rights on the one hand and growth rates on the other. He finds a positive correlation not only between individual liberty and economic growth but also between political and civil rights and enrollment in secondary schools and a negative one between political and civil rights and infantile mortality. Bhalla shows that the availability of human capital is a necessary but not a sufficient condition for sustained economic growth. This will only occur if economic liberties come along with human capital. His study is thus also a challenge of the so-called new growth theory.[11]

9. Conclusions and outlook

Section 8 has shown that positive constitutional economics is still in its infancy. Most of the (little) available knowledge is theoretical rather than empirical – and on top of this often based on plausibility rather than stringent models. The topics touched upon in the last section are, of course, not all-inclusive but rather the result of value judgments concerning their potential relevance. Promising questions for further research include, e.g., an analysis of the role of the judiciary for constitutional change as well as the relevance of international constitutional competition. If the last aspect is relevant, "sovereign" states might be forced to change their constitution due to changes in other societies' constitutions. Underlying these last two questions is the assumption that one can conceive of a general economic theory explaining constitutional change. This is, of course, an assumption that can be questioned, too.

Although these questions are very broad indeed, it is difficult conceptualizing constitutional economics as an economic subdiscipline in and of its own right. If constitutions are thought of as a group of rules constraining human behavior, the connection to the New Institutional Economics becomes obvious. Whereas mainstream economics has largely neglected the relevance of institutions, the New Institutional Economics has shown their relevance not only for the (static) analysis of allocation and distribution, but especially for the evolution of systems. The statement that institutions matter is hardly controversial whereas the statement that constitutions matter remains to be proven, at least if one is interested in knowing how exactly they matter. Additional insights might be gained by using most of the concepts of the New Institutional Economics for the analysis of constitutions.

John Neville Keynes (1955) proposed a tripartite division of political economy, introducing the "art of political economy" besides the more standard positive and normative branches. This art deals with possibilities of reducing differences between "Is" and "Ought." It is tempting to conceive of an "art of constitutional political economy" analogously. This art would itself have to have a positive foundation: knowledge about the possibilities to modify constitutions intentionally is primordial for such a third branch. A solidified New Institutional Economics *cum* constitutional economics can eventually become a serious challenge for neoclassical economy. One such example was given with neoclassical growth theory including its "new" variant.

Notes

1. Cf., e.g., Ackerman (1988: 173): "In response to the perception that public-regarding virtue is in short supply, *The Federalist* proposes a democratic constitution *that tries to economize on virtue*"; cf. also Schwartz (1989: 34f.) who observes three major differences to other theories hitherto available: (1) the importance of institutional detail, (2) the recognition of the incentives of individual actors, and (3) the notion of equilibrium albeit substantial differences in methodology. Cain and Jones describe Madison's methodology as "experimental, empirical, and circumstantial, not deductive and theoretical" (1989: 12).
2. This section is largely based on Voigt (1996).
3. The term has been coined by Burnham (1982: 78) who defines it as "the entire network of attitudes, norms, behaviors, and expectations among elites and publics that surround and support the written document."
4. Cf., however, Brennan and Lomasky (1993) and Wohlgemuth (1995) for recent critiques of the possibility of analogy.
5. As is common practice in economics, preferences are supposed to be stable. Institutional change that is brought about as the consequence of changed preferences is beyond the scope of economic explanations (cf. Brennan and Buchanan, 1985: 49).
6. From a public choice perspective, one could, however, argue that non-participation is rational as long as the absentees expected a clear result in either direction. The high turnout in referenda which were expected to have a close result (as, e.g., recently in Quebec or Ireland) would support this argument.
7. Some scholars seem to have slid a doubly split behavioral model into their arguments: on the one hand, legislators always transgress against the "public interest" because they auction off legislation to the highest bidders, i.e., provide rent-seeking groups with what they want. In an abstract way, judges are often seen as promoting the "public interest" by enforcing the rights and liberties laid down in the original text. Simultaneously, some of these scholars are ready to do some court bashing with regard to the U.S.-Supreme Court. According to them, the Court has not faithfully stuck to the Constitution at least since 1936. The custodian problem remains unsolved in this area (e.g., Dorn, 1988).
8. On the question of whether there is a systematic relationship between public sessions of the constitutional convention and the rules agreed upon, Macey (1986) advances the hypothesis that public deliberations make the obvious use of log-rolling and horsetrading less likely. In this setting, the representatives would at least try to formulate their arguments in terms of the common good.
9. An exception might be a constitutional provision to regularly check upon its contents.
10. Twight (1994: 190) defines political transaction costs as "the costs of reaching and enforcing political agreements regarding the role and scope of government. Political transaction costs thus include information costs, organization costs, agency costs and other costs that exist in a political situation because of the fact that individuals strive to act collectively."
11. Cf. also the study by Gwartney, Lawson, and Block (1996) which shows striking correlations between economic freedom and growth.

References

Ackerman, B. (1984). The Storrs Lectures: Discovering the constitution. *Yale Law Journal* 93: 1013–1072.

Ackerman, B. (1988). Neo-federalism? In J. Elster and R. Slagstad (Eds.), *Constitutionalism and democracy*, 153–193. Cambridge: Cambridge University Press.

Alessi, L. de (1980). The economics of property rights: A review of the evidence. *Research in Law and Economics* 2: 1–47.

Anderson, T. and Hill, P. (1986). Constraining the transfer society: Constitutional and moral dimensions. *Cato Journal* 6(1): 317–339.

Anderson, G., Shugart II, W. and Tollison, R. (1989). On the incentives of judges to enforce legislative wealth transfers. *Journal of Law & Economics* 32: 215–228.

Anderson, G., Martin, D., Shugart II, W. and Tollison, R. (1990). Behind the veil: The political economy of constitutional change. In W. Crain and R. Tollison (Eds.), *Predicting politics – Essays in empirical public choice*, 89–100. Ann Arbor: University of Michigan Press.

Arrow, K. (1951). *Social choice and individual values.* New York: Wiley.

Beard, C. (1913/1986). *An economic interpretation of the Constitution of the United States:* with a new introduction by F. McDonald. New York: The Free Press.

Becker, G. (1976). *The economic approach to human behavior.* Chicago: University of Chicago Press.

Bernholz, P. (1991). Institutional aspects of the European integration. In S. Borner and H. Grubel (Eds.), *The EC after 1992 – Perspectives from the outside.* London: Macmillan.

Bhalla, S. (1994). *Freedom and economic growth: A virtuous cycle?* Nobel Symposium. Uppsala University. August.

Blankart, C. (1985). Where are we in the economic theory of constitutions? *Economia delle Scelte pubbliche* 3: 147–158.

Boudreaux, D. and Pritchard, A. (1993). Rewriting the constitution: An economic analysis of the constitutional amendment process. *Fordham Law Review* 62: 111<->162.

Boudreaux, D. and Pritchard, A. (1994). Reassessing the role of the independent judiciary in enforcing interest-group bargains. *Constitutional Political Economy* 5(1): 1–21.

Brennan, G. and Buchanan, J. (1980). *The power to tax.* Cambridge: Cambridge University Press.

Brennan, G. and Buchanan, J. (1985). *The reason of rules.* Cambridge: Cambridge University Press.

Brennan, G. and Lomasky, L. (1993). *Democracy and decision – The pure theory of electoral preference.* Cambridge: Cambridge University Press.

Brennan, G. and Pardo, J. (1991). A reading of the Spanish Constitution. *Constitutional Political Economy* 2(1): 53–79.

Breton, A. (1987). Towards a theory of competitive federalism. *European Journal of Political Economy.* Special Issue 3(1+2): 263–329.

Brooks, M. (1994). The cost of being too cynical. Paper presented at the Public Choice Society-Meeting in Austin, Texas. April.

Buchanan, J. (1965). An economic theory of clubs. *Economica* 32: 1–14.

Buchanan, J. (1975). *The limits of liberty – Between anarchy and Leviathan.* Chicago: University of Chicago Press.

Buchanan, J. (1984). Sources of opposition to constitutional reform. In R.B. McKenzie (Ed.), *Constitutional economics – Containing the economic powers of government*, 21–34. Lexington: Lexington Books.

Buchanan, J. (1987). Constitutional economics. Entry in *The New Palgrave*, Vol. 1: 588–595. London/Basingstoke: Macmillan.

Buchanan, J. (1990a). The domain of constitutional economics. *Constitutional Political Economy* 1(1): 1–18.

Buchanan, J. (1990b). Europe's constitutional opportunity. In *Europe's constitutional future.* IEA: Readings/London.

Buchanan, J. (1991). The domain of constitutional political economy. In J. Buchanan, *The economics and the ethics of constitutional order*, 3–18. Ann Arbor: University of Michigan Press.
Buchanan, J. (1994). Choosing what to choose. *Journal of Institutional and Theoretical Economics* 150(1): 123–135.
Buchanan, J. and Tullock, G. (1962). *The calculus of consent: Logical foundations of constitutional democracy.* Ann Arbor: University of Michgian Press.
Burnham, W. (1982). The constitution – Capitalism and the need for rationalized regulation. In R. Goldwin and W. Schambra (Eds.), *How capitalistic is the Constitution?*, 75–105. Washington DC: American Enterprise Institute.
Cain, B. and Jones, W. (1989). Madison's theory of representation. In B. Grofman and D. Wittman (Eds.), *The Federalist Papers and the new institutionalism*, 11–30. New York: Agathon.
Chen, Y. and Ordeshook, P. (1994). Constitutional secession clauses. *Constitutional Political Economy* 5(1): 45–60.
Coleman, J.L. (1988a). The foundations of constitutional economics. In J.L. Coleman, *Markets, morals and the law,*, 133–152. Cambridge: Cambridge University Press.
Coleman, J.L. (1988b). Market contractarianism. In J.L. Coleman, *Markets, morals and the law,* 243–276. Cambridge: Cambridge University Press.
Cooter, R. (in print). *Constitutional law and economics.*
Cooter, R. and Ulen, T. (1988). *Law and economics.* New York: Harper.
Crain, W.M. and Tollison, R. (1979a). Constitutional change in an interest-group perspective. *Journal of Legal Studies* 8: 165–175.
Davidson, J. (1984). The limits of constitutional determinism. In R.B. McKenzie (Ed.), *Constitutional economics – Containing the economic power of government,* 61–87. Lexington: Lexington Books.
Denzau, A. (1985). Constitutional change and agenda control. *Public Choice* 47: 183–217.
Dorn, J. (1988). Public choice and the constitution: A Madisonian perspective. In J.D. Gwartney and R.E. Wagner (Eds.), *Publich choice and constitutional economics,*, 57–102. London: JAI.
Eggertsson, T. (1990). *Economic behavior and institutions.* Cambridge: Cambridge University Press.
Elster, J. (1984). *Ulysses and the Sirens.* Rev. ed. Cambridge: Cambridge University Press.
Elster, J. (1991). *Arguing and bargaining in two constituent assemblies.* The Storrs Lectures.
Elster, J. (1993). Constitution-making in Eastern Europe: Rebuilding the boat in the open sea. *Public Administration* 71(1/2): 169–217.
Elster, J. (1994). The impact of constitutions on economic performance. Paper presented to the Annual Bank Conference on Development Economics of the World Bank. April.
Eucken, W. (1952/1990). *Grundsätze der Wirtschaftspolitik.* Tübingen: Mohr (Siebeck).
Foyer, J. (1988). The drafting of the French Constitution of 1958. In R. Goldwin and A. Kaufman (Eds.), *Constitution-makers on constitution-making,* 7–46. Washington, DC: American Enterprise Institute.
Frey, B. (1979). Economic policy by constitutional contract. *Kyklos* 32(1/2): 307–319.
Frey, B. (1990). Institutions matter. *European Economic Review* 34: 443–449.
Frey, B. (1994a). Moral and institutional constraints. *Journal of Institutional and Theoretical Economics* 150(1): 136–141.
Frey, B. (1994b). Direct democracy: Politico-economic lessons from Swiss experience. *American Economic Review* 84(2): 338–332.
Friedman, M. (1962). *Capitalism and freedom.* Chicago and London: Chicago University Press.
Frohlich, N., Oppenheimer, J. and Eavey, C. (1987). Laboratory results on Rawls's distributive justice. *British Journal of Political Science* 17: 1–21.
Furubotn, E. and Pejovich, S. (1972). Property rights and economic theory: A survey of recent literature. *Journal of Economic Literature* 10: 1137–1162.

Furubotn, E. and Richter, R. (1991). The new institutional economics: An assessment. In Furubotn and Richter (Eds.), *The new institutional economics – A collection of articles from the* Journal of Institutional and Theoretical Economics, 1–32. Tübingen: Mohr (Siebeck).

Gifford, A. (1991). A constitutional interpretation of the firm. *Public Choice* 68: 91–106.

Goldwin, R. and Kaufman, A. (Eds.) (1988). *Constitution-makers on constitution-making*. Washington, DC: American Enterprise Institute.

Gordon, R. (1983). An optimal taxation approach to fiscal federalism. *Quarterly Journal of Economics* 98: 567–586.

Gwartney, J., Lawson, R. and Block, W. (1996). *Economic freedom of the world: 1975–1995*. Vancouver et al.: The Fraser Institute et al.

Hamilton, A., Madison, J. and Jay, J. (1788/1961). *the Federalist Papers* – With an introduction, table of contents, and index of ideas by C. Rossiter. New York: Mentor.

Hardin, R. (1989). Why a constitution? In B. Grofman and D. Wittman (Eds.), *The Federalist Papers and the new institutionalism*, 100–120. New York: Agathon Press.

Hardin, R. (1990). Contractarianism: Wistful thinking. *Constitutional Political Economy* 1(2): 35–52.

Hayek, F. (1944). *The road to serfdom*. Chicago: Chicago University Press.

Hayek, F. (1960). *The constitution of liberty*. Chicago: Chicago University Press.

Hayek, F. (1973). *Law, legislation and liberty, Vol. 1: Rules and order*. Chicago: Chicago University Press.

Hayek, F. (1976). *Law, legislation and liberty,* Vol. 2: The mirage of social justice. Chicago: Chicago University Press.

Hayek, F. (1979). *Law, legislation and liberty,* Vol. 3: The political order of a free people. Chicago: Chicago University Press.

Hayek, F. (1988). *The fatal conceit – The errors of socialism*. W.W. Bartley III (Ed.). London: Routledge.

Hechter, M. (1992). The dynamics of secession. *Acta Sociologica* 35: 267–283.

Heiner, R. (1983). The origin of predictable behavior. *American Economic Review* 73: 560–595.

Holmes, S. (1988). Precommitment and the paradox of democracy. In J. Elster and R. Slagstad (Eds.), *Constitutionalism and democracy*, 195–240. Cambridge: Cambridge University Press.

International Review of Law and Economics (1992). Special Issue on Constitutional Law and Economics 12(2): 123–288.

Keynes, J.N. (1955). *The scope and method of political economy*. New York: Kelley.

Kirchgässner, G. and Frey, B. (1990). Volksabstimmung und direkte Demokratie: Ein Beitrag zur Verfassungsdiskussion. In H.D. Klingmann and M. Kaase (Eds.), *Wahlen und Wähler – Analysen aus Anlaß der Bundestagswahl*, 42–69. Opladen: Westdeutscher Verlag.

Kiwit, D. and Voigt, S. (1995). Überlegungen zum institutionellen Wandel unter Berücksichtigung des Verhältnisses interner und externer Institutionen. *ORDO* 46: 117–147.

La Manna, M. and Slomp, G. (1994). Leviathan: Revenue-maximizer or glory-seeker? *Constitutional Political Economy* 5(2): 159–171.

Landes, W. and Posner, R. (1975). The independent judiciary in an interest-group perspective. *The Journal of Law and Economics* 18(3): 875–911.

Leipold, H. (1990). Neoliberal Ordnungstheorie and constitutional economics – A comparison between Eucken and Buchanan. *Constitutional Political Economy* 1(1): 47–65.

Leschke, M. (1993). *Ökonomische Verfassungstheorie und Demokratie*. Berlin: Duncker & Humblot.

Levmore, S. (1992). Bicameralism: When are two decisions better than one? *International Review of Law and Economics* 12: 145–162.

Macey, J. (1986). Promoting public-regarding legislation through statutory interpretation: An interest-group model. *Columbia Law Review* 86: 223–268.

Macey, J. (1988). Transaction costs and the normative elements of the public choice model: An application to constitutional theory. *Virginia Law Review* 74(1): 471–518.

McCormick, R. and Tollison, R. (1981). *Politicians, legislation, and the economy – An inquiry into the interest-group theory of government.* Boston: Nijhoff.
McDonald, F. (1986). A new introduction, to Charles A. Beard: An economic interpretation of the Constitution of the United States, vii–liii. New York: The Free Press.
McGuire, R. and Ohsfeldt, R. (1986). An economic model of voting behavior over specific issues at the Constitutional Convention of 1787. *Journal of Economic History* 46(1): 79–111.
McGuire, R. and Ohsfeldt, R. (1989a). Self-interest, agency theory, and political voting behavior: The ratification of the United States Constitution. *American Economic Review* 79(1): 219–234.
McGuire, R. and Ohsfeldt, R. (1989b). Public choice analysis and the ratification of the Constitution. In B. Grofman and D. Wittman (Eds.), *The Federalist Papers and the new institutionalism,* 175–204. New York: Agathon.
McKenzie, R. (1984). Introduction. In R.B. McKenzie (Ed.), *Constitutional economics – Containing the economic powers of government,* 1–18. Lexington: Lexington Books.
McKenzie, R. and Tullock, G. (1975). *The new world of economics.* Homewood, IL: Irwin.
Merville, L. and Osborne, D. (1990). Constitutional democracy and the theory of agency. *Constitutional Political Economy* 1: 21–47.
Milgrom, P., North, D. and Weingast, B. (1990). The role of institutions in the revival of trade: The law merchant, private judges, and the champagne fairs. *Economics and Politics* 2: 1–23.
Miller, G. and Hammond, T. (1989). Stability and efficiency in a separation-of-powers constitutional system. In B. Grofman and D. Wittman (Eds.), *The Federalist Papers and the new institutionalism,* 85–99., New York: Agathon Press.
Mueller, D. (1989). *Public choice II.* Cambridge: Cambridge University Press.
Mueller, D. (1991). Constitutional rights. *Journal of Law, Economics, and Organisation* 7(2): 313–333.
Niskanen, W. (1990). Conditions affecting the survival of constitutional rules. *Constitutional Political Economy* 1(2): 53–62.
North, D. (1981). *Structure and change in economic history.* New York: Norton.
North, D. (1990). *Institutions, institutional change and economic performance.* Cambridge: Cambridge University Press.
Nozick, R. (1973). *Anarchy, state, and utopia.* Oxford: Blackwell.
Oates, W. (1972). *Fiscal federalism.* New York: Harcourt.
Olson, M. (1965). *The logic of collective action.* Cambridge, MA: Harvard University Press.
Olson, M. (1984). Comment. In R.B. McKenzie (Ed.), *Constitutional Economics – Containing the economic powers of government,* 89–94. Lexington: Lexington Books.
Olson, M. (1991). Autocracy, democracy, and prosperity. In R.J. Zeckhauser (Ed.), *Strategy and choice,* 131–157. Cambridge: MIT Press.
Ordeshook, P. (1992). Constitutional stability. *Constitutional Political Economy* 3(2): 137–175.
Pejovich, S. (1990). *The economics of property rights: Towards a theory of comparative systems.* Dordrecht: Kluwer.
Pommerehne, W. (1978). Institutional approaches to public expenditure. *Journal of Public Economics* 9: 255–280.
Pommerehne, W. (1990). The empirical relevance of comparative institutional analysis. *European Economic Review* 34: 458–468.
Pommerehne, W. and Frey, B. (1992). The effects of tax administration on tax morale. Paper presented at the Conference on Tax Administration and Tax Evasion of the International Seminar in Public Economics (ISPE). El Escorial, June.
Posner, R. (1987). The constitution as an economic document. *George Washington Law Review* 56(1): 4–38.
Priddat, B. (1993). Constitutional economics – einige Fragen an die constitutional economics. Diskussionspapiere der Wirtschaftswissenschaftlichen Fakultät der Universität Witten/Herdecke.

Przeworski, A. (1991). *Democracy and the market – Political and economic reforms in Eastern Europe and Latin America.* Cambridge: Cambridge University Press.

Przeworski, A. and Limongi, F. (1993). Political regimes and economic growth. *Journal of Economic Perspectives* 7(3): 51–69.

Radnitzky, G. and Bernholz, P. (Eds.). (1987). *Economic imperialism.* New York: Paragon House.

Rawls, J. (1971). *A theory of justice.* Cambridge, MA: Harvard University Press.

Riker, W. (1983). Political theory and the art of heresthetics. In A. Finifter (Ed.), *Political science: The state of the discipline,* 47–67. Washington, DC: American Political Science Association.

Riker, W. (1984). The heresthetics of constitution-making: The Presidency in 1787, with comments on determinism and rational choice. *American Political Science Review* 78: 1–16.

Scharpf, F. (1991). Kann es in Europa eine stabile föderale Balance geben? In R. Wildenmann (Ed.), *Staatswerdung Europas: Optionen für eine Europäische Union,* 415–428. Baden-Baden: Nomos.

Schelling, T. (1984). Self-command in practice, in policy, and in a theory of rational choice. *American Economic Review* 74(2): 1–11.

Schwartz, T. (1989). Publius and public choice. In B. Grofman and D. Wittman (Eds.), *The Federalist Papers and the new institutionalism,* 11–30. New York: Agathon.

Sinn, H. (1990). The limits to competition between economic regions. *Empirica* 17(1): 3–14.

Steunenberg, B. (1992). Referendum, initiative, and veto power: Budgetary decision-making in local government. *Kyklos* 45(4): 501–529.

Streit, M. (1992). The Freiburg School of Law and Economics. *Journal of Institutional and Theoretical Economics* 148: 675–704.

Streit, M. (1995). Ordnungsökonomik – Versuch einer Standortbestimmung. Discussion paper 04/95 of the Max-Planck-Institute for Research Into Economic Systems, Jena.

Sunstein, C. (1987). The Beard thesis and Franklin Roosevelt. *George Washington Law Review* 56(1): 114–143.

Sunstein, C. (1991). Constitutionalism and secession. *University of Chicago Law Review* 58(2): 633–670.

Thaler, R. and Shefrin, H. (1981). An economic theory of self-control. *Journal of Political Economy* 89(2): 392–406.

Tocqueville, A. de (1840/1945). *Democracy in America.* New York: Knopf.

Tullock, G. (1987). The *calculus* after 25 years. *Cato Journal* 7(2): 313–321.

Twight, C. (1992). Constitutional renegotiation: Impediments to consensual revision. *Constitutional Political Economy* 3(1): 89–112.

Twight, C. (1994). Political transaction-cost manipulation – An integrating theory. *Journal of Theoretical Politics* 6(2): 189–216.

Ulen, T. (1992). An economic interpretation of the Bill of Rights. The limits and potential of law and economics in discussing constitutional issues. *University of Illinois Law Review* 1: 189–212.

Vanberg, V. (1988). 'Ordnungstheorie' as constitutional economics – The German conception of a 'social market economy.' *ORDO* 39: 17–31.

Vanberg, V. (1992). Organizations as constitutional systems. *Constitutional Political Economy* 3(2): 223–253.

Voigt, S. (1992). On the internal consistency of Hayek's evolutionary-oriented constitutional economics – Some general remarks. *Journal des Economistes et des Etudes Humaines* 3(4): 461–476.

Voigt, S. (1994). Die kontraktorientierte Theorie der Verfassung – Anmerkungen zum Ansatz Buchanans. *Homo Oeconomicus* 11(2): 173–209.

Voigt, S. (1996). Pure eclecticism – On the tool kit of the constitutional economist. To appear in *Constitutional Political Economy.*

Weingast, B. (1993). Constitutions as governance structures: The political foundations of secure markets. *Journal of Institutional and Theoretical Economics* 149: 286–311.
Weingast, B. (1995). The economic role of political institutions: Market-preserving federalism and economic development. *Journal of Law, Economics & Organization* 11(1): 1–31.
Wicksell, K. (1896). *Finanztheoretische Untersuchungen.* Jena: Fischer.
Young, R. (1994). The political economy of secession: The case of Quebec. *Constitutional Political Economy* 5(2): 221–245.
Wohlgemuth, M. (1995). Economic and political competition in neoclassical and evolutionary perspective. *Constitutional Political Economy* 6: 71–96.

Public Choice **90**: 55–72, 1997.
© 1997 *Kluwer Academic Publishers.*

Constitutions for new democracies: Reflections of turmoil or agents of stability?*

PETER C. ORDESHOOK
Division of Humanities and Social Sciences, California Institute of Technology, Pasadena, CA 91125, U.S.A.

Abstract. Despite the widely held view in newly emerging democracies that constitutions are mere words on paper or that parchment barriers cannot render a state stable or democratic, those who draft such documents commonly act as if words ARE of consequence. The difficulty, however, is that contemporaneous conflicts too easily intervene so as to corrupt the drafting process and to preclude optimal constitutional design. The specific principle of design most likely to be violated is the proposition that we treat all parts of the constitution as an interconnected whole and that we not try to assess the consequences of one part without appreciating the full meaning of all other parts. This essay illustrates this violation by looking at the new Russian constitution, ratified by direct popular vote in December 1993, with special attention paid to that document's treatment of federalism. We offer the additional argument, however, that even contemporary research in political institutional design pays insufficient heed to this principle.

1. Introduction

Constitutions are rarely written in a vacuum, insulated from the political conflicts that swirl about them. The delegates in Philadelphia in 1787 might have shuttered their windows and sprinkled straw on the streets outside Independence Hall to muffle the distractions of the external world, but that world, not merely political theory, weighted heavily on their decisions. Similarly, the uncertain and confused steps taken in drafting constitutions for Poland and Ukraine, for example, bear witness to the impact of contemporary disputes, just as the extraordinary powers granted the president by Russia's new constitution signal unambiguously whose orders tank commanders followed in 1993 and who was victorious there in the conflict between Yeltsin and the People's Congress. With the exception of states that had constitutions imposed on them by some occupying military force or by a dictator who sought to apply a democratic gloss to his regime, not only has the philosophy of the

* This essay was made possible through support provided by the U.S. Agency for International Development under cooperative agreement DHR-0015-A-00-0031-00 to the Center on Institutional Reform and the Informal Sector of the University of Maryland as well as through the support of The National Council for Soviet and East European Research.

American constitution been a template for others, but the process by which that document was prepared – contentious wrangling over contemporaneous sectional and substantive issues – has been replayed countless times as well.

There are three lessons to be learned from these wars of words. First, despite the view of many that constitutions are mere words on paper or that parchment barriers cannot render a state stable or democratic, they tell us that those who draft such documents act as if words ARE of consequence. Either constitutions allocate power, or contentious negotiation over their content is manifestly irrational. Second, the product of these wars need not correspond to any optimal or rational design. We may be able to understand that product in the same terms as we come to understand any social process, but we can appeal to theories of many types – to social choice theory or to the pitfalls of short-sighted vote trading – to predict that the resulting documents will only accidentally adhere to some definition of social rationality. The final lesson – actually, more an hypothesis – is that the observed failures of constitutional democracy should not be interpreted to mean that constitutions have little or no effect. Such examples are consistent with the contrary proposition that, absent of theory of constitutional design sufficiently compelling to overcome myopic self-interest, failed democracies illustrate the consequences of poor constitutional designs born of the imperatives of myopic self-interest.

Our purpose here is not merely to argue that constitutions matter or that the exigencies of contemporary politics can preclude the implementation of viable political institutions. Instead, we want to offer some advice to those who would craft such documents so that less is left to chance or surpise. Section 2, then, considers three examples, drawn from the Soviet experience, that illustrate the preceding lessons, and which show in particular that constitutions matter even for states without a democratic tradition. Section 3 briefly considers the process and conflicts that led to the ratification of Russia's current constitution and illustrates the principle most commonly violated when crafting new constitutions – the principle that the separate parts of a constitution should be treated as interdependent components of a unitary document. Section 4 focuses on federalism and describes how and why Russia violated this principle. Finally, Section 5 argues that although several (but hardly all) of the problems Russians created for themselves have been resolved subsequently, little guidance was provided by the comparative political science literature on constitutional and political institutional design and that until this literature develops further, we can suppose that states will continue to replicate Russia's experience.

2. Lessons from the Soviet Union

The constitution of the Soviet Union, both it's '36 Stalinist and '77 Brezhnevian versions, offered a panoply of constitutional rights as detailed and expansive as anything set to paper in the West. Chapter X of the 1936 document "guaranteed" the right to free speech, a free press, free assembly, equal protection, freedom of religion and thought, equal rights for women, the inviolability of the person and due process, and, conflating negative with "positive" rights, the right to work, rest, material security, and education. The USSR's failure to satisfy these constitutional prescriptions, then, is often taken to indicate a failure, if not of constitutionalism in general, then at least of its applicability to Russia and "Russian tradition."

The fault of those documents, though is not that they failed, but rather that they worked precisely as designed. Those who believe constitutionalism failed in the USSR owing to the gap between promise and reality are correct to assert that merely setting words to paper about rights and social welfare entitlements did not and, in general, cannot accomplish much. At best, such words merely coordinate people's expectations about legitimate and illegitimate governmental action and, in a functioning democracy, provide the courts with a rationale for opposing and rallying public sentiment against the actions of other governmental agencies. Ultimately, though, only appropriately designed and properly functioning institutions can ensure adherence to rights and the promulgation of legitimate governmental policy.

The presumption of constitutional failure in the USSR, though, is based on a preoccupation with only one of three questions we can ask about a constitution when evaluating its performance. In this instance the question asked is:

- Did the constitution lead to the realization of stated goals?

The answer, evident to everyone, is NO (at least insofar as rights and welfare guarantees is concerned), and therein lies the basis of pessimism about the prospects for a democratic society guided by constitutional principles among the citizens of the successor states of the Soviet Union. But before we concur in this judgement, we must answer two other questions:

- Did Soviet constitutions legitimize or contribute to the stability of the political institutions they prescribed?
- Were those institutions appropriate for the realization of the rights and guarantees each constitution identified as goals?

Only if our answers to these questions are NO and YES can we deem a constitution a failure. In fact, our answers are exactly the opposite.

The fundamental error of Soviet constitutions was that they were based on a social theory that assumed that people are perfectible and that beliefs and values can be changed fundamentally so that social goals become private ones, so that a government of offsetting or balanced powers becomes inessential. Thus, they enshrined a political system doomed to failure. However, although they failed to achieve what is beyond the reach of any constitution – guaranteeing the realization of lofty principles by mere proclamation – Soviet constitutions succeeded to the extent that the system and institutions they legitimized did in fact function as described. Setting Marxist-Leninist principles at the core of Soviet social organization, both the '36 and, even more fortrightly, the '77 constitutions legitimized democratic centralism in the form of the dictatorship of the Communist Party. Having done that, all the rest was mere window dressing. In fact, absent a Constitutional Court, neither constitution was intended as working law (Blankenagel, 1992). This is not to say that neither constitution played a role in forming political structures. Although those structures existed before either document was written, the '77 document codified many of the post-Stalinist changes in Soviet law and, by institutionalizing the role of the communist party more fortrightly in Article 6, signaled the transition from Stalin's personal dictatorship to that of the party. Both documents, then, gave legal sanction to what existed so that, with respect to our second question about their influence on political structures, we should judge Soviet constitutions as either irrelevant to events or we can infer that they contributed to the strength of institutions. In either case, the answer to our second question ought to be YES.

Turning to our third question, about the adequacy of that structure for realizing stated goals, we can, of course, debate whether the USSR's dissolution was inevitable and whether Gorbachev's "reforms" merely hastened the end (see Laqueur, 1994, for a critical survey of the literature). However, insofar as the gap between constitutional pronouncement and reality is concerned, the social theory on which Soviet constitutions were based – the '36 one, the '77 one, or the much-amended version of the '77 one that disappeared in 1991 – failed to anticipate the inevitable consequences of unchecked power: inefficiency and corruption. Nevertheless, this was the structure that Soviet constitutions legitimized, and this was the one that prevailed. Thus, Soviet constitutions failed to deliver on their promises not because constitutionalism is somehow alien to the "Russian soul" or because Russia had been ruled throughout its history by Czars and despots. Soviet constitutions "failed" because they legitimized a political system that could not channel self-interest so as to serve the public interest. So the answer to our third question is NO.

If there is a lesson to be learned from the USSR's constitutional experience, it is not that constitutions did not work. It is either that that experience is an irrelevant experiment or that even bad constitutions can, for a time at least, be stable. This argument does not challenge the view that history would have been unchanged if any of these constitutions was merely a blank piece of paper. It need not convince anyone that a new constitution can lead to something other than what exists. And it does not contradict the assertion that the USSR or any of its successor states must proceed along historical paths that can only be interrupted but not negated by attempts at developing a constitutional democracy. To counter these arguments requires consideration of the more general matter of how constitutions in fact influence political processes, how they ensure rights, and how they facilitate the establishment of stable political systems.

Our second example comes also from the Soviet experience, and illustrates more directly how even the Soviet constitution influenced things. Although both the '36 and '77 versions allowed for secession in principle (Articles 17 and 72, respectively), these words were understood to be void of content; indeed, both documents precluded such a possibility by their failure to offer any procedure for separation. However, thinking in 1990 that he could borrow time for his reforms, and viewing constitutions as a treaty among contending interests rather than as a device whereby society coordinates its expectations about legitimate governmental process (Hardin, 1989; Ordeshook, 1992), Gorbachev acceded partially to Lithuanian demands and allowed implementing legislation that specified a clear albeit tortuous path to secession. But instead of mollifying Lithuanian demands, the effect was to legitimize secession as part of Soviet law, thereby emboldening leaders of the Baltic republics to more vigorously pursue separation from the USSR (Sharlet, 1992). Thus, playing the coordinating role that is the ultimate basis of the enforcement of their provisions, we have an example here of a constitution (and its implementing legislation) that coordinated expectations so as to render what was deemed illegal under one set of words legal and attainable under a different set.

Our third example comes from Russia itself and the constitution, largely a reprint of the '77 Soviet text, that was superseded by the 1993 document. Although that constitution was amended to establish a president, to empower a Constitutional Court, and to proclaim the principle of a separation of powers, Article 104, consonant with the revolutionary slogan "all power to the Soviets," gave the Congress of People's Deputies (actually, the Supreme Soviet) the authority to legislate and govern in all important matters. Thus, following the demise of a communist party that could negate theoretical inconsistencies, the document's logical flaws found full play in the conflict between Yeltsin and parliament that resulted in a mini-civil war that was resolved ultimately only by military force. However, more clearly than earlier Soviet constitutions, the Russian one can be credited with empowering new institutions (notably, the presidency and the Constitutional Court). So, rather than argue that constitutions had little impact in the early years of an independent Russia, we can find good reasons for arguing exactly the opposite, provided we appreciate the ways in which its constitution encouraged political conflict.

3. A first principle of constitutional design

Admittedly, the evidence that Soviet-era constitutions influenced events is not wholly scientifically compelling. A strong case can be made for the argument that the Soviet Union's 70 or so year history was dictated more by the flawed theory upon which its institutions rested than on any post-hoc legalistic rationalization for those institutions. However, although Russians commonly lament that constitutions can never be much more than mere words, the drafting of Russia's current constitution, like most constitutional drafting processes, was approached as though it was critical to the resolution of several internal conflicts: "Constitutions are usually retrospective documents, not prospective ones. They are designed to solve the most pressing problems of the past, not the future. Yeltsin's constitution is no exception ..." (Holmes and Lucky, 1994) and "political institutions ... often get chosen more because of calculations made during the process of change ... than because certain versions of these institutions are uniquely appropriate ..." (Colomer, 1995). We cannot here review the events leading to the preparations and ratification of that constitution and to Yeltsin's Ukaz 1400 dissolving the old parliament (for overviews of those events see Tolz, 1993; Rutland, 1994; Semler, 1994). We need only note the basic issues that confounded Russia's constitutional drafting process. Briefly, those conflicts were,

- between those who accepted the view that constitutional rights were first and foremost limitations on the state, versus those who sought to compel the state to partake of a variety of welfare entitlements and to regulate not only the state, but society as well,
- between those who saw a constitution as a minimal document that concerned essential institutional details, versus those who viewed them more as a social contract in which as much detail as possible was included to preclude disputes over meaning,
- between those who argued for the strong hand most consonant with a presidential system, versus those who feared Russia's traditions of Czar rule and who preferred parliamentary government,

- between those who feared Russia's disintegration and preferred a unitary state, versus those who saw federalism as the only way to govern a heterogeneous state like Russia.

Several participants in the drafting process were familiar with Western practice, but opponents in these disputes were rarely motivated by principled notions of constitutional democracy. Yeltsin sought a strong presidency because he was president; conservatives in the People's Congress argued for a parliamentary system because they sought to undermine Yeltsin's policies (Thorson, 1993); leaders of the republics argued for federalism because they wished to maximize their autonomy and control of the resources on their territories; politicians in Moscow preferred a unitary state because they sought to maintain control of governmental revenues and because they knew no other governmental form (Sharlet, 1993); Oleg Rumayntesev and his Constitutional Reform Commission argued for an elaborate document since that was the style of their ill-prepared drafts and to argue otherwise was to hand the constitutional agenda to competitors; competitors such as St. Petersburg mayor Anatoly Sobchak and Yeltsin advisor Sergi Shakrai argued the opposite to seize the agenda and the label "the James Madison of Russia"; and those who argued for extensive welfare entitlements did so because doing otherwise was to reject their heritage of democratic centralism.

The details of these disputes concerned nearly every article of the various draft constitutions (Cohen, 1993), and their final resolution was a document that contradicts many of its loftily stated principles.

- Despite proclaiming Russia a federation (§ 5), federal subjects are precluded from establishing their own independent judiciaries (§ 118) or from controlling the method whereby deputies to either national legislative branch are elected or selected (§ 96); regional governments possess few if any exclusive policy jurisdictions (§ 71 and 72) and have no authority over local governments (§ 132 and 133); the president is empowered to overturn those regional executive acts he deems unconstitutional (§ 85); regional governments possess no independent taxing authority (§ 72); there is no guarantee of the obligation of contracts and no comity clause; and, in perhaps the clearest reincarnation of Lenin's idea of democratic centralism, the constitution provides that "federal executive bodies and the bodies of executive authority of the members of the Russian Federation shall form a single system of executive authority" (§ 77).]
- Despite proclaiming the people the ultimate sovereign (§ 3) and rights as inalienable (§ 17), citizens have no standing before the Constitutional Court (§ 125), constitutional rights are confused with citizen duties (§ 57–59), and the law is allowed to limit rights in order to uphold "the

foundations of the constitutional system, morality, or the health, rights and lawful interests of other persons or for ensuring the defense of the country and state security" (§ 55).]

– And despite proclaiming a governmental form based on a separation of powers (§ 10), in addition to the duties and powers normally associated with that office (appointment, legislative initiative, veto) and in addition to being anointed "guarantor of the constitution" (§ 80), the president of the Russian Federation is empowered to dissolve parliament (§ 84), to appoint ministers without legislative oversight (§ 83), and to issue decrees insofar as the law is silent (§ 90) – a power Yeltsin has already used under the guise of controlling rampant crime to abrogate constitutional rights in general and habeas corpus in particular (Cohen, 1995).]

This constitution, then, violates not only a good many ideas about democratic institutional design, but also its own stated objectives. Of course, many of those violations can be resolved through amendment, judicial interpretation, and evolving tradition. But if we want to argue that politics distorts the design of constitutions and precludes the implementation of appropriate institutions, we should consider what specific design principles are most likely to be violated. Only when we identify the "disease" can we offer a cure. And here our argument is that the principle most at risk is the following:

> all parts of the constitution are interconnected, so we cannot assess the consequences of one part without appreciating the full meaning of all other parts and their relationship to the part in question.

Violations of this principle are a consequence of the understandable inability to isolate writing a constitution from the conflicts that make constitutions essential and are manifest in the tendency to address each part of the document separately, as an arena for negotiation between competing interests. Thus, the presidential powers enshrined by Russia's constitution are best understood as a byproduct of the presidential-parliamentary conflict that preceded it and the fact that Yeltsin prevailed in that conflict. The president is empowered to name and fire his own ministers without parliamentary approval because of the Congress's recalcitrance at approving earlier presidential recommendations; the president can dissolve the Duma if it fails to approve his nomination for Prime Minister because of Yeltsin's earlier inability to secure the re-appointment of Yegor Gaider to that post; the president can issue decrees with the force of law because the dissolved Congress was unwilling to extend his emergency authority; and the constitution fails to provide for the office of vice-president because Yeltsin's first vice-president, Alexander Rutskoi, became a focal point for parliamentary opposition to his policies.

As with presidential-parliamentary relations, the treatment of federalism was isolated from other issues (except the president's authority to over-ride regional executive actions). The connection of this part of the constitution to the sections dealing with presidential and parliamentary powers, for example, comes only as background: Yeltsin originally offered the republics special privileges such as majority control of the upper legislative chamber, the Federation Council, to secure their support. But once victory over the People's Congress was achieved, he reneged on these "constitutional promises" and has since sought to render federal subjects mere administrative appendages of the central government (Sharlet, 1993). Only grudgingly, for example, has Yeltsin allowed regional governors to be directly elected rather than presidentially appointed.

Legislative and presidential election procedures were relegated to implementing legislation or decree in part to ensure flexibility, but also because Yeltsin's supporters could not agree on which procedures best served their interests. The issue at hand here was selecting an election method that offered the best chance of filling the new parliament with "democratic" reformers. Lip-service was paid to the idea that something must be done to facilitate the formation of national political parties and to avoid divisive ethnic and regional ones. But national party-list proportional representation was used to elect half the State Duma out of fear that communists would dominate the traditional single-mandate election districts and to take advantage of the fact that reformer's support was concentrated in the country's urban centers. Virtually no attention was paid to the influence of legislative election procedures on federal relations or to the consequences for party formation and the powers of the presidency of having presidential and parliamentary elections held at different times.

4. Federalism: Violating the first principle

It is understandable that contemporaneous conflicts should influence the actions of constitutional draftsmen. But such conflicts need not preclude good design. To see how this is possible, consider again the subject of federalism. Briefly, debate on this subject throughout 1992 and 1993 focused on three words: sovereignty, supremacy, and symmetry. Yeltsin's early drafts, written to accommodate the demands of Russia's ethnic republics, labeled those republics sovereign, which they interpreted as affording them the same status in international affairs as Stalin claimed for Ukraine and Byelorussia. Sovereignty also impacted on the issue of supremacy, and several republics asserted that their laws took precedence over federal ones or that republics could nullify federal laws on their territory. The current constitution proclaims the supremacy of federal law, but the issue remains a contentious one and contradicts several republic constitutions (as well as the treaties negotiated with those republics that proclaim equal status for all constitutions). Finally, the issue of symmetry arose in the debate over whether Russia's ethnic republics would enjoy privileges not possessed by its other regions (oblasts and autonomous regions). Yeltsin's early draft constitutions allowed federal subjects to renegotiate their status with Moscow on a bilateral basis, thereby confounding the meaning of the provision that all federal subjects "shall be equal in their relation with federal bodies of state authority" (§ 5). And although the final version makes no mention of the possibility of such negotiations, a variety of bilateral asymmetric agreements have been negotiated between the republics and Moscow in the attempt to smooth relations between Moscow and Russia's ethnic regions (Teague, 1994).

Although the draft ratified in December 1993 imposed a federal form that made only modest accommodation of regional and republic demands, there was little dispute throughout the drafting process over what parts of the constitution were the core federal provisions – namely those dealing with

- supremacy and secession;
- the admission of new federal subjects or alterations in the boundaries of existing ones;
- the role of federal subjects in amending the constitution;
- free trade within the federation;
- the policy jurisdiction of national and regional governments;
- democratic governance within federal subjects;
- the judicial system;
- representation in the national legislature.

Insofar as how the constitution treats these topics, we might prefer a more restricted grant of authority to the national government and a more explicit guarantee of democratic governance within federal subjects. But most items on this list are treated in ways that are not unlike their treatment in other national constitutions. Federal law is unambiguously supreme (§ 15, 76), secession is prohibited (§ 4), new federal subjects can be admitted in accordance with procedures specified by federal law (§ 65), no subject's boundary can be altered without the affected subject's consent (§ 67), approval by a super-majority of federal subjects if required to amend the constitution (§ 136), free trade is guaranteed within the federation (§ 74), and, paralleling Articles 73 and 74 of the German Basic Law, the national government has an explicit role in most issues of public policy (§ 71 and § 72).

The instinct to compartmentalize constitutional issues, though, led to an unsatisfactory accommodation of the last two items on this list, and to a failure to consider several additional parts of the constitution, namely those that concern the following:

- control over the methods of election to the national legislature as well as state legislatures;
- the timing of presidential and parliamentary elections;
- the method of electing the president;
- elections as a means of filling federal subject and local public offices;
- the content of federal subject constitutions.

Insofar as the judicial system is concerned, the constitution appears to foil the design of balanced regional governmental structures based on a separation of regional executive, legislative, and judicial powers insofar as it precludes independent regional courts. Instead, it requires that the country's judicial system "be established by the Constitution of the Russian Federation and federal law" (§ 118) and that "judges [be] ... subject only to the Constitution and federal law" (§ 120). To our knowledge, little thought was given to the role of the judiciary in a federal system. Instead, the primary concern was to avoid a repeat of Yeltsin's experience with a runaway Constitutional Court chaired by someone (Zorkin in the case of the old Court) who sided too frequently with opponents.

We can imagine ad hoc accommodations to the problems of a centralized judiciary, including the passage of federal laws that allow for reasonably independent regional judicial structures. But here we run afoul of the constitution's treatment of the last item on our first list – representation in the legislature – and its failure to consider fully the consequences of its treatment (or non-treatment) of the items on our second list. Briefly, the relevance to federalism of these things, which may be treated directly or only indirectly by a constitution, is that they influence the structure and role of parties, their degree of decentralization, the vertical integration of local parties with national ones, and correspondingly, the extent to which local, regional, and national governmental structures form an integrated whole in which local politicians "naturally" accede to the supremacy of federal law and national politicians are "naturally" protective of regional autonomy (Ordeshook and Shvetsova, 1995). If "political parties created modern democracy ... and modern democracy is unthinkable save in terms of political parties" (Schattschneider, 1941: 1), then it is also true, in William Riker's (1964: 136) words, that "Whatever the general social conditions, if any, that sustain the federal bargain, there is one institutional condition that controls the nature of the bargain in all instances here examined and in all others with which I am familiar. This is the structure of the party system, which may be regarded as the main variable intervening between the background social conditions and the specific nature of the federal bargain." Thus, the preceding provisions, in combination with those that treat representation in the national legislature, are as important to federalism as are the provisions relegated to those sections of a constitution labeled "The Organization of the Federation."

Unfortunately, unfamiliarity with party politics combined with contemporaneous political conflicts to preclude consideration of Riker's admonition about the role of parties and the ways to encourage the development of parties appropriate to a federal state. Instead, each of the items on this second list were attended to in the context of other issues. Thus,

- the basis of representation in the State Duma, as we note earlier, was considered only in the context of securing control of that chamber and minimizing the prospects of opponents. Unsurprisingly, the electoral system decreed by Yeltsin allowed Zhirinovsky to secure a plurality of PR seats in the first Duma election (December 1993), ensured a highly fractured party system in the contest for seats in the second Duma election (December 1995), and discouraged anything but a top-down Moscow-centered process of party formation that alienates many of Russia's regions from the main flow of partisian politics and party competition.
- fearful of regional bosses, the constitution merely states that "the procedure for forming the Federation Council ... shall be determined by federal law" (§ 96) and that the Council should "be composed of two representatives from each member of the Russian Federation; one from its representatives and one from its executive body of state authority" (§ 95). Thus, the constitution fails to provide for direct election of deputies to the Federation Council, and leaves the door open to defacto presidential appointment of the upper legislative chamber. Also, with "democrats" in the Kremlin concerned about the strength of regional communist party organizations, it centralizes full control of parliamentary elections (including the drawing of districts for the State Duma) in Moscow (§ 96).
- Because Yeltsin saw no reason to jeopardize his own position and because he sought to maintain a Czar-like distance from "normal" politics, he postponed the presidential election until June 1996. Thus, rather than hold that election at the same time as parliamentary ones, parliamentary elections will be held six months before the presidiential contest – thereby guaranteeing that those elections will be more like presidential primaries than a source of incentives for the formation of national parties. Unsurprisingly, 42 parties were listed on the December 1995 parliamentary election ballot, and virtually every attempt to consolidate parties with similar ideological positions was foiled by the egos and aspirations of potential contenders for the presidency in June 1996.

- The constitution requires only that the president be elected by direct vote (§ 81). Thus, there is no explicit (as in Nigeria) or implicit (as in the United States) constitutional requirement that presidents be elected with broad geographic support.

The last two items on our subsidiary list of constitutional provisions – regional and local elections and regional constitutions – are not normally addressed by a national constitution. But Yeltsin's subsequent policies here are consistent with a myopic view of constitutional democracy. Fearing the loss of political control that might accompany the rise of regional leaders with independent electoral mandates, Yeltsin has only recently (December 1995) allowed for the direct election of regional governors, and then only if such elections are held after the June 1996 presidential contest. Although it is assumed that regional Dumas and local Soviets will be directly elected, with attention focused on ensuring that local and regional governments rescind the mandated share of tax revenues to the federal government (Wallich, 1994), little if any thought has been given to the role elections might play in regional and local governance. The constitution makes vague reference to direct citizen involvement in local governance (§ 130), but it is clear that the authority of local governments will be closely controlled by Moscow. And although the constitution makes reference to "republic constitutions" and "regional charters" (§ 5), it offers no guidance as to the content of those documents. Moscow's attempt to control that content has focused on ensuring that they do not contradict the federal constitution, Yeltsin's decrees, or federal law – in particular, that they not undermine Moscow's attempt to control Russia's vast natural resources.

Of course, we should not be surprised to see manipulation of electoral procedures in the interests of those who have the power to do so. Much of the early history of American state and national politics focused on such manipulations (see, for example, Williamson, 1960; Hoadley, 1986), just as interests of the same type dictated the selection of procedures in Central and Eastern Europe after the fall of communism (Colomer, 1995; Holmes, 1994). On the other hand, aside from Yeltsin's dissolution of regional soviets after the overthrow of parliament in 1993, little thought appears to have been given to the role of elections at the regional and local levels, and even less to the procedures that might be used there. Certainly the encouragement of parties that would facilitate stable federal relations is not seen as a relevant consideration when the provisions on our second list were addressed. One might argue, perhaps, that the creation of a true federation was never the intent of those who drafted the final document. We suspect, though, that much of its democratic-centralist flavor is the result of the general belief that only traditional command-and-control devices could arrest the forces that threatened Russia's fragmentation – a belief that was the consequence of an inability to understand the role of parties in a federation and the failure to estimate the extent to which these provisions might usefully influence that role.

5. The failures of social science

It is one thing to assert that constitutions ought to be written as fully integrated documents; it is another thing to contend successfully with the political pressures and crises that normally surround their preparation and ratification. Nevertheless, referring again to the Russian case, there are solutions to this seemingly insurmountable problem. We can begin by noticing that several solutions were achieved "automatically" following the December '93 parliamentary elections.

- It was soon understood that Yeltsin's aloofness from the election was an error and for this reason he encouraged the formation of two electoral blocks in April 1995, one headed by Prime Minister Chernomyrdin and the other by State Duma Speaker Ivan Rybkin – blocks that could support his bid for reelection or that could support a centrist candidate if Yeltsin chose not to run. Only one of these blocks – Chernomyrdin's – has met with much success, but the general principles of party competition are beginning to be understood.
- The '93 elections also revealed the dangers of national party-list proportional representation, and Yeltsin has since argued for a reduction in the number of seats to be filled this way (although incumbent Duma deputies successfully resisted changing a system that led to their initial success). The presence of 42 parties on the December 1995 ballot is certain to occasion significant changes in election laws if not a complete overhaul of those laws and the basis of legislative representation.
- We can now envision a system in which regional authorities play a more direct role in the selection of deputies to the Federation Council. Indeed, Yeltsin has now signed a new law over the objections of the Federation Council (owing to an override vote of the Duma) which specifies that the Council will consist of regional governors as well as the leaders of regional Dumas, and,
- as part of the same law, rather than allow the President to appoint regional governors or to decide which governors will be appointed and which will be elected, all regional governors must be directly elected by December 1996.
- Much of the debate over electoral reform prior to December '95 examined the pros and cons of postponing parliamentary elections until 1996

> so that presidential and parliamentary contests could be held simultaneously. Parliamentary elections will not be postponed, but there is growing sentiment to alter the election schedule to allow for simultaneity in the future.

Also, although the republics, following Tatarstan's lead, adopted constitutions that contradicted the federal one (by proclaiming the supremacy of their constitutions and laws), Moscow muted this issue with a series of bilateral treaties so that, in exchange for increased autonomy, the republics have largely dropped their claims to sovereignty (Teague, 1994).

Thus, resistance to many of the things that would have led to a better integrated constitution and a more viable federal system in fact disappeared soon after the constitution's ratification. Of course, this is not to say that this resistance has disappeared altogether or that it has been muted by a better understanding of constitutional design. There is still serious resistance to many of the things that would facilitate a more viable federal state – regional governments with independent taxing authority, more extensive use of regional and local elections, regional governments with full control over their charters and constitutions, and regional control of elections to both chambers of the national legislatures. Earlier arguments for sequenced elections, party-list PR, and a president who was above politics gave way to political realities rather than more ready acceptance of reasoned arguments about political institutional design.

Thus, may of the errors of design, both today and in 1993, were not based on strongly held beliefs about the best way to organize the transition to democracy, but instead were the result of faulty judgements as to what procedures and tactics best served the self-interests involved and of the force of contemporaneous conflicts that compelled and continue to compel a divorced attention to constitutional issues. This is not to say that beliefs and actions can ever be easily changed, but especially with respect to beliefs about the consequences of certain choices, we can see with the benefit of hindsight where good social science arguments might have moved things in a different direction. Unfortunately, such arguments were not forthcoming, because political scientists in the West have largely ignored the subject of constitutional design or are guilty of the same error of compartmentalization that characterized Russian efforts. Despite Riker's (1964) seminal arguments and Horowitz's (1991) focus on the importance of electoral institutions in ethnically divided federal states, Sartori's (1994) recent discussion of presidential and parliamentary systems and of election laws, for example, devotes less than a page to federalism. Linz and Valenzuela's (1994) 2-volume study of the failures of presidential systems devotes a scant two pages to the subject, while Powell's (1982) analysis of democratic stability relegates federalism to two footnotes. Neither Lijphart's (1992) edited volume on presidential and parliamentary systems nor Shugart and Carey's (1992) book on presidential-legislative structures include the words "federal" or "federalism" in their indexes, the index to Ostrom's (1991) otherwise seminal analysis of American federalism makes no mention of "party," the World Bank's assessment of federal relations in Russia (Wallich, 1994) makes only passing reference to political structures and wholly ignores party competition, none of the essays in Elster and Slagstad's (1988) edited volume on constitutionalism pays heed to Riker's argument, and although Lijphart's (1984) widely used text devotes a chapter to federalism, that chapter offers no discussion of parties. Thus, even if Russia's constitutional fathers had been better schooled in contemporary social science, there is no reason to believe that they would have produced a document much different than the one they eventually wrote and ratified.

But while mainstream comparative texts fail to provide much guidance, Russians might have gained from their own experience. Our arguments about federalism are summarized by the proposition that political parties breath life into constitutional structures, that the parties which do this are those with strong local roots but which also have an incentive to integrate with national parties, and that election laws, the timing and procedures of presidential elections, and the autonomy given regional governments to manipulate the elections laws that pertain to regional and local offices (including representation in the national legislature) are important influences on these incentives. Interestingly, the communist party performed an equivalent function during the Soviet era. Although the party operated with a top-down command-and-control administrative apparatus and its authority did not rest on any electoral mandate, there was sufficient content to the theory of democratic centralism that our arguments here about parties and federalism might not have appeared wholly alien to those who drafted the Russian constitution. Thus, constitutional engineering consistent with our first principle of design, although unrealized, was not infeasible. It was more the imperatives of conflict in an unsettled environment rather than specifies that compartmentalized the drafting of Russia's constitution. Greater awareness of the need for integration, in combination with a better theory of federal constitutional design and the role of political parties in federal democratic governance, might have contributed discernably to the avoidance of many of that document's inadequacies. This is not to say that the instinct to write a document that favored democratic centralism and a unitary state could have been averted. It is naive to argue that theory and mere consciousness can compel political elites in Moscow to embrace fully the precepts of democratic constitutional federalism. Nevertheless, consciousness and better theory would have encouraged such a government and would have armed those who sought to implement a more democratic regime with more compelling arguments.

References

Blankenagel, A. (1992). Toward constitutionalism in Russia. *East European Constitutional Review* 1.2 (Summer): 25–27.

Cohen, A. (1993). Comparing Russia's constitutional drafts. *Eurasian Reports: What Is Russia,* Center for American-Eurasian Studies. 3.2 (Winter).

Cohen, A. (1995). Crime without punishment. *Journal of Democracy* 6.2 (April): 34–45.

Colomer, J.M. (1995). Strategies and outcomes in Eastern Europe. *Journal of Democracy* 6.2 (April): 74–85.

Elster, J. and Slagstad, R. (Eds.). (1988). *Constitutionalism and democracy.* Cambridge: Cambridge University Press.

Hardin, R. (1989). Why a constitution? In B. Grofman and D. Wittman (Eds.), *The Federalist Papers and the new institutionalism.* New York: Agathon Press.

Hoadley, J.F. (1986). *The origins of American political parties. 1789–1803.* Lexington: University Press of Kentucky.

Holmes, S. and Lucky, C. (1994a). Storm over compatibility. *East European Constitutional Review* 3.1 (Winter): 120–122.

Holmes, S. (1994b). Designing electoral regimes. *East European Constitutional Review* 3.2 (Spring).

Laqueur, W. (1994). *The dream that failed.* Oxford: Oxford University Press.

Lijphart, A. (1984). *Democracies.* New Haven: Yale University Press.

Lijphart, A. (Ed.). (1992). *Parliamentary versus presidential government.* Oxford: Oxford University Press.

Linz, J.J. and Valenzuela, A. (Eds.). (1994). *The failure of presidential democracy.* Baltimore: Johns Hopkins University Press. 2 vols.

Ordeshook, P.C. (1992). Constitutional stability. *Constitutional Political Economy* 3(2): 137-175.

Ordeshook, P.C. (1995). Institutions and incentives. *Journal of Democracy* 6.2 (April): 46–60.

Ordeshook, P.C. and Shvetsova, O. (1995). If Hamilton and Madison were merely lucky, what hope is there for Russian federalism. *Constitutional Political Economy,* 6.2 (Summer): 107–126.

Ostrom, V. (1991). *The meaning of American federalism.* San Francisco: ICS Press.

Powell, G.B. (1982). *Contemporary democracies.* Harvard: Harvard University Press.

Riker, W.H. (1964). *Federalism: Origin, operation, significance.* Boston: Little Brown.

Rutland, P. (1994). Has democracy failed Russia. In A. Leftwich, *Democracy and development.* Forthcoming: Polity Press.

Sartori, G. (1994). *Comparative constitutional engineering.* New York: New York University Press.

Schattschneider, E.E. (1941). *Party government.* New York: Holt, Rinehart, Winston.

Semler, D. (1994). The end of the first Russian republic. *East European Constitutional Review* 3.1 (Winter): 107–113.

Sharlet, R. (1992). *Soviet constitutional crisis.* Armonk, NY: M.E. Sharpe, Inc.

Sharlet, R. (1993). Russia's 'ethnic' republics and constitutional politics. *Eurasian Reports: What Is Russia,* Center for American-Eurasian Studies 3.2 (Winter).

Shugart, M.S. and Carey, J.M. (1992). *Presidents and assemblies: Constitutional design and electoral dynamics.* Cambridge: Cambridge University Press.

Teague, E. (1994). Russia and Tatarstan sign power-sharing treaty. *RFE/RL Research Report* 3.14 (8 April).

Thorson, C. (1993). The battle for central authority in Russia: A presidential or parliamentary system. *Eurasian Reports: What Is Russia,* Center for American-Eurasian Studies 3.2 (Winter).

Tolz, V. (1993). Drafting the new Russian constitution. *RFE/RL Research Report* 2.29 (July).

Wallich, C. (1994). *Russia and the challenge of fiscal federalism.* Washington, DC: World Bank.

Williamson, C. (1960). *American suffrage from property to democracy 1760–1860.* Princeton: Princeton University Press.

Public Choice **90:** 73–115, 1997.
© 1997 *Kluwer Academic Publishers.*

Toward a new constitution for a future country*

MARTIN J. BAILEY
Department of Economics, Emory University, Atlanta, GA 30322, U.S.A.

Abstract. This paper outlines a preliminary radical plan for a constitution based primarily on recent contributions on mechanisms for choice of public goods and on constitutional rules and concepts, but based also on experience with present constitutions, corporate charters, and private arbitration procedures. It uses the standard economic perspective, disregarding such motives as herd instincts and the desire to serve the public interest. The result is markedly different from existing constitutions.

> In this world of sin and woe, no one pretends that democracy is perfect or all-wise. Indeed, it has been said that democracy is the worst form of government, except all those other forms that have been tried from time to time.
>
> Winston Churchill

1. Introduction and summary

During the past several decades, many newly independent or newly formed countries have written their own constitutions, adapting them from existing ones. When they have done so, nothing remarkably distinctive has emerged and the problems and inefficiencies in the ensuing governments have resembled or, often, caricatured those of older countries. That does not surprise us, but it is a good time to ponder whether the lessons of experience and of sound analysis could offer the prospect of a better result.

Consider this question from the perspective of a strong national leader in a newly liberated country or in one undergoing fundamental reforms after the overthrow of a previous tyranny. Suppose that this leader, who can have a dominant influence in shaping the new constitution, views the country's

* The author is indebted to Peter Aranson, Paul Rubin, to students and other colleagues in the Emory University Economics Workshop, and to students and colleagues in the Clemson University Economics Seminar for helpful comments. Inasmuch as most disagree with what I propose, the usual disclaimer has more than the usual force. For the Churchill quotation, see *Hansard,* 11 Nov. 1947, col. 206–207.

challenges and opportunities from a long-term perspective and wants to leave as a monument a system of governance that achieves "the greatest good for the greatest number." Suppose also that the leader and the nation's people strongly desire a system of effective citizen sovereignty, with a government that serves the long-term best interests of all law-abiding households, including their descendants.

The leader, if truly well-informed, will know about several barriers to sound government. We may summarize these as follows. In existing nations the clash of interests often has powerfully wasteful and detrimental effects, among other reasons because elected professional politicians with almost unlimited authority to enact and administer laws are subject to enormous rent-seeking pressures. Indeed, they *seek out* groups that have been unable to solve their own organizational free rider problems and solve them through legislation – e.g., for labor in the 1930s through the National Labor Relations Act and more recently for the poor and the "homeless." Political discourse in all venues is routinely filled with fraudulent claims, slander and other misrepresentations. Even if they might wish to enact perfectly constructive, statesmanlike legislation, politicians have no reliable conduit with which to collect valid information about the preferences and values of their constituents. A fundamental reason for these symptoms is that citizens have no incentive to seek out the truth on public issues, but instead choose rational ignorance and, often, rational non-participation. See Downs (1957: 238–274). From this core problem emanate others that permeate government. Finding a corrective mechanism for this core problem is a necessary condition for overall improvement.

Aided by expert advisers, this leader might then search for a constitutional plan that would avoid most of these problems and that would lead to the best attainable results. Supposing that these experts provide the leader with all the relevant public choice literature, what help would it be? They could point out recent work on the relation of the rent-seeking problem to constitutional issues. (See Anderson and Hill, 1986; Merville and Osborne, 1990; Mueller, 1991; Mueller, 1989: Chs. 13, 16, and pp. 326–342; Spindler, 1990). There is a large literature on the functioning of various kinds of elected parliaments, which provides insights into the reasons for the problems one discerns in the functioning of governments. Neither literature offers persuasive solutions. There is the U.S. literature on ways to improve the functioning of those governments that have in place something like the U.S. constitution. Suggestions include an increase in the powers of the states relative to the federal government, the use of supermajorities or specific imbedded constitutional rules to limit income transfers among interest groups and returning to the way the Supreme Court interpreted the U.S. constitution in the 19th century. For example, see Anderson and Hill (1986), Buchanan and Faith (1987), Lowenberg and Yu (1992), Mueller (1991), Ordeshook (1992), Spindler (1990), Sunstein (1991). There is the inconclusive literature on mechanisms, other than balloting, for collective choice – notably the demand-revealing processes. There is little analysis of how one or another of these mechanisms could be fitted into an overall constitutional design, however, so as to produce better outcomes than those we observe now.

This paper seeks to show that we can provide such a leader with a novel but sound constitutional design that could produce markedly better overall performance of a country's economy and government than occurs with existing constitutions. Enough ideas on mechanisms are now available, along with sound ideas derived from the more traditional approaches, to provide the material for high-performance designs. This paper's main exercise is to provide a sample of such a design, with as much discussion of its main features as space permits.

The proposed constitutional design will produce collective decisions that much more closely resemble ordinary business and commercial transactions than do present political processes. Citizen households will buy those kinds and amounts of government projects and activities that they find it worthwhile to buy. Each household will have a substantial personal stake in each outcome and in the household's own contribution to each outcome. The concepts and procedures for such a constitutional design have already been published, but they have not been properly brought together in a coherent framework. The present paper is a first effort to that end.

To keep this paper to reasonable length we omit any discussion of local autonomy and federalism. A point that can only be mentioned is that the literature on local public goods has much to offer on this issue. The theory of this subject tells us that when labor and capital are perfectly mobile, efficient local government maximizes the aggregate of local property values (Brueckner, 1983; Starrett, 1988: 47–62 and 77–84; Wildasin, 1979). We note that from time to time a town is developed on bare land by a private developer, who maximizes profit by maximizing the value of the property involved. The lessons from this kind of experience could also contribute to constitutional design.

There are many other issues that we also must defer. After reading through the present effort, for example, a reader may well ask if this complicated structure is worth its cost. The question is relevant but premature. There is no attempt here to assess the overhead cost of legislatures, election machinery, voter participation, and so on, still less to weigh this cost against the expected benefits. The first priority is to design a plan whose outcomes would be as nearly efficient as possible, given the premises. Once that large task is completed, one can consider the balancing of cost against advantages for various parts of the plan and for plausible alternatives. This comparative exercise is closely related to possible compromises that might result from "political necessity" and it could help illuminate the approach to such compromises.

2. Objectives, postulates, and premises

The objective is to design rules and procedures for a government that comes as close as practicable to having these attributes and effects: (1) resources in each activity, public or private, would be employed in the quantities that satisfy the conditions for Pareto efficiency, subject to specified constraints on what is legal; (2) when determining what legal prohibitions and constraints to impose to protect intangible benefits, traditional values, and so on, households participating in these decisions would have full knowledge of and direct responsibility for the sacrifices of real income that such prohibitions and constraints would entail. That is, decisions about abstract, intangible, and moral values also would satisfy the conditions of Pareto efficiency.

With only limited explanation, I postulate that there are four necessary conditions for satisfying these objectives even approximately. (1) The redistribution of income through government-managed tax-transfers would be clearly specified in the constitution, in a manner as closely consistent as possible with the second fundamental theorem of welfare economics. The relevant constitutional provision could be changed only by constitutional amendment or by legislation that enacts "Pareto optimal redistribution" consistent with the next postulate. See Hochman and Rogers (1969). (2) Apart from constitutionally mandated redistribution, the tax-transfer packages that finance government budget expenditures would be as close as practicable to Lindahl taxes/subsidies: those who benefit from or favor the budget outlays should bear, in proportion to their willingness to pay, the full cost. (3) Decisions on intangible, abstract, and moral issues would also contain tax-transfer packages approximating Lindahl tax-transfers for those issues. (4) Every citizen should have an incentive to be well-informed, to participate in the decision process, and to provide truthful information on willingness to pay. That is, the decision mechanism should not only be incentive-compatible but also should provide effective incentives to take the mechanism seriously.

On the first postulate, I would note that some redistribution is Pareto efficient and some is not. Whether to put in force more redistribution than the efficient kind is as fundamental as the issue of whether to permit slavery; this issue must be decided at the outset as a constitutional matter. If some households will be compelled to pay more taxes to be redistributed to other households than they would approve as part of a Lindahl tax-transfer package, the nature and extent of this redistribution must not be part of the ongoing decision process. Constant political tinkering with taxes on income, wealth, and estates harms almost everyone's interests, so that this tinkering cannot be part of an efficient system of government. Therefore, it must be settled once and for all at the stage of writing the constitution. My own preference would be to hold as strictly as possible to Pareto-efficient redistribution. This view also rules out slavery and involuntary servitude in the armed forces. I would strongly advise a new nation's constitution-writing authority, if it disagrees with this perspective, to work out redistribution formulas that damage economic output and growth as little as possible.

The second postulate and the first are two sides of the same coin. The first settles the philosophy of coercive redistribution in the constitution and the second says that government purchases of goods and services shall, as nearly as possible, command unanimous consent.

The third postulate extends the first and second to the protection of minority (or majority) rights in issues other than those relating to public finance. Rather than delegate these decisions to supreme court justices or to legislatures, those who have their way must be willing and able to compensate those on the losing side, to the extent that such compensation is practical. This willingness can be determined only in an incentive-compatible referendum.

The fourth postulate, which concerns incentive compatibility and the incentive to participate, is a necessary condition for the achievement of the second and third. It involves concepts well developed in the public choice literature and will be a central feature of the constitutional outline proposed here.

In addition, this paper uses certain premises that we will discuss only briefly at this point and then use as given fundamentals. These include individual rationality and citizen sovereignty. Also, we can adopt some features of present government more or less unchanged or at least leave them outside the scope of the present paper.

First, the constitutional outline I present here is based on analysis of rational self-interest. I also take motives such as a modest amount of altruism implicitly into account as long as they are consistent with rational behavior, as economists understand that term. That is, we can represent citizens' preferences, monotonic in economic goods, by quasi-orderings that satisfy the generalized axiom of revealed preference (that is, we can represent these preferences by a utility function). We allow motives like statesmanship to play a role at the stage of designing and promulgating a constitution, but in its subsequent operation such motives would at most involve a minor variant on a standard utility function. Except insofar as it bears on the voter's response to misleading information, we also mostly disregard the herd instinct, the desire to conform to peer group preferences.

The rationality premise is a way to gain access to the solution of the problem. The "impossibility" school of public choice apparently would have us believe that there is no solution. However nonsensical the claim, we would wish to find out quickly whether there is anything to it. Therefore, we first must try to deal with the analytically most tractable case and, once the analysis has achieved a reasonable degree of success, we may proceed to analytically more difficult formulations of human motivation.

Second, a desideratum one takes as self-evident is that the electorate shall be sovereign – in some broad way the electorate shall have the last word. On this point, Churchill's remark about democracy, cited here on the title page, is right in two respects and wrong in one. One must agree that no way has yet been found – or is likely to be found – that beats voter/consumer sovereignty as a way to direct resources and to decide national policies. One also must agree that the forms of representative government with political freedom that have been established so far are all something less than poetry in motion. Being neither perfect nor all-wise, they are almost always replete with wasteful and even repugnant features. One need not agree, however, that no better way has been found to serve many of the purported aims of government. Those economies or economic sectors that have operated with little or no government regulation or other intrusion, though not perfectly nor all-wisely, have performed better than has any known form of government, democratic or other. That historic fact provides us with a model to emulate and a set of concepts to use in the search for a better way to govern.

Exactly how we can realize the principle of voter sovereignty and in what ways voters will delegate sovereign powers to government are matters for analysis. To expedite our inquiry, however, we take as compelling the case for having legislatures, in preference to requiring voters to formulate and to decide all legislative issues by an initiative mechanism. Although households are the ultimate authority on their own values and preferences, the costs of gathering and interpreting information make it impractical to decide every detail of government by referendum or in a town meeting.

Finally, we use traditional concepts for some aspects of government. For present purposes, to keep the problem within reasonable bounds, we assume that a certain minimum of civilized norms prevail, so as to make constitutional government possible. No "self-enforcing mechanism" can be designed into a constitution that will rule out all possibility of a military coup or of civil war. When we analyze self-enforcement, we must draw a plausible line between actions that we can rule out by assumption and those that we cannot. For present purposes, we draw that line as follows: we assume that we can deal with traditional crimes, such as sedition, armed robbery, theft, bribery, commercial fraud, and so on by traditional means.

Certain major problems nevertheless remain to be dealt with explicitly by our design effort. These include fraudulent policy promises and other extreme misrepresentations by public officials and candidates, encroachment by government agencies on constitutional and legal rights, organized attempts to transfer income and wealth, including difficult-to-police forms of extortion and bribery and other such hallmarks of actual governments.

Here is a summary of the givens of our exercise. The central objective is to design a constitution that promotes and sustains Pareto efficiency by requiring those who favor government projects and policies to pay the full costs, including compensation to those opposed, so far as practicable, and to show reliable willingness to pay such costs when actual compensation is not practicable. To do that, we postulate that a constitutional formula should strictly define coercive redistribution and that apart from this formula the tax system should be as close to Lindahl taxes as possible. The decision mechanism should be incentive compatible and should provide a positive incentive to voter participation. We assume a sovereign electorate of rational voters. To concentrate on essentials we accept several norms of government without discussion. Taking these postulates, premises, and norms as given, we now proceed to consider ways consistent with them to achieve the stated objectives.

3. Central ideas and concepts

We now consider the key positive, partly novel ideas on which we build our constitutional outline.

3.1. Representative legislatures

A critically important idea is to apply something like the present method for jury selection to the selection of official legislators. It is a simple alternative that can eliminate the charades of the election process and that in principle can eliminate all rent-seeking pressures: choose by lot a representative cross section of the population to legislate. This idea has found advocates from time to time (see Mueller, Tollison, and Willett, 1972), but no one, to my knowledge, has proposed it as part of a mechanism to eliminate rent seeking. The elimination of rent seeking is further assured by the achievement, to the closest extent possible, of Lindahl taxes.

To approximate the goal of Lindahl taxation, it is necessary that each official legislature must reliably represent all economically significant, identifiable interest groups. The efficient way to obtain such representation is by stratified random sampling, assuming that there is an acceptable way to stratify. For present purposes, we assume that one can find a workable way to identify and certify all the distinct interest groups that our approach says should have assured proportional representation.

3.2. Key procedures

Selection of legislators by lot can solve a few of the stated problems of government, but by itself it does not ameliorate the problem of transmitting information to and from the electorate nor that of the weak incentive for voters to participate in referenda or elections. Furthermore, one must seek efficient legislative outcomes. To promote voter participation and efficiency, one can turn to demand-revealing processes, discussed further in the next subsection. Moving beyond the seminal ideas of Buchanan and Tullock (1962), economists in recent decades have developed and elaborated on radically new concepts of mechanism design. Such mechanisms can find use both in legislative decisions and in referenda.

To address information problems and other challenges to the integrity of policy-making processes, one can use courtroom-like procedures to protect legislators from improper pressures. Legislators and their families, when necessary, would be sequestered. Rules such as present courtroom rules governing expert witnesses, relevance of evidence, and so on would apply to legislative hearings and deliberations.

Besides the foregoing internal procedures for legislative efficiency, competition would provide external control. The advantages now claimed for separation of powers would be provided instead by effective competition in almost all government functions and by a well-informed, motivated sovereign electorate. Various authors note the benefits of competition but do not explore its full possibilities. See Lowenberg and Yu (1992); Marlow (1992).

Therefore, consider the possibility of having two parallel official legislatures, each hearing testimony and examining other relevant evidence in a manner and under rules drawn from experience in the judicial branch. Each would develop a detailed plan for the government for a fixed term of years. Each legislature would also spell out the continuation of its plan in detail into the subsequent budget period to define a "status quo" for that period. It would be extremely important to protect legislators from outside pressures, that is from bribery attempts and from extortion. It also would be important to avoid collusion between or among legislatures to favor their own narrow interests against all others. Therefore, the sitting official legislatures should be prevented from any communication with each other except for certain formal communications after they have reached decisions.

In addition, a further constructive force can be the formation of private, for-profit legislative enterprises that would compete with the official legislatures for voter approval. Their communications to or from official legislatures should also be tightly restricted.

3.3. Decision mechanisms

The two decision mechanisms of interest for legislation are the Thompson insurance mechanism and the Vickrey-Clarke-Groves (VCG) tax mechanism, sometimes referred to as "the Clarke tax," both of which try to imitate the efficient outcomes of free markets. See Thompson (1966); Mueller (1989); Groves, Radner and Reiter (1987): esp. Ch. 2, by Groves and Ledyard; Bailey (1995b, c). Both mechanisms would have a role in referenda, whereas the VCG mechanism alone would be the principal mechanism in an official legislature. One can tailor both mechanisms both to decide "either-or" choices and to decide choices along a continuous scale, such as the choice of a budget size for a government activity.

Under the Thompson insurance mechanism, a central authority quotes odds and sets corresponding fair premia for insurance against the success of each proposal. Each voting household then insures against those outcomes that would harm its financial or material welfare. The central authority declares the winner to be that proposal that has the smallest total insurance against it – the one that would generate the highest profit to the central authority as insurer.

The information needed to set fair insurance premia would come from the decision process in each legislature. The excess of benefit over cost of a proposal that passes a legislature, together with statistical sampling theory, imply the required posterior odds that the proposal will pass a referendum. With multiple legislatures offering nonidentical proposals, there would be a corresponding improvement in the reliability of these odds. Voters would therefore have a sound basis for accepting the premia as fair.

Under the most plausible assumption about the effects of intangible issues on a household's marginal utility of wealth, however, households would not buy insurance or would buy less than full coverage against intangible harms such as enactment of a law the household regards as immoral or grossly offensive. For the pertinent analysis, see Calfee and Rubin (1992). One should turn, therefore, to the VCG mechanism to weigh intangibles. Although in a large society voters have little incentive to participate carefully and accurately in this mechanism by itself, linking it with the Thompson mechanism on all issues involving both tangible and intangible effects would provide the appropriate incentive. For a more detailed discussion of the incentive effects involved, see Bailey (1995a).

These mechanisms, along with competition and voter sovereignty, are the key features that offer the promise of an efficient system.

3.4. *Incentives*

The instruction to legislators must emphasize that conscientious maximization of their own interests, based on their regular non-legislative incomes and preferences, is the way to obtain a successful program. Then, after the referendum selects one of the programs, members of the winning legislature would receive a bonus (after they leave office) based on how accurately their program reflects public tastes and on how accurate the program's forecasts and promises were. We have noted, for example, that the legislature can estimate and propose, as part of its program, a set of Lindahl taxes for identified subgroups of the population. The more accurate this estimate is, the more nearly the referendum outcome will be unanimous. The bonus would be a strongly increasing function of the degree of unanimity as well as of the referendum measure of the dollar superiority of the winning legislative program over the nearest alternative. It also would depend on program outcomes, as in the case of a contract with penalty clauses.

Because the winning legislative program could be the status quo program, the bonus for the program could go to the members of an earlier winning legislature, no longer in office. This feature means that there would be at least three legislatures in competition with each other at the stage of the first budget of the legislative term, besides the competition of private legislative proposals, so that the risk of possible collusion among them would be easy to control.

3.5. *Competition in the judiciary*

It appears that the easiest general issue, under the broad headings indicated thus far, concerns the governmental judiciary. Either private arbitrators or government-supplied courts can settle civil disputes. Government-supplied courts have proved to be a necessary part of the system because sometimes a defendant in a dispute must be compelled to participate in adjudication and to comply with the result. For criminal cases this point is even more obvious.

For discussion purposes, let us assume that official courts of first resort should function in substantially the same ways as do those we now have in the U.S. and Britain. However, we do not assume that official courts should have a cartel to determine jurisdiction or venue for each case. Instead, they should compete for business. Experience, both with the medieval British legal system and, more recently, with private arbitrators indicates that competition between alternative judiciaries can bring major benefits (Kiralfy, 1956: 153, 160; 1990: 129–134; see also Berman, 1983: 268–269 for a philosophical argument favoring such competition).

4. Tentative draft of a constitution

We now pull these ideas together and provide further specifics. Items in brackets are to be filled in or made more specific at a later stage.

MODEL CONSTITUTION FOR NEW GOVERNMENTS

PREAMBLE

We the people of [*the nation of Cumulanis*] adopt this constitution as a solemn contract, binding ourselves and our successors in perpetuity. Although in some circumstances it compels some of us to accept the will of others, we accept that minimum amount of such compulsion that, when applied consistently and without favor in all circumstances, serves our best interests and those of our successors. It is our aim to harmonize each public decision with our interests under this constitution so that we support each such decision, as nearly as possible, unanimously.

Article I: Popular Sovereignty

Section 1. The government, a provider of services under contract with the people, implements and enforces such legislation as the people approve. The people delegate specified authority to its executive and judicial officers. Subject to the provisions of this constitution, officers and legislative programs shall compete for the people's approval.

Article II: Legislatures, Legislative Programs, and their Execution

Section 1. (a) There shall be two official legislatures and there may be private ones as provided in Subsection 10(d), each drafting a separate legislative program to be presented to the people in such a manner that they may approve one or another in its entirety or may approve a composite of parts of more than one program.

(b) Except as modified by Article V, Section 8, "by law" means by a statute enacted under the procedures prescribed in Article II, Sections 8, 9, and 10.

Section 2. (a) Each official legislature shall consist of citizens eligible to vote, selected by lot. The number selected shall be no fewer than [*200*] and no greater than 500. The selection procedure shall be a stratified random drawing in which each population subgroup, classified by gender, age group, region, employment status, income, and income source by industry and occupation, if any, including career government servants, shall be proportionately represented. The subgroups shall be mutually exclusive and exhaustive, so that each citizen shall be a member of exactly one subgroup. The selection shall be supervised by an

Election Commission of [*five*] members selected by the two official legislatures in joint session in the fourth year of their term of office from a panel of successful arbitrators and judges, to take office [*three*] months prior to the commencement of the term of office of the incoming official legislatures. The term of an Election Commission shall be four years. No Election Commissioner may serve consecutive terms.

(b) A new demographic subgroup other than those specified in Subsection (a) may be created by law by subdividing an existing subgroup, provided that it has first been established in official legislative proceedings (1) that membership and nonmembership of such a group can be independently verified by nonmembers of the original demographic subgroup and (2) that creation of the new subgroup will reduce the within-group variability of declared harms on some significant public policy referenda.

(c) Persons selected by lot shall be compelled to serve in an official legislature, except for those excused for overriding reasons. Such reasons are restricted to (1) terminal illness with a prognosis of less than [*two years*] of survival or permanently incapacitating ill health confirmed by a panel of doctors selected by the Election Commission, (2) indictment for a felony, in which case the person shall be temporarily excused until the case is concluded, including appeals, and if not convicted the person shall be available as an alternate for a vacancy during the legislative term, (3) election to high office under Article IV, or (4) [*other.*]

Section 3. Two official legislatures shall be selected every four years. If a legislator becomes ineligible to serve as a result of death, permanently incapacitating ill health, election to high office, or conviction for a felony, the Election Commission shall select an alternate if one is already available or if not conduct a special drawing to select a new legislator, in either case from the same population subgroup as that of the ineligible legislator.

Section 4. An official legislature shall have no authority to exclude a member for any reason, other than those prescribed by Section 3. Such exclusion shall not take effect until certified by the Election Commission. In the fourth year of each legislative term each official legislature shall propose a law defining felonious conduct in connection with legislative business, such as bribery, extortion, and obstruction, and such a law shall come into force at the beginning of the next legislative term, if it meets the requirements for legislation prescribed in this Article. Each such legislative proposal shall include provisions governing subsequent employment of legislators by employers who do business with or otherwise tangibly benefit from government programs.

Section 5. Each official legislator shall receive a salary while serving equal to [*1.2*] times the full value of his or her personal services as measured by prior earnings, together with a reasonable expectation of current increase. Under this section, members of the official legislator's immediate family shall be considered to be official legislators. In addition, each legislator may receive incentive pay as prescribed and pay incentive taxes as prescribed in other sections of this article. For the income from property, including intellectual property, that an official legislator would otherwise receive, said legislator shall exchange such property for a portfolio of equal value proportionately representing the same industry or

industries as that of the original property. Apart from these specified sources, no official legislator may receive royalties, honoraria, gifts of more than nominal value, or any other income while serving except as otherwise provided in this constitution.

Section 6. Each official legislature shall select a presiding officer to be called "Speaker" from among a panel of successful appellate judges. The Speaker shall have the same authority that a judge has in a civil trial to limit evidence and arguments presented on the grounds of relevance and reliability, to preserve order, and to determine specific rules of order pursuant to those prescribed by law. Upon receiving the Speaker's recommendation at the beginning of a session, the legislature shall determine its structure of committees, their membership, and the scope of their authority pursuant to the legislature's business. Each official legislature shall keep a journal of its proceedings and votes, which shall be published in a timely way prior to each referendum.

Section 7. The identities of legislators shall be kept secret until [*ten*] years after they have served. Under exceptional conditions as may be prescribed by the Election Commission all official legislators, together with their families, shall be sequestered from all contact with persons other than government officials and witnesses for a period to be prescribed by the Election Commission. Their access to news, other information, and messages from outside the legislature shall at all times be controlled by the Speaker in such a manner as to protect the integrity of the official legislative process. In particular, there shall be no communication between the two legislatures nor between their Speakers, and the proceedings of each legislature shall be kept secret until the subsequent referendum ballot is set. This provision shall not prohibit the Election Commission from arranging the presentation of evidence to both official legislatures simultaneously or from permitting relevant questions from legislators to experts and interested citizens who testify, in such a manner as to conform to the ban on communication. During periods of sequestration the Speakers and the members of the Election Commission, with their families, also shall separate themselves from all contact with persons other than government officials and witnesses.

Section 8. Each official legislator may initiate budget proposals and other legislative proposals and the Speaker may lay before the official legislature such proposals as have been presented to the Speaker by citizens. This provision shall not in any way compromise a citizen's right to initiate proposals in the manner described in Subsection 10(d) nor shall a citizen's participation in proposals under Subsection 10(d) compromise the citizen's right to offer proposals to Speakers.

Section 9. (a) Each official legislator shall be instructed to vote within the legislature in such a manner as to maximize his or her family's best interests, taking both financial and intangible considerations into account, based on the family's incomes and interests prior to serving and on the modifications of property income prescribed by Section 5. The legislator also shall be instructed that truthful voting in this stage will maximize the legislator's prospects for generous incentive pay. The manner of voting is that each legislator shall state, in

response to a proposal, how much money it is worth to that legislator's family to pass or to defeat the proposal, as the case may be. When an official legislature votes on several related issues, such that the votes on one issue may depend on the outcome of another issue, all such issues shall be considered together in a single procedure. All feasible outcomes shall be enumerated and each legislator shall state how much money it is worth to that legislator's family to obtain each outcome relative to each less preferred outcome. Each legislator also shall state by how much this money amount would be changed if the family's income were initially higher by the stated amount. If these amounts are inconsistent with a technically rational, self-consistent set of preferences, the legislator shall be required to bring them into conformity with same. Subject to adjustment procedures set out in part (a) of the Technical Annex, the amounts voted shall be summed and the proposal or package with the highest money amount voted in its favor is adopted as a formal proposal of the legislature. If the legislator's vote changes the outcome, compared to what it would have been had all others voted the same while this legislator did not vote, the legislator will pay an incentive tax equal to the minimum amount required from that legislator to produce a tie vote between the actual outcome and the alternative in a pairwise vote between the two. Alternative outcomes that are outvoted by a sufficiently narrow margin, as determined by criteria supplied by the Election Commission, also shall be presented by the legislature for possible inclusion in the referendum, in conformity with Subsection (b).

(b) An advisory committee of statisticians appointed by the Election Commission shall determine the probability that a referendum as prescribed in Section 10 will approve each portion of a legislative proposal and each alternative portion. Those noncompetitive portions that are found to have a probability of approval higher than [*95*] percent shall be grouped together for a single up or down vote. Those portions with lower probabilities of approval and acceptable proposals facing competing alternatives shall appear as separate proposals on the referendum ballot. A noncompetitive proposal is acceptable if the advisory committee of statisticians finds that the probability of acceptance exceeds [*ten*] percent. A group of competing proposals is acceptable as a group if the probability that a proposal from the group will pass exceeds [*ten*] percent and each competing proposal is acceptable if the probability of acceptance exceeds [*one*] percent. A budget proposal is defined to include every legislative proposal pursuant to the authority of Article III, Sections 3 and 4 and such other legislative proposals as are identified as budget proposals under Article II, Subsection 9(c). Budget proposals under Article III Section 4 shall include alternative funding levels for each kind of expenditure as separate proposals or as a continuous scale of options, over a range chosen on the basis of this probabilistic rule. Alternative budgets for inspection, auditing, and application of measures of performance of government programs shall be provided for as a set of separate budget proposals. When the official legislatures have decided their proposed legislative programs, the two Speakers shall advise the Commission on the appropriate subject grouping of items on the ballot. Every legislative proposal must conform to the grouping selected by the Commission and within each proposal group it must state what it proposes (possibly including "no action") for each subject and program in that group. However, a legislature may decline to propose legislation in an entire proposal group.

(c) Each legislative proposal pursuant to the authority of Article III, Sections 5, 6, 7, 8, or 9 shall be accompanied by a thorough, accurate analysis of its budget consequences. If said proposal requires a budget for its implementation, the legislature shall include it as a combined legislative and budget proposal as part of the overall proposal for the budget referendum ballot. Each such proposal, if included on the ballot, shall be subject to the rules of Subsection (b) on proposal groups.

(d) Using the official legislators' votes as guidance, each Speaker shall propose a set of taxes and, if necessary, positive transfers for each population subgroup represented in the legislature and where appropriate for each type of property, with a view to achieving a unanimous referendum vote for or against each legislative proposal including the "proposals" of the continuation budget that will appear in the same referendum. These taxes and transfers shall be itemized by proposal and by whether the tax basis is the household or an item of property. Upon receiving this proposal from its Speaker, each official legislature shall adopt a proposed schedule of taxes and transfers for each proposal group. The taxes to finance each proposal group must pay for its entire expected cost, period by period, and the budget proposals as a whole from each legislature must have exact balance, inclusive of debt service payments and payments to the financial reserve as prescribed in Subsection 12(e), based on estimation procedures prescribed by the Election Commission. The Election Commission, advised by its statistical advisory committee, shall determine these estimation procedures taking account of foreseeable demographic changes and other changes affecting the sizes and economic circumstances of the population subgroups represented in the official legislatures. For identical or substantially identical proposals, according to the data from the official legislatures, the Election Commission shall consolidate the tax schedules proposed by the legislatures for each such proposal into a single schedule having the maximum likelihood of attaining a minimum-harm outcome (nearly unanimous in value terms) and a balanced budget. This consolidation also shall apply to compensation to property owners for property and easements acquired by court order.

(e) A full and fair account of the facts and arguments for and against each plan, except for omissions or summaries required by consideration of military secrecy as prescribed by law, shall be assembled by the Election Commission, subject to the rules of evidence applicable to official legislative proceedings. These facts and arguments shall be distributed at least [*one month*] in advance of the referendum to all citizens eligible to vote.

(f) Beginning in the year [*2000*] and every [*twelfth*] year thereafter the budget proposals of the two official legislatures shall include provision for a census of the population, designed and conducted in such a manner as to facilitate accurate implementation of Section 2. In addition, each official legislature shall include in the [*first*] budget proposal of its legislative term the funding of an analysis of trends in voter residence and registration to vote, to provide an authoritative basis for revision of the census numbers. Provided that voters approve such a budget provision, these revisions shall be used to implement Section 2 in the selection of the official legislatures for the subsequent legislative term.

Section 10. (a) Each legislative proposal from both official legislatures shall be presented in a referendum to all eligible voters, together with other proposals

approved under Subsection (d). There shall be a biennial budget proposal for the functions of government, which shall include a two-year extension representing its continuation. Each budget proposal also shall offer as an alternative "no action" budget a set of programs representing a minimum program for public safety prescribed by a previously enacted law. This minimum program shall include provision for compensation of legislators, Speakers, Election Commissioners, the Chief of State, the Commander in Chief of the Armed Forces, for payment of government accounts payable, debt service, and scheduled payments to financial reserves as prescribed in this constitution. Each regular budget referendum shall include the continuation of the budget adopted two years earlier and the "no action" budget proposal for each proposal group. For non-budget proposals, the alternative of no action shall appear on the ballot. All no-action and continuation proposals herein prescribed shall appear on the ballot whether or not they meet the statistical tests prescribed in Subsection 9(b). Legislatures may propose supplementary budgets and budget reductions at any time whose costs shall include election costs; subject to these tests a referendum shall be held. Voting shall be secret, except that the matching of identified ballots to voters must be known to the Election Commission to carry out its duties under this Section and kept under permanent seal. The Election Commission also shall keep under seal all referendum-generated information about voter willingness to pay (by population subgroups) that could otherwise influence tax proposals under Subsection 9(d).

(b) For those proposals that the Election Commission places on the ballot, voters shall express their preferences among the proposals in monetary terms. They shall express such preferences in two ways. First, the Election Commission shall offer them insurance against each less-preferred outcome at a fair premium, based on the probabilities determined by the statistical advisory group. The voter is expected to purchase insurance against each outcome other than the voter's most preferred outcome. The voter will receive the face value of said insurance for an outcome that is not the voter's most preferred outcome. Second, each voter may declare, pairwise between every pair of mutually exclusive proposals, an uninsured harm that the voter would suffer if the outcome went against the voter's pairwise preference. The voter who declares uninsured harm also shall declare what the uninsured harm would be if (a) the outcome were the voter's least preferred rather than most preferred and if (b) the voter's income were higher by the amount of the greatest harm otherwise declared. Each such declaration of uninsured harm may not exceed [*ten*] percent of the voter's income and the sum of all declared uninsured harms on a ballot may not exceed [*twenty*] percent of the voter's income. The Election Commission shall set lower maximum declarations whenever legislative proceedings reveal that such maxima are appropriate. If these various amounts are inconsistent with a technically rational, self-consistent set of preferences, the voter shall be required to bring them into conformity with same or, failing that, part or all of the voter's ballot shall be disqualified. If more than one manner of partial disqualification would satisfy the test, the voter shall select which disqualification to accept. The Election Commission shall sum the insurance plus the uninsured harms, subject to adjustment procedures set out in part (b) of the Technical Annex, and declare the outcome that results in the least aggregate harm. It shall pay the insurance face value to those voters who insured against this outcome. It shall assess an

incentive tax on each voter whose uninsured harm was great enough to change the outcome, with other votes held constant, setting the incentive tax on that voter as the amount that would have produced a tie vote in the referendum. It shall pay members of each official legislature an incentive fee prescribed by law, based on the accuracy with which the income effects predicted by that legislature's valuations predict voter income effects, and also based on the accuracy with which the legislature predicts the variability of declared harms for each proposal group, within each population subgroup. Corresponding procedures set out in the Technical Annex, part (d) shall apply for a proposal presented as a continuous scale of options. However, if neither official legislature associates intangible values with some pairs of potential referendum outcomes, under part (a) of the procedure in the Technical Annex, then for such pairs no declarations of uninsured losses shall be accepted in the referendum procedure and the outcome shall be determined solely by the amounts of insurance purchased, without adjustments for income effects.

(c) Attempts to organize voter groups to misrepresent their harms shall be a felony with penalties prescribed by law.

(d) A citizen, nationally chartered corporation, or group of citizens may offer budget proposals and other proposed legislation to the Election Commission. The person or group offering such proposals shall post sufficient bond to cover incremental election costs due to the proposals, as defined pursuant to Subsection (f), and shall be liable for these costs whether the proposals succeed or fail, except in the case of proposals for measures of success under Subsection (h). All private proposals except those embodied in citizen petitions shall be kept secret from official legislatures until the ballot is set. If a private proposal has no competition from an official legislature, the Election Commission shall refer it to a legislature as a citizen "petition" to obtain information and shall exclude the legislature's answering proposal, if any, from the ballot while using that legislature's official report and tax proposal in the usual ways. The Election Commission shall apply the same procedures for determining chances of success of such proposals as the procedures used for proposals by official legislatures and shall allow those proposals to appear on the ballot that meet the criteria of Subsection 9(b).

(e) Each proposal for legislation under the authority of Article III, Sections 5, 6, 7, or 8 shall appear on two successive referendum ballots, except as otherwise provided under Article III Section 8. The first time it appears the legislation may be briefly though accurately summarized, as may the arguments for and against its adoption. The question put to the voters in this first referendum shall be, "Shall this proposal be considered for adoption in the forthcoming referendum of [*date*]?" If voters reject this proposition, the proposal shall not appear on a subsequent referendum ballot until and unless the first vote is reversed, and the legislature that originated the proposal shall receive a reduction in its incentive payments. This reduction shall consist of the costs of placing the proposal on the ballot plus [*20*] percent of the net total harms declared by voters in rejecting it.

(f) The Compensation of each Election Commissioner and of each Speaker for serving shall equal [*two*] times the average salary paid to official legislators; plus incentive pay of [*.02*] percent, for each subject group, of the net monetary value of the superiority, measured by total declared harms of the programs approved by referenda over "no action" net of the harms to those who prefer "no action" to the approved programs; less [*.003*] percent, for each subject group,

of the net total monetary value of the inferiority of the programs approved by referenda relative to "no action," for each population subgroup that on balance supported "no action"; plus the adjustment prescribed in Subsection 12(c), less [*.02*] percent of all costs, including private costs, of the conduct of and participation in referenda sanctioned by the Election Commission during its term. The method of reckoning these costs shall be prescribed by law prior to the Commission's term. An Election Commissioner's and Speaker's income from property and other sources shall be subject to the same rules and restrictions as those prescribed for legislators in Section 5.

(g) The Election Commission shall maintain an Election Fund in two parts, Fund A and Fund B. Fund A shall receive the insurance premia, pay the insurance claims, receive the supplementary taxes provided for by Subsection (b), receive the incremental cost payments for private proposals prescribed by Subsection (d), and pay the costs of administration of elections. At the end of each legislative term, the surplus or deficit in this fund shall be allocated to voters according to the following rule. For each voter the size of the fund shall be adjusted to the size it would have had if this voter had not participated in the election. The adjusted fund shall be divided by the number of voters and the quotient, if positive, shall be paid to this voter or if negative charged to this voter. Where applicable, the payment or charge to the voter shall be adjusted as indicated in the Technical Annex, part (d). If this method of division leaves a residual surplus or deficit in the fund, the residual shall be carried forward into the next legislative term and placed in Fund B. If the surplus or deficit in Fund B exceeds, in absolute value, [*one-half*] the planned amount in the financial reserve prescribed in Subsection 12(e), the excess shall be transferred to that reserve.

(h) Legislation approved by the voters shall be deemed in law to be a contract between the legislature that proposed it and the voters. Measures or indicators of the success or effectiveness of government proposals shall be prescribed by law and shall be binding on the government. These measures of success shall be enacted or renewed in a separate law in the fourth year of each legislative term, to take effect for first and subsequent budget legislation of the following term, except that the first continuation budget, if enacted in whole or in part, shall be subject to the previously enacted measures of success that applied to it when it was first enacted as a regular budget. This law also shall prescribe measures of success for the functions of inspection, auditing, and application of measures of performance. At any time the Election Commission may accept private proposals for revised measures of success to apply to a future budget, provided that a referendum on these measures is possible at least [*two months*] before the referendum on the budget to which they would apply and provided that the citizens offering such a proposal have no proprietary interest, direct or indirect, in a pending budget proposal for the budget referendum.

(i) Legislators shall be immune from lawsuits concerning their individual conduct in the course of legislative business. However, executive officers, the legislature that appoints them, and the legislature that performs inspection, auditing, and application of measures of performance shall not be immune from lawsuits arising from the outcomes of legislation once enacted. The criteria for standing and admissibility of suits shall be identical to those for suits against private parties as specified by the laws of torts and contracts, taking due account of the penalties prescribed in Article III, Section 4, that form part of the legisla-

tive contract. Judges shall be immune from lawsuits concerning their conduct of court business, so long as this conduct conforms to the canons of judicial ethics and so long as they interpret the applicable law in good faith as provided in this constitution. A reversal of a judge's decision on appeal shall not constitute grounds for a lawsuit against this judge unless the opinion in the reversal states that the judge's decision showed flagrant or malicious disregard of the law.

Section 11. (a) Incentive pay for legislators, official or private, shall be based on the accuracy with which their proposals approximate voters' preferences. In the case of proposals by official legislatures, the declared harms used to calculate this incentive pay shall be adjusted by the difference between the legislature's proposed tax assessments and the actual tax assessments, where applicable. Subject to the modifications prescribed by Sections 10 and 12 and by Article III, Section 4, the aggregate incentive pay to a legislature for each of its proposals that is adopted will be [*0.1*] percent of the budget amount contained in the proposal plus [*30*] percent of the total harm from non-adoption net of declared harms due to adoption, relative to the nearest distinct and different alternative proposed by another legislature, insured and uninsured, less [*5*] percent of the net total monetary value of the inferiority of those proposal subgroups relative to distinct and different alternatives on the ballot for each population subgroup that on balance would have supported alternative proposals in those subgroups under the legislature's proposed taxes. If, however, the only such alternative is "no action", the incentive pay shall instead be [*0.1*] percent of the budget amount contained in the proposal plus [*3*] percent of the total harm from non-adoption relative to no action, insured and uninsured, declared by voters who supported its adoption less [*.5*] percent of the net total monetary value of the inferiority of those proposal subgroups relative to "no action", for each population subgroup that on balance would have supported no action in those subgroups under the legislature's proposed taxes.

(b) The incentive pay for those proposals on which official legislatures make identical or equivalent new proposals shall be divided equally between or among them. If an official legislature and a private legislative enterprise have identical proposals that voters approve, the official legislature shall receive the entire amount of the incentive pay unless the Election Commission receives the private proposals before the official legislature has voted on them or on equivalent ones. If a portion of a continuation budget wins in the referendum, the entire resulting incentive pay shall be paid to the members of the legislature(s) of whose budget it is a continuation. If more than one legislature shared the incentive pay of said budget portion, they shall divide the continuation incentive pay equally.

(c) The incentive pay to each official legislature shall be divided among its members as follows: [*One half*] shall be divided equally among them and [*one half*] shall be divided among them in proportion to their minimum individual incomes as determined under Section 5. Incentive pay for a sitting legislature shall be placed in escrow and paid to its members at the end of their term.

(d) All official legislators shall be exempt from tax assessments under the budgets for which they have made proposals until the first regular budget enacted after they leave office.

Section 12. (a) The official or private sitting legislature whose budget propos-

als approved by referendum sum to the largest aggregate total shall appoint executive officers to administer the government's activities, except as provided otherwise under Subsection (b) and elsewhere herein. These executive officers shall serve at the pleasure of the legislature. Prior to a biennial budget referendum each legislature shall publish its proposed team of executive officers. In case both official legislatures have received approval for identical budget totals, the choice of legislature for this role shall be determined by the toss of an honest coin supervised by the Election Commission.

(b) An official legislature not responsible for executive functions shall be responsible for inspection, auditing, and application of measures of performance. If, pursuant to Subsection (a), neither official legislature is responsible for executive functions, the one gaining the larger incentive pay under Section 11 of this Article shall be responsible for inspection, auditing, and application of measures of performance. If in this circumstance both official legislatures have gained the same incentive pay under Section 11, the choice of legislature for inspection, auditing, and application of measures of performance shall be determined by the toss of an honest coin supervised by the Election Commission.

(c) The incentive pay of legislators in the legislature that appoints executive officers shall be reduced/increased by [*35*] percent of all cost overruns/underruns and shall be increased or reduced by specified functions of the indicators of government performance under the legislation provided for in Subsection 10(h), as prescribed by law. The legislature responsible for inspection and audit shall calculate adjusted budget revenues, at the end of the budget period, by correcting the total for unanticipated changes in the numbers of citizens in the official population subgroups due to changes in status such as from employed to unemployed. The Election Commission shall calculate the presumptive adjusted revenues and the presumptive planned revenues corresponding to the tax assessments that had been proposed by each official legislature for the budget just ending. The incentive pay of each official legislature shall be reduced by [*three*] percent of the absolute value of the discrepancy between presumptive adjusted budget revenues for that legislature and the presumptive planned budget revenues for the budget as enacted. For acquisitions of property and easements authorized by a referendum, the incentive pay of a legislature shall be reduced by [*five*] percent of the amount that the affected property owners have insured against financial harm (if any) arising from the success of this legislative proposal, after correcting the amount insured for the difference between actual compensation and the compensation the legislature had proposed for the property and easements. This reduction of incentive pay is additional to and separate from all other incentive pay adjustments herein prescribed. Cost overruns/underruns for a government program shall be assessed/allocated to voters in proportion to their taxes assessed for this program, adjusted by their individual net benefit for the marginal (last) unit or increment of that program as measured by the valuations declared in the referendum, provided that the result is positive. If a marginal net benefit is negative, it shall be considered to be zero for the purpose of this assessment or allocation. For this purpose a "program" means a budget proposal group or a portion of it that for each voter subgroup has a single tax assessment rate. The pay of an executive officer shall be a fixed salary plus a fraction or multiple of the incentive pay received by a legislator under this subsection and Subsection 10(h).

(d) The incentive pay for the legislature responsible for inspection, auditing, and application of measures of performance shall include [*30*] percent of all improper and unauthorized costs recovered by this activity and shall be a function of the performance measures for this activity as prescribed by law.

(e) The government shall plan to maintain a financial reserve of readily marketable assets equal to [*three*] percent of the approved biennial budget, for the purpose of payment of unanticipated budget deficits. These assets shall be located within the national boundaries and shall not include currency or financial claims issued by a foreign government nor shall it include the government's own bonds. Its balance of national currency shall not exceed [*0.2*] percent of the biennial budget. Whenever the financial reserve differs from [*three*] percent of the approved biennial budget by more than [*0.5*] percent but less than [*three*] percent, the next biennial budget proposal shall include a schedule of uniform payments to or from the financial reserve scaled to restore the reserve to the planned figure within [*four*] years. Whenever the difference is [*three*] percent or more, the next biennial budget proposal shall include a schedule of uniform payments to or from the financial reserve scaled to restore the reserve to the planned figure within [*six*] years. If the difference is a deficit and the reserve is exhausted, the government shall issue full faith and credit bonds with a maturity schedule to conform to the prescribed payment schedule. The incentive pay of each Election Commissioner shall be reduced by [*0.1*] percent of the absolute value of the discrepancy between adjusted budget revenues and the officially planned budget revenues that had been stated in the budget as enacted, for each biennial budget enacted under the Commissioner's supervision.

(f) Until the first budget referendum of the legislative term, the executive team from the end of the previous term shall continue in office in a caretaker role. In its proposals for the budget referendum each legislature shall specify the executive team it has selected. After the referendum the team chosen by the winning legislature shall take office until the next budget referendum unless an executive team is replaced by another team to serve the remainder of its term. No member of an official legislature may serve as an executive official or employee.

(g) Career government employees shall be limited to the following categories: (1) a secretariat for each legislature; (2) magistrates and judges provided for in Article V and such court officers as they may appoint; (3) military officers in the line of command, their operational staffs including intelligence, and combat personnel; and (4) officials and operatives responsible for such anti-terrorist and other police intelligence functions as are prescribed by law. Competition for the intelligence functions shall be provided by parallel, independent units within the government and by private firms, after the manner of legislatures. The roles of career military officers and of reservists shall be competitive in the development of military tactics, proposals for weapons selection, and troop training, but shall come under unified command for military operations as prescribed by law. Logistics and other military support functions shall be performed by military reserve units and private firms as prescribed by law. Promotion of career employees in categories (3) and (4) shall be decided by the legislature that selects executive officers, after receiving the advice of the Commander-in-Chief for category (3) and of the chief executive official for category (4).

Article III: Powers of the Government and Limitations Thereto

Section 1. (a) All powers herein permitted to "the government" refer to powers exercised in conformity with the procedures and restrictions specified in this constitution.

(b) The government may enact every law that receives unanimous consent or where a statement of indifference or voter absence may imply consent, provided (a) that the Election Commission conducts a diligent effort to locate every absent voter and to obtain an absentee ballot and (b) that a law that is inconsistent with Section 2 must have the freely given, voluntary written consent of each voter whose rights the law abridges.

Section 2. [*Bill of rights. Standard stuff, including strict prohibition of retroactive laws. Strict prohibition of involuntary servitude in any form, except that in the case of foreign invasion or an imminent threat of same, the government may use emergency powers to compel military service for up to a maximum of sixty days by citizens represented in official legislatures and qualified to vote, whose compensation shall be prescribed by law.*]

Section 3. [*Scope and terms of permitted forms of official income redistribution from rich to poor. Specified taxes for this purpose.*] These provisions may not be modified, amplified, or compromised by ordinary legislation.

Section 4. (a) Pursuant to laws enacted under Article II, the government may acquire property by compulsory court order for public purposes such as highway and sewer construction, provided that previous owners are compensated by [*five*] percent in excess of fair market value of the property acquired and of the diminution of fair market value of adjacent or associated property of the same owners that the government does not acquire. The government may purchase goods and services at market prices to further the purposes of this section, Sections 5, 6, 8, 9, and Article II, Section 9 and Subsection 12(b). The government may obtain by compulsory purchase easements from property owners restricting the private use and enjoyment of their properties for furtherance of the general welfare as provided by law, provided that all owners required to provide such easements are compensated by [*five*] percent in excess of the reduction of fair market value of said properties that results from the purchase of all such easements for a given specific purpose.

(b) The government may collect taxes in the manner prescribed in Article II, to finance the activities authorized herein. For this purpose it may require all citizens to file periodic reports of their incomes from all sources, to identify their property income by its industry and location, and to provide such other information as may be necessary to identify each citizen's membership in a population subgroup for the purposes of Article II, Subsection 2(a).

(c) In addition to the compensation provided for under Article II, the government may provide such additional compensation to officials as is prescribed by law.

(d) The government may issue full faith and credit bonds to finance budget deficits in conformity with Article II, Subsection 12(e).

(e) The government may coin money and issue currency up to a total not to exceed [—*pesos*]. It may not change the quantity of currency in circulation, either

by destruction, creation, or payment into or out of the financial reserve, by more than [*two*] percent of this amount in a year nor by more than [*three*] percent of this amount in a four-year period. Deviations of the amount in circulation shall be restored to the authorized amount according to its own schedule with the same trigger points and correction schedule as those prescribed for the national financial reserve in Article II, Subsection 12(e).

[*(f) The government may not operate, franchise, nor have a financial interest, direct or indirect, in a banking institution nor create nor authorize the creation of a Central Bank. The government may not buy, sell, nor have a financial interest in the currency or in other obligations of a foreign government or of foreign financial institutions.*]

(g) To the extent possible, all activities of the government, including the design and production of military weapons, postal service and other communications except only military communications within military operations, and transportation, shall be contracted out to private firms. The executive team, subject to independent inspection and audit as prescribed in Subsection 12(b) and elsewhere herein, shall supervise the fulfillment of these contracts. Streets and highways shall be private toll roads except where their value is greater without tolls, due to the costs of collecting tolls, as determined by law.

(h) The government may not collect money as taxes or fees nor disburse it in any manner except as prescribed by law. The government may not acquire goods and services nor lend, rent, or deliver to private hands goods and services it has acquired, except as prescribed by law.

(i) The government may issue patents and copyrights for limited periods to inventors, tradespeople, and authors to protect their discoveries, trademarks, writings, and other original works, except that, wherever monitoring and assessment of economic value is practicable, the government shall instead offer prizes or royalties for limited periods approximating the economic value of the discoveries, etc.

Section 5. Under the procedures of Article II, the government may enact and enforce laws that define ordinary crimes and misdemeanors, for the protection of public safety and for the implementation of specific laws authorized by this constitution. If laws enacted under this section harm owners of some properties or reduce the incomes of some citizens whose activities, previously legal, become unlawful, these effects shall be considered easements for the purposes of Subsection 4(a). The government may prohibit and punish the counterfeiting of its coin, currency, bonds, and of private securities and other private objects of value. In conformity with international law, the government may prohibit and punish felonies committed on the high seas.

Section 6. Under the procedures of Article II, the government may enact and enforce laws defining those kinds of contracts and contract provisions that will be enforced in official courts and, clarifying for new and unanticipated circumstances, those kinds of contracts that this constitution prohibits under Section 7. The government may not thereby create new prohibitions other than those listed in Section 7, however. In the case of contracts that are neither prohibited nor expressly sanctioned by law, the parties to such contracts shall exhaust every remedy that the contracts themselves provide before seeking recourse in an official court. Subject to this provision, the official courts shall interpret and

enforce all contracts not specifically prohibited by law. The government may enact and enforce laws governing bankruptcy. The government may prescribe by law uniform units of measure and definitions, measures or indicators of quality for private goods and services. Such units, definitions, etc., shall have no restrictive effect on goods and services offered for sale unless such restrictions are expressly provided for by easements in conformity with Subsection 4(a). The government may pay court fees and fees of private arbitrators arising from government business, including amicus curiae submissions.

Section 7. [*List of prohibited private contracts.*]

Section 8. (a) The government shall conduct foreign affairs as prescribed by law. No official or private person shall negotiate or conclude treaties with a foreign government, except as authorized by law. The government may negotiate treaties and propose their provisions as legislation. If approved in a referendum, a treaty or a part thereof may be revoked only in a manner provided for in a treaty itself or else under the procedure and requirements prescribed in Article VI, Section 1 for constitutional amendments. The government may enact and enforce laws governing immigration and naturalization. The government may enact and enforce laws delimiting the nation's territory and may acquire or cede territory in conformity with international law, except that a proposal to cede territory shall be subject to the procedures and requirements prescribed in Article VI, Section 1 for constitutional amendments.

(b) The government may establish and support armed forces.

(c) The government may declare war, following the legislative procedures prescribed in Article II. In the event of foreign invasion or an imminent threat to the armed forces, however, the Commander in Chief may order the armed forces to defend themselves and to defend the nation's territory, following emergency procedures prescribed by law. No private person or group of persons may make war or maintain troops, except that in the event of foreign invasion or an imminent threat to citizens' homes and property, they may form temporary militias in their own defense. This provision shall not restrict the right of citizens to organize private organizations of security guards or to supply police and military services to government as prescribed by law.

Section 9. [*The national government may delegate governmental powers to regional or local authorities, either created ad hoc from time to time or created on a permanent basis, as prescribed by law, provided that such regional or local authorities shall be governed by Article II and by all other applicable articles of this constitution and provided further that, in the referendum for the enabling legislation, the declared harms of both kinds of voters outside the participating regions or localities shall not exceed {10} percent of the net total declared harms from nonadoption in the participating regions or localities.*]

Section 10. No power or authority herein granted may be delegated to any person, commission, or other body except as expressly authorized in this constitution. Neither the executive authority nor the courts may impose rules, regulations, or other comparable restraints on private persons other than such rules, regulations, and restraints as are duly enacted in legislation. This constitution has the

force of law and may not be compromised nor amended except as provided in Article VI, Section 2.

Article IV: Chief of State and Commander in Chief

Section 1. Each official legislature shall, at the beginning of its term, nominate a candidate for the ceremonial function of Chief of State, a candidate for Commander in Chief of the Armed Forces, a candidate for Vice Chief of State, and a candidate for Vice Commander in Chief of the Armed Forces. These candidates shall be four different citizens. Private legislative enterprises may also nominate such candidates under the provisions of Article II, Subsection 10(d). These candidates shall be presented to voters under the same procedures as those for legislation, Article II, Sections 8 through 11, inclusive. The winner of each of these contests shall serve for a term of four years and may serve successive terms, except that the Commander in Chief may serve at most [*three*] terms, except in a time of war or of extreme emergency coming under the provisions of Article III, Section 8. If the Chief of State or Commander in Chief ceases to serve due to death or disability, the Vice Chief shall serve as Chief for the remainder of the term. In that event candidates for Vice Chief shall be nominated and presented in a referendum, to be elected to serve the remainder of the unexpired term. If the office of Chief falls vacant when there is no Vice Chief, the official legislature that appoints executive officials (or if neither does, the official legislature that performs the inspection and audit functions) shall appoint an Acting Chief to serve until a referendum to fill the positions of Chief and Vice Chief, for the remainder of the unexpired term, can be held.

Section 2. Each candidate for the office of Chief of State, for Commander in Chief, or for Vice Chief of either office shall be a native-born citizen of [*Cumulanis*] and shall be at least [*35*] years old. A candidate for Commander in Chief or for Vice Commander in Chief of the Armed Forces shall have had at least [*four*] years of experience in the active military service of [*Cumulanis*].

Section 3. (a) The Chief of State or when necessary the Vice Chief of State shall receive foreign ambassadors and higher-ranking foreign dignitaries in conformity with the foreign policy authorized by law and they shall perform such other ceremonial duties as may be prescribed by law. Neither the Chief of State nor the Vice Chief of State shall be an executive official for functions prescribed under Article II, Subsections 12(a) and (b) nor shall either serve as an official legislator. Financing and support for the activities of the Chief of State shall be provided by budget legislation and by executive officials as prescribed by law.

(b) The Commander in Chief of the Armed Forces shall have sole command of military operations subject to the foreign policy and military strategy prescribed by law, or as determined in extreme emergency under Article III, Subsection 8(c). Neither the Commander in Chief nor the Vice Commander in Chief shall be an executive official for functions prescribed under Article II, Subsections 12(a) and (b) nor shall either serve as an official legislator.

Section 4. The pay of the Chief of State and of the Vice Chief of State shall

be at least equal to that each of the Speakers or of an Election Commissioner, whichever is higher, under Article II. The pay of the Commander in Chief and of the Vice Commander in Chief shall be at least equal to that of the highest-paid executive among those appointed by the governing legislature.

Section 5. The Chief of State or the Commander in Chief may be removed from office upon the same grounds and procedures as those for removing an official legislator, except that the impeachment of either of these high officials shall be the responsibility of the legislature that controls the executive functions and that the trial of this official, for removal from office, shall be the held in the official legislature responsible for inspection and auditing. The procedures for these steps shall be the same as those for legislative proposals and final appeals.

Article V: The Judiciary

Section 1. (a) Magistrates and official courts shall have the power to compel attendance by defendants at their proceedings. In addition, official courts shall have the power to bring to trial and to sentence criminal offenders, to enforce contracts, to issue writs and injunctions [*etc.*] as prescribed by law, and to collect fees to support their operations.

(b) The courts shall interpret the law as it meant when enacted and shall not amend or modify the law. The only law, in addition to this constitution, shall be statute law. The courts shall interpret the constitution in terms of the meaning it had at the time it was ratified and similarly for the interpretation of each constitutional amendment.

Section 2. The courts shall be supported solely by their fees, which may include fees for amicus curiae submissions.

Section 3. (a) The legislature that selects executive officers also shall appoint judges and magistrates. Judges in courts of first instance and magistrates shall normally be selected from among successful arbitrators. The legislature shall appoint judges to appellate courts from among successful judges, which here and throughout this document means those judges whose lower courts have consistently covered their costs.

(b) Judges whose courts fail to be supported by fees and other income as provided by law shall be retired. Whenever, because of delays in the resolution of cases, a sufficient number of parties with standing in active disputes petition that a successful private arbitrator be appointed an official judge, the appointing legislature shall approve such an appointment unless it finds that the delays are temporary.

(c) The legislature shall appoint one magistrate for each judicial district.

(d) Rules for determining which persons have standing to participate in civil or criminal case before a court shall be prescribed by law.

Section 4. For each civil or criminal case that arises, there shall be at least three official venues that may accept jurisdiction. If the parties to a case reach timely agreement on a venue, the agreed court shall receive jurisdiction. If they

fail to reach timely agreement, the plaintiff or prosecutor shall ask the magistrate to select a venue by weighted random choice from a list consisting of (1) the venues proposed by the two sides and (2) as many as three additional venues that handle more cases than do any of those proposed by the two sides. To obtain the weights for this choice, the magistrate shall sum those cases handled by each proposed venue in the past year in which the two sides agreed on a venue and use the fraction of this total handled by each such venue as the weight or probability for the random selection. For these purposes the magistrate may restrict the calculation to cases of the particular class of which the case in question is a member.

Section 5. In addition to the functions prescribed elsewhere in this constitution, magistrates may perform marriages, notarize documents, [*and perform other customary routine functions of magistrates.*]

Section 6. The provisions of Sections 3(a), 3(b), and 4 apply also to appellate courts.

Section 7. If a party should choose to appeal an appellate court decision, the venue for the final appeal shall ordinarily be the official legislature whose legislative proposals approved by the electorate have the greatest aggregate value, measured by their budget amounts plus the declared net aggregate value of votes of the electorate. However, an official legislator who is a defendant or a member of whose family is a defendant in a suit as provided in Article II, Subsection 10(i) or in a criminal trial may not participate in the review of said suit or trial. In such cases the same rules regarding venue as those in Article V, Section 8 shall apply. The procedure for handling appeals shall be the same as that for legislation, except that such appeals shall not be subject to referendum; the decision of the legislature is final.

Section 8. A person with standing may contest a law or other action by any part of the government on the grounds of its constitutionality and courts at each level may accept the case and rule on this issue. If the official legislature that appoints executive officers and judges enacted the challenged law or was responsible for the challenged action, the other official legislature shall sit as the constitutional court for the case. If both official legislatures have a significant share of the responsibility for a challenged law, the previous legislature that appointed executive officers and judges in the most recent past term shall be convened to sit as the constitutional court for the case. The decision procedure shall be the same as that for legislation, except that the decision of the constitutional court shall be final.

Section 9. The compensation of an official legislature or constitutional court for deciding each appeal or constitutional issue shall be [*500*] times the court fees paid by all parties except the government in the court of first instance for the case at issue, plus such additional compensation as has been prescribed by law enacted prior to the first filing of said case.

Section 10. The grounds and procedures for removal of judges and magistrates shall be the same as those for disqualification of an official legislator.

Article VI

Section 1. This constitution shall come into force if it is ratified by a referendum in which at least [*80*] percent of citizens eligible to vote participate. Voting citizens shall declare the monetary value of the harm to them if ratification succeeds or fails. Ratification will depend on [*two*] criteria: (a) at least [*90*] percent of those voting shall have declared a harm if ratification fails, that is, shall have voted in favor of ratification; and (b) the aggregate amount of declared harm in case of failure shall be at least [*five*] times the aggregate amount of declared harm in case of ratification. No insurance against these harms shall be offered. The procedure shall otherwise conform to Article II, Subsection 10(b).

Section 2. This constitution may be amended by the procedures of Article II, including positive and negative tax assessments, except that in order to enter into force, an amendment must be approved by a voter declaration of net aggregate harm, in case it fails, of at least [*five*] percent of one year's value of the nation's aggregate production of goods and services. In addition, if those subgroups of the population, defined by Article II, Sec. 2, that oppose the amendment (that is, those in which the votes sum to aggregate declared harm) have an overall aggregate declared harm in excess of [*one*] percent of the nation's aggregate production of goods and services the amendment is disapproved. It must be proposed at least one year prior to the referendum to approve or disapprove it. When a constitutional amendment is under consideration, each official legislature considering it shall sequester itself at least until the completed proposal is published. A proposed amendment that is not adopted may not be considered again for at least [*ten*] years. The compensation of official legislatures for a constitutional amendment put to a referendum shall be determined according to the same formulas as that provided for legislation, except that the incentive fee for the total declaration of putative harm from non-adoption prescribed in Article II, Section 11 shall instead be [*50*] percent of the (positive or negative) excess of this total over [*five*] percent of one year's value of the nation's aggregate production of goods and services.

Section 3. (a) Upon ratification of this constitution, [*the existing proto-government*] shall serve in a caretaker capacity until the following provision creating an Interim Official Legislature can be implemented. [—] shall select [*two*] eminent jursts from [*Cumulanis*] and [*three*] from former members of [*the International Court of Justice*] to serve as the Interim Election Commission for [*two*] years, during the transition to its full implementation. As soon as it can be constituted, the Interim Election Commission shall choose a random sample of [*400*] citizens, from among those eligible to vote, to serve as the Interim Official Legislature. The Interim Official Legislature shall select a Speaker and shall function in the same manner as does an official legislature under Article II, except that there shall be no requirement for an Interim Legislator to exchange property as prescribed in Article II, Section 5.

(b) Using the procedure of Article II, Subsection 9(a), within six months of being constituted the Interim Official Legislature shall (1) propose a temporary "no action" budget containing the minimum for public safety, represented by a continuation of previous year's military and police budgets for the predecessor

government, plus interim family assistance as provided by Article III, Section 3, plus compensation of [*—pesos*] each for the Election Commissioners, plus compensation for government officials and private Legislators as herein provided until the first regular budget, plus provision for an audit of the interim "no action" budget, plus provision for an interim Census, designed and conducted in such a manner as to facilitate accurate implementation of Article II, Section 2, plus provision for a budget surplus of [*one*] percent of the budget total to commence building the national financial reserve prescribed in Article II, Subsection 12(e), and shall include proposed payroll taxes and property taxes to finance it; (2) propose legislation defining costs of elections and measures of success for subsequent budgets; (3) select an Election Commission to begin serving a regular four-year term within one year of the date at which the Interim Official Legislature was chosen; (4) nominate candidates for Chief of State, Commander in Chief of the Armed Forces, Vice Chief of State, and Vice Commander in Chief of the Armed Forces and appoint acting officials to fill these four positions; (5) appoint [—] judges and interim magistrates to proceed under the provisions of Article V; (6) propose a law defining felonious conduct in connection with legislative business, such as bribery, extortion, and obstruction, including provisions governing subsequent employment of legislators by employers who do business with or otherwise tangibly benefit from government programs; (7) propose an interim set of demographic subgroups to be used by the first regular Election Commission; and (8) propose an interim executive team to administer the interim budget.

(c) As soon as practicable, the Interim Election Commission shall conduct a referendum for approval of the proposals of the Interim Official Legislature. The referendum shall follow the procedures prescribed in Article II, Subsections 10(a), and 10(b), except that no insurance shall be offered and all declared harms shall be uninsured. Private proposals for these referendum issues shall be included, as provided in Article II, Subsection 10(e), for the two private proposals on each issue that post the largest bond among those competing. Compensation for the Interim Official Legislature shall be that provided in Article II, Section 5, plus [*0.1*] percent of the budget amounts contained in those of the Interim Official Legislature's proposals that the voters approve, plus [*3*] percent of the net total harm, of non-adoption of these approved proposals, declared by voters. Compensation for successful private proposals shall be [*0.1*] percent of the budget amounts contained in those proposals plus [*3*] percent of the net total harm of non-adoption of these approved proposals, declared by voters. No other proposals for legislation shall be included in the referendum unless an imminent threat of war requires implementation of Article III, Section 8.

(d) Members of the Interim Official Legislature shall not be exempt from the taxes prescribed in Subsection (b).

(e) Judges and magistrates shall enforce all laws, rights, and obligations that were in force prior to the ratification of this constitution that do not conflict with it for [*four*] years, after which all such laws, rights, and obligations mandated by those laws, shall be null and void, unless superceded or reinstated sooner by legislation enacted under the full provisions of this constitution. Private rights and obligations arising from existing contracts and customs shall continue in force on the same basis as if this constitution had always been in force, except that

previously legal contracts that this constitution prohibits and that were entered into before this constitution was presented for ratification shall be enforced for [*four*] years, after which all such contracts shall be null and void.

(f) Within [*three*] months of taking office, the Election Commission selected under Subsection (b)(3) shall select two official legislatures as provided under Article II. [*etc.*]

TECHNICAL ANNEX

Procedure for Adjusting Legislative Votes and Voters' Uninsured Harms

This Technical Annex is part of and has the same legal force as the Constitution.

If the rate of change, with respect to income [*the income effect*], of a legislator's willingness to pay to change an outcome is the same for all legislators in both official legislatures, there shall be no adjustments of the kind herein provided. The following procedure shall apply if this rate of change differs among legislators.

(a) ***Legislative Decisions on Finite Sets of Alternative Proposals.*** **Within each legislature, the official monetary effects on each legislator's family of each issue to be decided, in terms of taxes, changes in property values, and changes in prices and wages shall be calculated in a manner determined by the legislature subject to the rules of evidence. Each legislator, when stating a willingness to pay for an outcome relative to an alternative, shall state whether it includes perceived monetary effects that disagree with the official monetary effects. If a legislator's willingness to pay is equal to the perceived monetary effects for the legislator's family, there is no intangible value involved; otherwise there is such a value. The legislator's willingness to pay to change each pairwise choice will be used as stated for all issues having no intangible value for that legislator.**

For sets of issues, some of which include intangible values for one or more legislators, that are to be considered together in a referendum, the declarations of willingness to pay shall be adjusted for income effects and the outcomes ranked using the Cardinal Ranking Procedure and related steps using the legislator's stated pairwise income effects. The Election Commission shall use the resulting ranking of outcomes and their estimated net aggregate gains to determine the probabilities of success of the possible outcomes in the pending referendum.

(b) ***Legislative Decisions on Continuous-Scale Issues.*** **When a legislature considers a budget proposal or other legislative proposal whose outcome is to be chosen as a point on a continuation scale together with associated schedules of tax/transfers, each legislator shall declare two valuation schedules showing, at each point on the scale, what the legislator's family would be willing to pay to increase the outcome by one unit. The first of the two valuation schedules shall show the portion of the valuation that represents the family's financial interest in the outcome and the second shows intangible valuation. The legislator also shall declare by what amount the intangible valuation schedule would differ in**

the event of a specified increase in the legislator's family income.

(c) ***Referenda with Finite Sets of Outcomes.*** **When the legislative process reveals intangible values associated with a pairwise choice between outcomes, if the Election Commission finds that income effects can affect the outcome, the declarations of uninsured harms by voters shall be adjusted for income effects and the outcome determined according to the Cardinal Ranking Procedure and related steps. The income effects shall be estimated by efficient statistical procedures from legislative votes and procedures from both official legislatures.**

(d) ***Referenda with Continuous-Scale Outcomes.*** **When a referendum offers a budget proposal or other legislative proposal whose outcome is to be chosen as a point on a continuous scale together with associated schedules of tax/transfers, the Election Commission shall offer corresponding fair insurance whose premium varies continuously along this scale. If the legislative process reveals uninsurable intangible values, each voter shall declare two valuation schedules showing at each point on the scale what the voter would be willing to pay to increase the outcome by one unit. The first of the two valuation schedules shall show the portion of the valuation that the voter wishes to insure and the second shows the uninsured part of the valuation. The voter also shall declare an income effect for the uninsured valuation schedule. The voter's insurance payout will be the absolute value of the integral of the insured curve from the outcome to the voter's most preferred outcome. The voter's incentive tax will be the integral for all other voters of the areas under their uninsured curves from the value the outcome would have had, without this voter's uninsured valuation schedule, to the actual outcome. [*A further transfer to each voter will be determined by the applicable formula in Bailey (1995b).*]**

END OF DRAFT CONSTITUTION

5. Further discussion

5.1. The legislative and executive functions – general discussion

As I note at the outset, it seems almost self-evident that for every case except perhaps a small town, households can prepare for collective decisions most efficiently by using legislatures to work out the details of proposed programs and legislation. Legislatures can deliberate and educate themselves on technical issues and on efficient design of programs and can filter out the noise of unsound major and minor proposals. Statistical analysis of their proceedings can determine which issues are important enough to require separate consideration and which ones can be packaged together. It is reasonable to suppose that households, in the aggregate, can digest information about the costs and benefits to them of national highway programs of different sizes or of national defense programs of different sizes. It is not reasonable to suppose that they can or should try to compare the merits of alternative highway routes and surfaces, of alternative military missile and tank designs, or of alternative contractors to do the work. It is more efficient to delegate these kinds of decisions to legislatures and their agents, provided that these officials have enough incentive to do their work efficiently.

We have interlocking proposals here with interlocking effects, tending to promote outcomes more efficient than those that governments now permit. These include:

1. stratified random selection of official legislators;
2. a demand-revealing process in each official legislature;
3. estimated Lindahl taxes;
4. potentially generous compensation for legislators based on all relevant outcomes, combined with competition among legislatures;
5. protection from bribery and extortion;
6. sound incentives for Speakers and for the Election Commission;
7. referenda with combined demand-revealing mechanisms.

These provisions leave almost no opportunity for rent-seekers to influence outcomes. In arguing this point, I do not deny that sometimes a skillful salesperson can sell refrigerators to the Native Americans of Alaska. Present political systems do that kind of selling routinely, however. The question is, can we bring government closer to the efficiency of the marketplace, while recognizing that the marketplace is not perfect nor all-wise? It is from this perspective that I argue the case for the proposed constitution.

The system has tightly woven armor to keep improper influences out of legislation and to prevent direct or indirect waste. Consider, for example, why corn farmers and sugar beet growers under this constitution would not even attempt to lobby for any form of government subsidy or import protection for domestically produced sugar. If a program such as that now in place in the U.S. were to cost each household \$5 per year in higher food prices, the set of Lindahl tax-transfers for the program would pay each rational, self-interested household an average of \$5. Summing that up, however, legislators would find that the total potential gain to domestic producers, the basis for their Lindahl taxes, would be little more than half the total offsetting compensation to households. (For various estimates of the numbers, see Hufbauer, Berliner, and Elliott, 1986: 295.) The budget-balancing constraint would imply that sugar producers would have to pay the whole amount, in which case they would prefer to do without the program. When the taxes must approximate Lindahl taxes, no interest group will try to promote a legislative program involving an economically unsound subsidy, price regulation, or the like.

Perhaps a better way to describe the resistance of this system to "special interest" legislation is to point out that *every* interest in equally represented, in the sense that a dollar of value to one population subgroup has the same weight as a dollar of value to each other population subgroup. Because each citizen is a member of exactly one such subgroup, it is also true that a dollar of value to each citizen has exactly the same weight as has a dollar of value to each other citizen. The draft constitution applies dollar democracy not only to the private sector but to the entire economy. Because this constitution also provides for competition for all parts of the government except for the Chief of State, the Commander in Chief, the Electoral Commission, and the magistrates (and tightly circumscribes the authority of these officials), no interest group can take advantage of other citizens.

Because persons within interest groups disagree, the tax-transfers would be only approximately Lindahl taxes and could not match individual differences in detail. Some issues that are highly divisive in present-day societies would also be divisive under the constitution proposed here. But they would be less so: advocates of legislation on every sort of issue would be obliged to put their money where their mouths are. Such a requirement can have a calming effect. All the more obvious regional, occupational, and other such common interests would be accurately matched in the tax structure. Those persons who have the largest identifiable interest in a given program or project would pay for it; those who had no interest would pay nothing; and those tangibly harmed would be compensated. If this feature of the proposal is accurately implemented, the possibility of improper influence on legislation could arise only in cases of fraud and in cases of intangible and moral questions, such as whether abortion or narcotics should be outlawed. That narrows down the problem immensely.

The Thompson procedure itself also provides partial quasi-Lindahl compensation to those tangibly harmed by legislation. Households favoring losing proposals would receive full compensation for their harm, less the amount they pay in insurance premia. Those favoring the winning proposals would pay partial compensation in the form of their insurance premia. Therefore, the procedure partly offsets any deviation in the tax-transfer program in legislation from true Lindahl taxes. This combination of features implies that all voters have an incentive to participate and to purchase their insurance carefully. The rules about published official analysis of legislative proposals would reduce the cost to voters of obtaining the information they need to participate properly. Consequently, voters would provide the necessary information to the election process for sound economic decisions.

The provisions interact in other ways as well. For example, the information generated by the use of the VCG process in the legislature makes it possible to use the Thompson mechanism in referenda. In the reverse direction, the information generated by referenda plays a large role in the incentive system of compensation of legislators. For a more elaborate discussion of several of these points, see Bailey (1995a).

Such compensation answers the concern that a representative sample of voters could not understand the technical issues in a government budget. Indeed, present-day juries deal with complex technical issues in civil lawsuits involving sophisticated scientific, statistical, and engineering issues. No one supposes that juries are perfect or all-wise, but we have not found a better way to handle such disputes, other than alternative arrangements agreed to by the parties. We certainly have not found a better way to handle legislation. Present legislators have little incentive to understand either the technical or the efficiency aspects of what they do. If a country pays its legislators for well-monitored results, it can expect to get better results than if it pays them and reelects them with little systematic attention to the results.

These mechanisms are complicated to explain and justify, so one can ask, "are they worth the trouble?" In responding to this question, one must first recall that all that the voter needs to understand is what to do and that is not so complicated. For Thompson insurance, one decides how much insurance to buy against an unfavorable referendum outcome. For the VCG mechanism, one declares how much uninsured harm one would suffer from an unfavorable outcome, on the understanding that one will pay at most the amount one declares in the event that one's vote changes the overall outcome favorably. In that case the amount paid will be the amount that would have produced a tie vote. (A slightly longer explanation, along the same lines, would be necessary if the referendum tries to pick an optimal budget size as a continuous variable, rather than choosing among a specified set of increments.) The complicated part is explaining the VCG decision mechanism and its incentive-compatibility, which is something one need do only at the stages of designing and adopting a constitution.

That said, we recount three reasons why these mechanisms are worth the trouble. First, using them in a referendum in the way proposed gives voters an incentive to participate and to inform themselves. This incentive comes from the Thompson mechanism and it spills over into the modified VCG procedure that goes in tandem with it. Second, each legislature is a sample of the population so that even if the members were mechanically perfect and reliable there would be sampling error. Correcting this sampling error requires all the information provided by the referendum. Third, legislators need the proper incentive to do their work well, so as to promote efficient outcomes. The referendum information, used in the right way, makes the system incentive-compatible for them.

It is nevertheless not self-evident that electioneering would entirely cease to have mischievous effects, despite the Lindahl tax-transfer system. Although this system would prevent rent-seeking on budget issues and on takings of property easements (such as zoning and other restrictions), divisive issues (such as abortion and narcotics) could be a problem. We assume that in public discussion the norms of free speech would apply in that everyone would be free to publicize competing opinions and arguments. Certainly, interested persons and groups could attempt to influence opinion, using arguments that sometimes would have all the veracity and reliability of present-day political and commercial advertising. Almost the only evidence, however, that such advertising has any effect is that some people spend a lot of money to do it. Recent economic analysis of advertising provides no basis for a belief that, on balance, anything is gained or would be gained by restricting it.

I would emphasize further the benefits of having competition in almost every function of government. Although choosing the legislature by lot and having it choose the executive would eliminate the role of polical parties, these provisions would not by themselves assure efficiency. Existing legislatures respond to rent-seeking pressures and create jobs to reward the political supporters of the legislators and their political parties while doing these things in ways beneficial to their friends and families. This friends-and-family effect is a problem of all governments and putting political parties out of business would not eliminate it. A single legislature, even if checked by referendum, can always control the agenda presented to voters in wasteful ways beneficial to legislators. But if several legislatures independently develop programs for a referendum in which one program will be selected and if legislators receive the powerful incentives proposed here for planning and executing efficient programs, then this combination of incentives would reduce venality and nepotism to trivial proportions.

It is obvious that I have drawn upon the experience of corporate governance in addressing the principal-agent problem with respect to the executive branch. A successful legislature, under this constitution, functions like a corporate board of directors that accurately represents shareholder interests. Unlike the United States under the SEC, in a country under this constitution the shareholders easily can get rid of a mediocre management team and the directors have strong incentives to do it first when that is needed. Indeed, the legislator-"directors" would choose executives with excellent management skills at the outset, attracting them with the level of pay and benefits that their services are worth.

Concerning constitutional amendments, we should note that a rule requiring ratification by a supermajority of interest groups provides such groups with bargaining leverage to demand excessive "Lindahl" compensation for the change. Therefore, the constitution needs the rule in Article VI, Section 2 requiring a time delay before a rejected amendment can be reconsidered, say ten years. The proposed sequestration also protects against this problem during legislative review of such amendments.

5.2. The legislative function – incentive compatibility

The various features of the draft constitution interact in further ways. The more accurately the proposed legislation specifies Lindahl taxes, the more reliably the demand-revealing processes of referenda will function. This tax plan almost eliminates redistributive effects of legislation and so it reduces the risk that income effects will give rise to anomalies in the VCG process in referenda. Anomalies in the case of discrete choices are completely avoided if the number of likely winning proposals narrows down to at most two. That is, even in the presence of income effects, an "up or down" vote with the VCG mechanism is incentive compatible. Important issues for which the VCG process would be needed, such as crime and punishment, environmental protection, and so on, may often come in this form. Although the mechanism can be manipulated when there are more than two possible outcomes, I have tried and failed to construct a plausible example fitting the present context. For all varieties of proposals, sophisticated corrections for income effects are possible but complicated. On these points, see especially Bailey (1995a and c).

As noted earlier, the use of the Thompson mechanism also narrows down the problem of income effects. For those proposals that solely affect voting households' material and financial interests, that is, proposals involving no esthetic, moral, or other intangible concerns, there is no problem and the Thompson mechanism does not need to be supplemented with a VCG mechanism. Standard classroom analysis of risk and insurance tells us that risk-averse households would buy exactly full coverage of fair insurance. See Varian (1992) at 180f; see also Thompson (1966). Hence, the winning proposal would always be the one with the greatest total excess of benefits over costs. With full compensation and usually even without it that proposal would be the Pareto-efficient choice.

When an issue also involves intangible values, the Thompson mechanism lacks incentive compatibility in the sense that voters will not generally insure against the exact amount of perceived harm from a proposed plan or from its failure. Denote by $\underline{x}_0{}^i$ voter i's initial wealth (including all discounted future income), by y_0 the status quo government program, and by y_1 and alternative program. Suppose that the taxes to finance the alternative program exactly equal voter i's financial gains from that program (where both taxes and gains may be either positive or negative), so that $\underline{x}_0^i$ remains unchanged if the program is adopted. Because positive and negative cases are symmetrical, without loss of generality we assume that voter i favors the adoption of the alternative program. For simplicity, we disregard relative prices, in effect assuming that they remain unchanged. Denote by $V^i(\underline{x}^i;y_j)$ the voter's indirect utility function. Denote the first partial derivative of indirect utility with respect to $\underline{x}^i$ by V_x^i and the second derivative by $V_{xx}{}^i$. Suppose also that voter i is risk averse so that $V_{xx}{}^i < 0$. Denote by $\Delta' t^i$ voter i's willingness to pay to have y_1 adopted; that is, $V^i(\underline{x}_0^i - \Delta' t^i; y_1) = V^i(\underline{x}_0^i; y_0)$. The amount of insurance that voter i buys under the Thompson mechanism is I^i and the probability of adoption of y_1 is p so that the insurance premium is $(1-p)I^i$. If there were no income effect, we would have $\Delta' t^i$ constant as $\underline{x}_0^i$ changes: for every value of $\underline{x}^i$, $V^i(\underline{x}^i - \Delta' t^i; y_1) \equiv V^i(\underline{x}^i; y_0)$, so that $V_x{}^i(\underline{x}^i - \Delta' t^i; y_1) \equiv V_x^i(\underline{x}^i; y_0)$. In that case voter i, maximizing expected utility, would respond to the Thompson mechanism in a referendum by insuring $\Delta' t^i$ in full against the possibility that y_1 would be rejected.

$$\text{Max } E(V^i) = \text{Max}\{pV^i(\underline{x}_o^i - [1-p]I^i;\ y_1) + [1-p]V^i(\underline{x}_o^i + pI^i;\ y_o)\}$$

$$\Rightarrow p(1-p)V_x^i(\underline{x}_o^i - [1-p]I^i;\ y_1) = p(1-p)V_x^i(\underline{x}_o^i + pI^i;\ y_o),$$

that is,

$$V_x^i(\underline{x}_o^i - [1-p]I^i;\ y_1) = V_x^i(\underline{x}_o^i + pI^i;\ y_o), \tag{1}$$

which holds when $I^i = \Delta' t^i$.

When there is a positive income effect, however, so that $\Delta' t^i$ increases with $\underline{x}^i$, we instead have $V_x^i(\underline{x}_0^i - \Delta' t^i; y_1) > V_x^i(\underline{x}_0^i; y_0)$ so that condition (1) is met at some smaller amount of insurance $I^i < \Delta' t^i$. For a full development of this analysis for a logically equivalent problem, see the appendix of Calfee and Rubin (1992). In this case, the voter is willing to declare an uninsured harm when the referendum has the VCG mechanism in tandem with the Thompson mechanism and will declare the correct amount $\Delta' t^i - I^i$. On an up or down vote for a program y_1, the VCG mechanism is incentive compatible, as I noted earlier.

Although it is appropriate to prohibit all attempts to organize voter coalitions, in the case of issues having tangible, financial effects the Thompson mechanism has the added benefit of making such attempts unprofitable. Any voter who senses that an attempted coalition may affect the outcome will change the amount of Thompson insurance he or she purchases in a direction that offsets the coalition's goals because of the coalition's effect on the fairness of the insurance premium.

Consider this point first for a pure budget issue involving no intangible policy issues. An attempt at collusion might be promoted, for example, by aggressive misrepresentation. Under the Thompson mechanism, however, voters have roughly the same incentive to inform themselves as they now have for a major private expenditure, such as the purchase of a consumer durable. Scare tactics and other misinformation, moreover, would have a tendency to be self-defeating, as in the case of coalition formation. Assuming that the incentive system and rules of evidence work in the intended ways for the legislatures, the official statements about the merits of the proposed legislative programs will contain reliable information about them and the Thompson insurance premiums will be based on the legislative history. If misinformation creates an apparent groundswell of opinion in favor of added spending, say $\$\Delta X$ more than the $\$X$ proposed for a program by either legislature, the insurance premiums the system offers against this contingency will be too low. Those persons who, influence by the misinformation, would want to insure against the failure of larger spending will face official insurance premiums that are too high. If the official probability is p that the extra spending will succeed, the insurance premium against harm $H arising from the failure of $\$\Delta X$ to be approved would be $(1 - p)\$H$. The true probability being $p' > p$, an actuarially fair premium would be $(1 - p')\$H < (1 - p)\$H$.

An alert citizen of whatever opinion would then want to speculate on this discrepancy and "insure against" the success of the larger expenditure by a claimed harm of $\$H'$ (which is the same financially as betting on its success). The premium for this insurance would be $p\$H < p'\$H$. Buying this insurance would not be gambling but profitable speculation. Such speculation also would tend to neutralize the effect of the misinformation on the outcome of the referendum. Thus, whenever misinformation tended to provoke a voter stampede, contrarians could profit from reducing the probability that the stampede will change the outcome.

The same reasoning applies to an issue involving the tandem mechanism, where a proposal with substantial financial effects has intangible side effects. A putative coalition would know (a) that shifting the amounts of Thompson insurance that voters purchased would induce counterspeculation; (b) that it might be easier to encourage false declarations of uninsured harm, although each voter would have an incentive to tell the truth, that is, to cheat on the coalition; and (c) that successful solicitation of false declarations by changing the probability of the affected outcome would induce counterspeculation through the Thompson mechanism. Enforcing laws more restrictive than present laws against vote selling, so as to rule out collusive voting, would therefore be a low-cost, effective operation in most cases.

Another apparent problem to be considered is the possibility that some voters will be gamblers, rather than risk-averse – they will "insure against" the proposal they favor, perhaps thinking that they know the odds better than do the official statisticians. Whenever such gamblers have legislative representation, however, the legislative process assuredly will lead to the use of the VCG mechanism in tandem with Thompson insurance during the following referendum. The VCG mechanism provides a correction to the false reporting through the Thompson mechanism. A voter pays the VCG tax only if the outcome hinges on the voter's willingness to pay to reverse the outcome. A gambling voter will not want to lose the bet and so will declare an uninsured harm for a possible unfavorable outcome equal to its perceived harm *plus* the amount of the gamble. It is worth paying that much if so doing would prevent losing the bet. This declaration more than offsets the gambler's "insurance" in the official tally and so it corrects the perverse effect of the gamble.

Now consider further the incentives for legislators. First, if there were no incentive pay for efficient legislative performance, a legislator's incentives would depend exclusively on the VCG tax within the legislature. We have no set of devices for the legislature comparable to those we propose for voters to achieve incentive compatibility for multiple options involving intangible values. There could be circumstances, therefore, in which a legislator would have an incentive to engage in strategic voting. The VCG tax in legislative proceedings is thus merely a device to help focus the legislator's mind.

The proposed legislative incentive pay is an approximation to a legislator's marginal social product and therefore it should dominate by orders of magnitude the comparatively trivial incentive of the legislature's own VCG tax. The proposed constitution bases legislative incentive pay not only on the efficiency of proposed programs and on the approximation to Lindahl taxes by the tax proposals but also on how well the legislature estimates the variability of deviations from Lindahl taxes. I leave this incentive to be filled in Article II, Subsection 10(b) because its specification depends on characteristics of the electorate. If the constitution sets the optimal percentages for this component of legislative incentive pay, the legislator will maximize bonus income by telling the truth. Finding the optimal formula to imbed in the constitution requires more technical work, but it would appear to be a straightforward matter.

If the reward structure were to parallel that in the private sector, members of a successful legislature that improved national economic efficiency substantially would legitimately become some of the wealthiest people in the nation. Successful entrepreneurs like Aristotle Onassis and Sam Walton became billionaires by finding minor ways to lower cost and improve efficiency in shipping and distributing goods. The gains from efficient government can be a quantum jump larger than that. The intent of the draft proposal is to give correspondingly larger incentive pay to successful legislators. Hence, the reward structure would provide a powerful incentive to excellent performance by the competing legislatures.

Apart from these brief remarks, I do not discuss here in detail the particulars of the compensation of legislators and of members of the Election Commission. The intent of the carefully considered provisions of Article II, Sections 10(f), 11, 12(c) and 12(d) is to provide each of these officials with optimal incentives to maximize expected aggregate national welfare. A number of points in these specifics undoubtedly deserve further study and elaboration.

5.3. The judicial function

Although judicial appointments would be the responsibility of the successful legislature, judicial tenure would be determined by judges' success under the market test. Competition, where multiple venues are available and both parties have equal influence on the choice of venue, has the same effect in this case as in legislative affairs. For civil cases, moreover, private arbitrators would intensify this competition.

Most modern systems establish a judicial cartel that is only partly effective. Wherever the system offers more than one possible venue for a lawsuit, the plaintiff who can convince a court to accept jurisdiction can choose that court, regardless of the defendant's preferences. The same is true in criminal cases, where the official side has the initiative if more than one venue is available. This system results in many avoidable abuses. Experience both with this system and with private arbitration suggests that it is much better to have multiple, competing venues and to give both parties a veto of the choice.

To prevent a denial of justice by an obstructive defendant and to expedite agreement, there must be some recourse in the event the two parties do not reach timely agreement on a venue. Therefore, the plaintiff or prosecutor could appear before a magistrate, who could compel the defendant to attend. Then if there is no agreement on a venue, the magistrate could assign such cases by random selection from lists proposed by the two parties. Courts of appeals should be subject to the same multiplicity and rules of selection.

This competition would mean that parties to disputes would select judges known for their impartiality. The random selection rule to be applied by magistrates, where the parties fail to agree, would protect and reinforce this tendency. To preserve their reputations, moreover, judges also would take care to avoid reversals on appeal, so that there would be fewer appeals than otherwise and parties to disputes would avoid appellate costs. These considerations would reinforce the predictability and hence the efficiency of the law. As in the case of Speakers and Election Commissions, the incentive structure is intended to elicit impartiality, dedication to rules of evidence, and dedication to the rule of law.

In a system with competing official courts, there necessarily must be a final court of appeal to preserve a settled, consistent order in the law. In England this final court evolved to a selected subset of members of the House of Lords, the "Law Lords," who also participate in the legislative role of the whole House of Lords (Carter, 1994; Jackson, 1972). The United States chose not to follow the British example in this matter. One can make a case for making this task a legislative function, both because one can say that the ultimate interpretation of the law is too important to leave to the judges and because it would blend well with the role of creating new statute law. Similarly, it would be a legislative function to determine which disputes are actionable and who has standing to sue.

A further compelling reason for having an official legislature handle final appeals is that a highly motivated legislature would precisely and proportionately represent all interests in the law. Persons with each kind of interest in a legal rule would be members of the legislature in the same proportions as in the population and with the same financial interest (prior to receiving incentive compensation for their work as legislators). This proportionality is what the opposing sides commonly lack in a case to be decided. See Bailey and Rubin (1994). Sending final appeals to a legislature also would alert legislatures to deficiencies in the law that would require correction by legislation. Therefore, legal interpretation controlled by a representative legislature would move toward efficient law, both through interpretation and through new statutes.

By requiring all courts to support themselves by fees, this system would tend to eliminate biased views. It would force convergence toward an equilibrium balance between the interests of plaintiffs and defendants in judicial interpretations and in applications of the laws. All judicial systems have some amount of judge-made laws by practical necessity. However, one cannot say whether such law will converge on an economically sound, efficient structure. That will depend on the frequency of appeals to an official legislature, among other things. There is as yet no lower-level procedural solution to this normative problem in a self-contained judicial system, except perhaps to reduce the amount of judge-made law to the minimum efficient proportions. Presumably, the proposed plan for the final court of appeal, together with judges' incentive to anticipate its rulings, would keep this problem under control.

Unfortunately, space does not permit a full discussion of all the issues raised here and prevents discussion of many other issues not specifically raised or not spelled out. That will be a task for a larger work.

References

Anderson, T.L. and Hill, P.J. (1986). Constraining the transfer society: Constitutional and moral dimensions. *Cato Journal* 6(Spring/Summer): 317–339.

Bailey, M.J. (1995a). Implementation of the Thompson mechanism. *Public Choice* forthcoming.

Bailey, M.J. (1995b). A Vickrey-Clarke-Groves mechanism for non-separable utility. Unpublished manuscript.

Bailey, M.J. (1995c). Lindahl taxes and demand revelation: How to apply the Vickrey-Clarke-Groves mechanism. Unpublished manuscript.

Bailey, M.J. and Rubin, P.H. (1994). A positive theory of legal change. *International Review of Law and Economics* 14: 467–477.

Berman, H.J. (1983). *Law and revolution: The formation of western legal tradition.* Cambridge, MA: Harvard University Press.

Brueckner, J.K. (1983). Property value maximization and public sector efficiency. *Journal of Urban Economics* 14: 1–15.

Buchanan, J. and Tullock, G. (1962). *The calculus of consent.* Ann Arbor: University of Michigan Press.

Buchanan, J. and Faith, R.L. (1987). Secession and the limits of taxation: Toward a theory of internal exit. *American Economic Review* 77 (December): 1023–1031.

Calfee, J.E. and Rubin, P.H. (1992). Some implications of damage payments for nonpecuniary losses. *Journal of Legal Studies* 21: 371–411.

Carter, A.T. (1944). *An English history of the courts.* 7th Ed. London: Butterworth.

Downs, A. (1957). *An economic theory of democracy.* New York: Harper & Brothers.

Green, J. and Laffont, J.-J. (1977). On the revelation of preferences for public goods. *Journal of Public Economics* 8: 79–93.

Groves, T., Radner, R. and Reiter, S. (1987). *Information, incentives, and economic mechanisms.* Minneapolis: University of Minnesota Press.

Hochman, H.M. and Rodgers, J.D. (1969). Pareto optimal redistribution. *American Economic Review* 59: 1348–1362.

Hamilton, A., Madison, J. and Jay, J. (1961). *The Federalist Papers.* New York: The New American Library.

Hufbauer, G.C., Berliner, D.T. and Elliott, K.A. (1986). *Trade protection in the United States: 31 case studies.* Washington, DC: Institute for International Economics.

Jackson, R.M. (1972). *The machinery of justice in England.* 6th ed. Cambridge, U.K.: Cambridge University Press.

Kiralfy, A.R. (1990). *The English legal system.* 2nd ed. (1956) London: Sweet & Maxwell, 8th ed. (1990).

Lowenberg, A.D. and Yu, B.T. (1992). Efficient constitution formation and maintenance: The role of exit. *Constitutional Political Economy* 3 (Winter): 51–72.

Marlow, M. (1992). Intergovernmental competition, voice and exit options and the design of fiscal structure. *Constitutional Political Economy* 3 (Winter): 73–88.

Merville, L.J. and Osborne, D.K. (1990). Constitutional democracy and the theory of agency. *Constitutional Political Economy* 1 (Fall): 21–47.

Mueller, D.H. (1989). *Public Choice II.* Cambridge, U.K.: Cambridge University Press.

Mueller, D.H. (1991). Choosing a constitution in Eastern Europe: Lessons from public choice. *Journal of Comparative Economics* 15 (June): 325–348.

Mueller, D.H., Tollison, R.D. and Willett, T.D. (1972). Representative democracy via random selection. *Public Choice* 12 (Spring): 57–68.
Ordeshook, P.C. (1992). Constitutional stability. *Constitutional Political Economy* 3 (Spring/Summer): 137–175.
Rubin, P.H. and Bailey, M.J. (1994). The role of lawyers in changing the law. *Journal of Legal Studies* 23: 807–831.
Spindler, Z.A. (1990). Constitutional design for a rent-seeking society. *Constitutional Political Economy* 1 (Fall): 73–82.
Starrett, D.A. (1988). *Foundations of public economics.* New York: Cambridge University Press.
Sunstein, C.R. (1991). Constitutionalism, prosperity, democracy: Transition in Eastern Europe. *Constitutional Political Economy* 2 (Fall): 371–394.
Thompson, E.A. (1966). A Pareto optimal group decision process. In G. Tullock (Ed.), *Papers on non-market decision making.* Charlottesville: University of Virginia.
Varian, H.R. (1992). *Microeconomic analysis.* 3rd ed. New York: Norton.
Wildasin, D.E. (1979). Local public goods, property values, and local public choice. *Journal of Urban Economics* 6: 521–534.

Appendix

Setting the insurance premium for the Thompson mechanism

Consider the issue of whether to approve a single proposed project y_1. Suppose that the variety of views among voters, normally distributed, is known in a rough way to voters themselves and to the Election Commission. Then we may think of the total voter population as a random sample of size N, drawn from a hypothetical population whose individual willingness to pay for the project has known mean μ and variance σ^2, with a normal distribution $\mathcal{N}$. The voter population has unknown mean m whose known variance is σ^2/N. An official legislature is a sample size n with observed mean m. Then for this case the Bayesian posterior distribution on m is (Green and Laffont [1977])

$$\mathcal{N}\left(\frac{\mu + nN\mathit{m}}{1 + nN}, \frac{\sigma^2}{1 + nN}\right) = f(\mathit{m}).$$

The probability of acceptance of the project, for an up or down choice, then becomes

$$p(y_1) = \int_0^{\infty} f(\mathit{m}) d\mathit{m}.$$

(Where σ^2 is unknown, one would use a similar formulation with the Student "t" distribution.) If y_1 is a continuous variable, $f(\mathit{m})$ is the posterior distribution of the optimal m, given m. Then, for each increment to the value of (amount spent upon) y_1, the appropriate odds for the insurance premium are given by

$$p(\Delta y_1) = \int_{y_1^0}^{y_1^1} f(\mathit{m}) d\mathit{m}.$$

Public Choice **90:** 117–138, 1997.

© 1997 *Kluwer Academic Publishers.*

The balanced budget amendment: Clarifying the arguments

JAMES M. BUCHANAN
Center for Study of Public Choice, George Mason University, Fairfax, VA 22030, U.S.A.

Abstract. From the perspective of a supporter, this paper responds to the several criticisms that have been raised to the proposed constitutional amendment to require budget balance. Economists have concentrated on the loss of fiscal flexibility. This objection is countered by reference to the political inefficacy of attempted budgetary manipulation. Lawyers have concentrated on problems of enforcement. This objection is countered by reference to observed respect to other constitutional rules.

PART ONE

1. Introduction

On 26 January 1995, the U.S. House of Representatives approved a proposed constitutional amendment that requires balance in the budget of the federal government by the year 2002. On 2 March 1995, the U.S. Senate, by a single vote, failed to approve such an amendment. As this monograph is written (March 1995), the proposal for constitutional constraints on deficit financing appears certain to occupy the attention of the public and politicians alike over several years.

This monograph is intended as a possible contribution to the ongoing discussion, at several levels of dialogue, during 1995, 1996 and beyond. It is prompted specifically by the recognition that much of the expressed opposition to the amendment for budget balance is based on serious misunderstandings rather than upon interest-motivated desires to maintain high levels of debt-financed governmental outlay.

As early as 1954, in an unpublished paper, I identified a political flaw in Keynesian macroeconomic policy, and I predicted the regime of continuing fiscal deficits that we have witnessed over the half-century. I did not call explicitly for a constitutional amendment, but by the time I published my 1958 book on public debt, the constitutional implications were clear. In the early 1960s, Gordon Tullock and I examined the constitutional foundations of democracy in general terms, and also in the early 1960s, I discussed more explicitly the proclivity of democratic process to generate regimes described by "easy budgets and tight money". As we came to observe continuing deficits, Richard Wagner and I spelled out both the history and the analysis in our 1978 book, *Democracy in Deficit*. Various proposals emerged in the 1970s, 1980s and 1990s, all aimed at constitutional correction. I expressed my personal support in legislative hearings, documents, papers and books.

I do not parade this long record of personal involvement to promote my books or to establish my bona fides. I do so to suggest that my current position, along with that of a relatively small number of coauthors, colleagues and students, does not reflect some belated recognition of the deficit as an issue, born out of concern about the fiscal profligacy of the 1980s. The structural flaw in our fiscal politics did not arise in the 1980s, and it will not go away in the ordinary politics of the 1990s and beyond. The structural flaw requires structural correction, that is, constitutional constraint that will, effectively, change the basic rules for the fiscal game.

I shall proceed as follows. In Section 2, I summarize the history of attitudes toward budget balance in order to tell us where we are and how we got to the here and now. In Section 3, I show that the ordinary politics of majoritarian democracy cannot get the deficit under control, despite the noblest of efforts. The incentive structure of this politics is such as to insure the dissipation and any gains that might be achieved temporarily. Section 4 presents the basic analysis of the constitutional rule for budget balance, with emphasis on the necessary distinction between choices among rules and choices within rules – a distinction that is missed by many in the current political dialogue. More specifically, stress is put on the intertemporal feature that makes any budget balance rule especially difficult to put in place. In Section 5, the critical distinction between the fiscal adjustments that the adoption of such a rule makes necessary over a transition period and the adjustments that are required on a permanent and continuing basis is examined. And I advance the argument for temporally lagged implementation of any constitutional rule for budget balance.

Part Two shifts attention to possible criticisms that have been advanced against adoption of the constitutional amendment. The first argument, treated in Section 6, is the one that suggests rejection of the proposed amendment based on the notion that it is inappropriate for inclusion in the general constitutional structure. In this section, I make a separation between the "clean" amendment for budget balance and the sometime proposals that include constitutional requirements for qualified majorities in tax legislation. I suggest that complementary advocacy of such tax and/or spending limits serves to sow confusion – even among those who have been among the strongest advocates of the basic amendment.

In Section 7, I move on to consider the argument most often advanced by economists – an argument that suggests academic residues of the Keynesian rationale for fiscal fine tuning. Section 8 examines the arguments that emerge from legal-political sources that defend the status quo by reference to issues involved in the enforcement of any fiscal rule. In Section 9, I briefly analyze a sophisticated "supply-side" argument that was advanced in the 1980s and which reappeared in the 1990s in support of the complementary tax and spending limit supplements in the basic rule. Section 10 briefly discusses capital budgeting as it may apply to the proposal rule. Section 11 examines the specious social security argument that was used by opponents to defeat the amendment in the U.S. Senate in early 1995.

In Part Three, Section 12 returns to positive discussion with examination of some of the macroeconomic implications of an operative regime of budget balance. In Section 13, the monograph is concluded with a general discussion of the symbolic significance of the adoption of a constitutional rule for budget balance.

2. How and why we got here

The budget of the United States federal government has not been balanced since 1969. And despite rhetoric about fiscal responsibility and despite occasional short periods during which the size of the deficit has been reduced (the Gramm-Rudman years of the second Reagan term and the Clinton years after the 1993 budgetary legislation), there is little or no expectation that a regime of budget balance will somehow emerge to replace the quasi-permanent regime of fiscal deficits.

How and why did the United States political structure get into this pattern of acknowledged fiscal irresponsibility? If we understand how and why we got here, we may begin to understand how we might get out.

The first century and one-half of our national political history did, indeed, embody a norm of budget balance. This rule was not written into the constitutional document, as such, but rather it was a part of an accepted set of attitudes about how government should, and must, carry on its fiscal affairs. Politicians prior to World War II would have considered it to be immoral (to be a sin) to spend more than they were willing to generate in tax revenues, except during periods of extreme and temporary emergency. To spend borrowed funds on ordinary items for public consumption was, quite simply, beyond the pale of acceptable political behavior. There were basic moral constraints in place; there was no need for an explicit fiscal rule in the written constitution.

The balanced budget norm is ultimately based on the acceptance of the classic principles of public finance. Government borrowing offers a means through which burdens of paying for current public spending can be transferred forward through time and placed on the shoulders of those "future generations" who will be subjected to the taxes required to service and amortize public debt.

These elementary principles were overlooked in the Keynesian macroeconomic theory developed in the 1930s and 1940s. The government budget was seen to offer an instrument through which a wise and benevolent government could fine-tune the economy so as to promote the commonly-desired objectives of full employment and economic growth. In this vision, any constraint on the exercise of governmental discretion in setting rates of taxes and spending could only reduce the efficacy of the macroeconomic enterprise.

In order to sell the Keynesian policy prescriptions, the moral onus on government debt and deficits had to be exorcised from public consciousness. For this purpose, the intergenerational effects of public debt-financing had to be denied. Such a denial was allegedly accomplished by concentration on macroaggregates to the neglect of the necessary reduction of costs and benefits to the individuals who lose and gain. By the claim that debt financing did not impact negatively on future-period taxpayers, the moral constraint that had acted to insure fiscal responsibility was eroded and nothing emerged to take its place. The natural proclivities of democratically elected and constituency respondent politicians to spend and not to tax were allowed free play.

The economists were converted to the Keynesian mind-set by the 1940s, and they launched their advocacy of fiscal profligacy in the name of the potential achievement of widely acclaimed objectives, while wearing romantic blinders concerning the motivations of those who must make fiscal choices. The politicians themselves were, at first, reluctant to shed off the shackles of the old-time fiscal religion, but, by the 1960s, they too had come to realize that there were no dramatic negative feedbacks. The regime of permanent and accelerating deficits became a part of our political reality.

Understanding why and how we got here is easy. How to get back to where we were, as described in our moral attitudes toward imposing burdens on future taxpayers, becomes central to the whole debate about the proposed constitutional amendment.

3. Why ordinary politics cannot balance the budget

If fiscal irresponsibility could, indeed, be laid at the feet of particular politicians or parties, there might be some expectation that, with electoral rotation, those who stand for fiscal integrity might eventually replace those who are fiscally profligate. But such expectation could only be utopian. The fault lies not in ourselves, as participants in the ordinary politics of modern majoritarian democracy, but in the structural rules within which this politics takes place.

As they now exist, these rules allow our political agents to escape the discipline of opportunity cost. Government spending for a wide array of "goods" may be authorized, and every one of these "goods" may be valued positively by some or all constituents. The approval of these rates of spending may, however, proceed without explicit regard to the genuine opportunity cost that must ultimately be measured in the sacrifice by someone, sometime, of other values that might have been produced. It is not the public spending, as such, that is the proper focus of attention here. (The normative question of the dividing line between political and private resource use may be important in its own right, but its introduction into the argument on the decision structure can only be misleading.) That which makes the existing rules generate patterns of outcomes that we deem to be irresponsible is the political agents' authority to *spend without taxing*. Little or no sophistication is required to recognize how different the dynamics of fiscal choice would be in a constitutional setting that forced politicians to levy taxes to cover outlays.

The residual Keynesians in our midst, who remain locked into macroeconomic illusion, may continue to suggest that the opportunity costs of public spending must always be borne contemporaneously with the spending itself. They suggest that the valued resources are used up as the outlays are made. But they forget that those who actually give up resources do so in exchange for valued claims (interest-bearing government securities) against future taxpayers.

A more sophisticated denial of the simple logic of deficit financing is located in the argument that citizens, and their political agents, do, indeed, face the full opportunity cost of debt-financed outlay because they will, quite rationally, discount the future tax obligations that any issue of public debt embodies. In this argument, the temporal displacement of the costs of public spending need not affect fiscal choices. Within this "Ricardian logic", there need be no concern about failures in the basic rules of fiscal politics.

Politicians may be observed to spend without taxing, while the shortfall is made up by public borrowing. But, it may be asked, why is government different in this respect from a private person, or a firm, who may also be observed sometimes to borrow in order to meet spending needs? An important difference lies in the absence of any assigned liability for future payment for servicing and amortizing public debt. The owner of a government bond holds a claim against the general tax base of the political community, not against the income or assets of some identified person or group. There is no effective presence of future-period taxpayers in current-period political choice settings, a presence that might exert some rough balance into the fiscal benefit-cost calculus.

The incentives are such as to generate a regime of fiscal deficits as a necessary consequence of fully rational responses of political agents to the demands of their constituents. This result remains quite robust under many possible variations in the definitions of political rationality and in the composition of political coalitions. There are, of course, upper limits on the natural proclivity of constituency responsive political agents to create fiscal deficits. But the margin between tax and debt financing that comes to be established in a political equilibrium is well beyond any margin that might be dictated by choices that fully incorporate the present-period interests of future-period taxpayers.

To this point, I have discussed only the direct incentives that exist to bias fiscal choices toward deficit financing of public outlay. These incentives are supplemented by a secondary set which serve to make efforts to behave responsibly in some long-term fiscal sense seem folly. Assume, heroically perhaps, that a majority of elected political agents, acting on behalf of their constituents, comes to acknowledge the long-term damage of continued deficit financing, and that this majority takes effective action toward reducing or eliminating the imbalance in the budget. Such praiseworthy enterprise would necessarily remain vulnerable in the face of electoral rotation. If the responsibly-acting majority coalition could be assured permanence or quasi-permanence in positions of fiscal authority, the deficit-reduction effort might well succeed. But, with constitutionally guaranteed electoral periodicity, there is no assurance that deficit reducing actions (tax increases or spending cuts) taken currently will not be dissipated, wholly or in part, by the actions of other majority coalitions in future periods.

To reduce the budget deficit, costs must be imposed on current-period taxpayers and/or current-period beneficiaries of governmental programs. Taxes must be increased, and/or rates of spending must be reduced. There will be predictable electoral feedbacks on those political agents who impose such burdens. Why should current-period agents, even those who fully acknowledge the long-term damage generated by continuous deficit financing, take on the political costs of deficit reduction if they, at the same time, fear that all of their current-period efforts are vulnerable to dissipation by differing political coalitions in future periods? In ordinary majoritarian politics, there is no way through which currently serving political agents can "lock in" or make secure the salutary effects that any action might produce.

This set of secondary incentives reinforces the primary ones. The natural proclivity to spend without taxing becomes even more dominating an influence on choice when current-period political agents recognize that the same proclivity exists for and will possibly be influential on those political agents who will become their replacements in later periods.

4. The relevance of rules

Political choices are made within rules. Elections to the U.S. House of Representatives take place every other year. This rule is only one among many that describe the operation of our politics. Who could deny that political outcomes would be different with congressional election cycles of, say, one year, or four years? This illustration suffices to show that rules matter. And because they do matter, we are obligated to consider changes in rules as well as particular policy options available within the set of rules that exist.

We must make a careful and categorical distinction between *choices among rules* (constitutional politics) and *choices within rules* (ordinary politics). The whole discussion about the constitutional amendment for budget balance is marred by a failure to recognize the importance of making this distinction. The proposal is aimed at changing the rule for the game of ordinary fiscal politics. Supporters of the change predict that, under the new rule, fiscal outcomes will be different, and better, than those outcomes now observed to emerge under existing rules that do not require budget balance.

The point of emphasis is simple. Rules constrain the set of admissible choice alternatives. Different constraints (different rules) must thereby generate different patterns of outcomes. And this direct relationship holds even with no change in the identification of the decision makers. The person who sets her alarm clock (a rule) gets up at a different hour from the person who does not set the clock (another rule). It is, therefore, little more than obfuscatory confusion to suggest that, because we shall have the same or similar political agents in authority with or without a formal balanced budget rule, there will be no predicted difference in fiscal behavior.

The rule for budget balance is, however, different in one critically important respect from ordinary rules for ordinary games. Consider an illustrative comparison. Think of a set of poker players who have been playing for some time under a rule that allowed for only stud games. Someone proposes that the rules be changed to allow draw poker to be called by the dealer. The proposed change may or may not be approved, but the point to note is that the *same* persons who played under the old rules are considering the new rules under which they will also expect to continue playing.

A budget balance rule differs in the temporal composition of membership as between the operation of the existing rules and that of proposed alternatives. Under the rule that allows for the generation of continuing deficits, those citizens and their legislative agents who enjoy the current benefits of spending without paying current taxes impose costs on all taxpayers who will be around in future periods. The rule for deficits allows current players in the fiscal game to secure differential gains at the expense of future period players. A change in fiscal rules that would require budget balance removes such differential gains for current-period citizens. The primary beneficiaries of such a change are all those persons who will hold membership in the political community in future periods.

This temporal differentiation among prospective losers and gainers under alternative rules for fiscal politics makes any change from the status quo rule for deficit financing difficult to achieve. It is not as if the same set of players are changing the rules under which play will continue. Those persons who expect to leave the game soon – those who have high rates of time discount, and, in particular, those who gain from benefit most directly from debt-financed spending – will oppose any change that promises its benefits only in future periods. The aged pensioner, or her political agent, must oppose the constitutional amendment for budget balance if her position is motivated by economic self-interest.

5. Lagged implementation and transitional adjustment

It is clearly more difficult to secure agreement on a change in the rules of any game while the game is being played than it is to secure agreement on a set of rules before play begins. This relationship applies to the rules of fiscal politics as well as ordinary games. To the extent that is possible, alternative rules should be considered in a setting where individual positions cannot be identified in terms of prospective gains and losses under the operation of particular rules. Ideally, basic change in rules, constitutional change, should be made only behind some veil of ignorance and/or uncertainty that is sufficiently thick to allow the individual to choose among the alternatives without explicit consideration of the particularized distributional impacts.

This consideration alone suggests that proposals for constitutional change should be lagged in the time for full implementation, that they should never be applied immediately when identified distributional effects are maximally predictable. Critics of the balanced budget amendment who suggest that the introduction of time lags for implementation reflect political cowardice either misunderstand the simple logic of constitutional choice or deliberately seek to sow confusion.

Time lags for implementation should be distinguished from extensions in the time period allowed for transition to a new rule. All of the proposals for the balanced budget amendment include a specific period of transition, and, in the version passed by the U.S. House of Representatives in January 1995, this adjustment period was set at seven years. The purpose of a transition period is to allow for a gradual adjustment in rates of spending and taxing so as to minimize disruptions in established expectations of citizens, whether as program beneficiaries, taxpayers or their political agents.

There is no logical argument that suggests, say, a seven-year lag in implementation of a balanced budget rule. Clearly, uncertainty about distributional effects will be reduced as the time period for adjustment is extended, and, relatedly, there will be less required adjustment during each particular period. With a deficit of, say, $210 billion, a $30 billion first-year adjustment becomes reasonable with the proposed seven-year lag, provided that the constitutional rule operates to insure a continuance of the initial year discipline.

PART TWO

6. Budget balance as a procedural rule

In Part One, I have laid out the arguments in support of the proposed constitutional amendment that requires the federal government to balance its fiscal budget. In Part Two, I propose to discuss separately and in some detail the most prominent objections and criticisms that have been advanced in opposition to the amendment, or in favor of the status quo, which we may think of as the rule for deficit financing. In this section, I shall address the argument based on the claim that a rule for budget balance is inappropriate for inclusion in the "law of the land" that the U.S. Constitution is supposed to represent, and that adoption of any such rule would amount to constitutionalizing a specific economic philosophy. I shall defer until Section 8 the more familiar economists' objection that the proposed rule embodies a particular stance on macroeconomic policy.

The essential distinction that must be made is that between a rule that acts on the *procedures* through which participants are allowed to reach and to carry out decisions and a rule that acts directly on the *outcomes* that any such decisions might describe. A simple example: A rule that all motor vehicles must drive on the right side of two-way roads in the United States is *procedural*. It does not, in any way, dictate or prohibit any particular pattern of road usage. By contrast, a rule that prohibits large trucks from usage of residential streets is nonprocedural or *substantive* because it operates directly on the set of permissible outcomes that may be generated by the behavior of the vehicle operators.

In the context of democratic politics, most of the rules that we normally classify to be constitutional are procedural. The constitutional rules define the processes within which political action takes place. Every citizen is granted the voting franchise; legislative agents are chosen by pluralities or majorities in elections that are scheduled regularly on predictable calendars. Once these and other procedural conditions are met, the basic rules remain silent on the wide ranges of outcomes that may be produced within their limits.

When viewed in this perspective, a constitutional rule for budget balance is procedural rather than substantive. Such a rule does not constrain either the overall size of the public sector (the budget) or the composition of the activities within that sector. Outcomes are allowed to emerge from the interaction of the various cooperative and conflictual pressures that describe the workings of ordinary majoritarian politics. Both proponents and opponents of the balanced budget amendment may, of course, apply their own evaluative standards to specific patterns of outcomes, however these may come about. But it is not legitimate to introduce evaluative criteria applicable for outcomes when directly assessing alternative procedural constraints.

The proposed balanced budget amendment lays out a new rule for making fiscal choices; it does not lay down guidelines for what these choices might be. In one sense, the proposal may be too simple to be understood. In its bare-bones formulation, the amendment requires only that congressional majorities, within the other constraints through which they are authorized to act, pay for what they spend, with "pay for" being defined in a willingness to levy taxes on those citizens who make up the current membership of the polity. By extension from everyday private life, the procedural norm here is simple indeed. Each person or family knows that it must pay for what it buys, and the background law that enforces this precept seldom enters into private consciousness.

Why should the body politic, through government, be allowed to behave differently? They are enabled to do so, in the absence of a constraining rule, only through the legally recognized organic life of the collectivity. A person or family cannot place future persons in indebtedness. Existing claims on a decedent are honored only against the value of assets held at death. There is no burden of private debt that may be transmitted intergenerationally.

Not so with government or public debt. Government remains alive through time, and their obligations are legally honored and enforced, even as the membership of the polity transforms itself through birth, life and death. Recognition of this basic distinction between the private and the collective economy provides the ultimate foundation for the budget balance rule which converts the collectivity into an analogue of its private counterpart.

At this point it is appropriate to discuss briefly that version of the balanced budget amendment that was debated, but not passed, by the U.S. House of Representatives in early 1995 – the version that included the supplementary constitutional provision that all taxes should be approved by a three-fifths majority in both houses of Congress. Advocates of this version failed to make the procedural-substantive distinction that I have noted in this section. A constitutional rule that requires a three-fifths majority for *all* fiscal actions would remain procedural, since there is nothing constitutionally sacrosanct about simple majority decision making as such. But, as presented, the qualified majority was aimed to apply only to taxing decisions, a requirement that clearly represented an attempt to introduce substantive direction as to how the federal budget was to achieve and to maintain balance. Such a supplementary rule would have been inappropriate for inclusion in a constitutional structure that is best confined to procedural rules. And this evaluative conclusion holds quite independently of any separate judgment about the urgent need to keep the growth of the public sector within bounds.

7. Politics, policy, and budget imbalance: Response to the Keynesians

The argument that is most frequently advanced in opposition to the amendment centers on the loss of flexibility under a regime that requires budget balance. There is no dispute about the claim that the proposed rule would act to constrain fiscal choices. At issue is whether or not such constraint is desirable.

Whose choices are constrained by the enforcement of a balanced budget rule? The direct influence is exerted on the choices of those persons who are placed in the roles of fiscal agents for the collectivity, the politicians and bureaucrats who are authorized to make decisions on taxing and spending. The question to be resolved concerns the model to be used in understanding and predicting the behavior of these political agents, both individually and as they interact in complex institutional structures.

There is a long philosophical tradition in which the whole activity or enterprise of politics is modeled in an idealistic way. Political agents are implicitly presumed to be both benevolent and omniscient. They seek only to further "the public interest" in some inclusive, aggregative sense, and, perhaps more importantly, they are presumed to know precisely what this interest is. In the extreme version of this conceptualization of politics, *any* constitutional constraint on potential choices of agents must act to forestall or prevent some actions that would otherwise be beneficial for members of the community. Why, for example, should benevolent and omniscient governments ever be required to seek electoral approval for their actions? And, of course, such political agents should never be constrained in their access to particular institutional tools that might be used to further the public interest, as defined. Clearly, the budget, described as the composition of taxing and spending flows chosen on behalf of the collectivity, is a tool that might be used, in whole or in part, to achieve designated objectives. Any constraint imposed constitutionally necessarily reduces the ability of political agents to use the budgetary tool. By the very presupposition of this romantic model of politics, a constitutional constraint *could never* improve patterns of fiscal outcomes; at best, such a constraint would simply be ineffective.

It is from within this time-honored tradition of idealized politics that the whole Keynesian theory of fiscal policy emerged during the middle decades of the twentieth century. Keynes did not seriously think about the political institutions through which budgetary decisions are implemented. The "presuppositions of Harvey Road" embodied the notion that macroeconomic policy is to be made by a small, select and sophisticated elite, whose members are both fully informed and personally disinterested in securing private advantage.

The Keynesians – the whole group of economists, publicists and politicians who adopted the proffered nostrums as guidelines for practical policy – were particularly naive in their extension of the norms to the American political setting described by the division of power between the executive and legislative branches and without the party discipline of the British parliamentary regime. In a post-public choice retrospective evaluation, it is difficult to understand how anyone could have imagined that fiscal fine-tuning could be within the politically possible.

Quite apart from the neglect of political-institutional practicability, basic macroeconomic obstacles to the efficacy of fiscal fine-tuning were recognized early in the post-Keynesian dialogues. The fiscal budget, even if all issues of political pressures are overcome, remains a crude instrument, and the effects of budgetary manipulation emerge only after significant time lags. An observed deficiency in aggregate demand may prompt tax cuts or spending increases, thereby increasing the deficit, but by the time the effects of such changes take place, other forces may obviate the presumed need for the fiscal action.

A more persistent, and coherent, source of opposition to the balanced budget amendment is concentrated on the potential efficacy of built-in budgetary flexibility. If elements in the tax and expenditure structures are such that increased or reduced deficits (reduced or increased surpluses) emerge as a matter of course during either recessions or inflations, these budgetary changes serve as stabilizing forces that influence the macroeconomy to return to its predisturbance equilibrium.

This argument has considerable persuasive force if the balanced budget rule is framed and interpreted so strictly that *ex post* or end-of-period accounting equality between revenue intakes and outlays is enforced. If the rule requires that, in the event of an *unanticipated* shortfall of revenues behind outlays, due to a reduction of anticipated revenue collections or to an unanticipated increase in rates of outlay, corrective adjustment must be introduced retrospectively as it were, then the operation of the rule would exacerbate the macroeconomic disturbance that might have generated the budgetary shortfall in the first place.

A more acceptable, and less stringent, interpretation of budget balance, as a basic choice rule to be constitutionally implemented, involves no such difficulty. The rule might require only that the final budget resolution, as approved by the Congress and the President, contain revenue and outlay estimates that are equal, as based on competently prepared and unbiased projections at the time of fiscal choice. If, subsequent to choice, that is, to the approval of the budget, the macroeconomic setting should change so as to generate shortfalls or surpluses, these shifts, in themselves, need not be considered to violate the constitutionally mandated rule for maintaining budgetary balance.

In the event that the budget for subsequent periods must be chosen under modified macroeconomic circumstances, implementation of the rule, as such, might require budgetary tightening (on either the taxing or spending side) relative to the prior period, whereas the standard Keynesian prescriptions dictate the opposing direction of change. But the whole hypothetical scenario here can only be grounded on some presupposition about the inefficacy or inoperability of monetary policy instruments in combination with assumptions about the tendencies of the economy toward macroeconomic instability. In a setting in which the central bank fulfills its primary responsibility and keeps the value of the monetary unit stable (within narrow limits) and in which the government budget is balanced, major internal sources for instability are eliminated. The balanced budget rule would, in itself, be an important stabilizing element that would provide an expectational anchor against the fiscal adventurism of impermanent political coalitions.

8. Enforcement and implementation

The opposition to the proposed constitutional amendment for a balanced budget discussed in Section 7 stems directly from economists who have not fully escaped from the intellectual straitjacket imposed on their discipline by the Keynesian revolution of mid-century. A second main source of opposition emerges primarily from the legal community, from constitutional lawyers and legal practitioners, whose human capital has been invested in understanding and interpretation of the constitutional status quo. To members of this group, *any* change in existing rules of the political-legal order must act to create a setting that remains unexplored and unfamiliar. Natural instincts suggest opposition to any radical change, which, indeed, the proposed amendment represents.

At the intensely practical level, the legal opposition to the balanced budget rule targets the alleged ambiguities surrounding the enforceability of the amendment. Much of the argument here seems to be deliberately obfuscatory and appears to be a smoke screen for suppressed ideological objections. By contrast with the economic arguments discussed above – arguments that do express serious misgivings about how the proposed rule might work in its effects on macroeconomic policy – the enforceability arguments seem, at base, to be relatively empty and not worthy of consideration except for their apparent success in introducing uncertainties in the attitudes of persons who might otherwise support the amendment.

The first, and elementary, point to be made is that any rule (law, constraint), once put in place, will necessarily provide incentives for violation, either openly or covertly. This effect is inherent in the notion of a rule. The logical grounds for imposing a rule for budget balance is the need to constrain government's proclivity to spend without taxing. The enactment of the rule will not, directly, reduce or eliminate the pressures brought to bear on fiscal decision makers. They will remain vulnerable to demands for spending increases and tax cuts. Faced with the presence of an operative rule for budget balance, these political agents will try to accomplish their purposes by avoidance and evasion when opportunities permit. Efforts will be made to shift programs off budget and to secure regulatory objectives through nonfunded mandates aimed at both private and public units. The acknowledgement that a rule for budget balance would increase the activities of political coalitions along avoidance-evasion dimensions does not, however, support the conclusion that such a rule would not succeed in imposing fiscal constraint. No law could pass that demands perfect enforcement.

A more suspect argument against the amendment takes the form of scare stories about possible means through which enforcement might take place. At issue here is not the predicted efforts of legislative and executive officers to avoid the force of the rule, but rather the processes that may be called into being when and if such agents openly defy or disregard the constitutional prohibition on deficit financing of governmental outlay. What would happen if the Congress and the President simply proceed to approve a budget that violates the constitutional prohibition on deficits? Would the Supreme Court then act on its own and order cuts in rates of spending and increases in taxes? Or would it direct the President to impound funds as necessary to bring the budget into compliance with the constitutional requirement?

When such concerns as these are raised, the implications for the ultimate division of political authority may seem to become threatening. Who could support a constitutional change that promises to open up yet another area for judicial intrusion?

Such concerns seem misplaced when we look at the operational experience of American democracy. The institutions of governance – executive, legislative, judicial – have long operated within established, and time honored, constitutional limits. The basic "rules of the game" have only rarely been breached. Elections are organized on schedule; majorities or pluralities effectively determine outcomes; the electoral succession of political representatives occurs peacefully; military authority defers to civilian control.

Why should anyone predict that the Congress and the President would behave differently under the constraints imposed by a new rule that requires budget balance? Why should a Congress defy this rule any more readily than it would refuse to honor electoral results? The very fact that such a rule would be *constitutional*, and understood as such, would seem to be sufficient to guarantee basic adherence.

9. Budget deficits and tax increases

In this section, I shall examine an argument that was important in persuading the Reagan administration against promoting a balanced budget amendment in the early 1980s – an argument that also fostered acquiescence in the mounting fiscal deficits of that period. The same argument resurfaced in support for the inclusion of direct tax or spending limits in the amendment as proposed in 1995. For identification of the argument addressed here, the fiscal stance associated with Milton Friedman may be noted.

In a sense, the argument is not correctly classified among those advanced in opposition to the constitutional amendment for budget balance. The argument is less direct, and it is aimed at reasons for advocacy of the rule. The argument challenges the basic presupposition behind the support for the rule of budget balance – the presupposition that budget deficits, as such, are the center of normative concern. Instead, the claim is that deficit financing, in itself, is irrelevant. The modern variant of the ancient Ricardian theorem is adduced – a theorem that equates debt and tax financing of public outlay through the rational calculus of citizens who fully discount the expectations of future period taxes that any issue of debt embodies. The variable that deserves exclusive attention is the rate of government spending rather than the manner of its financing. Will aggregate outlay be larger or smaller under debt financing? The argument of the early 1980s was to the effect that the Congress might fear increases in the deficit more than increases in taxes, and, as a result, deficit financing might actually slow down rates of approval for ever-larger budgets.

This position is seriously flawed on at least three counts. First of all, and as noted earlier, it ignores the burden that the payment of interest charges places on future-period taxpayers. Second, it presumes, quite naively, that political agents are more willing to levy current taxes on constituents than they are to authorize public borrowing. Finally, there is the implicit failure to separate fiscal choice-making at the postconstitutional and the constitutional level.

In retrospect, the political-fiscal experience of the early 1980s seems bizarre. The diversion of attention from budget imbalance almost guaranteed that the deficits would increase rather than decrease over time. In the 1995 discussion, the Friedman argument offered analytical encouragement to those who sought to append the proposed amendment with tax or spending limits, thereby shifting the proposal from the procedural to the quantitative category and providing occasion for totally different sources of opposition.

10. The case for capital budgeting

Critics of the balanced budget amendment often identify the failure to include an exemption for capital spending as a major flaw. Such critics suggest, at least by inference, that the constitutional amendment for balance in the current budget might deserve serious consideration upon the establishment of a separate capital budget account.

The classical (pre-Keynesian) theory of public debt included a normative argument in support of debt financing of lumpy or extraordinary spending on projects that promise to yield benefits over some finite sequence of periods subsequent to that in which the initial outlay is made. By analogy, individual families and business firms finance long-lived assets with debt extending over the income yielding lives of the assets. Persons finance consumer durables, including houses, by debt, and mortgage payments are a large share in household budgets. Firms finance capital improvements by bonds. The argument suggests that governmental units should be constitutionally empowered to behave under roughly similar rules.

Two issues emerge, however, that suggest caution in setting too much emphasis on capital budgeting. First, a distinction must be made between capital assets that will yield income to government (via the taxable income base) over some effective life, and those assets, although physically durable, that may not yield measurably productive increments to the income stream. Such assets should, in principle, be treated quite differently from the first sort in any sound accounting. The argument for separate treatment applies only to the first sort of capital investment assets. Servicing and amortization of debt used to finance the second sort of assets impose net burdens on future-period taxpayers that are indistinguishable from burdens imposed by servicing the debt used to finance ordinary public outlay. The fact that there may exist marble monuments that last forever offers no basis for a claim that such edifices are appropriately financed by debt issue.

A second problem emerges even if the capital budget is defined to include only those public investments that do, in fact, generate streams of income, thereby providing sources for debt service. The classical theory of public finance supported debt issue for capital projects only when the spending was predicted to be extraordinary rather than continuous over a whole sequence of budgetary periods. If rates of spending on capital projects that are fully eligible for exemption from period-by-period budget balance requirements are roughly uniform over time, the operation of separate current and capital budget accounts, with only the first subject to the balance mandate, would not be different, in effect, from combination into a unified account – all of which is subject to the balance requirement. In this setting, which seems empirically descriptive of modern fiscal institutions, the argument for the establishment of a separate capital budget, with exemption from the constitutional rule for balance, seems much ado about nothing.

11. Social security trust fund accounting and the amendment for budget balance

This Section was not in the initial outline for this monograph. It has been added only as a response to the U.S. Senate debates in February–March 1995 that resulted in a one-vote failure of the proposed amendment to secure the votes necessary for approval. Opponents of the amendment justified their position by introducing alleged threats that ultimate implementation of the constitutional change would carry for social security programs.

There are two, quite different, claims advanced. The first is to the effect that trust fund revenues should not be used to balance the fiscal budget. This claim is bizarre at best, since all estimates for the size of deficits for the 1990s do include OASI revenues, which, in isolation, generate a surplus over outlays (some $60 billion in 1995). To move to budget balance in seven years, or by 2002, as projected in the program advanced in the U.S. House of Representatives proposal of 1995, both revenues and outlays under the social security program are included. To argue for exclusion of trust fund accounting revenues from the achievement of the initial target for budget balance is to argue that the objective be made more rather than less difficult to achieve.

A second, and quite different, argument is both more direct and more reflective of interest-group pressures on political choices. If the amendment, as proposed, should be ultimately approved, both by the Congress and the required number of states, reductions in rates of projected federal outlays and/or increases in rates of taxes will be necessary over the years of transition. Opponents sought to secure specific exemption of social security outlays from any spending reductions made necessary under the generalized austerity regime that implementation of the balanced budget rule would cause. The debate over the efficacy or inefficacy of a constitutional rule for budget balance, a debate that is properly joined along the dimensions already discussed above in Sections 6 through 10, was effectively shifted to argument about budgetary composition, argument that seems totally inappropriate at the level of constitutional discourse.

PART THREE

12. Budget balance and macroeconomic stability

Opponents of the constitutional amendment for a balanced budget have "pulled out all the stops" in describing the horrible consequences that the rule could produce. As discussed earlier in Section 7, much of the argument is grounded in outdated Keynesianism, as this shows up in nonsophisticated models of the economy and in naive models of democratic politics. In part, however, the generalized macroeconomic opposition to the balanced budget rules stems from an elementary misunderstanding of the positive feedbacks on macroeconomic stability that the presence of such a rule would exert. In the language of competitive sports, "the best defense is a good offense". The most effective counter to the macroeconomic opposition arguments may be that which traces how the operation of such a rule will, first, introduce a stabilizing force in the economy, and second, will make the task of the monetary authorities much easier.

Who could challenge the claim that, if it were not for the expectation of continuing deficits, with the ever-present danger-threat of ultimate monetization of public debt, the efforts of the Federal Reserve authorities to squeeze the inflationary premium out of long-term interest rates would be more successful. Lower long-term rates would almost surely accompany implementation of the balanced budget rule, not only because of reduced inflationary expectations, but also because governmental demand for loanable funds would be reduced. And, with lower long-term rates, private investment would be encouraged.

A regime of budget balance, by comparison with a regime of continuing deficits, must embody lower rates of government spending and/or higher rates of taxation. Both of these changes reduce aggregate demand for consumption, private and public, and allow resources adjustment toward increased investment. Given any specified level of macroeconomic activity, under the two regimes compared, the postrule composition of resource use must involve a shift toward more investment and less consumption. Only if the "secular stagnation" thesis of the 1930s and 1940s should be revived could such results be denied.

It is perhaps too easy to become strictly provincial in discussions and debates about the possible efficacy of the constitutional rule for budget balance in the United States. Rudimentary attention to the historical experience of other countries and in other times may offer new insights. In almost all cases where economic-social-political stability has been undermined by hyper or near-hyperinflation, generated by disproportionate increases in the quantity of money, the source has been fiscal. Governments have been motivated to spend revenues at rates in excess of their willingness or ability to collect taxes from constituents. To meet emerging revenue shortfalls, governments have, first, made efforts to borrow funds, that is, to finance deficits, by issue of public debt. As revenue shortfalls accelerate, however, lenders of funds (both domestic and foreign) have become wary of governmental credit worthiness. At this juncture, governments face increasing difficulty financing deficits with interest-bearing debt. Faced with such a dilemma, governments have, almost everywhere, resorted to the printing presses, subverting the allegedly independent monetary authorities (national central banks) for political purpose.

These historical experiences from other places and times should never be forgotten when we engage in current constitutional policy discussion in the United States. Participants on all sides of the debates, are likely to presume that "it cannot happen here". But the potential macropolitical disaster that threatens when and if we fail to correct the structural flaw in our decision-making procedures must inform any reasoned attitude.

Finally, related observations concerning possible default on public debt are in order. As interest charges mount under the regime of continuing deficits and in the absence of corrective action as reflected in the proposed amendment, more and more questions must be raised about the moral-ethical status of those claims against productive income earners. Why should taxpayers in, say, 2010, be obligated to pay for public use of resources in, say, 1995? Why should future-period taxpayers be coerced in order to meet fiscal charges that are incurred by present-period program beneficiaries?

These questions, once posed at all, themselves suggest that the moral and, hence, political bases for "fiscal responsibility", as defined by both historical tradition and international agencies, become increasingly insecure as the regime of continuing deficits persists. It is scarcely an exaggeration to suggest that the collective choice is starkly simple: Adopt the constitutional amendment that requires budget balance *now*, or face fiscal-economic-political disaster in the rapidly approaching day of reckoning. Sooner or later, the piper must be paid.

13. The rule as symbol

The symbolic significance of a constitutional rule for budget balance should not be overlooked. Each person constructs her own image of the society in which she lives, and of her own role in that society relative to those of others through the use of symbols. And these symbols may only in some part mirror the realities that may be revealed by empirical science in its ordinary sense. In the United States, we presume that our society embodies "the rule of law", which, in its familiar representation, means that all citizens are subject to equal treatment under the law. But we also recognize that this interpretation of the rule of law remains in part only symbolic, as expressive of an idealized conception, and that, in the reality of legal practice, the equality norm is often violated. "The law" for O.J. Simpson in 1995 is not that which would have been faced by an ordinary citizen, black or white.

Recognition of the divergencies between the observed realities of social interaction and the idealization of these realities through their symbolic representations does not, however, offer legitimate grounds for rejecting the value of the latter. It may be suggested that the principle for budget balance, as such, remains symbolic of governmental fiscal responsibility. With few exceptions, even the most ardent opponents of the constitutional rule express adherence to budget balance as a norm for sound fiscal policy. And, prior to the Keynesian epoch, the symbolic status of budget balance, as an ideal, was in itself sufficient to limit violation of the implicitly-accepted rule in political reality. There was then little, if any, need to formalize that which was almost universally accepted as a practicable norm.

Viewed from this perspective, approval of the proposed constitutional amendment becomes a reaffirmation of the symbol for governmental fiscal responsibility. The emplacement of this rule, interpreted as a fiscal norm, in the actual written constitution serves dual purposes. Such a rule positively modifies public expectations about the fiscal stance of government in future periods, and, at the same time, modifies the personalized cost-benefit calculus of those politicians who must make ordinary fiscal choices.

In the political climate of the 1990s, before any approval of the constitutional amendment for budget balance, the politician who responds to constituency pressures toward increased spending does so with some conscious recognition of the effects of his or her action on the size of the deficit, and, indirectly, in the burden thereby placed on future-period taxpayers. Continued deficit financing does, indeed, impose *some* opportunity cost on those whose decisions produce such results. But who can challenge the claim the constitutionalization of the moral norm of fiscal responsibility would act so as to increase such cost dramatically? To violate a moral norm is one thing, and especially as one decision maker in a large group. To violate a moral norm that also involves breaking a constitutional law is quite another.

Prior works by James M. Buchanan on public debt, deficits and the constitutional amendment for a balanced budget

Buchanan, James M. (1958). *Public Principles of Public Debt.* Homewood: Richard D. Irwin.

Buchanan, James M. (1960). *Fiscal Theory and Political Economy.* Chapel Hill: University of North Carolina Press.

Buchanan, James M. (1966). *Public Finance in Democratic Process: Fiscal Institutions and Individual Choice.* Chapel Hill: University of North Carolina Press.

Buchanan, James M. (1964). Concerning future generations. In J.M. Ferguson (Ed.), *Public Debt and Future Generations*, 55–63. Chapel Hill: University of North Carolina Press.

Buchanan, James M. (1964). Public debt, cost theory, and the fiscal illusion. In J.M. Ferguson (Ed.), *Public Debt and Future Generations.* Chapel Hill: University of North Carolina Press.

Buchanan, James M. (1965). Critique of the public debt. In A.L. Grey and J.E. Elliot (Eds.), 185–190. New York: Houghton-Mifflin.

Buchanan, James M. (1966). 'Fiscal policy' and fiscal choice: The effects of unbalanced budgets. In *Public Finance in Democratic Process*, 98–112. Chapel Hill: University of North Carolina Press.

Buchanan, James M. (1968). Public debt. In *International Encyclopedia of the Social Sciences*, Vol. 4: 28–34.

Buchanan, James M. (1986). The economic consequences of the deficit. In C. Cox (Ed.), *Symposium on Budget Balance*, 11–18. Washington, DC: Committee for a Responsible Federal Budget.

Buchanan, James M. (1986). Public debt and capital formation in the United States. In D. Lee (Ed.), *Taxation and the Deficit: Fiscal Policy and Capital Formation in the United States*, 177–194. San Francisco: Pacific Institute.

Buchanan, James M. (1986). First, the academic scribblers – Democracy in deficit: The political legacy of Lord Keynes. In A.C. Kimmins (Ed.), *The Federal Deficit*, 42–54. *The Reference Shelf*, Vol. 57, No. 4. New York: H.W. Wilson Co.

Buchanan, James M. (1987). The fiscal constitution. In P. Peretz (Ed.), *The Politics of American Economic Policy Making*, 225–228. New York: M.E. Sharpe.

Buchanan, James M. (1987). Keynesian follies. In D. Reese (Ed.), *The Legacy of Keynes*, 130–145. New York: Harper and Row.

Buchanan, James M. (1989). The political economy of the budget deficit. In *Essays on the Political Economy*, 1–12. Honolulu: University of Hawaii Press.

Buchanan, James M. (1984). *Politiek schuldbesef.* ("Political debt consciousness" and "The deficit and American democracy"). Rotterdamse Monetaire Studies, Erasmus University, Rotterdam, No. 16, 39 pages.

Buchanan, James M. (1957). External and internal public debt. *American Economic Review* 47 (December): 995–1000.

Buchanan, James M. (1959). The real debt. *Challenge* 7 (July): 58–61.

Buchanan, James M. (1962). Easy budgets and tight money. *Lloyds Bank Review* 64 (April): 17–30.

Buchanan, James M. (1966). The icons of public debt. *Journal of Finance* 21 (September): 544–546.

Buchanan, James M. (1984). Democracy in deficit. *Manhattan Report* 4: 6–9.

Buchanan, James M. (1985). The moral dimension of debt financing. *Economic Inquiry* 23 (January): 1–6.

Buchanan, James M. (1987). The political economy of the deficit: A 1987 perspective. *Florida Policy Review* 3 (Summer): 5–10.

Buchanan, James M. (1987). Debt – An economic and moral crisis. *IPA Review* (May–July): 56–57.

Buchanan, James M. (1987). The deficit and obligations to future generations. *Imprimis* 16 (January): 1–6.

Buchanan, James M. (1988). Reining in the deficit. *The Owen Manager* 9 (Spring): 27–31.

Buchanan, James M. (1979). The budget balance amendment: Statement to the New Hampshire House of Representatives, 2 April. *Congressional Record*, 4 April: S-3858.

Buchanan, James M. (1979). In defense of budget balance. *Congressional Record* 125 (30 April), No. 51: S4940–S4944.

Buchanan, James M. (1995). Statement. House Judiciary Committee, 5 January.

Buchanan, James M. (1979). Budget balance proposal. Unpublished paper.

Buchanan, James M. (1984). The deficit and American democracy. Unpublished paper.

Buchanan, James M. (1984). Budgetary bias in post-Keynesian politics: The erosion and potential replacement of fiscal norms. Unpublished paper.

Buchanan, James M. (1985). The secondary economic consequences of the deficit. Unpublished paper.

Buchanan, James M. (1987). The budget deficit in modern democracy. Unpublished paper.

Buchanan, James M. and Geoffrey Brennan (1980). Toward authentic tax reform: Prospects and prescriptions. In *The Power to Tax: Analytical Foundations of a Fiscal Constitution*. New York: Cambridge University Press.

Buchanan, James M. and Marilyn Flowers (1987). Public debt and public finance. Unpublished paper.

Buchanan, James M. and Jennifer Roback (1987). The incidence and effects of public debt in the absence of fiscal illusion. *Public Finance Quarterly* 15 (January): 5–25.

Buchanan, James M., Charles Rowley and Robert Tollison (Eds.) (1987). *Deficits*. New York: Blackwell.

Buchanan, James M. and Robert Tollison (Eds.) (1972). *Theory of Public Choice: Political Applications of Economics*. Ann Arbor: University of Michigan Press.

Buchanan, James M. and Robert Tollison (Eds.) (1984). *Theory of Public Choice II: Political Applications of Economics*. Ann Arbor: University of Michigan Press.

Buchanan, James M. and Gordon Tullock (1962). *The Calculus of Consent: Logical Foundations of Constitutional Democracy*. Ann Arbor: University of Michigan Press.

Buchanan, James M. and Viktor J. Vanberg (1986). Organization theory and fiscal economics: Society, state, and public debt. *Journal of Law, Economics, and Organization* 2 (Fall): 215–227.

Buchanan, James M. and Richard E. Wagner (1977). *Democracy in Deficit: The Political Legacy of Lord Keynes*. New York: Academic Press.

Buchanan, James M. and Richard E. Wagner (1966). *Public Debt in Democratic Society*. Washington, DC: American Enterprise Institute.

Buchanan, James M. and Richard E. Wagner (1978). Dialogues concerning fiscal religion. *Journal of Monetary Economics* 4 (July): 627–636.

Buchanan, James M., Richard E. Wagner and John Burton (1978). *The Consequences of Mr. Keynes*, Hobart Paper 78. London: Institute of Economic Affairs.

Public Choice **90:** 139–163, 1997.

© 1997 *Kluwer Academic Publishers.*

The prohibition-repeal amendments: A natural experiment in interest group influence*

MICHAEL MUNGER[1] & THOMAS SCHALLER[2]
[1]*Department of Political Science, University of North Carolina, Chapel Hill, NC 27599-3265, U.S.A.;* [2]*Department of Political Science, University of Ohio, Athens, OH 45701, U.S.A.*

Abstract. The pattern of state support for Prohibition (18th Amendment, 1919) and Repeal (21st Amendment, 1933) is analyzed and compared. This comparison is important because Prohibition is the only amendment ever to be repealed. The main thesis is that there was no wholesale change in preferences of citizens. Instead, producer interests failed to mobilize effectively in 1919, and the coupling of moral and economic arguments that worked in 1919 broke apart in 1933. Regression analysis is conducted on state legislatures (for Prohibition) and state referenda on convention delegates (for Repeal), so states are observations in the cross-sectional regression analysis. The results broadly support the main thesis.

1. Introduction

The U.S. Constitution, to use a hackneyed phrase, is a "living document". Though the rules codified in the Constitution were designed to be permanent and constant, the framers of the Constitution recognized the need for adaptability. On the other hand, the framers clearly sought to avoid making the constitution simply a scorecard for finding out interests were most powerful. As Madison made clear in *The Federalist*, fear of uncontrolled pressures of faction (more commonly now called "interest groups") weighed heavily on the framers' minds as they devised the rules to govern government. They tried to strike a balance between making amendments too hard, or too easy, to adopt.

> The designers of Article V had two goals in mind. First, recalling that the impossibility of amending the Articles of Confederation had made them ineffective as a form of government, the Constitution's framers hoped to render the new document adaptable to changing circumstances and needs. At the same time, they sought to ensure that the amending process

* The authors wish to thank Kevin McGuire, Thomas Oatley, and Peter VanDoren for helpful comments. We especially thank Charles Rowley for helping conceive the topic. The usual caveat, of course, applies.

> would operate only when the polity had reached a consensus that it was necessary to change the constitutional text. They tried to strike a balance, seeking to create a process more easily used than that of the Articles of Confederation, yet not so easy as to leave the Constitution prey to passing majorities ... (Bernstein, 1993: 15)

The procedure the framers settled on makes the U.S. Constitution the most stable in the world (Lutz, 1994). Successful amendments are rare, both for practical reasons and because tinkering with the Constitution is seen by Americans as serious business, not something to be done frivolously. Any amendment must first be proposed by a 2/3 majority at the federal level (either both chambers of Congress, or a national constitutional convention called in response to requests from 2/3 of the states). Proposed amendments must then be ratified by 3/4 of the states, either through passage of resolutions by the state assemblies or by state conventions where delegates are chosen in special state elections. (For the text of the amendment procedure, see Article V in Appendix 1 in this paper.)

More than 10,000 amendment resolutions have been introduced in the U.S. Congress. Of those, 33 have been formally "proposed", or received 2/3 majorities in the House and Senate. Of these, 27 have been ratified by 3/4 of the states through one of the processes outlined in Article V. The first step is the hardest: most of the amendments succesfully proposed are ratified. Even discounting the first 10 amendments (the "Bill of Rights") still leaves 17 out of 23 proposed amendments (74%) actually being ratified.

This paper is an analysis of two "successful" amendments, the Prohibition Amendment (18th, 1919) and the Repeal of Prohibition Amendment (21st, 1933). There are several reasons these two stand out, and why a comparative analysis of their passage is worthwhile. First, the 18th is the only amendment ever repealed in its entirety. Second, the method of ratification of the 21st Amendment is unique: no other Amendment has been ratified using the votes of state convention delegates. Finally, the set of interests and preferences brought into conflict over Prohibition and Repeal are amenable to analysis using statistical techniques, as we shall see.[1]

1.1. *Historical background*

On 18 December, 1917 the U.S. Congress passed a resolution proposing an amendment to the Constitution prohibiting the manufacture, sale, or transportation of alcoholic beverages. The 18th Amendment was declared ratified on 19 January, 1919, and became operative one year later (for text of 18th Amendment, see Appendix 1). The Amendment left enforcement to statute, so the Volstead (National Prohibition Enforcement) Act was passed, over

President Wilson's veto, on 28 October, 1919. Prohibition had wide support in government: as late as 1929, Congress passed the Jones Act, increasing the penalties for the federal offense of making or transporting liquor, wine, or beer.

In 1931 the "Wickersham Commission"[2] report was delivered to the U.S. Congress. The report concluded that enforcement of the 18th Amendment had broken down. One problem was the difficulty of coordinating state and federal enforcement of the strictures against alcohol (the Amendment made enforcement powers "concurrent;" see Appendix 1). Another problem was the enormous rents created by Prohibition. Al "Scarface" Capone and other gangsters collected tens of millions of dollars in the 1920s; the total net rents created by Prohibition may have amounted to more than $100 million (Nelli, 1985). These quantities of money were so enormous, and the desire for illegal beer and other acholic beverages so widespread, that bribery and pervasive corruption in the enforcement apparatus were inevitable. The Commission did not recommend outright repeal (President Hoover, who appointed the Commission, strongly opposed repeal), but did recommend extensive revisions, including a centralization of enforcement powers in the federal government. Congress debated amending the Volstead Act, but did nothing substantive in response to the Commission report.

Four years later, with the Depression growing worse and an increasing need for revenue to finance the incoming Roosevelt administration's "New Deal" economic stimulus programs, all political will to maintain Prohibition had disappeared.[3] In February, 1933 Congress passed a resolution proposing an amendment to repeal Prohibition. Unwilling to wait for formal repeal, Congress also amended the Volstead Act, in an impressive display of cynicism. After all, the 18th Amendment outlawed production, sale or transportation of all alcoholic beverages. This amendment had been duly ratified, and should have bound Congress.

The amendment had left enforcement to the Congress and states, however. In March 1933, Congress amended the Volstead Act with the Beer and Wine Revenue Act, in effect *nullifying* much of the Prohibition Amendment before it was formally repealed. The Act allowed wine, beer, and other beverages with less than 4% alcohol content by volume to be sold and transported freely (subject only to state restrictions), provided a tax of $5 per barrel was collected and paid to the federal Treasury.[4] The Prohibition Amendment was finally formally repealed later that year, on December 5, 1993.[5]

What in the world were these people doing? It wasn't easy to pass the Prohibition Amendment, and the economic costs were enormous. Tens of thousands of workers lost their jobs, millions of dollars in investments in breweries and distilleries disappeared almost overnight in 1919, and further millions in tax revenues were lost to state and national governments. Why pass an Amendment to the Constitution that does this sort of damage, only to repeal it just 14 years later? To analyze these questions, and begin to answer them, we must turn briefly to some background on constitutions and amendments.

2. On constitutions and amendments

The contract among citizens, and between citizens and government, spelled out by a constitution is not implicit, or hypothetical. Constitutions, as elaborated by the institutions of a nation, are the explicit rules that circumscribe the activities of citizens and the scope of government. Consequently, these rules are not (or should not be) constantly rearranged in response to temporary political forces or the congealing of a particular set of political interests in one majority or another. In a legitimate constitutional system, the constitution admits of flexibility, but has an air of constancy.[6]

The case, or difficulty, of constitutional amendment have important implications for the performance of political economies. As Buchanan and Tullock (1962) pointed out, the rules have direct effects:

> The Constitutional approach indicates clearly that the anticipated costs of reaching decisions will cause some collective activities to embody specific decisions made with less than-than-unanimous approval .... These variants will be rationally chosen, not because they will produce 'better' collective decisions (they will not), but rather because, on balance, the sheer weight of the costs involved in reaching decisions unanimously dictates some departure from the 'ideal' rule. (pp. 94–96)

The rules based on the costs of decision, however, will have important indirect effects, because of the importance of predictability and consistency in rules governing the definition of property and exchange relations.

> Property rights especially can never be defined once and for all, and there will always exist an area of quasi property rights subject to change by the action of the collective unit. The relevant point is that the individual will foresee that collective action in this area may possibly impose very severe costs on him. In such cases he will tend to place a high value on the attainment of his consent, and he may be quite willing to undergo substantial decision-making costs in order to insure that he will, in fact, be reasonably protected against confiscation. (pp. 73–74)

Later work that has built on the tradition established by Buchanan and Tullock (see, for example, North, 1981; Brennan and Buchanan, 1985; Holcombe,

1994) has elaborated this fundamental insight that stability and predictability in property rights is a key feature in explaining the performance of societies over time.

> The forms of cooperation and competition that human beings develop and the systems of enforcement of these rules organizing human activity are at the very heart of economic history. Not only do these rules spell out the system of incentives and disincentives that guide and shape economic activity, but they also determine the underlying distribution of wealth and income of a society .... Ultimately, it is the state that is responsible for the efficiency of the property rights structure, which causes growth or stagnation or economic decline. (North, p. 17)

In short, threats of expropriation, or even just variability, in the state's definition of property rights, reduce the expected present value of investment. Societies that prosper are able to guarantee stability, and predictability, of property rights, so that economic agents have some confidence they can retain the rents that accrue to long-term investment and innovation.

Viewed in this light, the experiment with Prohibition in the United States doesn't just seem unusual. It seems bizarre! There don't seem to be *any* net gainers from the expropriation of rights to brew beer, or distill liquor, and then restore these rights less than fifteen years later. Did voters simply change their minds? Or was there some change in the set of interest group forces exerted on the Congress and States? In the following two sections, we will develop the two hypotheses of preference change and interest group influence at greater length.

3. The "public" interest: Did voters *change* their minds?

Because we are analyzing the effects of interests on the pattern of state support for the Prohibition, and (later) for repeal of the same amendment, it is important that we define what "interest" is. But such a task is deceptively difficult. It is fashionable (outside *Public Choice*, at least) to distinguish *economic* interests, or groups formed around hoped-for profits accruing to some collective action, from *public* interests, or groups formed around higher, more selfless motives.

This distinction may have some value analytically, but it is hard to sustain empirically. In both cases, the groups are trying to affect public policy, or to alter the Constitution, to make it conform with their political preferences. The psychological basis of the political preference for change is a potentially interesting datum, *but the preference itself is simply political.* Consider the following discussion by one of the fathers of modern interest group theory, Truman (1951: 98–99):

> Economic groups ... are not isolated, discrete phenomena, though we may treat them as such for convenience in analysis. Changes directly affecting them will also influence ... patterns of interaction in religious groups and even in college faculties. Other types of disturbances, moreover, may have their primary focus in other institutionalized groups, only secondarily or insignificantly affecting ecnomic groups ...
>
> As an example of this sort one readily thinks of one of the most powerful associations in recent American history, the Anti-Saloon League, whose activities were a major factor in the country's politics for two decades .... The circumstances from which the league emerged, moreover, fit the familiar patterns, as did its later activities. The Oberlin (Ohio) Temperance Alliance, out of which the league grew, was formed in 1874 "to deal with a crisis in the local temperance situation". A State-wide organization was set up in 1893, and two years later a number of such groups were merged into the Anti-Saloon League of America, which grew steadily. *From the beginning the strategy of the "Ohio idea" was not to secure abstinence pledges from individuals, but to operate through political institutions toward the objective of abolishing all traffic in liquor. It was a political interest group from the start.* (emphasis added)

This passage illustrates our point admirably. Anti-drinking activists had access to the means of persuasion. They could have harangued drinkers, and tried to elicit promises of temperance. But this the activists did not do, at least not *primarily*. Instead, the Anti-Saloon League used the coercive tool of majoritarian populism: Carrie Nation's hatchet was to be transferred from the hand of a strong woman to the much stronger hand of government.[7] Consequently, whatever else it was, the Anti-Saloon League was a *political*, not public, interest group.

We haven't answered the question that motivates this section, of course. What changed? In 1919, many (perhaps most) citizens in more than three-quarters of the states did not actively oppose the Anti-Saloon League's open political agenda. Yet, in 1933, Prohibition was flayed and gutted before it was even truly dead. Can we explain change in citizen preferences of this magnitude?

We may not have to. The preferences expressed through the political process, under pressure from political interest groups, may be different from preferences held by citizens. One basis for this claim can be found in Brennan and Lomasky (1993). This argument can be paraphrased as follows:

- Citizens have two sets of preferences: (1) The preferences they feel, and act on in private; and (2) The preferences they feel they should have, and act on in public. For example, a citizen might sometimes drink too much, though he thinks it is morally wrong to get drunk.
- Both sets of preferences are "real", in the sense that they motivate behavior consistent with maximizing satisfaction. The fact that behavior seems inconsistent at different points in time implies conflict between moral and primitive preferences, not changing preferences or irrationality.
- Decisions on moralistic policies affect not just the citizen himself, but others as well. Thus, citizens may act paternalistically in decrying in others behavior in which they themselves engage. For our purposes, this means that, though our one citizen may think he can withstand the temptations of alcohol on his own (though he might have a nip on weekends), his weaker brethren need more help.
- The conflict between the two types of preference is particularly severe when political decisions are being made, because citizens (rationally) do not perceive that their own statements have any nonnegligible influence on the collective outcome. Since the probability of any one person's vote, or opinion, determining the outcome is zero as the number of decision-makers grows large, each individual simply accepts the outcome as given and decides what preference they should project to others in their church, community, or other group.

Brennan and Lomasky (1993) give an example of voting on Prohibition that relies on a Prisoner's Dilemma problem. We have adapted their argument in Table 1.

The citizen has no control over the support, or opposition, of others to Prohibition. The best situation (ranked "1", as the entries in the table are ordinal rankings) for the citizen is to offer public support of Prohibition (so our guy can be moral and upstanding in the eyes of other members of his church and community), but have Prohibition fail to be passed (so he can still drink!). Since everyone can only control their own public stand on Prohibition (they want to appear "for"), but has preferences over the actual policy (they want it to fail), the result is apparent support for Prohibition.[8] Of course, this is simply a collective action problem (isomorphic with an n-person Prisoner's Dilemma), since if no one opposes Prohibition, the damned thing passes. This framework offers an explanation of the apparent switch in preferences that does not rely on either voters changing their minds en masse, or on some collective irrationality. Brennan and Lomasky's argument applies with particular force to the kind of sumptuary restrictions we are considering here.[9] The U.S. Constitution is generally a set of restrictions on what government

Table 1. Brennan and Lomasky's prisoner's dilemma in voting for Prohibition.

Strategies for Citizen j	Actions of all other citizens: Majority favors Prohibition	Majority opposes Prohibition	Tie, so j's vote determines outcome
Publicly support Prohibition	5	1	4
Publicly oppose Prohibition	6	2	3

Note: Numbers in Table are ordinal rankings of outcomes. Since columns are exactly equivalent to plays by "Nature", this is not a game in any important sense. Rather, this is simply a graphical decision problem for an arbitrary Citizen j. It appears there is no "best" strategy for Citizen j. However, Brennan and Lomasky argue that

$$\lim_{n \to \infty} [P(\text{tie, or} n/2 \text{ ``for''} = n/2 \text{ ``against''})] = 0$$

Consequently, for Citizen j, and for each citizen, "Publicly support Prohibition" is a dominant strategy.

can do to citizens. The 18th Amendment is different: it restricts what citizens can do. As Ostrom (1987) asserts in his study of the construction of the Constitution, articles that supersede the proscription of government actions and outlaw actions by citizens face great difficulties.

> Moral sentiments are much too fragile to maintain the enforceability rules of constitutional law .... Formulating a constitution which was intended to have legal force in *limiting the legal and political competence of government authorities* poses quite a different problem in legal draftsmanship than the *formulation of a set of general moral principles* which serve only as a set of moral sentiments. (Ostrom, p. 67; emphasis added)

The framers of the U.S. Constitution showed great will in expressly avoiding the temptation to inject moral sentiments in the guise of limiting authority into the original document. As Swindler (1985: 55) points out, the 18th Amendment "was then, and remains to date, the only constitutional attempt to incorporate a sumptuary provision into the fundamental law of the land".

The language of the 21st Amendment, unfortunately, is also no model of what Ostrom called "legal draftsmanship". Twenty-nine states maintained their own policies of complete prohibition after the Repeal Amendment.[10] Solicitous of the *retained* powers of states to restrict alcohol on their own, the drafters of the 21st Amendment actually botched the attempt to *remove* federal restriction. As Tribe (1995: 219–220) gleefully points out:

> The text [of Section 2 of the Repeal Amendment] actually forbids the private conduct it identifies, rather than conferring power on the States as

> such. This has the singular effect of putting the Twenty-first Amendment on a pedestal most observers have always assumed was reserved for the rather more August Thirteenth Amendment, which is typically described as the *only* exception the principle that our Constitution's provisions, even when they don't say so expressly, limit some appropriate level of *government*.
>
> ...The upshot is that there are two ways, and two ways only, in which an ordinary private citizen, acting under her own steam and under color of no law, can violate the United States Constitution. One is to enslave somebody, a suitably hellish act. The other is to bring a bottle of beer, wine, or bourbon into a State in violation of its beverage control laws – an act that might have been thought juvenile, or perhaps even lawless, but *unconstitutional*? (emphasis in original)

To sum up: We cannot, in general, be sure that the genuine preferences of a majority of citizens will be expresssed in public debates over sumptuary restrictions. Consequently, changing a constitution to express moral sentiments of a (temporary) majority, even an apparently large majority, is very difficult to justify. Further, the practical legal difficulties in defining and enforcing the outlawed consumption are likely to defeat the best of intentions. For all these reasons, it is not necessary to resort to an argument of "preference reversal", where millions of voters simply changed their minds, to explain the passage, and subsequent repeal, of Prohibition.

We still need to establish what did happen, of course. The main argument below rests on the influence of political entrepreneurs, and the changing circumstances of economic interest groups. In the model section, we will try to proxy the influences of complex and conflicting preferences using religious and economic variables. First, however, we elaborate on the nature of the political interest groups in conflict over Prohibition, and Repeal.

4. Political interests: Did producers *lose* their minds?

Dozens of groups mobilized to advance, or hinder, the cause of Prohibition. The successes of the Anti-Saloon League (ASL), Women's Christian Temperance Union (WCTU) and its allies would ultimately be reversed by the concentrated efforts of the Association Against the Prohibition Amendment (AAPA), the Voluntary Committee of Lawyers (VCL) and the Women's Organization for National Prohibition Reform (WOPNR), among others. We will consider first those groups *supporting* Prohibition (the "Drys"), and then those who first *opposed* Prohibition and then mobilized to pass the Repeal amendment (the "Wets").

4.1. *The Drys*

Dry groups can classified in one of three categories, based on the degree to which the issue for them was conceived as moral or economic. Protestant-based prohibition groups, most notably the Anti-Saloon League, founded in Ohio in 1893, depicted alcohol as a vice that would tarnish the American soul if its consumption went unchecked (Odegard, 1928; Kerr, 1985). Encouraged by the passage of earlier state prohibition statutes – most notably Neil Dow's Maine law, the first state prohibition statute, passed in 1850 – the ASL and its dynamic lead counsel, Wayne B. Wheeler, championed the fight against the evils of liquor and the saloons that served as vehicles for promoting alcoholism.

The female-led Womens' Christian Temperance Union, an alliance of state movements formed in 1874, promoted a far more sweeping agenda than the ASL (Donovan, 1995). Prohibition was part of the larger, "progressive" reforms of the day, linked to womens' suffrage and electoral reform. Where the ASL, despite its Protestant undergirding, portrayed Prohibition as a political problem requiring political change (Kingsdale, 1973), the WCTU saw drinking as part of a broader moral decay. Both groups agreed, however, on the need for a Prohibition amendment, and so worked as close political allies.

On the opposite end of the moral-economic spectrum were the bootleggers who, envisioning the unimaginable rent-seeking opportunities that prohibition would undoubtedly provide, promoted the prohibition movement on strictly economic aims. Specific activities, and levels of influence, are difficult to measure, of course (Haller, 1985). Nonetheless, it is clear that bootleggers, hoping to traffic illegally in the distribution and sale of alcohol, stood to gain substantially from Prohibition.

Bootleggers had no interest whatsoever in the salvation of the American soul. Moreover, as Nelli (1985) shows, the criminal syndicates that controlled illegal gambling were well-suited for the transition into the newly-illegalized alcohol markets. Entrepreneurs with a taste for risk had a clear-eyed vision of what Prohibition would mean:

> The early 1920s were a period of intense competition among criminal entrepreneurs attracted by Prohibition's economic opportunities. The small capital outlay required to enter the business, and the potential for high financial returns, convinced formerly law-abiding citizens as well as small-time criminals to try their luck. (Nelli, p. 125)

There was one other set of groups that favored Prohibition, for reasons of economics as well as morality. These were owners of large industrial enterprises, who joined with the ASL and WCTU in concern for the decaying morals of the American workers. It could be argued, of course, that "morality" in workers was valued because it made them more productive (Rumbarger, 1989). Magnates (such as Standard Oil heir John D. Rockefeller, Jr.) led captains of the banking, insurance, steel, coal, petroleum and railroad industries, on Yale Professor Irving Fisher's "Committee of Sixty". This group appointed itself as overseers of workers' character, bringing their significant political resources to bear in attacking the saloons and alcohol that kept workers home, or haggard, on the "blue Monday" of each week. The activities of the industrial elite, says Rumbarger (1989: 175)

> [d]ispel comfortable assertions that the thrust of reform in these years was toward an abstract, albeit moralistic, ideal of human welfare and well-being. Such ideas, as well as those of social betterment and human uplift, *were functionally related to the exigencies of industrialization* carried on at the discretion of business enterprise. (emphasis added)

In short, industrialists had morals on their tongues, but labor productivity on their minds. Nonetheless, the framing of the issue as moralistic, rather than economic, had key consequences for the outcome of the debate. As we shall see in the next section, the "Wets" never effectively organized against the moral arguments of the Drys, and they lost badly as a result.

4.2. *The Wets*

The organized interests opposed to Prohibition in the nineteen-teens were actually neither organized nor particularly interested. Prohibitionists, of course, had been caterwauling in the streets since before the Civil War, but to little apparent political effect. Indeed, many of the state-level prohibition victories won in the late 19th century had already been reversed by 1919, and the Prohibition Party itself had long since dissolved.

So the industries that would be most severely damaged by alcohol prohibition – the beer makers of the Unites States Brewers' Association and the hard liquor distillers of the National Wholesale Liquor Dealers Association – were not prepared when the womens' suffrage and Prohibition movements coalesced in 1918. Major brewers such as Pabst and Budweiser failed to pool resources or coordinate their individual efforts.[11] In military terms, Prohibitions achieved strategic surprise against alcohol producers. By the time it became clear the Prohibition threat this time was real, it was too late to mobilize to mount an effective defense. Another possible source of opposition, the drinking public, also failed to organize effectively.[12]

The passage of Prohibition, of course, represented a classic "disturbance", in the jargon of Truman (1951). Having lost the battle, former alcohol producers resolved to win the war. They were able to convert their assets to the production of other beverages or products in the short run (Plavchan, 1976), but began to organize politically now in earnest. They found allies in the form of broader-based economic interests (Goff and Anderson, 1994) such as the Association Against the Prohibition Amendment (AAPA) and the Federal Dispensary Tax Reduction League (FDTRL), which argued on behalf of repeal for the purpose of recovering the lost tax base caused by Prohibition. The American Federation of Labor (AFL), lamenting the loss of unionized labor in brewing trades, and almost responding to its members' very real desire to drink legally, joined with the Wet forces. By the early 1930s, many of these groups, along with the Women's Organization for National Prohibition Reform (WOPNR) and the Voluntary Committee of Lawyers (VCL), combined their efforts into the United Repeal Council (URC).

It may seem surprising that it took fourteen years to correct the Prohibition "disturbance". From a financial perspective, prohibiting the sale of alcohol was clearly not an equilibrium, because of the deadweight losses imposed on producers and consumers, and the tax revenue losses suffered by government. Politically, however, it proved possible to defend Prohibition long after general support for the policy had faded. One reason, of course, is that the policy was based on a constitutional amendment, and not a statute. The gravity of constitutional change, and the practical difficulties posed by the complex supermajority requirements of amendment, advantage any constitutional edict against change.

Ultimately, two outside factors proved decisive in the victory of the Wet counteroffensive. The first, paradoxically, was the successful passage of the 19th Amendment, which forced states to grant female suffrage. Now that women could vote, womens' political organizations lost membership and energy. Denied this link between womens' rights and Prohibition, which had been instrumental in passing Prohibition in the first place, the Dry forces lost a crucial organizing principle. Second, as was pointed out in the historical overview in Section 1.1, the Depression and the New Deal political agenda made the federal government desperate for new revenue sources.

In the previous section, we argued that the "preferences" expressed in Prohibition were actually a failure to solve a collective action problem. Since repeat play was possible, the sub-optimal outcome was reversed 14 years later. This is no explanation, of course, unless we can say *how* citizens avoided the dilemma at the second stage. The answer is that the Wet forces succeeded in framing the issue very differently in 1933. Prohibition looks to us like the same issue in 1919 and 1933, but for contemporaries it was different in at least two important ways.

The Drys had managed, either out of shrewdness or luck, to frame the alcohol issue exclusively as a way to save the moral character of the working class in 1919. Against the backdrop a nation still committed to the self-abnegation of WWI, abstemiousness and industriousness were powerful arguments (Wasserman, 1989; Donovan, 1995). Second, the Drys managed an impressive feat of political legerdemain: with the support of only about 31%[13] of the U.S. population, they managed to put together what looked like a supermajority. It is important to remember that the U.S. Constitution requires only 3/4 of the states, not the population, for ratification. Winning narrow majorities (often through threats and intense lobbying of legislators) in 36 states, mostly rural or sparsely populated, the Drys were able to impose their will on all the people.

The tactical and strategic advantages enjoyed by Drys evaporated quickly, however. By 1993 it was clear the debate had more to do with economics than with moral character. Groups like WOPNR, who supported both Repeal and temperance, are evidence that the unintended consequences of Prohibition were uncompensated by moralistic gains. By the 1930s, the Drys could no longer portray Prohibition as a question of defending the morals of the individual. Finally, when Congress prescribed ratification of Repeal by state convention – a prescription hailed by practically every state assembly (Brown, 1938) – any chance of repeating the intimidation and lobbying practices of 1919 was lost.

In 1919 the American public was duped into making a "moral" choice. In 1933 the economic and moral aspects of Prohibition were uncoupled. The decisions were therefore different in important ways. In the next two sections, we offer some measures of these differences, and consider the consistency of the patterns we find with the theory outline so far.

5. Model and data

We have argued that the passage of the Prohibition Amendment, followed by the Repeal Amendment fourteen years later, can be explained by a change in the importance of political interests. We will offer only a very simple test of this claim, comparing coefficients in similar regressions, using states as observations, from 1919 and 1933. The model to be estimated tests whether preferences of citizens and economic interests in the state explain support for Prohibition, and for Repeal:

$$\text{Support}_i = f(\text{preferences of citizens}_i,\ \text{economic interests}_i)$$

It is important to note what we are not doing: we are not claiming to explain which people supported Prohibition, and which opposed it. Rather, we will determine whether a simple model incorporating some proxies for preferences of citizens, and economic interests, can explain varying levels of support for Prohibition across states.[14]

5.1. *Dependent variables*

We estimate regression models for three different dependent variables:[15] *Lower Chamber* Percent for Prohibition, *Upper Chamber* Percent for Prohibition, and *Special Election* Percent for Repeal (the italicized portions will serve as names hereafter). Lower Chamber and Upper Chamber are the percentage of the state legislative assemblies (House of Representatives, and the Senate, respectively) that voted to ratify the Prohibition Amendment in 1919. These data were obtained from various issues of the *New York Times*.

The third dependent variable is *Special Elections*, a measure of support in state conventions for ratification of the Repeal Amendment. We considered analyzing the convention votes themselves, but almost all of these were unanimous in favor of Repeal, because most states chose to use "at large" elections. Further, the number of delegates ranged from 3 (in New Mexico) to 329 (in Indiana), so that the conventions were hard to compare. Fortunately, 38 states had elections for delegates where citizens voted directly for, or against, Repeal.[16] For these 38 states, we were then able to use the percentage support for Repeal as a dependent variable. The source for these variables was again the New York Times, especially on November 8th 1933.

5.2. *Independent variables*

We have argued above that preferences and economic interests affect support for constitutional amendments. A simple reduced form set of variables to proxy for preference should account for religion (especially given the moralistic tenor of the argument for Prohibition) and per capita income in the state. We considered both overall income per capita, and farm income per capita, in an effort to capture both the level of income and something of its composition. Finally, we need some proxy for the economic interests of the state. The difficulty is that we wanted a measure that is (a) available for both 1919 and 1933, and (b) a reasonable proxy for how much production of alcohol was foregone during Prohibition.

Here is the list of dependent variables used in the analysis:

Pct Catholic: The proportion of the population of the state listed as Catholic in 1919 (*World Almanac*, 1920), and 1930 (*Official Catholic Directory*, 1931).

Farm Income/Pop: Agricultural Production data come from the *Census of Manufactures* (1919 and 1929, respectively). Population data come from the *Census of Population* (1920 and 1930).

Total Income/Pop: Total state Value of Products comes from *Census of Population* (1920 and 1930, respectively).

Alch Tax Rev/Pop: This variable is total federal revenue (per capita) from acholic beverage sales, from the last year (1919) before Prohibition, and the first year after Repeal (1934). This variable proxies for deadweight losses for both producers (since taxes were ad valorem) and for the federal government. The Alcohol Tax Revenue data come from the *U.S. Office of the Internal Revenue Service: Annual Report* (1919 and 1934, respectively).

Female Suffrage Dummy: Since the linkage between female suffrage and female support for Prohibition was a key factor in the passage of Prohibition (Goldstein, 1973), states that allowed women to vote before passage of the 19th Amendment had a different electorate. This is a dummy variable, taking a value of 1 if the state had womens' suffrage at the time of voting on the Prohibition Amendment, zero otherwise. The data are taken from the *Historical Abstract of the U.S.: Colonial Times to 1970, Part 2*.

"*Already Passed*" Dummy: All 48 states had votes in their legislatures on Prohibition. However, some states voted only after the requisite 3/4 (that is, 36 states) had voted to ratify. Votes after ratification may have had more symbolic than substantive value. This dummy variable takes the value 0 for states that voted *before* the 3/4 majority was achieved, and 1 for states that voted *after* it was clear Prohibition would be ratified.

The descriptive statistics, and correlation tables, for the numeric dependent variables are given in Table 2.

To make clear the expected relations between the dependent variables and the independent variables, we offer the following set of predicted signs, and summary explanations.

Table 2. Descriptive statistics and simple correlations of dependent variables.

Panel (a): Prohibition (1920, N=48)

Descriptive Statistics

Variable	Mean	Std Dev	Minimum	Maximum
Pct Catholic	15.62	14.07	0.0	68.1
Farm Income/Pop	198.47	116.97	18.49	545.10
Total Income/Pop	481.40	307.41	49.55	1236.0
Alch Tax Rev/Pop	0.0062	0.0014	0.0	0.058

Table of Correlations

	Pct Catholic	*Farm Income/Pop*	*Total Income/Pop*	*Alch Tax Rev/Pop*
Pct Catholic	1.0	–0.351	0.558	–0.154
Farm Income/Pop	×	1.0	–0.556	–0.0393
Total Income/Pop	×	×	1.0	0.00857
Alch Tax Rev/Pop	×	×	×	1.0

Panel (b): Repeal (1932, N=38)

Descriptive Statistics

Variable	Mean	Std Dev	Minimum	Maximum
Pct Catholic	14.53	11.77	0.0	46.5
Farm Income/Pop	132.0	95.94	14.71	499.43
Total Income/Pop	487.56	256.79	107.85	947.22
Alch Tax Rev/Pop	0.0031	0.0037	0.0	0.016

Table of Correlations

	Pct Catholic	*Farm Income/Pop*	*Total Income/Pop*	*Alch Tax Rev/Pop*
Pct Catholic	1.0	–0.141	0.696	–0.0151
Farm Income/Pop	×	1.0	–0.288	–0.130
Total Income/Pop	×	×	1.0	0.217
Alch Tax Rev/Pop	×	×	×	1.0

	Prohibition	*Repeal*	*Summary Explanation*
Pct Catholic:	Neg	Pos	Catholics generally did not support Prohibition, and even the Church hierarcy offered only lukewarm support.
Farm Income/Pop:	Pos	Neg	Rural states with high farm populations were more likely to support Prohibition. Farm communities were closer knit, and it was more difficult to take a public stand for alcohol.
Total Income/Pop:	???	???	Wealthy industrialists favored Prohibition. But income per capita in the state is an ambiguous measure of both economic interest and preference, if the wealthy believe alcohol is only a problem for lower classes.
Alch. Tax Rev/Pop	Neg (0)	Pos (Pos)	The more alcohol produced in the state, the greater the political to oppose Prohibition, and then to support Repeal. However, the subsidiary hypothesis is that produces were caught by surprise, and did not exert any effective pressure in the Prohibition process.
Female Suffrage	Pos	–	Women were more likely to favor Prohibition. More accurately, organized womens' groups were more likely to favor Prohibition.
Already Passed	Pos	–	States that only voted on Prohibition after it had been ratified were only making a symbolic gesture. Therefore, legislators were free to vote their public, or moral, consciences.

6. Discussion of results

The results of the three regressions are presented in Table 3. The overall performance of the models is satisfactory, with R^2s of .637, .529, and .66 respectively for the Lower Chamber, Upper Chamber (both Prohibition), and State Convention votes (on Repeal). The F-statistics indicate the models are highly significant in the aggregate, against the null hypothesis that all the estimated coefficients are zero.[17]

The specific hypotheses outlined in the previous section are largely supported as well.

Pct Catholic: States with high proportions of Catholic citizens appear somewhat less supportive of Prohibition (though the t-statistics for this relationship are only around 1.00). High Catholic states were *significantly* more supprotive of Repeal, however, as predicted.

Farm Income/Pop: States with relatively more farm income per capita were

Table 3. Regressions Comparing State Legislature Votes for Prohibition, and State Convention Votes for Repeal (*: .10 significance, **: .05 significance, 2-tailed tests).

	Prohibition Amendment				Repeal Amendment	
	Lower Chamber[a]		Upper Chamber[a]		Special Elections	
Variable	Coeff. Est.	t-stat	Coeff. Est.	t-stat	Coeff. Est.	t-stat
Intercept	0.92**	12.91	0.875**	10.89	0.584**	16.02
Pct Catholic	–0.00166	–1.00	–0.0020	–1.05	0.0042**	2.76
Farm Income/Pop	0.000231	1.17	0.00033	1.48	–2.9E-4**	7.12
Total Income/Pop	–0.0003**	–3.76	–0.0002**	–2.03	9.8E-5	1.32
Alch Tax Rev/Pop	1.540	1.018	1.741	1.019	11.74**	3.59
Female Suffrage	0.1087**	2.38	0.097	1.873	b	
Already Passed	–0.081*	–1.78	–0.108**	–2.103	b	
Dep Var Mean	0.803		0.823		0.708	
N	48		48		38	
F/R^2	11.96/.637		7.69/.529		15.99/.660	

[a]For the purposes of this study, Nebraska's unicameral assembly was double-counted, appearing in both the upper and lower chamber regressions.
[b]Both these dummy variables are inappropriate for the Repeal Amendment, and were omitted. Female Suffrage was universal after 1921, and no state conventions were formed after the Repeal Amendment was ratified.

somewhat more likely to have supported Prohibition, and much less likely to have supported Repeal, again as predicted.

Total Income/Pop: Interestingly, wealthy states (that is, with high income per capita) were strongly less supportive of Prohibition. They were also somewhat more favorable toward Repeal, though with a t-statistic of only 1.32.

Alch Tax Rev/Pop: The estimates for this variable are the most interesting in all of Table 3. Based on tax collections before Prohibition, producer states were if anything *more likely* to have favored Prohibition, though the relationship is not statistically significant. That is, producers were either not effectively organized, or there was a public backlash against saloons and manufacturers. The vote on Repeal, however, appears to indicate that producers had effectively organized by 1933. States that could expect to have more alcohol production after Repeal were much more likely to favor Repeal.

Female Suffrage: This dummy variable is defined only before the 19th Amendment, and so is used only in the Prohibition regressions. States where women could vote were significantly more supportive of Prohibition, as predicted. This effect, of course, could be attributable either to the direct effect of women voting, causing a different set of preferences to be represented, or ideological differences among states. That is, states that allowed women to vote before the 19th Amendment clearly had different ideas about how societies should be organized, so a dummy variable for one policy difference may simply be picking up this difference in political preferences overall.

Already Passed: Again, this dummy variable is only included for the Prohibition regressions. The logic of the prediction that the effect would be positive is based on the symbolic, or moralistic, nature of the debate. However, the effect is clearly negative and significant. Most of the states that voted late did, in fact, vote in favor of Prohibition; they just did so in lower proportions. An obvious explanation is that those states that voted late were generally opposed. What the dummy is picking up is this temporal order reflecting intensity of preference. It is quite possible that if this same state had voted earlier, it would actually have voted *against*.

Our results should be compared with those of a previous study, Hersch and Netter (1989). They considered prohibitions of alcohol by states, rather than state voting on the federal Prohibition Amendment, but they used several variables similar to ours, and obtained qualitatively similar results. In the Hersch and Netter work, "urbanization" was used to proxy for differences in taste and for concentations of hotel interests, which were of course very hostile to Prohibition. Our Total Income variable may be picking up parts of this effect. Their "female suffrage" dummy variable shows the same general effect as ours, but the t-statistics on their coefficient indicated only marginal statistical significance. The explanation for the difference may be that the Hersch and Netter sample considers state action across time: Their dependent variable is the "year of adoption" of state-level prohibition, using TOBIT to control for the fact that many states never adopted such a law. Because our sample examines cross-sectional variation in support, and the year of our sample is 1919, when female suffrage was an important issue, the effect may indeed have been more significant both substantively and statistically.

7. Conclusions

This paper has had many parts, and has tried to present a variety of evidence on the passage of the Prohibition and Repeal amendments. It is well summarize the historical argument we have made, and to assess the consistency of that argument with the results of the simple statistical model in Section 6.

The Prohibition Amendment passed in 1919, with overwhelming support in the U.S. Congress and the State Legislatures. Forty-five states ratified the Amendment, though only 36 were required to approve it for ratification to become official. Just 14 years later, the Amendment was repealed, again with overwhelming support. This is the only instance in U.S. history when an Amendment was passed and later repealed. Why, given the popular scepticism of constitutional tinkering, and the practical difficulties in passing Amendments, did this happen?

We have claimed that the personal preferences of citizens were relatively constant throughout the period, so the source of change is not simply that voters "changed their minds". No test of this claim was offered directly. We did, however, summarize the argument of Brennan and Lomasky (1993) that personal preferences and public positions may differ, so that changes in public positions in public positions may occur with no real preference shift. Because of the moralistic aspects of the arguments for Prohibition, it was possible for citizens to take public positions, or accept public positions of others, they did not stronlgy support.

This collective action problem by voters left the determination of policy to organized interests. The support for the Prohibition Amendment was organized around Protestant religious groups, groups working for womens' suffrage, manufactuers' groups hoping for a more productive labor force, and entrepreneurial bootleggers. These groups, operating in tacit alliance, achieved strategic suprise against the interests that, by rights, should have opposed Prohibition. Brewers, distillers, their employees appeared to believe that there was no real threat of Prohibition, until it was too late to mobilize. By the time Prohibition had passed, the financial resources available to producers were greatly reduced, and bootleggers depending on Prohibition for their livelihoods were well entrenched in key cities.

A decade later, much of the appeal of Prohibition had worn off, and the organized interests that had passed the amendment had broken up. The womens' suffrage movement had succeeded in passing the 19th Amendment. The Protestant-oriented "Progressive" reform groups of the early 1920s had changed electoral practices and municipal governments all over the country, and was likewise a victim of its own success. Enforcement of Prohibition proved largely impossible, because of the widespread desire for alcoholic beverages among citizens, and the enormous rents to satisfying those desires. Corruption was rampant in every level of the enforcement apparatus except (arguably) the federal government, breeding disrespect for the law and the legal system among citizens. Finally, the political entrepreneurs of the New Deal saw an opportunity for an infusion of tax revenues to finance their Keynesian stimulus programs.

Many of these factors are beyond our ability to measure, or to account for, in any systematic fashion. We were able to corroborate key parts of the argument, however. First, those states that already had womens' suffrage were actually more likely to support Prohibition, affirming the linkage between the womens' movement and political restrictions on alcohol. Second, the religion and per capita income proxies we used (Pct Catholic, Farm Income/Pop and

Total Income/Pop) did have significant effects, and attest to the power of moralistic arguments and paternalistic preferences in sumptuary restriction policies.

Finally, the economic interest of states in alcohol production *before* Prohibition had no effect on support for the 18th Amendment. This is quite consistent with the historical evidence we were able to find. In fact:

> Prior to ratification of the 18th Amendment . . . most brewers were confident that the federal government would remove the wartime restrictions on cereal beverages as soon as possible. August A. Busch himself believed the brewing ban would be readily lifted. (Plavchan, 1976, p. 151)

The revenues created by alcohol production immediately *after* Repeal are strongly correlated with support for repeal, however. This contrasting evidence (no effect on Prohibition, strong effect on Repeal) tends to confirm our main claim. Producers were surprised by the passage of Prohibition, but were eventually able to organize for Repeal.

In sum, Prohibition was not a political-economic equilibrium. Nonetheless, it survived for over a decade, and changed the course of American history. Further, the Prohibition "experiment" offers a clear instance of the disturbance-response pattern of classical interest group theory. For students of rent-seeking, however, it is clear that this classical model must be argumented. The most powerful force in the Repeal movement may well have been the desire of New Deal reformers to finance their programs. Alcohol, not then taxed but widely consumed, offered a chance for a substantial transfer from bootleggers and consumers to the federal coffers. This unrelated, but perhaps ultimately necessary force of an entrepreneurial, rent-seeking administration tipped the balance of interest group pressures. Without this coincidential alignment of historical forces, Prohibition might have lasted for decades.

Notes

1. For background on constitutional analysis using the techniques of economics, see Brennan and Buchanan (1985).
2. Named after former Attorney General George W. Wickersham, chair of the commission.
3. This desire for new tax revenues to finance programs designed to win votes is simple rent-seeking (Tullock, 1967; Krueger, 1974). For reviews of this literature see Tollison (1982), or Rowley, Tollison, and Tullock (1987).
4. "Barrels" were standardized at 31.5 gallons (25 imperial gallons), or one-half hogshead.
5. In the proposed resolution passed by Congress appeared language (underlined below) never seen before or since:

   SECTION 3. This article shall be inoperative unless it shall have been *ratified as an amendment to the Constitution by conventions in the several states, as provided in the*

> *Constitution*, with seven years from the date of the submission hereof to the States by the Congress.

Every other amendment has either contained no restriction on the means of ratification, or has specified the state legislatures as the focus of decision.

6. Rousseau was one of the first to elaborate a basis for a hierarchy of decision:

> There is but one law which, from its nature, needs unanimous consent. This is the social compact .... Apart from this primitive contract, the vote of the majority always binds all the rest. (Rousseau, 1974: Book IV, Chapter 2).
>
> There are two general rules that may serve to regulate [rules for choosing]. First, the more grave and important the questions discussed, the nearer should the opinion that is to prevail approach unanimity. Second, the more the matter in hand calls for speed, the smaller the prescribed difference in the number of votes may be allowed to become: where an instant decision has to be reached, a majority of one vote should be enough. (Rousseau, 1974, Book II, Chapter 2).

7. Carrie Nation (1846–1911) was an activist in the Womens' Christian Temperance Union. She carried a hatchet for chopping open barrels of beer and whiskey, and anyone who got in her way.
8. For an in-depth analysis of state-level interest group and voter preference effects on voting by legislators, see Hersch and McDougall (1988).
9. Sumptuary laws or practices restrict the amount, or content, of consumption decisions by citizens.
10. As of December 5, 1933, sixteen states were dry by statute (Alabama, Arkansas, Georgia, Iowa, Massachusetts, Michigan, Minnesota, Mississippi, Missouri, New Hampshire, North Carolina, North Dakota, South Carolina, Tennessee, Vermont, and Virginia), and thirteen were still dry by state constitutional restriction (Florida, Idaho, Kansas, Kentucky, Maine, Nebraska, Ohio, Oklahoma, South Dakota, Texas, Utah, West Virginia, and Wyoming).
11. See Plavchan (1976) and Cochran (1948).
12. The standard "free rider" explanation (Olson, 1965) may be sufficient to explain this failure to organize. On the other hand, we have argued that the power of the Drys' moralistic arguments about the preferences people *should* have actually resulted in a general Prisoner's Dilemma problem (Brennan and Lomasky, 1993), over and above the usual Olsonian collective action problems.
13. This figure was obtained by multiplying the majorities "for" Prohibition in the state lower chambers by the state populations for the first 36 states to pass the amendment.
14. Hersch and Netter (1989), and Toma (1988) examine micro-level motives in local polities for regulation of alcohol production and consumption.
15. Two other dependent variables were also analyzed, but were not included in this paper. The first was the vote by the states' Congressional delegation. The second was a logistic analysis of whether the state supported Ratification. In the first case, the regression analysis showed very little, quite likely due to the pathological variance structure of a proportion that can take only a few discrete values. The second omitted analysis closely replicate the regression on special elections included in the paper.
16. Several other states also held special elections on Repeal, but we were unable to find reliable data on the totals.
17. The reader intent on getting in touch with his or her "inner Grier" will have (at least) two questions at this point. We offer these observations in no particular order. First, it is quite true that the Prohibition regressions are run on a sample of 48 states, while the Repeal regressions are run on only 38. Could the differences in results be attributed simply to different samples? The answer is no: running the Lower Chamber regression (Prohibition) on the 38 state sample used for Repeal yields results very similar to those reported for Lower Chamber in Table 3. Second, both the Female Suffrage and Already Passed

dummies are really dummies for a set of states. Would estimating a separate intercept for these states have mattered in the Repeal regression? The answer is again no: both dummies are insignificant in the later Regression.

References

Bernstein, R.B. (1993). *Amending America.* New York: Random House.

Brennan, G. and Buchanan, J. (1985). *The reason of rules: Constitutional political economy.* New York: Cambridge University Press.

Brennan, G. and Lomasky, L. (1993). *Democracy and decision: The pure theory of electoral preference.* New York: Cambridge University Press.

Brown, E.S. (1978). *Ratification of the Twenty-First Amendment to the Constitution of the United States: State convention records and laws.* New York: Da Capo Press.

Buchanan, J. and Tullock, G. (1962). *The calculus of consent: Logical foundations of constitutional democracy.* Ann Arbor: University of Michigan Press.

Buchanan, J., Tollison, R. and Tullock, G. (1980). *Toward a theory of the rent-seeking society.* College Station: Texas A&M Press.

Cochran, T. (1948). *The Pabst Brewing Company.* New York: New York University Press.

Donovan, B. (1995). Framing and strategy: Explaining differential longevity in the Woman's Christian Temperance Union and the Anti-Saloon League. *Sociological Inquiry* 65: 143–155.

Goff, B. and Anderson, G. (1994). The political economy of prohibition in the United States, 1919–1933. *Social Science Quarterly* 75: 270–283.

Goldstein, J.H. (1973). *The effects of the adoption of Woman Suffrage.* New York: Praeger Press.

Haller, M.H. (1985). Bootleggers and businessmen. In D. Kyvig (Ed.), *Law, alcohol and order,* 139–158. Westport, CT: Greenwood Press.

Hersch, P.L. and Netter, J.M. (1989). State Prohibition of alcohol: An application of diffusion analysis to regulation. *Research in Law and Economics* 12: 55–70.

Hersch, P.L. and McDougall, G.S. (1988). Voting for "sin" in Kansas. *Public Choice* 57: 127–139.

Holcombe, R. (1994). *The economic foundations of government* New York: Publisher?

Kerr, K. 1985). *Austin organized for Prohibition.* New Haven: Yale University Press.

Kingsdale, J.M. (1973). The "Poor man's club": Social functions of the working class saloon, *American Quarterly* 25: 472–484.

Krueger, A. (1974). The political economy of a rent-seeking society. *American Economic Review* 64: 291–303.

Lutz, D.S. (1994). Toward a theory of constitutional amendment. *American Political Science Review* 88: 355–370.

McCormick, R. and Tollison, R. (1981). *Politicians, legislation, and the economy: An inquiry into the interest group theory of government.* Boston: Kluwer Academic Publishers.

Mitchell, W. and Munger, M. (1991). The economic theory of interest groups: An introductory survey. *American Journal of Political Science.* Vol. ?: pp. ?

Nelli, H. (1985). American syndicate crime. In D. Kyvig (Ed.), *Law, alcohol and order,* 123–138. Wesport, CT: Greenwood Press.

Olson, M. (1965). *The logic of collective action: Public goods and the theory of groups.* Cambridge, MA: Harvard University Press.

Ostrom, V. (1987). *The political theory of a compound republic.* 2nd edition. Lincoln: University of Nebraska Press.

Odegard, P. (1928). *Pressure politics: The story of the Anti-Saloon League.* New York: Columbia University Press.

Plavchan, R.J. (1976). *A history of Anheuser-Busch, 1852–1933* New York: Arno Press.
Rowley, C., Tollison, R. and Tullock, T. (1987). *The political economy of rent-seeking*. Boston, MA: Clair Academic.
Rumbarger, J. (1989). *Profits, power and Prohibition: Alcohol reform and the industrializing of America, 1800–1930.* Albany: SUNY Press.
Swindler, W. (1985). A dubious constitutional experiment. In D. Kyvig (Ed.), *Law, alcohol and order*, 53–66. Westport, CT: Greenwood Press.
Tollison, R. (1982). Rent-seeking: A survey. *Kyklos* 35: 525–602.
Toma, E. (1988). State Liquor Licensing, Implicit Contracting, and Dry/Wet Counties. *Economic Inquiry* 26: 507–524.
Tribe, L. (1995). How to violate the Constititution without really trying: Lessons from the Repeal of Prohibition to the balanced budget amendment. *Constitutional Commentary* 12: 217–221.
Truman, D. (1951). *The Governmental process: Political interest and public opinion.* New York: Knopf.
Tullock, G. (1967). The welfare costs of tariffs, monopolies, and theft. *Western Economic Journal* 5: 224–232.

Appendix: Article V (amendment process), and the 18th and 21st Amendments

Article V

The Congress, whenever two thirds of both Houses shall deem it necessary, shall propose amenments to this Constitution, or on the application of the legislature of two thirds of the several states, shall call a convention for proposing amendments, which, in either case, shall be valid to all intents and purposes, as part of this Constitution, when ratified by the legislatures of three fourths of the several States, or by conventions in three fourths thereof, as the one or the other mode of ratification may be proposed by the Congress . . . .[1]

Article XVIII

SECTION 1. After one year from the ratification of this article the manufacture, sale, or transportation of intoxicating liquors within, the importation thereof into, or th exportation thereof from the United States and all territory subject to the jurisdiction thereof for beverage purposes is hereby prohibited.

[1] The article continues: ". . . provided that no amendment which may be made prior to the year one thousand eight hundred and eight shall in nay manner affect the first and fourth clauses of in the Ninth section of the First article; and that no State, without its consent, shall be deprived of its equal suffrage in the Senate".

SECTION 2. The Congress and the several States shall have concurrent powers to enforce this article by appropriate legislation.

SECTION 3. This article shall be inoperative unless it shall have been ratified as an amendment to the Constitution by the legislatures of the several states, as provided in the Constitution, with seven years from the date of the submission hereof to the States by the Congress.

Article XXI

SECTION 1. The 18th article of amendment to the Constitution of the United States is hereby repealed.

SECTION 2. The transportation or importation into any State, Territory, or possession of the United States for delivery or use therein of intoxicating liquors, in violation of the laws thereof, is hereby prohibited.

SECTION 3. This article shall be inoperative unless it shall have been ratified as an amendment to the Constitution by conventions in the several states, as provided in the Constitution, with seven years from the date of the submission hereof to the States by the Congress.

Public Choice **90:** 165–184, 1997.

© 1997 *Kluwer Academic Publishers.*

Term limits and electoral competitiveness: Evidence from California's state legislative races*

KERMIT DANIEL[1] and JOHN R. LOTT, JR.[2]
[1]*The Wharton School, University of Pennsylvania, Philadelphia, PA 19104;* [2]*School of Law, University of Chicago, Chicago, IL 60637, U.S.A.*

Abstract. California's legislative term limits have dramatically reduced campaign expenditures. Real expenditures during the three general elections after the term limits initiative passed in 1990 were lower than in even 1976. This drop has occurred at the same time that races have become closer contests and more candidates are running for office. By any measure, term limits have coincided with large changes in the level of political competition, even before term limits have forcibly removed a single politician from office. The changes are so large that more incumbents are being defeated, races are closer, more candidates are running, and fewer single candidate races than occur at any other time during our sample period from 1976 to 1994.

1. Introduction

Term limits are not just binding during a politician's last year in a particular office. They also change the returns to political behavior during all earlier periods in a politician's career. Shorter terms seem likely to reduce the returns to campaign spending. Lower expenditures will undoubtedly affect other variables, such as a politician's stock of reputation, which has further implications for entry barriers. Making the date that incumbents leave office more certain encourages the entry by challengers even before the seat becomes vacant, if only to be better positioned once the incumbent does leave. Incumbents may also more frequently be pitted against politicians who hold other offices but who do not want to wait for the incumbents to retire, as these challengers may be facing the end of their terms. Reducing the importance of seniority may also lower the returns to running for reelection. Term limits may thus make elections more competitive even before politicians find them binding.

Economists have used historical continuation rates to predict the effect term limits will have on the composition of Congress (e.g., Reed and Schansberg, 1994 and 1995).[1] In particular, this work has asked how limits would

* We would like to thank Gertrud Fremling and Beth Garrett for their helpful comments. Jennifer Mayer and Michelle The also provided helpful research assistance.

affect expected tenure, and whether the limits would benefit Republicans or Democrats. While it is a reasonable first approximation to assume that past continuation rates will continue to apply during the years in which term limits are not binding, this paper points out that some of the more obvious predictions may have to be tempered. For example, though there is little doubt that term limits would produce large "superclasses" of freshman in legislatures, current estimates will be shown to overestimate their size. Reed and Schansberg (1995: 710) predict that a six year congressional term limit will produce a "superclass" of 309 freshman (71 percent), almost three times greater than the highest congressional turnover rate during the last 44 years. Yet, to the extent that term limits make incumbents more vulnerable prior to when the term limits become binding, the smaller will be this initial "superclass" and the faster we will see legislative retirements converging towards their long-term steady-state.

Other issues, such as how effectively legislatures operate, may turn on the answers to these preceding questions. For example, Garrett (1996: 60) points out that, "The certain prospect of large freshman classes at regular intervals would challenge the seniority system; indeed, supporters of term limits probably intend for the adoption of federal term limits to eviscerate the seniority system ...". Even if freshman classes do dominate for a while, it is not obvious whether this will be a long-term pattern. If not, the returns to seniority may increase in the future, albeit, even then in a much more limited form to what we currently observe. The main issue is whether term limits reduce tenure, and thus legislative experience, by more than the direct limit imposed.

Despite the Supreme Court decision in *U.S. Term Limits, Inc* v. *Thornton*, that state imposed limits are unconstitutional, the debate seems very much alive. Term limit supporters are threatening more congressional votes on a constitutional amendment, and if that fails, they promise to force the issue by using the states to call for a constitutional convention. Twenty-one states now also have term limits for state legislators.[2] Unfortunately, only very limited evidence currently exists on whether term limits will enhance electoral competition (Lott, 1995). While state legislative term limits only started being passed in 1990, with initiatives in California and Oklahoma, no legislators will be forced from office until this year; nevertheless reductions in the value of holding office should already be influencing the behavior of legislators and their opponents. This paper analyzes California state assembly and senate races between 1976 and 1994 to examine the effect of term limits on four areas: campaign expenditures, the closeness of races, the number of candidates running for office, and whether candidates run unopposed.

2. The theory

2.1. *Limited property rights, entry barriers, and the timing of when to run for office*

The value of a political office depends upon what can be achieved by controlling it and how long lived the property rights to it are. This rent-seeking view of political competition holds that offices with longer terms are more valuable, and more time and money will be spent to obtain them. Crain and Tollison (1977) provide some suggestive cross-sectional evidence that campaign expenditures are greater for gubernatorial elections to serve four year terms than two year terms, though their results imply that two 2-year terms produce greater total expenditures than one four year term. More recent evidence using state level time-series cross-sectional data from gubernatorial and state house and senate races confirms their ealier findings (Lott, 1995).

One possible explanation for why two 2-year terms are more valuable than one 4-year term is that there are diminishing returns to creating transfers, and that when a politician is elected the transfers with the greatest marginal return are made first. The second 2-year term would thus not be worth as much as the first 2-year term, and the return to getting one's favorite politician into office for four years is not worth twice as much as getting one in there for two years. Two consecutive two-year terms are worth more because the group that values producing transfers the most during each period has an opportunity to win office.[3] By tending to produce the highest valued transfers, two two-year terms should increase the return to, and thus the level of, campaign expenditures. Jung et al. (1994) provide evidence supporting a similar explanation for why voters do not elect identically voting senators from the same state. Their explanation focuses on how obtaining wealth transfers reduces successful constituencies' returns to obtaining additional transfers through electing another senator to represent them.

The discussion of term limits is slightly more complicated than simply increasing the length of a term, since there is some chance of being defeated between terms. If the probability that a candidate wins the first election is independent of the probability that he will win the second election, campaign expenditures should not depend upon the presence of term limits. Alternatively, if the preceding notion of diminishing marginal returns to creating transfers were the entire story, the probability of winning the first and second elections would even be negatively correlated. Yet, the investments made in political reputations during the first race do positively effect the probability of winning later elections. It is also important to note that political reputations are nontransferable to the extent that it is a politician's preferences which guarantee his performance (Lott, 1987b). Term limits then effectively act as a tax on campaign expenditures because the politician's specific investments would be lost when the term limit becomes binding, and they will discourage rent seeking from taking the form of campaign expenditures. Obviously, politicians can still run for other offices and thus preserve at least some of this investment, though there is undoubtedly a higher probability of being defeated when switching offices as the constituents and issues faced in different offices are not always identical.

Though they make a different argument, Crain and Tollison also found some weak evidence that restricting the number of successive terms a governor could hold office reduces campaign expenditures (see also Besley and Case, 1995b: 793). However, Crain and Tollison's (1977) cross-sectional study was limited by not controlling for other factors which could affect the level of campaign expenditures. More recent evidence using state level time-series cross-sectional confirms both the effect of term limits and term lengths on expenditures (Lott, 1995).

While California's term limits do not actually remove politicians from office until 1996, it should have begun to impact the returns to campaign expenditures when it passed in 1990, or possibly even before to the extent that they were anticipated. Proposition 140, limiting members of the California Assembly to three 2-year terms and State Senators to two 4-year terms passed by a relatively close 52 to 48 percent vote in the November 1990 general election. The uncertainty over whether the initiative would pass and, to a lesser extent, questions over whether the California Supreme Court would find it constitutional should have limited the impact of the initiative on the 1990 election.

If term limits do reduce campaign expenditures, the effects are not limited to just a particular term. Past investments in a candidate's reputation lower his costs of raising future campaign funds and reduce the return to campaign spending. Past reputations also make it harder for opponents to mount successful challenges. This last point involves the issue of entry barriers in political markets: to the extent that political reputations are nontransferable, past investments in reputation can produce differential costs of production between challengers and incumbents in producing political support. For U.S. Congressional races, previous studies (Lott, 1987b and 1989) indicate that a politician's past campaign expenditures raise his current campaign expenditures and lower his opponent's expenditures.[4] In the short run, reductions in campaign expenditures will favor incumbents who have acquired a stock of reputation. The larger is an incumbent's preexisting reputational stock, the greater the relative advantage produced by the incumbent from similar reductions in current expenditures by both incumbents and challengers.[5] If these effects continue over time as term limits eliminate incumbents with larger pre-1990 campaign expenditures (and thus a larger stock of political reputation), the difference between the incumbent's and the challenger's reputational investments should decline. Thus, we should observe future races becoming more competitive.

The effect of term limits should also vary across incumbents based upon when they entered office. A reduction in a politician's reputational stock from lower current expenditures is likely to be greatest for political newcomers. Politicians entering prior to 1990 should be relatively less vulnerable to any effect term limits have.

Term limits also obviously change the timing of a candidate's decision to run for office. An ambitious politician can challenge an incumbent, though that is obviously a relatively risky strategy. However, just as incumbents can acquire reputational investments from past campaign expenditures, so too can challenger. Prior to term limits challengers might ideally have wanted to run for office against an incumbent despite near-certain defeat to position themselves should the incumbent choose to retire. In the past, the difficulty with this was that the incumbent may have chosen to remain in office longer than anticipated by the challenger, and any reputational investments made by the challenger would thus depreciate before the incumbent eventually does leave office. While politicians do sometimes announce when a particular election will be their last (e.g., Lott, 1987a), it is relatively unusual. Making the date that incumbents must leave office by more certain (through term limits), may encourage challengers to enter into races before the seat actually becomes vacant.

A politician's returns to campaign expenditures systematically change over the course of the politician's tenure, though short-term limits will compress these changes. If politicians leave public life after reaching the term limit and if campaign expenditures do not depreciate instantly, incumbents will have a relatively lower return to investing in campaign near the ends of their terms since they will have fewer terms over which to recoup any investment. If term limited politicians run for other offices, the scenario becomes more complicated as campaign spending will be useful for future campaigns. However, there is still one difference limiting the returns to earlier campaign spending for the politician planning to run for another office: the constituency for the possible future office will be different. Thus term limits should definitely reduce the return to campaign expenditures.

Although not yet extremely relevant for the time period that we study, there is still another reason to suspect that term limits will increase electoral competition. A politician facing term limits may no longer be able to wait until the incumbent for the next office that he plans on moving to leaves. Experienced politicians "kicked out" by term limits thus will challenge and occasionally defeat other incumbents sooner than those incumbents would have been removed through term limits. This problem is further compounded since the terms for California's Assembly and Senate seats do not match up particularly well. For example, a member of the Assembly may not have to leave until 1996, but if the Senate seat he desires is only open in 1994 and 1998, he may feel compelled to run in 1994 and thus vacate his office early.[6]

One serious caveat should be mentioned. Removing long-serving politicians is not necessarily the same thing as increasing "efficiency". Tenure can also be related to higher reelection rates simply because those politicians who differ from their constituents' interests are most likely to have been defeated already. Sorting by voters of their desired representatives could produce similar results to entry barriers with respect to either tenure or past campaign expenditures. The explanation for tenure is obvious. The longer incumbents survive the closer they may be to their constituents' values and the lower the probability that a challenger would be preferred. Incumbents who do deviate from their constituents may thus be sorted out of office quickly, and while no evidence yet exists for state level offices, recent studies for both the U.S. Senate (Lott and Davis, 1992) and the U.S. House of Representatives (Lott and Bronars, 1993) indicate that this sorting does occur extremely quickly. Likewise, the higher an incumbent's past campaign expenditures, the lower might be his costs of raising future expenditures simply because constituents are better matched with the preferred candidate and face a greater loss if represented by somebody else.[7]

Term limits can also weaken the effectiveness of electoral sorting. If running for office requires a large initial sunk investment, politicians who more closely match the positions of their voters are more likely to run because they face a longer expected horizon over which to recoup this investment. In the extreme, it may only pay for those politicians whose views perfectly match their constituents to run in the first place (Lott and Reed, 1989). Yet, even though politicians can run for other offices after they reach their term limits, as long as politicians are not able to transfer all of their investment between elected offices (e.g., the offices encompass different districts) or as long as they face a higher probability of being defeated whenever they switch offices, term limits will weaken those forces which discourage "mismatched" politicians from running for office.

The bottom line for this discussion is that term limits will reduce campaign expenditures, but the effect that reduction has on how competitive races will be is, at least in the short run, somewhat more ambiguous. In the short run the effects can go either way with the entry barrier story possibly making races less competitive if incumbents have large stocks of reputation. In the longer run, even the entry barrier story tends to work towards increasing electoral competition.

2.2. *Other factors that determine the level of campaign expenditures and political competition*

Other papers have suggested factors that explain the levels of campaign contributions/expenditures. For example, Snyder (1990, 1992) has dealt with how past investments in reputation influence future contributions and how these actions vary over a politician's life cycle. Lott (1987b, 1989) has asked the same questions regarding expenditures. While Snyder finds that contributions decline with age and Lott shows that higher past expenditures by an incumbent reduces his opponent's expenditures and both look at the effect of tenure, no implications were drawn for how total campaign expenditures have been changing over time.

Following this literature, we assume that campaign expenditures are a function how close elections are expected to be, and the characteristics of the incumbent which involves both questions of sorting and entry barriers. This paper attempts to control for the expected closeness by measuring the closeness of the incumbent's past elections, whether the election is contested, and whether an incumbent is running for reelection. Issues of entry barriers and sorting are measured by including variables for tenure and the incumbent's past campaign expenditures, though these past campaign expenditures will not be used in all the regressions because this reduces our sample size by about 20 percent.

Campaign finance rules also changed during the period. In June 1988, Californians passed Proposition 73 which imposed Federal style campaign donation restrictions on candidates for state office (a $1,000 limit on individual contributions to candidates for state office, a $2,500 limit on contributions from political action committees, and a $5,000 limit on contributions by political parties). The rules went into effect on 1 January 1989, but were overturned by a U.S. District Court decision in September 1990 and were thus in effect for only part of one election cycle (Rabin, 1988: part 2, p. 4 and Stansky, 1992: 1). To control for this all the specifications include a dummy variable that equals one for the 1990 election. To the extent that these rules make it more costly to raise donations, campaign expenditures will be reduced. One problem with interpreting any result with this dummy variable is that term limits also passed in 1990 and will also have the same effect campaign expenditures. However, term limits and campaign donation limits are likely to have the opposite effects on making campaigns competitive. Most work by economists and political scientists argue that campaign donation limits raise the costs of challengers running for office relative to that for incumbents.

Redistricting, which occurred during both 1982 and 1992, results in established candidates facing new constituents and sometimes results in forcing incumbents to run against each other. Presumably, to the extent that the normal advantages of incumbency are weakened by incumbents facing new constituents, it will encourage new and possibly stronger than normal candidates to run for office. Any differences in state senate versus state assembly races and whether the race is a general or primary election must also be controlled for. Nor only do the two bodies have different numbers of seats and different constitutional responsibilities (in other words, there are different values to holding a seat in the different chambers), but their terms are of different lengths. In addition, just as altruism may be important in explaining why people vote, it may also explain the level of campaign donations. Presumably, higher campaign contributions include the possibility that giving to campaigns is like giving to charitable organizations in that it increases with income (e.g., Roberts, 1984). However, the existing evidence linking campaign contributions and income is inconsistent across stories (Snyder, 1992; Lott, 1987b, 1995).

Finally, we recognize the possibility of technological change. Over the time studied, innovations include computers, polling, and mass mailings. While the paper does not include specific variables that reflect such changes since neither measures of how much district level campaigns spent on different portions of their campaigns nor indexes of these costs are available, it is hoped that the district dummies and either a time trend or year dummies will proxy for these changes. If changes in campaign techniques are disseminated and adopted quickly across districts, the year dummies should pick up any effects that may exist. We are less concerned about identifying what changes in campaign technology may have affected expenditures than we are about making sure that term limits are not accidentally proxying for some left out effects. A separate dummy variable that only equals one in 1982 and 1992 is used to help us pick up any increased competition resulting from redistricting.

3. Data

Our data set consists of all the California State Assembly and Senate general and primary elections involving Democrats and/or Republicans that occurred between 1976 and 1994. Unfortunately, time limitations prevented us from including data from the 1994 primary elections, and the California Fair Political Practices Commission no longer had records for expenditures during the 1978 general elections. Each general and primary election represents a separate observation. Thus most offices involve 3 observations during each election cycle (one general election and two primary elections, one Repub-

Table 1. List of variables and descriptive statistics

Variable name	Description	Mean	S.D.
Margin	Margin of victory in primary and general elections	69.63	36.63
Lagged margin incumbent	Margin of victory by the current incumbent in the last similar type of election	49.01	44.29
ln (Lagged margin incumbent)	Margin of victory by the current incumbent in the last similar type of election	3.959	0.9473
Incumbent dummy	Equals one if there is an incumbent in the race	0.564	0.4959
Unopposed dummy	Equals one if there is only one candidate in the race	0.561	0.4964
Incumbent's tenure	Incumbents tenure in number of years (mean for years 1982–94)	4.6086	4.901
Presidential year dummy	Equals one if it is a presidential election year	0.4986	0.5001
Total district campaign expenditures	Total campaign expenditures by type of election in 1982 dollars	94,970.77	200,666.70
Number of major party candidates	The total number of major party candidates running for office in either a general or primary election in a particular district	1.382	1.135

Sources:
Primary election results
California Secretary of State, *Statement of Vote and Supplement Primary Election*, 8 June 1976; 6 June 1978; 5 June 1984; and 3 June 1986.
Los Angeles Times, 8 June 1978; 5 June 1980; 9 June 1982; 10 June 1982; 9 June 1988; 7 June 1990; and 4 June 1992.

General election results
California Secretary of State, *Statement of Vote and Supplement Election*, 7 November 1978
California Secretary of State, *Statement of Vote General Election*, 2 November 1976; 4 November 1980; 2 November 1982; 6 November 1984; 4 November 1986; 8 November 1988; 6 November 1990; and 3 November 1992.

Campaign expenditures California Fair Political Practices Commission, *Campaign Contribution and Spending Reports*. State of California: Sacramento, CA, various years.

lican and one Democrat). Tenure was calculated only from the 1974. The variable and their sources are listed in Table 1.

4. The results

4.1. *Campaign expenditures*

1996 is shaping up as an important year for campaign finance reform in California. One or possibly two ballot initiatives are scheduled to appear on the

November ballot that propose to dramatically limit campaign expenditures for legislative and statewide offices (Sacramento Bee News Service, 28 February 1996). When California first passed intitiatives limiting campaign spending in 1988, State Assembly and Senate general election races averaged costing \$345,218 in real 1982 dollars and had reached their peak in real terms. As the following regressions show, the irony of these new campaign finance initiatives is that term limits have already greatly reduced campaign expenditures in California. By 1992 and 1994, the first two full election campaigns to take place after term limits had passed, State Assembly and Senate general election races had fallen to \$232,805 in real 1982 dollars. Real campaign expenditures for the three general elections from 1984 to 1988 averaged \$309,144, or 44 percent higher than the \$215,019 spent on the three general elections that took place after the term limits initiative passed.

To systematically test the effect of term limits on campaign expenditures, a dummy variable is added to all our regressions that equals one for the 1992 and 1994 election cycles. The simple specifications in Table 2 attempt to explain the total level of a district's campaign expenditures in the general and primary elections. It includes exogenous variables on the expected closeness of the race: whether there is an incumbent in the race, lagged margins by which the incumbent has won the district in either the primary or general election, whether the incumbent is unopposed, the incumbent's tenure, and whether redistricting has occurred. Other exogenous variables are: per capita state income, dummy variables to distinguish general from primary elections and whether it is an Assembly or Senate race, a time trend, and a dummy variable for 1990. Total campaign expenditures includes expenditures by all candidates in either the general or primary elections. There are two sets of specifications. One that distinguishes whether the endogenous variable for total expenditures is in natural logs or not and another breakdown by whether the squared values of lagged vote margin and tenure are used. We have no strong beliefs about whether these variables enter in linearly in the specifications so it is best to report both sets of results.

One very strong conclusion can readily be drawn from Table 2: there was a definite break in the growth of campaign expenditures that probably started in 1990, but had definitely occurred by 1992 and 1994. The most surprising finding is how extremely large the effect is. The results imply that the 1992 and 1994 drop in campaign expenditure offset between 7.5 (specification 1) and 9.4 (specification 4) election cycles worth of growth in campaign expenditures. Given that the data only encompasses 10 election cycles, specifications 3 and 4 imply a reduction in expenditures that puts us just back before the very beginning of our sample. If fact, real general election

Table 2. Campaign expenditures and term limits (OLS is used to produce these estimates and State Assembly and Senate district dummies were included in all specifications. All dollars are in real 1982 dollars. Absolute t-statistics are in parentheses)

Exogenous variables	Endogenous variables: ln (Total district campaign expenditures)		Total district campaign expenditures	
	(1)	(2)	(3)	(4)
Term limit dummy 1992–94	−1.2013	−1.2535	−132248.2	−134124.4
	(4.623)	(4.776)	(3.859)	(3.889)
Dummy 1990	−1.10827	−1.1300	−140133.1	−133537.6
	(1.795)	(1.828)	(1.714)	(1.638)
Time trend	0.15955	0.1594	15278.16	14344.51
	(2.762)	(2.759)	(1.992)	(1.876)
Lagged margin incumbent	−.00213	−.01728	−337.05	−4614.63
	(1.241)	(2.103)	(1.494)	(4.259)
Lagged margin incumbent sq.	...	.00013	...	36.98172
		(1.905)		(4.050)
Unopposed	−.78149	−.7767	−61908.63	−62670.14
	(7.357)	(7.307)	(4.499)	(4.566)
Presidential year dummy	0.1888	0.17275	23361.2	21595.52
	(1.357)	(1.241)	(1.299)	(1.204)
Incumbent dummy	−.1641	−.2235	−28273.52	−50901.05
	(0.913)	(0.938)	(1.195)	(1.624)
Incumbent's tenure	0.00928	−.04686	2782.98	−794.818
	(2.619)	(1.071)	(1.433)	(0.142)
Incumbent's tenure squared	...	.00358	...	251.2856
		(1.428)		(0.796)
Redistricting year dummy	−.59429	−.4500	−70517.07	−30948.57
	(2.184)	(1.735)	(1.971)	(0.865)
Per capita income at state level	−.00017	−.00016	−8.0890	−5.7393
	(1.275)	(1.229)	(0.456)	(0.325)
Senate dummy	1.16869	1.1247	296860	294291
	(1.647)	(1.585)	(3.121)	(3.104)
General election dummy	.06634	0.7552	62991.26	84030.7
	(5.228)	(5.701)	(3.768)	(4.829)
Intercept	12.3214	12.2025	120518.2	78489
	(5.789)	(5.736)	(0.427)	(0.279)
Number of obs. =	1749	1749	1841	1841
F-statistic =	4.32	4.31	4.78	4.88
Adj. R^2 =	.1979	.2000	.2107	.2178

expenditures in 1976 were $245,613, about $30,000 more than the 1992–94 average.

With the exception of specification 1, the economic importance of the 1992–94 dummy is larger than the dummy for 1990. Again, as noted earlier, the 1990 year dummy is somewhat difficult to interpret because the term limit initiative was not passed until November 1990 and, also, because the 1990 election cycle was the only time that campaign donations were limited by law. The coefficient for 1990 is very similar in size to the drops in spending implied by the term limit dummy. However, it is difficult to know what if any of the reduction in expenditures one can attribute to the temporary change in campaign finance laws.

Given that the court decision invalidating Proposition 73's limits on campaign was delivered in September, 1990 and that the initiative was passed in November, 1990, we tried rerunning the all regressions presented in this paper with a term limit dummy that equalled one starting with the 1990 general election. The 1990 year dummy equalled one only for the primary election. The results remained very similar to those presented here with the exception that the new 1990 year dummy was never statistically significant. These results indicate that the campaign donation limits were not the driving force behind any drops in campaign expenditures during 1990.

Overall the results are consistent with what the theory predicts, though the coefficients are not always significant. The greater the incumbent's victory margin in past elections, the less that is spent in the current election (though there are diminishing returns to that effect). As expected, more money is spent in State Senate races and in general elections. Less money is spent by incumbents, and less is spent when there is only one candidate in a race. The most surprising results are that redistricting either has no significant effect or a negative and significant effect on campaign expenditures, tenure is not significantly related to expenditures, and that per capita income is never both positively and significantly related to campaign expenditures. It would be interesting to see whether this last effect continues even when constituency income by district is also controlled for.

Table 3 puts the effect of term limits in equally sharp contrast. In this table, we use yearly dummy variables instead of a time trend to control for other factors that might account for changing campaign expenditures over time. All the other variables that were controlled for in Table 2 are again controlled for here though they are not reported since the results are extremely similar to those already reported. While many of the year dummies are signficant, only the term limit dummy is negative and significant. All of the term limit dummies imply economically large drops in campaign expenditures of over $100,000.

Table 3. Campaign expenditures and term limits: Using year dummies for 1978 to 1990 instead of a time trend (Specifications 1 through 4 use OLS and correspond to their number counterparts in Table 2. The same variables that were controlled for in Table 2 are controlled for here with the exception of year dummy variable for redistricting years. Some year dummies were dropped because of collinearity. State Assembly and Senate district dummies included in all specifications. All dollars are in real 1982 dollars. Absolute t-statistics are in parentheses)

Exogenous Variables	Endogenous variables ln (Total district campaign expenditures) (1)	(2)	Total district campaign expenditures (3)	(4)
Term limit dummy 1992–94	–.8012	–.8627	–108033	–115667.8
	(5.995)	(6.311)	(6.231)	(6.551)
Year dummy 1990	0.9098	0.8833	–3552.24	–4779.02
	(4.119)	(4.000)	(0.144)	(0.194)
Year dummy 1988	Dropped due to collinearity		Dropped due to collinearity	
Year dummy 1986	0.5478	0.5423	Dropped due to collinearity	
	(2.326)	(2.301)		
Year dummy 1984	0.2980	0.3018	21004.82	20662.22
	(1.515)	(1.537)	(0.798)	(0.788)
Year dummy 1982	0.36247	0.3510	–36121.8	–37607.6
	(1.701)	(1.643)	(1.418)	(1.482)
Year dummy 1980	Dropped due to collinearity		Dropped due to collinearity	
Year dummy 1978	Dropped due to collinearity		–61707.82	–56804.22
			(1.980)	(1.701)
Intercept	7.10805	8.459	–302497.7	–321696.4
	(7.848)	(9.966)	(2.323)	(1.827)
Number of obs. =	1749	1749	1841	1841
F-statistic =	4.29	4.28	4.75	4.85
Adj. R^2 =	.1977	.1997	.2106	.2177

Finally, while we have attempted to control for the incumbent's stock of brand name capital through such things as tenure, this is a relatively imperfect measure. Table 4 attempts to control this stock by using the depreciated stock of past campaign expenditures over the two preceding election cycles. This variable is controlled for separately because including it reduces our sample size by over 300 observations. While Table 4 only reports the results using a 20 percent annual depreciation rate, we also ran regressions with depreciation rates of 10, 30, and 40 percent, but the results were all very similar to those shown in Table 2. The regressions show that the larger the incumbent's depreciated stock of campaign spending the greater current total campaign spending. Specifications 3 and 4 imply that a one dollar increase in

Table 4. Campaign expenditures and term limits: Rerunning the specifications in Table 2 by including a term for each incumbent's depreciated brand name capital using a 20-percent depreciation rate (Specifications 1 through 4 use OLS and correspond to their number counterparts in Table 2. While the results for the other variables are not reported, the same variables that were controlled for in Table 2 are controlled for here. Again, State Assembly and Senate district dummies included in all specifications. All dollars are in real 1982 dollars. Absolute t-statistics are in parentheses)

Exogenous variables	Endogenous variables: ln (Total district campaign expenditures)		Total district campaign expenditures	
	(1)	(2)	(3)	(4)
Term limit dummy 1992–94	−1.20236 (4.168)	−1.2742 (4.367)	−133196.1 (3.580)	−137049.5 (3.655)
Dummy 1990	−1.1799 (1.640)	−1.0743 (1.491)	−158906.4 (1.705)	−132964.7 (1.428)
Time trend	0.1585 (2.394)	0.1494 (2.254)	15135.67 (1.761)	12805.11 (1.492)
Incumbent's depreciated past campaign exp.	3.38e-7 (1.672)	3.44e-7 (1.702)	.1202 (4.782)	0.1215 (4.856)
Number of obs. =	1415	1415	1498	1498
F-statistic =	3.66	3.69	4.84	4.91
Adj. R^2 =	.1980	.2018	.2514	.2584

this depreciated stock of past expenditures raises that total current spending by about 12 cents.

4.2. *The probability that an incumbent will be defeated*

While term limits are expected to make incumbents more vulnerable in the long run, the short-term effects are more ambiguous. For example, while challengers may be induced to run before the term limits become binding simply to be well positioned for when the incumbent leaves, initial entry barriers are likely to be even greater than usual because current campaign expenditures are reduced without reducing the large stock of reputations incumbents have acquired. Which effects dominate in the short run can only be answered empirically. Table 5 attempts to answer that question by running a dummy variable for whether an incumbent was defeated on the variables used in Table 2 (with the exceptions of the dummy for unopposed incumbents and the state income variable). The logit regressions are restricted to only those observations where an incumbent is running for reelection and the specifications use both the time trend and the individual year dummy variables to explain the changes in the probability.

Table 5 implies that the probability of incumbents being defeated fell from at least 1980 to 1988 and then rose dramatically during 1990, 1992, and 1994. The results using the time trend imply that the 1992 and 1994 increase in the probability that incumbents will be defeated offset between 15.7 (specification 1) and 13.8 (specification 2) election cycles worth of decline in that probability. Given that the data only encompasses 10 election cycles, these two specifications imply an increase in the probability that incumbents will be defeated that is outside our sample period. The specifications 3 and 4 using the year dummy variables implied a less dramatic those still strong result: term limit increased the probability of incumbents being defeated back to where it had been in 1980.

Given the very short-lived nature of Proposition 73's campaign donation limits and that the probability of incumbents being defeated was between 14 and 37 percent higher in 1992 and 1994 than 1990, it appears very difficult to attribute much if any of the drop in reelection rates to the campaign donation limits. If anything, the results weakly suggest the reverse occurring: that term limits lowered the probability, but not by as much as would have occurred without the donation limits. This result is also consistent with much of the political science and public choice literatures that view donation limits as making it relatively more difficult for challengers than incumbents to raise money.

The other coefficients have signs that are consistent with our earlier discussion, but they are not always significant. Incumbents who did well in previous elections have a lower probability of being defeated, though this effect increases at a decreasing rate. Incumbent's tenure significantly reduces the probability that an incumbent will be defeated, though this declines at a decreasing rate. State senators and those running in the general election both face higher probabilities of being defeated. Redistricting and presidential elections raise the probability of an incumbents being defeated, though only in one specification is one of these coefficients significant.

4.3. *The number of major party candidates, vote margins, and whether candidates run unopposed*

Table 6 presents other evidence on the increased legislative competition that has arisen under term limits, and the results are consistent with those in the preceding section and our theoretical discussion. The regressions use the same specifications that we used earlier except that the dummy for whether candidates are running unopposed is excluded from the first and fourth regressions since those regressions are themselves attempting to explain the number

Table 5. Term limits and the probability that an incumbent will be defeated (Logit regressions were used to explain a dummy variable that equalled one when an incumbent was defeated. The sample is restricted to only those observations where an incumbent was running for reelection in either the primary or general elections. Though they are not reported, the same variables that were controlled for in Table 2 are controlled for here. Again, State Assembly and Senate district dummies included in all specifications. All dollars are in real 1982 dollars. Absolute z-statistics are in parentheses)

	Endogenous variable: Whether incumbent was defeated			
Exogenous variables	(1)	(2)	(3)	(4)
Term limit	2.8097	2.0601	1.0215	0.8289
dummy 1992–94	(3.007)	(2.086)	(2.350)	(1.873)
Dummy 1990	2.0512	1.7657	0.8999	0.71157
	(2.878)	(2.257)	(1.477)	(1.040)
Time trend	–.1793	–.14897	...	...
	(2.161)	(1.721)		
Year dummy 1988	...	...	–1.4734	–1.0414
			(1.612)	(1.221)
Year dummy 1986	...	...	–.93819	–.93179
			(1.078)	(1.017)
Year dummy 1984	...	...	–.8193	–1.2763
			(1.048)	(1.520)
Year dummy 1982	...	...	Dropped due to collinearity	
Year dummy 1980	...	...	0.9928	0.65817
			(1.648)	(1.041)
Year dummy 1978	...	...	Dropped due to collinearity	
Lagged margin	–.0114	–.0554	–.01160	–.05627
incumbent	(2.178)	(2.224)	(2.190)	(2.237)
Lagged margin	...	0.0004	...	0.0004
incumbent sq.		(1.853)		(1.849)
Presidential	0.6748	0.90977	0.51296	0.9326
year dummy	(1.612)	(2.063)	(1.051)	(1.774)
Redistricting	0.2741	0.40096	0.6472	0.6313
year dummy	(0.658)	(0.922)	(1.478)	(1.348)
Incumbent's	–.1107	–.6543	–.11460	–.6835
tenure	(2.331)	(4.945)	(2.388)	(4.987)
Incumbent's	...	0.0334	...	0.034999
tenure squared		(4.386)		(4.406)
Senate dummy	18.3647	16.473	18.376	17.453
	(10.264)	(6.407)	(11.436)	(6.663)
General election	0.4377	1.1723	0.4820	1.2269
dummy	(1.128)	(2.541)	(1.223)	(2.616)
intercept	–18.1459	–16.0628	–20.35	–18.769
	(6.997)	(6.464)	(9.695)	(8.099)
Number of obs. =	846	846	846	846
Log likelihood =	–162.98	–146.65	–160.37	–143.42
Chi-squared =	107.23	139.89	112.44	146.33
Pseudo R^2 =	.2475	.3229	.2596	.3378

Table 6. Term limits, the number of major party candidates, vote margins, and whether candidates run unopposed (OLS is used for the first three specifications and a logit specification is used for the fourth. State Assembly and Senate district dummies are included in all specifications. All dollars are in real 1982 dollars. Absolute t-statistics are in parentheses)

Exogenous variables	Endogenous variables Number of major party candidates (1)	Absolute vote margin between top two candidates (2)	ln (Absolute vote margin between top two candidates) (3)	Dummy variable equalling in only one candidate in race (4)
Term limit	0.2666	–4.3199	–.2084	–.4406
dummy 1992–94	(2.684)	(3.070)	(3.102)	(1.584)
Dummy 1990	0.0715	–4.1463	–.1686	0.03116
	(0.861)	(3.533)	(3.010)	(0.128)
Time trend	–.0160	0.0867	0.0081	0.0030
	(1.836)	(0.701)	(1.670)	(1.321)
Redistricting	0.0456	–1.5382	–.0357	–.1073
year dummy	(0.889)	(2.115)	(–1.028)	(0.739)
Lagged margin	–.00212	0.02798	0.0004	–.0030
incumbent	(2.623)	(2.452)	(0.737)	(1.228)
Unopposed	...	68.3369	1.4871	...
		(95.223)	(43.403)	
Presidential	0.0205	–.07829	–.00578	–.11936
year dummy	(0.447)	(0.120)	(0.186)	(0.892)
Incumbent	–.4880	3.1412	0.2229	1.5963
dummy	(5.983)	(2.708)	(4.026)	(6.015)
Incumbent's	0.0007	0.07575	0.0025	0.0147
tenure	(0.114)	(0.823)	(0.577)	(0.776)
Senate dummy	–.3453	–6.4917	–.47717	0.15599
	(0.998)	(1.329)	(2.047)	(0.142)
General election	0.33566	1.5615	0.1226	–4.4633
dummy	(6.526)	(1.811)	(2.979)	(19.960)
Intercept	1.94659	27.4718	2.8897	1.2373
	(8.561)	(8.459)	(18.635)	(1.614)
Number of obs. =	2338	2325	2325	2338
F-statistic or Chi-square =	3.34	126.73	27.36	1215.76
Adj. R^2 or Pseudo R^2 =	.1138	.8747	.5941	.3757

of candidates. Term limits appear to have dramatically reversed weak time trends indicating that the number of major party candidates in races were falling, races were becoming less close, and more races involved just a single candidate. Imposing limits increases the number of major party candidates by 24 percent of a standard deviation, decreases the vote margin in elections by 10 to 22 percent of a standard deviation, and decreases the number of races where there is only one candidate by 89 percent of a standard deviation. As with the earlier results, all these regressions imply that term limits produce more electoral competition than existed earlier during the entire sample period. These four specifications were also rerun with year dummies and with the squared values of the lagged vote margins for incumbents and tenure, and they resulted in very similar results.

5. Conclusion

California's legislative term limits have dramatically reduced campaign expenditures, while at the same time that more candidates are running for office and races are becoming more competitive. By any measure, term limits have coincided with large changes in the level of political competition, and these changes have occurred even before term limits have even forcibly removed one politician from office. The regressions imply that term limits have reduced real campaign expenditures to less than what was spent in 1976 when campaign expenditure data was first collected. The changes are so large that more incumbents are being defeated, races are closer, more candidates are running, and there are fewer single candidate races than at any other time in our sample.

Notes

1. See also Reed and Schansberg (1992).
2. The states are: Arizona, Arkansas, California, Colorado, Florida, Idaho, Maine, Louisiana, Massachusetts, Michigan, Montana, Nebraska, Nevada, Ohio, Oklahoma, Oregon, South Dakota, Utah, Washington, and Wyoming.
3. To make this point clearer, suppose that there are two well-defined groups of constituents: A and B. Group A values winning the office more during the first two years than B does. But conditional on winning the office the first two years, group A does not value winning the second two-year term as much as group B values winning its first two-year term. If there are two consecutive two-year terms, group A will then win the first election and group B will win the second. The interest groups will be willing to spend more money with two two-year terms than with one four-year term simply because more total value is being produced for groups A and B.
4. For some historical evidence on these questions see Coates and Dalton (1992) and Yen et al. (1992).
5. Incumbents with large reputations however may experience larger (absolute or percentage) reductions in current campaign expenditures simply because the marginal returns to them making expenditures will be lower.
6. While no direct link was drawn to term limits, Alexander (1995) writes that: "In 1994, California politicians engaged in a massive game of 'musical chairs'; several constitutional

officers either retired or ran for other statewide offices, resulting in many 'open' statewide seats with no incumbent running. 27 legislators chose not to seek re-election to the same office, many opting instead for statewide bids, while some chose to run for other elective offices. This turnover resulted in 22 'open' Assembly seats and four open Senate seats, where no incumbent was running. One of the goals of term limits was to return seasoned politicians to the private sector. However, of the 27 legislators who did not seek re-election, only five retired from public office. The other 22 ran for other elective positions, often against other incumbents, resulting in even more costly and bitter contests". Alexander's discussion implies that this was an unusually high level of "musical chairs", though it would be useful to document how this has changed over time.

7. However, this last point on campaign expenditures is particularly difficult to separate from an entry barrier type story since matching a politician to a particular donor undoubtedly represents at least to some extent a nontransferable investment. Donors make contributions to the particular candidate because they become convinced that he strongly holds certain intrinsic preferences, preferences that are nontransferable.

References

Alexander, K. (1995). *The Great Money Chase*. Published by California Common Cause, April.

Besley, T. and Case, A. (1995). Does electoral accountability affect economic policy choices? Evidence from gubernatorial term limits. *Quarterly Journal of Economics* 110: 769–798.

Coats, M. and Dalton, T. (1992). Entry barriers in politics and uncontested elections. *Journal of Public Economics* 49: 75–90.

Crain, W.M. and Tollison, R.D. (1976). Campaign expenditures and political competition. *Journal of Law and Economics* 19: 177–188.

Crain, W.M. and Tollison, R.D. (1977). Attenuated property rights and the market for governors. *Journal of Law and Economics* 20: 205–212.

Dick, A.R. and Lott, J.R. Jr. (1993). Reconciling voters behavior with legislative term limits. *Journal of Public Economics* 50: 1–14.

Garratt, E. (1996). Political ambition and term limitations. University of Chicago Law School Working Paper.

Jung, A.-R., Kenny, L.W. and Lott, J.R. Jr. (1994). An explanation for why Senators from the same State vote differently so frequently. *Journal of Public Economics* 54: 65–96.

Lott, J.R. Jr. (1987a). Political cheating. *Public Choice* 52: 169–186.

Lott, J.R. Jr. (1987b). The effect of nontransferable property rights on the efficiency of political markets: Some evidence. *Journal of Public Economics* 32: 231–246.

Lott, J.R. Jr. (1989). Explaining challengers' campaign expenditures: The importance of sunk nontransferable brand name. *Public Finance Quarterly* 17: 108–1118.

Lott, J.R. Jr. (1995). A simple explanation for why campaign expenditures are increasing: The government is getting bigger. University of Chicago School of Law Working Paper.

Lott, J.R. Jr. and Bronars, S.G. (1993). Time series evidence on shirking by members of the U.S. House of Representatives. *Public Choice* 76: 125–150.

Lott, J.R. Jr. and Davis, M.L. (1992). A critical review and an extension of the political shirking literature, co-authored with M.L. Davis. *Public Choice* 74: 461–484.

Lott, J.R. Jr. and Reed, W.R. (1989). Shirking and sorting in a model of finite-lived politicians. *Public Choice* 61(1): 75–96.

Rabin, J.L. (1988). With Prop. 73, it won't be politics as usual next year. *The Los Angeles Times*, Sunday, 2 June, Part 2: 8.

Reed, W.R. and Schansberg, D.E. (1992). The behavior of congressional tenure over time: 1953–1991. *Public Choice* 73: 183–203.

Reed, W.R. and Schansberg, D.E. (1994). An analysis of congressional term limits. *Economic Inquiry* 32: 79–91.

Reed, W.R. and Schansberg, D.E. (1995). The House under term limits: What would it look like? *Social Science Quarterly* 76: 699–716.

Roberts, R.D. (1984). A positive model of private charity and public transfers. *Journal of Political Economy* 92: 136–148.

Sacramento Bee News Service. (1996). Reform initiative OK'd for ballot. McClatchy Newspapers, Inc., 28 February.

Snyder, J.M. Jr. (1990). Campaign contributions as investments: The U.S. House of Representatives, 1980–1986. *Journal of Political Economy* 98: 1195–1227.

Snyder, J.M. Jr. (1992). Long-term investing in politicians; or, give early, give often. *Journal of Law and Economics* 35: 15–44.

Stanksy, L. (1991). Campaign finance limits argued at 9th Circuit. *The Recorder*. Wednesday, 24 April: 2.

Yen, S.T., Coats, R.M. and Dalton, T.R. (1992). Brand-name investment of candidates and district homogeneity: An ordinal reponse model. *Southern Economic Journal* 58: 988–1001.

Public Choice **90:** 185–200, 1997.

© 1997 *Kluwer Academic Publishers.*

Choosing free trade without amending the U.S. Constitution*

WILLEM THORBECKE
Department of Economics, George Mason University, Fairfax, VA 22030, U.S.A.

Abstract. This paper documents the functioning of the market in trade protection. It uses a narrative approach to demonstrate that politicians respond to the demands of special interests by forcing open foreign markets and by closing domestic markets. In the process government officials violate property rights, disregard economic logic, damage the world trading system, multiply rent-seeking costs, and destroy wealth. Such outcomes imply that there is a constitutional failure, and that the rules and institutions governing international trade need to be reformed. This paper discusses several such changes and considers how consumers could be mobilized to support them.

> Protectionism is a constitutional failure.
>
> – Jan Tumlir
> Quoted in Robert Hudec (1993)

1. Introduction

Buchanan (1975) distinguished between two roles for government. The *night-watchman* or *protective* state enforces contracts, secures property righs, punishes criminals, and provides for the national defense. The *productive* state supplies public goods that cannot be produced easily through private trades. As Tullock (1993) has noted, rather than producing genuine public goods the government often provides private goods desired by politically-influential groups at the public expense. This abuse occurs because politicians face problems of incentive and knowledge.[1] Since they desire re-election, they have an incentive to see a situation as their strongest supporters see it. Since knowledge is incomplete, they can use general interest arguments to defend this brokering of particularist benefits to constituents.

The use of common interest arguments to justify transferring wealth to constituents is prevalent in international trade. Interferences with international

* Parts of this paper draw on Rowley, Thorbecke, and Wagner (1995). I thank Jae Chung, Yujiro Hayami, and the editor, Charles Rowley for helpful comments. Any errors are the responsibility of the author.

exchanges are justified by arguments about unfair foreigners, labor market externalities, predatory practices of foreign high-tech industries, national defense, and similar reasons. As discussed in Rowley, Thorbecke, and Wagner (1995, henceforth RTW) and in Thorbecke (1995a), politicians are unable to implement these policies in the ways that economists recommend. Rather, these arguments often function as smoke screens facilitating the transfer of wealth to constituents. This paper documents the pernicious ways in which the political marketplace has used arguments such as these to redistribute wealth to special interests. The resulting transfers jeopardize both the property rights of individuals and the wealth of the nation.

This paper then considers how the rules and institutions governing decision making in international trade could be reformed to protect the liberty and wealth of individuals. It does this first by considering several specific reforms. It then considers how to mobilize consumer interests to support these reforms.

Section 2 presents narrative evidence concerning how the market for trade protection in the U.S. opens foreign markets and closes domestic ones. It demonstrates that current outcomes violate property rights, disregard economic logic, damage the world trading system, multiply rent-seeking costs, and destroy wealth. Section 3 considers reforms that could reduce the incentives of politicians to engage in such practices, interests that could be harnessed to implement these reforms, and ideological issues that must be addressed to persuade the American electorate to embrace free trade. Section 4 contains concluding comments.

2. The market in trade protection

The public choice approach posits that trade policies are determined in a political market. Those seeking particularist benefits lobby politicians, offering campaign contributions and blocks of votes. Politicians pursuing reelection broker these benefits, often using public interest explanations to justify them. Consumers and others harmed by the redistributional policies provide these benefits, frequently without knowing that they are doing so. The structure of the market in trade protection is discussed in detail in RTW and in Thorbecke (1995a).

2.1. *Protectionism and the opening of foreign markets*

Recent unilateral attempts by the U.S. government to open up Japan's market in autos and auto parts well illustrate the workings of the market in trade protection. When President Clinton ran for election in 1992, he advocated a tough approach on trade issues with Japan. His arguments (and those of his advisors, were often couched in public interest terms. One argument held that unfair Japanese practices allowed Japanese high-tech firms facing increasing returns to expand output and produce at lower average costs, driving U.S. competitors out of the market. In 1993, he implemented his get-tough approach by seeking to raise tariffs on Japanese minivans 1000 percent. As the *New York Times* discusses, this move could not be justified by countering foreign threats to high-tech industries or by helping industries harmed by foreign competition (U.S. firms had over 90 percent of the market). Rather, it was "rank protectionism" that would "reward Chrysler" and "increase prices to consumers by thousands of dollars".[2]

On July 10, 1993 President Clinton and Japanese Prime Minister Miyazawa agreed to ground rules for a series of talks on automobiles and auto parts, as well as on four other areas. President Clinton's goal was to force Japan to purchase more American products in order to reduce America's trade deficit with Japan. He demanded specific market share targets, although the final agreement merely stated that the negotiations would be "results-oriented".[3] The talks led to agreement by the end of September on medical equipment, insurance, glass, and telecommunications equipment. As the talks were concluding, United States trade representative Mickey Kantor demanded that Japan increase its imports of auto parts from the United States to $40 billion from its existing level of $19 billion. When Japan balked, President Clinton cited Japan as an unfair trader under the "Super-301" clause of U.S. Trade Law. This clause would impose punitive sanctions if consultation with Japan failed to remove the "unfair" practices.

On January 4, 1995 the U.S. and Japan agreed that the consultation should cover three categories, increasing opportunities for Japanese car makers to purchase foreign auto parts; revising Japan's rules for auto maintenance and repairs; and permitting access of foreign cars to the Japanese market. The Clinton Administration decided on April 12, 1995 to adopt a highly confrontational approach with Japan, imposing billions of dollars of punitive tariffs unless Japan made enormous progress in negotiating over the next three weeks.[4] Officials said that these tariffs would be at least 20 percent.

U.S. negotiators made several demands. First, the Japanese government should adopt a "voluntary" plan to accept numerical targets for the amount of U.S. car parts that Japanese auto makers purchase. Second, Japan should deregulate its rigorous auto inspection system because, U.S. officials alleged, it discriminated against foreign autos. Third, the Japanese government should commit to help the Big Three U.S. auto makers (General Motors, Ford, and Chrysler) to increase the number of dealers allowed to sell foreign cars.

U.S. auto makers had a large hand in determining the demands made by the negotiators. They spent "months of building support in Washington with administration officials and congressional leaders".[5] They and others likely to gain from a tough approach to Japan also gave generously to politicians.[6] The U.S. auto industry came up with the idea of forcing Tokyo to accept numerical targets for buying U.S. made auto parts.[7] They also emphasized that these targets should include tough enforcement mechanisms.

Japan responded to these demands in several ways. First, it said that Japan's auto makers, struggling with a three-year recession and the high Yen, could not afford to increase sales by the amount demanded. Second, it said that numerical targets for increases in auto parts constituted managed trade and were thus contrary to the rules of the World Trade Organization (WTO). Third, it said that a voluntary plan should be voluntary and that the U.S. should not force it (under threat of tariff) to adopt a voluntary plan. Fourth, it said that its auto inspection system was necessary to maintain high safety standards. Fifth, it offered to send a letter reassuring dealers that they were free to deal in competing cars. Sixth, it offered to continue negotiations using the WTO as a neutral referee.

Rather than taking its case first to the WTO, the U.S. opted on 16 May to impose 100 percent punitive tariffs on thirteen models of Japanese luxury cars sold in the U.S.[8] The tariffs would affect imports totaling $5.9 billion. Although the tariffs would not be imposed until 28 June, if imposed they would apply retroactively to any cars reaching the U.S. after 19 May. These tariffs would almost eliminate new Japanese luxury cars from the U.S. unless Japanese auto makers bore the cost.[9] In the process they would devastate U.S. auto dealers selling Japanese luxury cars and their employees.[10] The *Wall Street Journal* described this policy as an attempt to reward those constituent groups that had supported President Clinton in 1992 and perhaps would do so again.[11]

U.S. auto makers were the big gainers from the threat of sanctions, with stock prices of the Big Three surging 5 percent when they were announced.[12] On the announcement, all three issued jubilant statements.[13] The *Wall Street Journal* stated that U.S. auto makers seemed likely to raise their prices.[14] Andrew Card, president of the American Automobile Manufacturers Association, refused to pledge that auto makers would not.[15]

The U.S. actions were clearly contrary to the spirit and rules of the WTO, which President Clinton had championed less than one year before. John Jackson, an expert on international economic legal relations, stated that Japan had a "cold, flat out, easy case .... If the U.S. feels it has been aggrieved, it has an obligation to go to the WTO" before applying sanctions.[16] Renato Ruggiero, Director-General of the WTO, declared that Washington was not living by the trading rules that it had the biggest hand in construction.[17] Bob Davis, summarizing what many observers from other countries thought, stated that "applying sanctions after a victory [at the WTO] is considered lawful activity; applying sanctions first is considered bullying".[18]

After flirting with a trade war, the two sides reached an agreement hours before the sanctions were scheduled to go into effect on 28 June. Shortly before the agreement, Japan had begun discussing imposing counter-sanctions on U.S. products. In the final agreement, Japanese car makers produced multi-year business plans that projected large increases in the use of U.S. auto parts. Japan's Ministry of International Trade and Industry (MITI) sent a letter to Japanese auto dealers confirming their rights to sell foreign cars. The Japanese government also agreed to deregulate the Japanese spare parts and inspection system and reduce the number of parts that it deemed critical. U.S. firms and negotiators continued to demand written numerical agreements for purchases of auto parts by Japanese companies and for increases in the number of car dealers selling foreign made cars. In the end they announced these numbers without any commitment from the Japanese government.

Several parties issued noteworthy statements about the trade confrontation. President Clinton called the agreement "a major step towards free trade".[19] U.S. trade representative Mickey Kantor said that the aggressive approach was good for the WTO.[20] The *Wall Street Journal* said the President has attempted to "use U.S. power to win votes from Detroit".[21] Lexus dealer Ron Salhany declared his anger that his employees were being used as "pawns for his [President Clinton's] 1996 re-election bid".[22]

This story highlights several elements of the public choice approach to trade protection discussed above. The Big Three auto makers invested time and money in developing relationships in Washington. President Clinton, responding to these constituents, offered them protection. His offers were often cloaked in public interest arguments such as the need to help high-tech industries or punish unfair foreigners. However, as the *New York Times* said of his proposed tariff on minivans and as the *Wall Street Journal* said of the sanctions threat his offers were often pure protectionism aimed at rewarding constituents. Consumers would have been major losers in both the minivan and the sanctions cases, since they would have paid higher prices. By thus seeking reelection through brokering benefits to U.S. auto makers, the Clinton Administration disregarded property rights, recent history, the world trading system, economic logic, and rent-seeking costs.

The property rights of owners and employees at U.S. auto dealers selling Japanese luxury cars were trampled on. The U.S. government came within hours of imposing 100 percent tariffs on these cars. All sides agreed that these tariffs would have produced large layoffs and operating losses in this industry. Those working in the industry were correct in arguing that they were being used as pawns in President Clinton's reelection bid.

The attempts to force Japanese auto makers and consumers to purchase more U.S. goods also ignored lessons from the massive failure of economic planning in Eastern Europe. Rather, it sought to implement a more pernicious form of planning; U.S. auto makers, who have an interest in their Japanese competitors failing, setting targets for the quantities of the U.S. auto parts that Japanese auto makers had to buy. Further, the results-oriented approach of the Clinton Administration and the U.S. auto makers they were trying to please would declare success only when Japanese consumers bought a quantity of American cars that the Big Three considered appropriate. If an increase in Japanese dealers selling American cars did not produce enough sales, then further pressure for results would follow. The facts that all but two models of U.S. cars had steering wheels on the left-hand side (the wrong side for Japan), that U.S. cars were too large to fit in Japanese parking spaces, and that U.S. cars had a reputation until very recently for bad quality were ignored by U.S. negotiators. Rather, they demanded that the Japanese government remedy the trade surplus in autos. How the Japanese government could persuade Japanese consumers to buy oversized, wrong-hand side drive American cars with a reputation for poor quality rather than correctly-sized, right-hand side drive, good quality Japanese cars was not specified.

The multilateral trading system was also damaged by the attempts to bully Japan. As Krueger (1995) argues, the multilateral system has been central to stimulating economic growth and increasing living standards in the post-War period. Following the Uruguay Round, it provided a binding dispute settlement mechanism ideal for claims by the U.S. that the Japanese auto inspection system discriminated against foreign autos. If Japan applied tougher standards to imported cars than domestic cars, it would be violating the national treatment obligation of the WTO. Thorbecke (1995a) provides several examples of cases where multilateral panels have successfully dealt with these types of issues. The advantage of such a multilateral approach is that it provides both parties with a greater sense of fairness since rulings are made by a neutral arbitrator. A unilateral ruling against Detroit's competitors by the Clinton Administration, actively seeking re-election support from Detroit, spreads cynicism and encourages other countries to similarly flaunt the rules. The ability to maintain what Bhagwati (1991) called a "fix-rule" trading regime, where rules are agreed on and the chips fall where they may, is thus reduced.

Using bureaucratic negotiation to eliminate the trade deficit flies in the face of economic logic. As Krueger (1995) has discussed, a country's trade deficit reflects its saving-investment balance. Since these aggregate variables are little affected by protectionism, bureaucratic management will not eliminate the trade deficit. Rather, by seeking to reduce the deficit in the auto sector, it will cause the deficit in other sectors to increase. In the process, it will deprive consumers in the U.S. and Japan of the benefits of purchasing products that firms in the other country produce efficiently. Political power rather than comparative advantage becomes the determinant of what goods consumers are able to purchase.

The trade deal reached with Japan will embolden the Clinton Administration to seek similar deals in the future, encouraging firms to rechannel resources towards lobbying politicians and away from satisfying consumers' preferences. Marcus Noland, a former Clinton trade economist, said that Clinton's deal with Japan strengthens the hand of administration officials advocating the use of unilateral sanction.[23] The *Wall Street Journal* reported that the next target for an aggressive unilateral approach will be Korean auto makers.[24] The increased willingness of the Clinton Administration to use political muscle to redistribute wealth gives some firms an incentive to spend time and money gaining transfers from the government and other firms an incentive to spend time and money resisting these transfers. These rent-seeking and rent-protecting expenditures waste scarce resources in non-value-adding pursuits. These resources are thus unavailable for cost reductions, product-enhancements, or market research. The rent-seeking losses could equal the full present value of the transfers that are available (Tullock, 1980). Thus, by encouraging rent-seeking waste, the Clinton Administration is reducing the wealth of the nation.[25]

The attempts by the U.S. to pry open Japan's auto and auto parts markets thus illustrate the dangerous and illogical outcomes produced by the market in trade protection. Property rights are trampled on as the President seeks reelection by transferring wealth to constituents. Economic planning is resurrected in the pernicious form of U.S. auto makers setting targets for their competitors' inputs. The world trading system is weakened by the cynical disregard for the WTO exhibited by U.S. negotiators. Political power replaces comparative advantage as the main factor determining the flows of trade. U.S. firms are given incentives to devote even more money and senior management time to rent-seeking rather than producing high-quality, low cost products. Over time these practices will drastically reduce the liberty and prospertiy of American citizens.

2.2. *Protectionism and the closing of domestic markets*

The insidiousness of the market in trade protection is not limited to aggressive attempts to open up foreign markets; it applies equally to attempts to close domestic markets. RTW have presented a narrative account similar to the one presented above documenting the pernicious ways in which the market in trade protection has closed domestic markets recently. The antidumping laws are particularly instructive in this regard. These laws defy economic logic, violate property rights, and contribute to massive rent-seeking. Space constraints permit only a cursory discussion here. RTW and Finger (1993) present detailed evidence.

While economics implies that dumping occurs when the export price is less than the home price, the antidumping laws mandate biased and illogical dumping determinations. When foreign prices are compared with U.S. prices, the Commerce Department throws out high prices in the U.S. and low prices in the foreign market, biasing the calculations towards a finding of dumping (Krueger, 1995). Of the foreign prices that it does not throw out it calculates an average and compares this with individual prices in the U.S., a process that can lead to a dumping findings when foreign and domestic prices are identical simply because an average of several numbers will be higher than some of its components (Palmeter, 1989). In 60 percent of U.S. cases, constructed costs rather than foreign prices are compared with domestic prices (Horlick, 1989). These constructed costs include the provision that the foreign firm earn at least 8 percent to cover profits and overhead. This provision ignores the fact that in slack times firms will continue to produce if they can meet marginal costs. In 1989, for instance, only two of the fifteen largest American firms had an 8 percent margin (Krueger, 1995). Similarly this constructed cost criterion would cause every after-Christmas sale by American firms to be ruled unfair (Bhagwati, 1988). Thus, the antidumping laws convict foreigners of practices that are considered fair and normal when engaged in by domestic firms. In the process they deceive the public by labeling these foreign traders "unfair".

The property rights of import-using firms and consumers are also violated by the AD laws. These laws permit no consideration of the effects of higher prices on import users or consumers. But just as import protection through the AD laws temporarily increases profits and employment in the protected industry, it reduces profits and employment in industries using the import as an input. The often arbitrary AD rulings thus not only harm foreign firms, they impede the ability of domestic employees and firms in import-using industries to earn wages and profits.

The antidumping laws are also ideal for rent-seeking. Lawyers and lobbyists have developed multi-case strategies. They "file a large number of cases against a large list of exporters, covering the spectrum of the industry's products" (Finger, 1993: 3). If they receive a negative ruling under one specification, they change the technical definitions of dumping, injury, and industry and try again. In the process, they saddle foreign competitors with large legal costs and massive uncertainty. Foreign firms producing steel, automobiles, semiconductors, and many other products have responded to threats from antidumping and similar laws by negotiating "voluntary export restraints" (VERs).

These VERs are another example of the senseless outcomes of the market in trade protection. They involve the U.S. government negotiating with foreign producers to limit their sales in the U.S. This raises prices for domestic consumers and transfer the quota rents to foreign producers. As Finger (1993) discusses, the VER on Japanese cars in the early 1980s cost U.S. consumers $7 billion per year to save about 35,000 jobs. This amounts to a cost of $200,000 per job. Hufbauer and Elliott (1994), examining the 31 most protected sectors, have similarly documented that the loss of consumer surplus per job saved averaged $170,000. The losses calculated by Finger and Hufbauer and Elliott would be much larger if rent-seeking costs were included. This money, if spent elsewhere, could have produced many times more jobs in areas where American firms possess comparative advantage.

VERs not only raise prices to consumers and inflict losses on society, they also violate property rights. As RTW discuss, property rights include the right to trade the fruits of ones labor. If an import quota prevents certain consumers from obtaining the autos of their choice, a property right is violated since the individual is unable to trade the fruits of his labor for the car of his choice.

Thus attempts to protect U.S. firms from import competition further highlight the pernicious workings of the market in trade protection. A complicated bureaucratic process is constructed that labels foreign producers unfair for practices identical to those engaged in by U.S. firms. Property rights are violated as the ability of import users to conduct business and consumers to purchase what they want is restricted. Rent-seeking waste multiplies as lawyers flood the system with antidumping petitions. VERs transfer billions of dollars from domestic consumers to foreign and domestic producers. The jobs saved in these domestic industries are only a small fraction of the jobs that would have been created in industries where the U.S. enjoys a comparative advantage if consumers had been able to spend their money elsewhere. Over time these senseless practices will eat away at what remains of the liberal trading order, threatening the property rights of individuals and the wealth of the nation.

3. Changing the rules and harnessing consumer interests

The discussion above indicates that rent-seeking special interests often succeed in obtaining protection from competition at the general expense. Politicians interested in getting re-elected broker this protection. In brokering it they tend to provide misleading explanations to the general public, who are usually unaware of the details of trade policy. They also violate the property rights of the individuals and firms who pay for the protection. The loss of consumer surplus alone in the 31 most protected sectors, as Hufbauer and Elliott

(1994) documented, averages $170,000 for each job saved. Public choice and not public interest provides a better explanation for these types of outcomes.

Buchanan (1987) argued that when making constitutional decisions, whereby choices are made regarding the rules guiding future day-to-day decisions, individuals should act as though they are behind a veil of uncertainty. Such a veil makes it difficult for them to predict their position relative to others in society and makes it hard for them to determine who would benefit from redistributional policies. It is impossible to believe that individuals confronted with such uncertainty would accept the rules and institutions currently in place in the market in trade protection. The usurping of property rights by politicians seeking re-election, the proliferation of rent-seeking waste, the nonsensical antidumping procedures, and the erosion of the wealth of the nation are all contrary to what self-interested individuals entering long term commitments would choose.

The market in trade protection thus suffers from a constitutional failure, one which requires constitutional solutions. Wagner (1993) has discussed two complementary ways to address constitutional failures. One is to articulate on parchment appropriate rules and institutions governing political decision making. The other is to place the guns of individual and group self-interest so that they reinforce the principles articulated on parchment. Wagner also emphasized the importance of correct ideology to make clear to individuals where their self-interest lies.

3.1. *Reforming the rules and institutions of international trade*

RTW have suggested one change in the rules underlying international trade. They have argued that the U.S. Constitution should be amended to guarantee unilateral free trade.[26] This would defend the property rights of individuals to engage in transnational exchanges. Currently the courts have interepreted the constitutional clause authorizing Congress to regulate commerce with foreign nationas to imply that the people have no vested right to foreign trade. The Court of Appeals for the Federal Circuit, for instance, stated:

> When the people granted Congress power 'to regulate Commerce with foreign Nations' ... they thereupon relinquished whatever right they, as individuals, may have had to insist on importation of any product.[27]

However, as discussed in RTW and in Section 2 above, the ability of special interests to usurp liberty and destroy wealth, so feared by the founding fathers, has been endemic in international exchanges. A constitutional amendment guaranteeing free trade could help ameliorate these problems.

Passage of such an amendment appears impossible in the near future, however. When Friedman and Friedman (1981) suggested a free trade amendment

15 years ago they stated that it was chimerical to believe that it could be passed then. Since then many Americans have expressed consternation about deindustrialization and the migration of high-paying manufacturing jobs abroad. While free trade is not to blame for these phenomena, convincing this to a supra-majority of rationally-ignorant voters would be difficult. The popular perception that foreigners are unfair, and that workers are losing jobs because of this, would add to the difficulty. The concept of fairness is so deeply ingrained in Americans, starting with Little League, that an opponent of such an amendment would just have to mention the need to retaliate against unfair foreigners and many would be convinced. Other opponents would say that, even if foreigners are not unfair, the U.S. needs to negotiate on a bilateral basis to obtain reciprocal market opening abroad. This would persuade another substantial subset of the polity. Thus, convincing two-thirds of Congress and three-fourths of the states to support such an amendment in the near future seems impossible.

More modest reforms in the rules and institutions governing international trade might be attainable, and many of these have been proposed. Krueger (1995) has argued that the U.S. eschew unilateral demands for market-openings, and replace the irrational procedures used by the Commerce Department to issue dumping decisions with the same criteria applied to American firms under U.S. antitrust laws. Bhagwati (1988) has argued that there should be penalties imposed on antidumping petitions judged to be frivolous or intended for harassment, that no relief should be provided for dumping margins below a threshold, and that firms gaining from VERs and similar protectionist measures should be required to return some of the rents to the government before distributing bonuses to CEOs. Finger (1993) has argued that antidumping rulings should take account, not only of the import-competing interests seeking protection, but also of the import-users and consumers who would be harmed. Thorbecke (1995b) has argued that the Section 301 statutes should be amended to require the U.S. to honor its international obligations under the Uruguay Round agreement to first seek redress using WTO dispute settlement procedures before imposing sanctions.[28] Each of these reforms would act, in various degrees, to loosen the grip that rent-seeking special interests have on the market for protectionism.

3.2. *Harnessing consumer interests*

The more difficult issue concerns aligning interests, or more precisely mobilizing consumer interests, behind these and similar reforms. Consumers tend to be rationally-ignorant about issues such as trade policy unless it concerns an industry that they are working in. Thus they are unlikely to support the reforms mentioned above.

Jones (1994) has offered a suggestion to motivate consumer interests to join the import-using interests, foreign exporters, and other groups currently resisting protectionism. He has argued that there be a statutory requirement mandating that all trade restrictive measures (including antidumping measures) be accompanied by an economic impact statement. This statement would cover several areas, including primary market impact, changes in consumer and produce surpluses, production upgrading effects, prospects for retaliation, conformity with WTO obligations, secular market trends in the industry, and environmental impact of domestic output.

While Jones's suggestion would increase transparency in political decision making, it suffers from the problem that the mass of voters (i.e., the median voter) does not read detailed economic analyses. A better way to mobilize consumers would be the simple requirement that every product that has benefitted from protection contain a sticker stating in large letters, "Trade protection has increased the price of this item by xxx dollars", and in smallest letters below, "This dollar figure is an average from several studies". An address could then be given from which a more detailed economic analysis including factors such as those discussed by Jones could be obtained. This simpler approach could tap into the anger that citizens are feeling towards Washington and the perception that government policies are eroding their prosperity. The use of an average over several studies could mitigate the problem that occurs when investigators using different data sets and different assumptions obtain different results.

To secure passage of such an economic impact statement, and to maintain consumer interest in the issue of protectionism, anti-protection lobbies need to change their tactics. Prior to the vote ratifying U.S. entrance into the WTO in November 1994 they purchased advertising in newspapers extolling the virtues of the multilateral trading system. The problem with this approach is that it is about as interesting to the average reader as advertising providing notification of the redemption of municipal revenue bonds that also appears in newspapers. A better approach would be to place an advertisement that stated in large letters "Why is the Average Price of a New Car $20,000?" Below this could be a simple explanation of how VERs caused Japanese manufacturers to upgrade their products and how these policies enriched Japanese and U.S. manufacturers. Similar advertisements could be taken out documenting how consumers are paying for other protectionist abuses.

By increasing transparency and tapping in to anger over the abuses of politicians, economic impact statements and consumer-oriented advertising could help tip the scales in the free trade direction. Import-using firms, importers, and foreign exporters and associated interests are currently leading the anti-protection lobby. Support from consumers upset about higher prices due to protectionism could help them succeed by activating what Bhagwati (1988: 85) called the Dracula Effect, "Exposing evil to sunlight helps to destroy it".

3.3. *Ideological issues*

It is also crucial to recognize the ideology that economists have developed supporting managed trade and the misleading rhetoric that politicians have employed concerning trade issues. Recently economic arguments for managed trade have arisen predicated on nationally-limited externalities, labor market imperfections, and the unfair practices of trading partners. These are discussed in detail in RTW and in Thorbecke (1995a). Further, politicians have developed a rhetoric about trade issues that rivals anything used by the government in George Orwell's *1984*. A "voluntary" agreement is one that foreign trading partners accept after being threatened with 100 percent tariffs. "Unfair" antidumping practices by foreign firms are identical to after-Christmas sales and other procedures that are considered normal business practices by domestic firms. Unilateral rulings against Detroit's competitors by the Clinton Administration, actively seeking re-election support from Detroit, are labelled "good for the WTO". The allocation of market share by Japanese and American bureaucrats cloistered in hotel rooms becomes "a major step towards free trade".

It is imperative to counter the rationales for managed trade with political economy reasons for free trade and to resist politicians' Orwellian abuse of language. The case for free trade becomes compelling because of the political influence over trade policy in the United States. Political markets in the grip of rent-seeking forces are unable to implement economists' recommendations concerning policies to exploit nationally-limited externalities, internalize labor market externalities, or curtail unfair foreigners. Thus interventions justified by these arguments would not produce the benefits claimed by proponents but would produce the costs that come when governments interfere with voluntary exchanges. These facts are discussed in RTW and in Thorbecke (1995a). One way to counter politicians' abuse of language is through the use of humor. Bhagwati (1988), for instance, made fun of claims that the Japanese are unfair by presenting a cartoon showing trade negotiators with a 50 pound Walkman complaining that Japanese consumers will not buy it. Strengthening the political economy rationales supporting free trade and debunking politicians misleading vocabulary concerning trade issues are necessary to make clear to American citizens that free trade rather than managed trade will contribute to a prosperous society.

4. Conclusion

This paper has used a narrative approach to document the workings of the market in trade protection. It demonstrated that rent-seeking special interests often succeed in receiving particularist benefits at the general expense. In brokering these benefits government officials violate property rights, disregard economic logic, damage the world trading system, and multiply rent-seeking costs. It is impossible to believe that individuals making decisions behind a veil of uncertainty would accept rules producing outcomes of these kinds. The market in trade protection thus suffers from a constitutional failure.

As Wagner (1993) has dicussed, constitutional failures can be addressed through the articulation on parchment of appropriate rules and through the positioning of the guns of self-interest to reinforce these constitutional rules. This paper argues that a constitutional amendment guaranteeing free trade could restrict special interests from usurping liberty and destroying wealth in international exchanges. Securing passage of such an amendment at present, however, appears impossible. Several changes in the regulatory rules governing international trade that fall short of full constitutional reform, on the other hand, appear within reach. This paper discusses several such changes. It then considers how to mobilize consumer interests behind these reforms. If consumer indignation can be aroused against the high costs of protectionism, it will help import-using firms, importers, foreign exporters, and others who are currently resisting protectionist demands. By thus strengthening the anti-protection lobby, the grip of protectionist special interests on the political marketplace would be loosened. Such an outcome would defend the property rights of Americans to engage in transnational exchanges and increase the wealth of the national. If this opportunity to advance free trade is not seized, the loss of liberty and prosperity over time will be enormous.

Notes

1. These problems are discussed in Wagner (1993).
2. *New York Times*, 3 May, 1993, p. A14.
3. *New York Times*, 10 July, 1993, p. 1.
4. *New York Times*, 13 April, 1995, p. A1.
5. *Wall Street Journal*, 28 June, 1995, p. A2.
6. As discussed in the Congressional Quarterly *Fax Report*, 19 June, 1995, pp. 2–4.
7. *Wall Street Journal*, 10 May, 1995, p. A14.
8. The U.S. simultaneously took its case to the WTO alleging nullification and impairment of U.S. access to the Japanese auto market.
9. *Wall Street Journal*, 17 May, 1995, p. A1.
10. *Wall Street Journal*, 10 May, 1995, p. B1.
11. *Wall Street Journal*, 10 May, 1995, p. A14.
12. *Wall Street Journal*, 11 May, p. A11.

13. *Wall Street Journal*, 17 May, 1995, p. A10.
14. *Wall Street Journal*, 29 June, 1995, p. A6.
15. *Wall Street Journal*, 11 May, 1995, p. A11.
16. *Wall Street Journal*, 11 May, 1995, p. A2.
17. *Wall Street Journal*, 18 May, 1995, p. A16.
18. *Wall Street Journal*, 15 May, 1995, p. A1.
19. *Wall Street Journal*, 29 June, 1995, p. A1.
20. *New York Times*, 3 October, 1994, p. D8.
21. *Wall Street Journal*, 29 June, 1995, p. A16.
22. *Wall Street Journal*, 29 June, 1995, p. A6.
23. *Wall Street Journal*, 30 June, 1995, p. A1.
24. *Wall Street Journal*, 30 June, 1995, p. A1.
25. The relationship between rent-seeking and trade protection is clearly discussed by Rowley and Tollison (1986).
26. They argued that Article 1, Section 8 should be amended to prevent Congress and the President from levying duties or imposing quantitative restrictions.
27. *Arjay Associates Inc. v. Bush*, 891 F.2d 891, 898 (Fed. Cir. 1989), quoted in Petersmann (1993).
28. See Jackson (1994) for a lucid discussion of the relationship between the 301 statutes and the Uruguay Round Agreement.

References

Bhagwati, J. (1988). *Protectionism*. Cambridge: MIT Press.

Bhagwati, J. (1991). *The world trading system at risk*. Princeton: Princeton University Press.

Buchanan, J. (1975). *The limits of liberty: Between anarchy and Leviathan*. Chicago: The University of Chicago Press.

Buchanan, J. (1987). The Constitution of economic policy. *American Economic Review* 77: 243–250.

Finger, M. (1993). *Antidumping: How it works and who gets hurt*. Ann Arbor: University of Michigan Press.

Friedman, M. and Friedman, R. (1981). *Free to choose*. New York: Avon Books.

Hudec, R. (1993). The role of judicial review in preserving liberal foreign trade policies. In M. Hilf and E. U. Petersmann (Eds.), *National constitutions and international economic law*. Boston: Kluwer Publishers.

Hufbauer, G. and Elliott, K. (1994). *Measuring the costs of protection in the United States*. Washington DC: Institute for International Economics.

Jackson, J. (1994). Testimony prepared for U.S. Senate Finance Committee Hearing on Uruguay Round Legislation, 23 March.

Jones, K. (1994). *Export restraints and the new protectionism: The political economy of discriminatory trade restrictions*. Ann Arbor: University of Michigan Press.

Krueger, A. (1995). *American trade policy*. Washington DC: American Enterprise Institute.

Palmeter, N.D. (1989). The capture of the antidumping laws. *Yale Journal of International Law* 14: 182–198.

Petersmann, E.U. (1993). National constitutions and international economic law. In M. Hilf and E. U. Petersmann (Eds.), *National constitutions and international economic law*. Boston: Kluwer Publishers.

Rowly, C.K. and Tollison, R. (1986). Rent seeking and trade protection. *Swiss Journal of International Relations* 141–166.

Rowly, C.K., Thorbecke, W. and Wagner, R. (1995). *Trade protection in the United States*. Brookfield, VT and Aldershot, U.K.: Edward Elgar Publishing.

Thorbecke, W. (1995a). Free trade versus managed trade: A constitutional political economy perspective. *Journal of Institutional and Theoretical Economics* 151: 373–389.
Thorbecke, W. (1995b). Preserving the multilateral trading system. George Mason University.
Tullock, G. (1980). Efficient rent-seeking. In J. Buchanan, R. Tollison, and G. Tullock (Eds.), *Towards a theory of the rent-seeking society*. College Station: Texas A&M University Press.
Tullock, G. (1993). *Rent seeking*. Brookfield, VT and Aldershot, U.K.: Edward Elgar Publishing.
Wagner, R. (1993). *Parchment, guns, and constitutional order*. Brookfield, VT and Aldershot, U.K.: Edward Elgar Publishing.

Public Choice **90**: 201–213, 1997.

© 1997 *Kluwer Academic Publishers.*

Marginal cost sharing and the Articles of Confederation*

KEITH L. DOUGHERTY[1] and MICHAEL J.G. CAIN[2]
[1]*Department of Government and Politics, University of Maryland, College Park, MD 20742;*
[2]*Political Science Department, University of Mississippi, University, MS 30677, U.S.A.*

Abstract. Between 1781 and 1789 the American states attempted to share the costs of national, public goods through a system of requisitions. This paper uses a simple public goods analysis to show why rational states would not share costs as intended by the Articles of Confederation. This normative argument illustrates a potential flaw in the constitutional design of the Articles and provides insight into the decline of the American Confederation.

1. Introduction

Even before the imperial arm of mother Britain was broken, the American states sought a national government to provide common defense, secure liberty, and promote general welfare. Borders were poorly defined and enemies too strong for the thirteen states to maintain their affairs privately and independently. What the states needed was a "perpetual union" (Article III) to bind them together into a "league of friendship" (Article II) and mutual assistance. This league was established by the Articles of Confederation which organized the American states from 1781 to 1789.

The framers of the Articles of Confederation created a Congress to provide for common state interests: maintain national defense, preserve state liberties, and promote mutual and general state welfare. These tasks advanced the interests of all states and could not be accomplished adequately or effectively without national organization. As Cornelius Harnett, a delegate from North Carolina, wrote, "many assert that the very salvation of these States depends upon [the Articles]; and that none of the European power will publicly acknowledge them free and independent until they are confederated".[1]

Since gains from Congressional services were shared by all states, a system of requisitioning the states for Congressional revenue was written into the Articles of Confederation in order to divide the costs of national, public goods.

* The authors would like to thank David Lalman, Joe Oppenheimer, Piotr Swistak, and Rick Wilson for invaluable feedback on this article. Katrhyn Doherty, Mark Graber, Paul Hernson, Daniel Simon, and Eric Uslaner provided useful comments as well.

All states ratified this agreement and were legally bound to contribute their share. However, after several requisitions, states learned to withhold their payments, leaving Congress without the resources needed to carry out its constitutional responsibilities. Lack of revenue prevented Congress from forcefully responding to British non-compliance with the 1783 Anglo-American peace treaty, reacting to the Spanish blockade of the Mississippi River between 1984 and 1987, enforcing treaties with the Indians by limiting western movement of settlers, and averting the piracy of the Barbary states (Brown, 1993). These problems might have been avoided if Congress had obtained the money it requested from the states.

Perhaps one reason why the states did not pay their quotas was that the Articles of Confederation failed to organize a union where state and national interests coincided. Although the system of requisitions was designed to share costs, there was no endogenous reason for states to behave consistent with national interests and no enforcement mechanism to ensure that states paid their share. Without these mechanisms, the Articles offered little relief from a classic collective action problem (Olson, 1965). State legislatures learned to withhold their payments and ultimately rendered Congress incapable of providing the most basic goods and services.

This paper builds on a simple public goods argument to suggest how the constitutional design of the Articles of Confederation affected the nation's ability to provide public goods through its established institution – the Continental Congress. To do this, we argue that the goods provided by Congress were public and show how the institutions created by the Articles attempted to facilitate their production. We then use a formal model of state decision-making to analyze whether the institutional design of the Articles promoted or hindered state compliance with Congressional requisitions. We find that states fully complying with their requisitions, when others did not, incurred a greater portion of the national costs than originally intended. This made the cost of contributing greater than the amount specified in a requisition. More importantly, we find that rational states would contribute where marginal benefits equalled marginal national costs. Since this is the same outcome predicted for unorganized groups, we conclude that the Articles did not affect a state's decision to contribute. In other words, the Articles did not provide any incentive for states to pay their requisitions nor a better means of financing Congressional goods and services.

2. Public goods and the system of requisitions

Authors of the confederation limited Congress to tasks which they believed advanced the interests of all states. Inadvertently, they gave Congress the responsibility of providing goods which were both non-excludable and non-rival. Congress maintained the authority to provide national defense, preserve open commerce, and foster international diplomacy. All of these goods were arguably non-excludable and non-rival.[2] However, the most important duties of Congress and clearest examples of public goods were the national war effort and reducing the public debt. Every dollar paid by a state to raise another soldier or to reduce the debt by an additional dollar improved the well-being of all states. During the Revolution, Congress spent almost the entire national budget on the military (Ferguson, 1961), while after the war, it spent roughly 88% of its budget on war debt.[3] Since Congress' primary functions were martial and most of its subsequent expenses were spent on other non-excludable and non-rival goods, Congressional goods and services can be treated as public goods. By design these goods required state support in order to be provided.

Under the Articles of Confederation Congress did not have the power to tax. Almost all Congressional revenues came from requisitions on the states, public bonds, or loans from abroad.[4] Since loans and bonds depended upon future revenues, Congress frequently relied upon requisitions to finance its expenditures. Requisitions were an appropriation of state monies for the purpose of funding Congressional acts, similar to an unenforced tax upon the states for national goods and services.

After an act passed Congress, monies were appropriated from the national treasury to pay for it. The treasury was then replenished by annual requisitions on the states which varied according to the estimated expenditures for the following year. However, when the coffers were depleted and immediate action was required, Congress had the authority to request funds through special requisitions. Special requisitions went to specific public goods such as the army needed to suppress Shays' Rebellion in 1786. Estimated expenditures in annual requisitions, or the total costs of a particular good in special requisitions, were then divided among the states according to each state's land value. These proportions were distributed to the states with a specified due date. As directed by Article VIII:

> All charges of war and all other expenses that shall be incurred for the common defence or general welfare, and allowed by the United States in Congress assembled, shall be defrayed out of a common treasury, which shall be supplied by the several states, in proportion to the value of all land within each state, granted to or surveyed for any person . . . The taxes for paying for that proportion shall be laid and levied by the authority and direction of the legislatures of the several states within the time agreed upon by the United States in Congress assembled.

This Article provided clear constitutional authority for Congress to requisition the states and legally required them to comply. In practice, however, each state decided whether or not to send monies requested by Congress. Since Congress had no means of enforcing its requisitions, the decision to support national policies depended upon the willingness and ability of thirteen separate state legislatures. This process was nicely summarized by Jonathan Arnold and David Howell, delegates from Rhode Island, in a letter to their governor:

> The Continental treasury is to be supplied from the several states agreeable to Article eight, by successive requisitions. When a new requisition is made, the purposes for which it is to be appropriated are to be pointed out to you;. and it is to be accompanied with particular estimates. You are at the same time, to be informed what has been done, with your last quota, and on a full consideration of the representation so made to you, you are to grant your money like freemen . . .[5]

Despite legal obligations to pay requisitions, many believed that states maintained the authority to independently choose whether to comply. In effect Congress determined the size of the requisition, while the states decided how much of it to pay.

3. Allocation of costs

To clarify the incentive problem under the Articles, we use basic theories of collective action and historical evidence to formalize state decision-making within the requisition process. For this analysis each state legislature is treated as a unitary actor which chooses its dollar contribution after receiving its portion of a requisition from Congress. The benefits a state gains depend upon the amount of non-excludable good produced from all state payments. The costs to each state are solely the monetary amount the state contributed. Thus, norms of cooperation, reputation, and external factors affecting utility are set aside from the analysis in order to illustrate the monetary incentives associated with the system.

After the total cost of the requisition was determined, it was divided among the states in proportion to the percentages specified by Article VIII. For example, Maryland was obliged to pay roughly 9.4% of any requisition (see Table 1, column three for each state's quota).[6] Since the amount requested was fixed after the size of the national requisition was determined, each state's quota did not vary with the amount returned by others.

Given the lack of enforceability it is easy to show why the system of requisitions did not distribute cost consistent with the proportions outlined by Article VIII. States faced costs consistent with their constitutionally defined shares only when all other states combined paid n-1 shares of the requisition. When other states paid too little or too much, costs would not be divided as intended. To illustrate this point, consider the following definitions:

X is a set of all possible amounts of the public good supplied, such that $X = [0, +\infty]$. $x^* \in X$ is the amount of the public good actually supplied, while x^r is the amount of the public good requisitioned. In general, superscripts denote constants, while subscripts differentiate nation from state.

Y is a set of all possible dollar amounts associated with X, such that $Y = [0, +\infty]$.

C_N is a monotonically increasing function from X to Y. It specifies the cost to the nation for x units of the public good.

Using the inverse of C_N, the amount of public good actually supplied can be derived from the total dollar amount received using $x^* = S(y) = C_N^{-1}(y_i^* + y_{-i}^*)$, where y_i^* and y_{-i}^* are the dollar amounts donated by states i and not i respectively. A state can choose any y such that $y \in Y$.

C_i is a monotonically increasing function from X to Y. It specifies the cost assigned to state i for x units of the public good.

The variable π_i is state i's proportion of the costs for x units of the good supplied such that $\pi_i = [0, 1]$ and $\pi_i = \frac{C_i(x)}{C_N(x)}$. This designates the relationship between C_i and C_N. Following the notation previously established, π_i^r is state i's proportion of the costs of goods requisitioned and π_i^* is state i's proportion of the costs of goods actually supplied.

π_i^r was used to determine the costs assigned to each state in a requisition. For x^r units of the public good requisitioned state i was assigned a cost of $y_i^r = C_i(x^r) = \pi_i^r \cdot C_N(x^r)$. Remember, since π_i^r and x^r are established before a requisition is sent to the states, y_i^r does not vary with the actual amount of the public good supplied; it only varies with the amount requisitioned and the cost of those goods. Figure 1 depicts these relationships for a marginally increasing cost function.

Noting the distinction between the amount of public good supplied and the amount requisitioned allows us to show cases where fully complying states would pay more or less than their constitutionally assigned share. When $y_i^* = y_i^r$ and $y_{-i}^* = y_{-i}^r$, the full amount of the requisition was paid and $\pi_i^* = \pi_i^r$.[7] But when $y_{-i}^* \neq y_{-i}^r$, state i does not pay its constitutionally defined share by paying the full amount of its requisition. If state i paid the full amount of its requisition while the other states paid less than the amount allocated to all

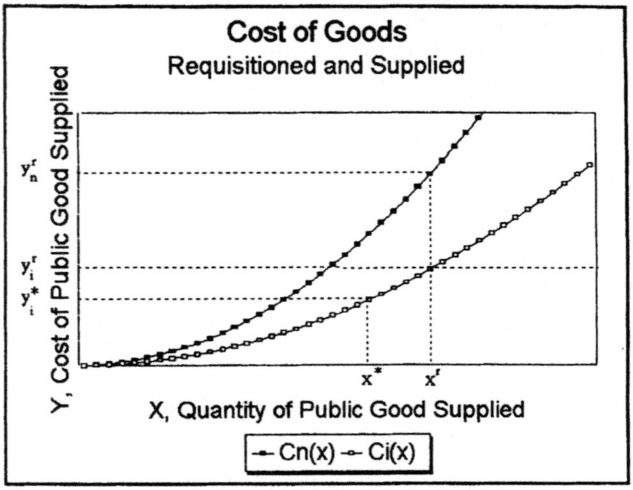

Figure 1.

other states, state i would pay more than its fair share.[8] Likewise, if state i paid the full amount of its requisition while the other states paid more than the amount allocated to all other states, state i would pay less than its fair share. This result stems from the simple fact that the proportion a state paid depended upon the amount donated by states, not the amount requisitioned.

Although states rarely paid more than their requisitions, they frequently paid less. This implies that the amount of public goods supplied frequently fell short of the amount requisitioned and any state willing to contribute its quota would pay a higher marginal cost. This point can be clarified by an example. On 21 October 1786 Congress requested $530,000 from the states in a special requisition to suppress Shays Rebellion (see Cain and Dougherty, 1995). This money was raised to provide for 2,040 soldiers at a unit cost of roughly $259.80/soldier. The $530,000 was then divided among the states according to each state's constitutionally defined share (see Table 1). Maryland, for example, was assigned roughly 9.4% of the requisition corresponding to $C_{MD}(x^r)$ = $49,979. The system was supposed to produce 2,040 soldiers for Maryland's benefit when Maryland donated this amount. However, like any public good, the amount supplied depended upon the amount contributed by others as well as the amount donated by Maryland. Congress would raise enough money to provide 2,040 soldiers, only if the other states paid the remaining $480,021. In which case, $\pi_i^* = \pi_i^r$ and national costs would be divided as planned.

However, if Maryland paid the full amount of its requisition while other states withheld their contributions, Congress would raise a smaller force

Table 1. Each state's portion of the requisition on 21 October 1786.

State	Requisition	Percent of total cost
VA	$90,630	17.1%
MA	79,288	15.0
PA	72,504	13.7
MD	49,979	9.4
CT	46,746	8.8
NY	45,368	8.6
NC	38,474	7.3
SC	33,973	6.4
NJ	29,415	5.6
NH	18,603	3.5
RI	11,395	2.2
DE	7,950	1.5
GA	5,671	1.1
Total	~ $530,000	100.0%

Source: *Journals of the Continental Congress*. Washington: National Printing Office, 1934. 21 October 1786, 31: 894; 7 April 1783, 24: 230–231.

than originally intended. In addition, Maryland would pay a much larger percentage than constitutionally required and perhaps more than it was willing to pay for this particular public good. As history revealed, Virginia was the only state which paid any portion of its requisition, donating roughly $40,000. Maryland did not comply, but let's consider a hypothetical example where it did. Suppose Maryland paid its full share of $49,979 along with the $40,000 provided by Virginia. Congress would then receive a total of $89,979 from the states and raise a force of roughly 346 soldiers. In this example, Maryland's actual share of the total costs then would be $\pi_i = \frac{C_i(x)}{C_N(x)} = \frac{49,979}{89,979}$, or roughly 56%. This is a much higher percentage than Maryland's constitutionally assigned share of 9.4%. Assuming that marginal costs were constant, this meant that Maryland would pay $145.49/unit for 346 soldiers, instead of the $24.42/unit for 2,040 soldiers assigned to it in the requisition. Such a large amount may have been more than Maryland was willing to pay, given that it would receive a smaller, less effective force in return.

Although Congress divided costs among the states under the assumption of full compliance, the marginal costs a state incurred depended upon the donation of others. If some states failed to pay their portion of a requisition, marginal costs would increase from a state's perspective and contributors would pay more of the marginal burden. This gave states good reason to ignore the costs assigned to them by Congress and to use more autonomous criteria in determining their optimal donations.

4. Rational contributions and national costs

The preceding observation does not imply that rational states would consider their portion of goods supplied nor their portion of the goods requisitioned in their decision to contribute. Since benefits from Congressional goods and services were non-excludable, rational states would consider marginal national costs, $C_N'(x)$, in determining their optimal donation. This is the unit price asked for by government suppliers and the rate at which money received from the states was transformed into units of the public good.

To illustrate this point consider some additional definitions and a reasonable conjecture about rational contributions under the system of requisitions.

B_i	is an increasing function with diminishing marginal returns from X to Y. It specifies the benefit to state i in dollars terms for X units of the public good.
C_i and C_N	are restricted to increasing functions with non-decreasing marginal returns to illustrate the point.
V_i	is a fully differentiable payoff function for state i such that $V_i(y_i, y_{-i}) = B_i(x) - y_i$. It specifies the payoff to state i for the total dollar amount contributed by it and other states.
	If a state receives no additional benefit or cost from the collective good or from the act of contributing, V_i represents the state's utility from each amount of the public good purchased. A rational state then donates where V_i is maximized.

Taking the partial derivative of V_i with respect to y_i, the unconstrained optimum of V_i is obtained where

$$\frac{\partial V_i}{\partial y_i} = \frac{\partial B_i}{\partial x}\frac{\partial S}{\partial y_i} - 1$$

is set equal to zero, or

$$B_i'(x) = C_N'(x).^9$$

This suggests that a state maximizes its payoff by contributing where marginal state benefits equal marginal national costs – not the marginal costs assigned to it in a requisition, nor the marginal cost of its donation. This is because the amount assigned to a state in a requisition is not the amount a state actually pays. A state actually pays y_i which must buy a single unit of the good before it can be applied to further units. Since a state pays the entire cost of each additional unit, marginal *national* costs are relevant to its decision. Rational states would not voluntarily contribute under this process unless the benefits produced from contributing were at least as great as the national costs. Since this is the same requirement for states in any unorganized, privileged group (Olseon, 1965; Frohlich and Oppenheimer, 1978; Mueller, 1989), the cost-sharing scheme provided by the Articles does not affect a state's incentive to contribute to collective goods.[10]

The Article of Confederation provided a central authority to determine the money needed for national goods and services. Guided by Article VIII, this authority signaled each state about how much of the cost to pay, but it could not enforce its edicts nor offer any concrete reasons for the states to comply. More importantly, the Articles failed to provide any endogenous incentives for states to treat the costs assigned to them in a requisition as their own. This meant that states which benefitted less than the amount needed to provide public goods on behalf of the union yet more than their portion of the costs were not encouraged to comply. Without these key contributors, the goal of maintaining a decentralized government based on voluntary taxation remained elusive.

These institutions were not conducive to "a league of friendship" among the states that the Articles extolled. By not encouraging states to consider the costs assigned to them in a requisition, states were left to choose between paying the entire unit cost on behalf of the nation or withholding their contributions altogether. This ineffectual means of raising revenue from the states may partially explain why requisition payments were consistently low.

5. State compliance

The effect of this system was that it placed unfair burdens on states that actually contributed. These burdens forced states to choose between their constitutional obligations and their monetary self-interest. Since state and national interests did not coincide, Congress had to depend upon strong written guarantees and civic obligation in order to induce cooperation. This may have encouraged payments in early years of the confederation, however, civic duty was insufficient to prevent cooperation from eroding in the 1780s.

Data to support such conjectures is limited, and it is not clear how much other factors influenced state decision-making. Nevertheless, there is evidence that state compliance with Congressional requisitions declined during the confederation. By 1787 the thirteen states paid the following requisitions: 66% of the 30 October 1781 and 27 April 1784 requisitions, 35% of the 10 September 1782 requisition, 20% of the 27 September 1785 requisition, and only 2% of the 2 August 1786 requisition.[11] In addition, the $40,000 paid by Virginia towards the special requisition to suppress Shays' Rebellion, 21 October 1786, represents 7% compliance. Although the amount returned to Congress was always less than desired, it declined to an almost non-existent rate in 1786. This decline is consistent with states gradually coming to understand the financial incentives involved in the requisition process and the fact that net benefits depended upon the contribution of others.

There may be another reason why cooperation declined. In the early years of the confederation, Robert Morris, Superintendent of Finance (1781–1784), pressured states to comply with national requisitions. Morris sent circulars to the states urging them to pay their outstanding debts, he met with Congressional delegates to encourage passage of laws that helped states meet their quotas, and continually reminded states about how much each owed (Brown, 1993: 14–16). When several states attempted to pay the salaries of their continental troops directly, Morris refused to credit their accounts for a requisition payment. He declared that direct payments were mere gifts and that salaries paid to the Continental army must come from a common treasury (Ferguson, 1961; Jensen, 1965). This policy was intended to encourage compliance with requisitions and to give Congress greater control over national finance. Such social sanctions may have stimulated requisition payments in the early part of the period. However, Morris' persistent pressure was insufficient to maintain steady compliance in the mid-1780s. By the time Morris retired in 1784, requisition payments were already in steady decline.

In the summer of 1786 receipts from requisitions dwindled to almost nothing. This left Congress incapable of providing the security, diplomacy, and open commerce the nation relied upon. In early 1787 this state of affairs led Madison to write:

> Indeed the present System neither has nor deserves advocates; and if some very strong props are not applied will quickly tumble to the ground. No money is paid into the public Treasury; no respect is paid to the federal

> authority. Not a single State complies with the requisitions, several states pass them over in silence, and some positively reject them. The payments ever since the peace have been decreasing, and of late fall short even of the pittance necessary for the Civil list of the Confederacy. It is not possible that a Government can last long under these circumstances.[12]

Perhaps Madison's quote was more of a prophecy than an observation. By late 1786 Congress received no money from the states for current expenditures and could neither pay its own civil officers nor borrow from its citizens (Brown, 1993: 27). This desperate state of affairs persuaded the founders to amend the Articles. However, in May 1787, they went much further than that. They framed a new nation.

6. Conclusion

This analysis suggests how specific properties of constitutional design can affect the decision of state actors and the solvency of a central government. Although the Articles of Confederation included cost sharing provisions, these arrangements were insufficient to guarantee that states paid their shares. The costs a state incurred were higher than the amount assigned and distributed unfairly. Instead of providing institutions which alleviated problems of collective action among the states, the Articles adopted a system of requisitions where incentives to free-ride were unaffected. This does not suggest that the constitutional design of the Articles was the only reason for states to resist Congressional requisitions; rather, it merely suggests how poor constitutional design can affect both short and long-term cooperative behaviors among confederated states. Such analysis contributes to our understanding of the institutions which preceded the Constitution.

Understanding what went wrong under the Articles is the first step toward understanding the constitutional designs of other confederacies as well. If problems of state cooperation are inherent to other confederacies, then future unions will want to know which institutions make state and national interests coincide an which institutions leave collective action unaffected. Unless requisition systems can be devised which provide adequate cost sharing among states, these systems should be avoided. Individual state interests are likely to leave central governments with inadequate revenues when enforcement mechanisms are not present. With the emergence of the Commonwealth of Independent States, the Baltic Assembly, and the United Nations, understanding the relationship between constitutional design and issues of federalism is of increasing concern.

Notes

1. Cornelius Harnett to Richard Caswell, 10 October 1777 *Letters* 8: 97–98.
2. Other responsibilities assigned to Congress by the Articles include: 1) coining money, 2) settling disputes between states, 3) fixing the standards of weights and measures, and 4) maintaining an efficient postal service. All but the last were non-excludable and non-rival goods.
3. This percent is the average of annual estimated expenditures allocated to the national debt from 1784 to 1789. See *Journals* 26: 186–196; 29: 765–771; 31: 459–466; 33: 569–583; 34: 432–443.
4. Some revenues between 1774 and 1789 came from the creation and selling of a national bank or the printing of unbacked currency, but these resources were short-lived and were not considered a stable source of revenue during the confederation (see Ferguson, 1961; Jensen, 1965).
5. Jonathan Arnold and David Howell to Governor Greene, 15 October 1782 *Rhode Island in Congress*: 397.
6. Although the Articles of Confederation apportioned requisitions according to the value of land within each state, Congress never received adequate surveys to establish quotas on the basis of property. Instead Congress divided requisitions according to a rough approximation of each state's population. The distribution represented in Table 1, column three was adopted on 7 April 1783 and remained unaltered thereafter. See *Journals* 2: 220–224; 24: 230–231, 256–262; and 30: 100–107.
7. This statement follows because $y_i^* = y_i^r$ and $y_{-i}^* = y_{-i}^r$ imply $y_i^* + y_{-i}^* = y_N^* = y_N^r$ and from the definition of π_i,
$$\frac{y_i^*}{y_N^*} = \Pi_i^* = \frac{y_i^r}{y_N^r} = \Pi_i^r.$$
8. If $y_i^* = y_i^r$ and $y_i^* < y_{-i}^r$, then $y_{-i}^* + y_i^* = y_N^* < y_N^r$, which implies that $y_i^*/y_N^* = \pi_i^* > \pi_i^r$. The case for $y_{-i}^* > y_{-i}^r$ is shown similarly.
9. Recognizing that $B_i(x) = B_i[S(y)] = B_i[C_N^{-1}(y_i+y_{-i})]$, the payoff function can be written as $V_i(y_i, y_{-i}) = B_i[C_N^{-1}(y_i+y_{-i})] - y_i$ from which the first order condition can be derived as follows:
$$\begin{aligned}\frac{\partial i}{\partial y_i} &= \frac{\partial B_i}{\partial x}\frac{\partial S}{\partial y_i} - 1\\ &= \frac{\partial B_i}{\partial x}\frac{1}{C_N'(x)} - 1\end{aligned}$$
setting the equation equal to zero
$$B_i'(x) = C_N'(x).$$
The second order condition is met by further assumption.
10. It can be shown that the rational supply is sub-optimal by comparing the individual optimum to the national optimum. Using the implicit summation technology, the first order condition for the unconstrained national optimum is obtained by maximizing
$$V_n(y_i, y_{-i}) = \sum_{i=1}^{13} B_i(x) - C_N(x)$$
with respect to y_i.
$$\frac{\partial i}{\partial y_i} = \sum_{i=1}^{13} \frac{\partial B_i}{\partial x}\frac{\partial S}{\partial y_i} - \frac{\partial C_N}{\partial x}\frac{\partial S}{\partial y_i}$$
$$\frac{1}{C_N'(x)}\left[\sum_{i=1}^{13}\frac{\partial B_i}{\partial x}\right] = \frac{\partial C_N}{\partial x}\frac{1}{C_N'(x)}$$
$$\sum_{i=1}^{13} B_i'(x) = C_N'(x).$$

11. Schedule of Requisitions on the Several States by the United States in Congress Assembled, 31 March 1787 *Papers of the Continental Congress* 2: 174. Subsequent reports suggest that requisition payments picked-up after March 1787 (see 31 March 1788, 1: 75; and 31 December 1787, 2: 484 – same title and reference).
12. Madison to Edmund Pendleton, 24 February 1787 *The Papers of James Madison* 9: 294–295.

References

Articles of Confederation. Reprinted in R. Ketcham (Ed.) (1986). *The Anti-Federalist Papers and the constitutional convention debates*. New York: Mentor Books.

Brown, R.H. (1993). *Redeeming the Republic*. Baltimore: Johns Hopkins University Press.

Cain, M. and Dougherty, K. (1995). Suppressing Shays' Rebellion: Collective action and constitutional design under the Articles of Confederation. Mimeo.

Ferguson, J. (1961). *The power of the purse*. Chapel Hill: University of North Carolina Press.

Frohlich, N. and Oppenheimer, J. (1978). *Modern political economy*. Englewood Cliffs: Prentice-Hall.

Jensen, M. (1970). *The Articles of Confederation*. Madison: The University of Wisconsin Press.

Jensen, M. (1965). *The new nation: A history of the United States during the Confederation 1781–1789*. New York: Knopf.

Journals of the Continental Congress (1910–1937). W.C. Ford (Ed.). Washington, DC: Government Printing Office.

Letters of Delegates to Congress, 1774–1789 (1976–). P. Smith (Ed.). Washington, DC: Library of Congress.

Madison, J. *The Papers of James Madison* (1977). R. Rutland (Ed.). Chicago: University of Chicago Press.

McLaughlin, A. (1969). The Articles of Confederation. In L.W. Levy (Ed.). *Essays on the making of the Constitution*. New York: Oxford University Press.

Mueller, D. (1989). *Public choice II*. Cambridge: Cambridge University Press.

Olson, M. (1965). *The logic of collective action*. Cambridge: Harvard University Press.

Ordeshook, P.C. and Schwartz, T. (1994). The architecture of democracy: Problems of constitutional design in Russia. Mimeo.

Papers of the Continental Congress #247, roll 154, item 141. Washington DC: National Archives.

Sandler, T. (1992). *Collective action: Theory and applications*. Ann Arbor: University of Michigan Press.

Stables, W. (1870). *Rhode Island in the Continental Congress, 1765–1790*. Providence: Providence Printing Co.

Public Choice **90:** 215–233, 1997.

© 1997 *Kluwer Academic Publishers.*

On the (relative) unimportance of a balanced budget*

LAURA RAZZOLINI and WILLIAM F. SHUGHART II
Department of Economics & Finance, University of Mississippi, MS 38677, U.S.A.

Abstract. This paper explores the reasoning underlying Milton Friedman's preference for a small, unbalanced budget over a large, balanced one. Because the marginal return from government spending is less than the marginal cost (measured in terms of the amount of income private individuals remain free to spend), government expenditures have more of an adverse impact on the economy in his view than does the method of financing that spending. Using a panel data set comprising the 50 states plus the District of Columbia, we report evidence from the years 1967 through 1992 that growth rates in income per capita tend to be higher in states with smaller public sectors. Moreover, we find that while both deficits and taxes reduce the rate of income growth in a state, the negative impact of government spending is considerably larger at the margin.

1. Introduction

Various proposals to balance the U.S. federal budget have been advanced by liberals and conservatives alike over the past ten years or so. The plans of deficit "hawk" and "doves" differ considerably in terms of the mixes of spending cuts, tax increases, and reductions in fraud and waste contemplated – as well as the length of time over which revenues and expenditures will be placed on a "glide path" that gradually brings the budget into balance – but there is virtually no disagreement about the ultimate goal: A near consensus exits that the continued accumulation of federal debt must be stopped before it triggers an economic apocalypse.

A balanced federal budget had become such a token of fiscal responsibility by late 1995 that the leadership of the Republican-controlled Congress was able to block a routine increase in the debt ceiling which limits the amount the government is authorized to borrow. This action was part of Congress's attempt to force the president to agree a reduction in the rate of growth of federal spending sufficient to achieve a balanced budget in seven years.

* We thank Charles Rowley for inviting us to contribute to this special issue. Comments on an earlier draft by Mike Belongia and Milton Friedman were quite helpful, as were discussions with John Conlon. J.G. Chen and Tinni Sen provided able research assistance. As is customary, however, we accept full responsibility for any errors.

The president, in turn, vetoed a number of appropriations bills, warning of the "dire consequences" of the bond market's reaction to a sudden halt in Treasury borrowing. Political pundits speculated at length about the effects of the fiscal "train wreck" that twice caused the federal government to partially shut down. During the first episode nearly 800,000 "nonessential" federal workers were furloughed for six days; a month later a quarter of a million federal employees spent two weeks at home.

Milton Friedman disputes the conventional wisdom about the importance of a balanced budget. He has remarked on a number of occasions recently that he would prefer living in a world in which the government spends $1 trillion a year and finances this spending partly by borrowing to one in which the government spends $2 trillion a year but keeps its budget in balance (Friedman, 1995: A12).[1] *Current* spending and *current* taxes, in other words, are the root of government's harmful effects on the economy: "Taxes and spending are the real culprits, not deficits and debt" (Friedman and Friedman, 1984: 27).

This paper explores the reasoning underlying Friedman's view that how government spending is financed makes a difference, but only of the second order. We begin by laying out a simple two-period model that describes the preferences of a representative voter and a Niskanen-type budget-maximizing bureaucrat over two hypothetical states of the world. In one stylized situation, the budget remains in balance and spending is financed entirely with the revenues raised by a broad-based head tax. In the other situation, by contrast, deficit spending is possible and government expenditures are financed partly by tax revenues and partly by funds borrowed in the bond market. Under the assumption that the bureaucrat behaves like a monopolist, charging a (tax) price in excess of the marginal cost of public good supply, the model implies that the bureaucrat will consistently produce more of the public good than voters prefer and, moreover, that such overproduction is exacerbated when the bureaucrat's fiscal policy toolbox contains both deficits and taxes. The model also implies that if the slack-maximizing bureaucrat exercises his or her monopoly power and enjoys slack from using borrowing as a means of financing public expenditure, then deficits make the voter unambiguous worse off – in the second period, the marginal disutility associated with the deficit is greater than the marginal utility of the spending financed with it in the first period. Ricardian equivalence no longer holds (individuals are no longer indifferent between debt and taxes), in other words, when we assume that the bureaucrat behaves self-interestedly.

We next explore this issue empirically. Using a panel data set comprising the 50 states plus the District of Columbia, we regress annual rates of growth in income per capita over the years 1967 through 1992 on state government spending, measures of the size of the state's budget deficit and its tax burden, and a number of other explanatory variables. We find that while the estimated coefficients on all three fiscal variables are invariably negative, at the data means taxes and spending restrain growth to a considerably greater extent than do deficits. We conclude from this evidence that, at least in terms of our measure of economic welfare, a smaller, unbalanced public budget is indeed preferable to a larger, balanced one. As such, a relatively low level of government spending financed partly by borrowing seems to be the best way of promoting economic growth.

2. Budgets and bureaucrats

We consider an economy with two periods and n consumers with identical preferences. In any period t(=1, 2), the representative consumer's preferences are symbolized by a concave utility function

$$U(x_t, G_t), \tag{1}$$

where x_t is the consumption of a private good at time t and G_t is the quantity of a public good consumed in that period. We assume that the economy can borrow and lend at a given interest rate equal to zero. Hence, the present value of the private good in either of the two periods is $p_1 = p_2 = 1$.

The cost of providing the public good is given by the function $c(G_t)$, increasing and convex in G_t. Assuming that the cost of the public good is shared equally by all consumers, the voter's budget constraint is

$$y_t = x_t + T_t/n_t;\ t = 1, 2, \tag{2}$$

where T_t is the total tax bill at time t, y_t is income at t, and n_t is the number of consumers in the economy in period t. The indirect utility function is therefore given by

$$V(T_t, G_t) = U(y_t - T_t/n_t, G_t). \tag{3}$$

Given standard assumptions on the utility function (i.e., U_x, $U_G > 0$; U_{xx}, $U_{GG} < 0$; and $U_{xG} = U_{Gx} \geq 0$, where the time subscripts have been dropped for simplicity), the indifference curves are positively sloped and convex.

On the supply side, we model a bureaucrat who derives utility from the slack he or she can extract from the budget when providing a public good.[2] We define slack at time t as the difference between the actual expenditure on the public good in that period and the good's cost of provision:

$$S_t = p_t G_t - c(G_t);\ t = 1, 2, \tag{4}$$

where p_t is the per unit expenditure and p_tG_t is the actual expenditure on the public good.[3]

With these preliminaries in mind, we are now in position to explore two alternative fiscal policy regimes. In the first regime, the budget must be balanced in every period; deficit spending becomes possible in the second regime.

2.1. *The balanced budget case*

In maximizing slack, the bureaucrat faces the following constraints: First, the budget must be balanced, that is,

$$p_tG_t = T_t;\ t = 1, 2, \tag{5}$$

where T_t represents the total tax revenue collected from consumer-voters. Substituting this constraint into the bureaucrat's slack function, we obtain $S_t = T_t - c(G_t)$. Given the assumptions on the cost function, the bureaucrat's "iso-slack" curves are positively sloped and concave. Second, the bureaucrat must guarantee a minimum level of utility to the voter-consumer, that is,

$$V(T_t, G_t) = U(y_t - T_t/n_t, G_t) \geq V_t^{min};\ t = 1, 2. \tag{6}$$

Notice that, by using $G_t = T_t/p_t$, the indirect utility function can be written as

$$V(T_t) = U(y_t - T_t/n_t, T_t/p_t).$$

To make the problem interesting, we assume that there exists a preferred level of taxation by the consumer. (Given our assumptions on the utility function and the budget constraint, it is easy to argue that the function $V(T_t)$ is single-peaked in T_t.) That is, there exists a $T_t \in (0, n_ty_t)$ that solves

$$dV/dT_t = U_{Gt}/p_t - U_{xt}/n_t = 0. \tag{7}$$

The problem for the bureaucrat is therefore in each period to choose optimally the variables G_t and T_t to maximize slack, subject to the constraints (5) and (6). After some substitutions, the problem reduces to one of maximizing the Lagrangean function

$$\mathcal{L} = T_t - c(G_t) + \lambda[U(y_t - T_t/n_t, G_t) - V_t^{min}];\ t = 1, 2. \tag{8}$$

The first-order conditions are the following (for t = 1, 2):

$$\mathcal{L}_{Tt} :\ 1 - \lambda U_{xt}/n_t = 0,\ \text{and} \tag{9}$$

$$\pounds_{Gt}: \ -c'(G_t) + \lambda U_{Gt} = 0. \tag{10}$$

From equation (9) it follows that $\lambda_t = n_t/U_{xt} > 0$. That is, the consumer's participation constraint is binding. In each period, the utility of the voter is always pushed to the minimum level, V_t^{min} (see Inman, 1987; Wyckoff, 1990; and Hayes et al., 1995 for a similar conclusion). Furthermore, from equation (9), we get

$$U_{xt}/n_t = U_{xt+1}/n_{t+1},$$

that is, the per capita marginal utility from consumption of the private good is equalized across time. Combining the two first order conditions (9) and (10) we obtain:

$$n_t U_{Gt}/U_{xt} = c'(G_t). \tag{11}$$

Equation (11) is the Samuelsonian condition stating that the sum of marginal rates of substitution between the public and the private good must be equal to the marginal rate of transformation. Comparing equation (11) with equation (7), we see that in any period t the bureaucrat may overprovide, underprovide or provide the same level of public good (taxation) preferred by the consumer according as $c'(G_t)$ is greater than, less than, or equal to p_t. In particular, if the per unit price of the public good is greater than marginal cost (i.e., $c'(G_t) < p_t$) so that the bureaucrat behaves like a "monopolist", then in each period t the public good is overproduced with respect to the level preferred by the voter.

2.2. *Deficit spending*

Let us now introduce the possibility of the bureaucrat financing current public expenditures by borrowing from voter-consumers. We assume that in the second period the government always honors its inherited debt obligations. The bureaucrat's budget constraints in the two periods are:

$$p_1 G_1 - T_1 = D_1 \text{ and } p_2 G_2 + D_1 = T_2, \tag{12}$$

where D_1 is government borrowing in period 1.

Using (12), the bureaucrat's objective function becomes

$$S = T_1 + D_1 - c[(T_1 + D_1)/p_1] + T_2 - D_1 - c[(T_2 - D_1)/p_2].$$

Differentiating slack with respect to T_t (t = 1, 2) and D_1, we obtain the following:

$$dS/dT_t = 1 - c'(G_t)/p_t, \ t = 1, 2; \text{ and}$$

$$dS/dD_1 = 1 - c'(G_1)/p_1 - 1 + c'(G_2)/p_2.$$

These relations suggest, on the one hand, that slack is increasing in, decreasing in, or unaffected by T_t according as p_t is greater than, less than, or equal to $c'(G_t)$, for $t = 1, 2$. On the other hand, slack is positively, negatively, or not affected by borrowing in the first period according as p_1/p_2 is greater than, less than, or equal to $c'(G_1)/c'(G_2)$.

If the bureaucrat exercises his or her monopoly power by pricing the public good above the marginal cost of producing it, then $dS/dD_1 < dS/dT_1$ (since $dS/T_2 = 1 - c'(G_2)/p_2 > 0$). In other words, the bureaucrat's slack increases more when expenditures in the first period are financed by current taxes rather than by borrowing. However, if the bureaucrat behaves like a benevolent social planner acting solely in the interest of the voters (i.e., sets $p_t = c'(G_t)$ in each period), then slack is not affected by the deficit. This result conforms to *a priori* expectations, since a selfless social planner will always balance the budget.

The bureaucrat's problem is to choose optimally T_1, T_2, and D_1 (the optimal values of G_1 and G_2 will follow automatically from the budget constraints) to maximize slack in the two periods, given the voter's participation constraint:

$$U(x_1, G_1) + U(x_2, G_2) \geq V_1^{min} + V_2^{min}. \tag{13}$$

Using (12), (13), and the voter's budget constraints (2), we obtain the following Lagrangean function:

$$\begin{aligned}\mathcal{L} = \ & T_1 + T_2 - c[(T_1 + D_1)/p_1] - c[(T_2 - D_1)/p_2] + \lambda\{U[y_1 - T_1/n_1, \\ & (T_1 + D_1)/p_1] + U[y_2 - T_2/n_2, (T_2 - D_1)/p_2] - V_1^{min} - V_2^{min}\}.\end{aligned}$$

The first-order conditions are the following:

$$\mathcal{L}_{Tt} : \ 1 - c'(G_t)/p_t + \lambda(U_{Gt}/p_t - U_{xt}/n_t) = 0, t = 1, 2; \text{ and} \tag{14}$$

$$\mathcal{L}_{D1} : \ -c'(G_1)/p_1 + c'(G_2)/p_2 + \lambda(U_{G1}/p_1 - U_{G2}/p_2) = 0. \tag{15}$$

In equation (14), the first term, $1 - c'(G_t)/p_t$, represents the bureaucrat's net marginal benefit from taxing, whilst the second term, $\lambda(U_{Gt}/p_t - U_{xt}/n_t)$, is the voter's net marginal disutility from the tax times the shadow price associated with the voter's participation constraint. Again, if $dS/dT_t > 0$, then $\lambda(U_{Gt}/p_t - U_{xt}/n_t) > 0$, which implies that in each period the voter is pushed onto the lowest possible indifference curve and the level of expenditure-taxation chosen if too high with respect to the voter's preferred level.

In equation (15), the first two terms, $-c'(G_1)/p_1 + c'(G_2)/p_2$, represent the bureaucrat's net marginal benefit from having a deficit in period 1, while the last term, $\lambda(U_{G1}/p_1 - U_{G2}/p_2)$, represents the voter's net marginal (dis)utility from period 1's deficit. If the slack-maximizing bureaucrat exercises his or her monopoly power (i.e., $\lambda > 0$) and also enjoys slack from using borrowing as a means of financing public expenditure (i.e., $dS/dD_1 > 0$), then the last term in equation (15), $U_{G1}/p_1 - U_{G2}/p_2$, is necessarily negative. That is, in the second period, the marginal disutility from using the deficit to finance provision of the public good is greater than the marginal utility associated with the first period's increased expenditure.

This last result implies that whether or not Ricardian equivalence holds depends on the assumptions made about bureaucratic behavior. When self-interested (i.e., slack maximizing) rather than public-interested motives are assumed, voters are no longer indifferent to the method of financing government expenditures.[4] Deficits begin to matter.

3. Empirical model and results

The previous section described the theoretical tradeoffs faced by a slack-maximizing bureaucrat between taxes and deficits. In what follows, we explore this issue empirically from the private sector's point of view. Which fiscal policy regime imposes smaller costs on the economy: a small, unbalanced government budget or a large, balanced one?

3.1. *The model and data*

The 50 states furnish a useful laboratory setting for examining the impact of government's "fiscal stance" (Chrystal and Dowd, 1989). Some state governments are frugal; others are spendthrift. There is, moreover, substantial variation in the extent of reliance on deficits and taxes as means of public finance both across states and over time. This wide variety of fiscal policy regimes in part reflects significant differences in governmental use of fiscal discipline management tools. While nearly all states are required to balance their budgets, a broad assortment of constitutional and statutory provisions have been adopted in recent years to constrain the fiscal policy choices of state governments. These fiscal discipline tools include tax and expenditure limitations, legislative supermajority voting requirements for enacting tax increases, gubernatorial line-item veto authority, and restrictions on indebtedness (Rowley, Shughart, and Tollison, 1986). The diversity in fiscal management tools at the level of the states supplies a rich institutional backdrop against which to explore the economic effects of various fiscal policy regimes.

Assessing the impact of various public spending, deficit, and tax mixes on the private economy requires adopting a welfare standard for rank-ordering the fiscal policy alternatives. The annual growth rate in income per capita, GROWTH, provies a broad measure of economic well-being, and we have chosen it as our dependent variable in that spirit. A linear regression equation designed to explain time-wise, cross-sectional differences in state growth rates is specified as follows:

$$\mathrm{GROWTH}_{it} = \beta_0 + \beta_1\mathrm{GOVSIZE}_{it} + \beta_2\mathrm{DEFPCT}_{it} + \beta_3\mathrm{BURDEN}_{it} + \\ + \beta_4\mathrm{TRA86}_t + \beta_5\mathrm{NORTHEAST}_i + \beta_6\mathrm{YEAR}_t + \in_{it}$$

where the subscripts denote the jurisdiction, i (= 1,. . .,51), and year of observation, t (=1967,. . ., 1992).

The key explanatory variables control for the relative size of the state government, GOVSIZE, measured as the ratio of total direct general expenditures to total state personal income; the current-year difference between total direct general expenditures and total general revenues (which includes intergovernmental transfers) as a percentage of total general revenues, DEFPCT; and the percentage of total general revenues raised by taxes, BURDEN.[5] Besides holding state fiscal policy regimes constant, the regression includes two dummy variables, TRA86 and NORTHEAST. The first of these, which is set equal to one beginning in 1986 and zero otherwise, controls for the effects of the Tax Reform Act of 1986. This law, which lowered federal marginal personal income tax rates substantially, simultaneously increased the (after-tax) burden of deductible state taxes. The second dummy variable, NORTHEAST, controls for regional differences.[6] A linear trend, YEAR, is also included to account for otherwise unexplained time-wise variations in the dependent variable.

The data were gathered from standard government sources. In particular, the observations on state per capita income are from the *Survey of Current Business* (U.S. Bureau of Economic Analysis, various issues).[7] Data to construct the fiscal policy variables are from *Government Finances* (U.S. Bureau of the Census, various issues).

The means of the key variables, averaged across the 50 states plus the District of Columbia, are shown in Table 1 for each year in the data set. (GENEXP is total state direct general expenditures; note also that because DEFICIT is defined as expenditures minus revenues, budget deficits are positive in sign and budget surpluses are negative.) The data suggest that the typical state ran a budget surplus over the period in question (surpluses have especially been the norm since the mid 1970s), a secular increase in state government spending coupled with a secular decline in the extent of reliance on taxes as a method of state public finance, and a great deal of year-to-year variation in growth rates in per capita income.

Table 1. State growth rates and fiscal characteristics, annual averages, 1967–92[a]

YEAR	GROWTH	GENEXP	GOVSIZE	BURDEN	DEFICIT	DEFPCT
1967	–	492.3333	.014307%	62.72141%	14.84314	2.622848%
1968	8.241914%	530.4314	.014105	62.50845	14.15686	2.439919
1969	10.99934	585.8627	.013483	62.89758	18.27451	2.711553
1970	7.388982	653.2353	.013465	62.38291	–44.78431	–2.678044
1971	6.631531	741.0000	.014161	61.27730	26.54902	2.907322
1972	9.270551	807.8235	.013934	61.34203	10.43137	.004581
1973	12.80308	874.1373	.013034	59.74739	–23.31569	–4.446575
1974	8.879879	944.1373	.012412	59.27553	–37.72549	–5.262046
1975	7.957658	1,087.804	.012651	57.99655	2.098039	–.427063
1976	9.285952	1,210.078	.012802	57.79722	–14.90196	–.951247
1977	9.432036	1,284.490	.012239	57.98879	–70.47059	–4.766769
1978	11.99229	1,387.980	.011758	57.48619	–99.96078	–6.965391
1979	10.87939	1,542.824	.011836	57.25862	–92.00000	–5.575428
1980	9.459043	1,714.118	.012217	55.39029	–123.4592	–4.793090
1981	10.55907	1,890.490	.012027	54.88571	–224.0784	–6.469498
1982	4.656812	2,046.353	.012349	56.18821	–283.8627	–8.029868
1983	4.943191	2,123.686	.012030	55.63776	–177.2941	–5.809518
1984	7.883933	2,273.026	.011984	56.30659	–247.0135	–8.709375
1985	6.048771	2,460.941	.012226	55.74942	–252.8039	–8.198223
1986	4.489368	2,632.863	.012390	55.36689	–210.1569	–6.175966
1987	5.373231	2,804.137	.012587	56.02407	–136.4902	–4.454892
1988	6.589118	2,943.157	.012121	57.10145	–163.2353	–4.411782
1989	7.621343	3,156.667	.011925	56.78916	–137.3137	–3.968639
1990	6.149429	3,410.431	.012006	56.28108	–134.2157	–3.654537
1991	3.337721	3,658.529	.012162	55.53238	–74.84314	–1.080130
1992	5.243592	3,911.118	.012233	54.53595	–27.49020	–.350594

[a]Millions of dollars (except percent).

Table 2 displays summary statistics for the per capita income growth and fiscal variables averaged over the 1,275 observations in the sample (51 of the original 1,326 observations were lost in computing per capita income growth rates). Substantial variation in the data over time and across states is evident.

The thrust of Friedman's point is that the size of the public sector, rather than how it is financed, is the chief determinant of the government's impact

Table 2. Summary statistics[a]

Variable	Mean	Median	Minimum	Maximum	Std. deviation
GROWTH (%)	7.844693	7.728772	−13.83351	44.85915	3.684489
GENEXP	1,867.107	1,591.000	340.0000	10,047.00	1,290.627
GOVSIZE (%)	.012566	.005488	.000594	.117515	.017005
BURDEN (%)	57.74990	57.90390	10.00480	97.58687	7.134719
DEFICIT	−100.1522	−45.0000	−7,081.000	787.0000	392.8173
DEFPCT (%)	−3.564612	−3.108108	−208.7407	43.17060	9.822519

[a]Millions of dollars (except percent).

on the private economy. The fiscal policy transmission mechanism operates primarily through the expenditure side of the budget, in other words, and while the taxes and borrowing required to finance that spending also have negative consequences, their effects are of secondary importance.

Hence, a negative *ceteris paribus* relationship between growth rates in state income per capita and total direct general expenditures as a percentage of total personal income is predicted. The direction of causality is assumed to go in one direction only, namely from increased government spending to lower rates of income growth.[8] The negative effects of greater government spending may operate directly – by channeling scarce resources to relatively unproductive sectors of the economy, for example – or indirectly – by making it more likely that taxes will be increased in the future, thereby lowering the expected after-tax rates of return to private investments. The level of spending may also be an indicator of the extent of regulatory and other off-budget government intervention into the private economy. If "big-government" states (as measured by the ratio of total direct general expenditures to total personal income) also tend to pursue active regulatory agendas that short-circuit competitive market forces and interfere with the efficiency of resource allocation in the economy, then growth rates should be lower in those states. Our model does not allow us to distinguish between the direct and indirect effects of state government spending, however.

Friedman's argument also implies that while higher taxes and greater reliance on deficit finance both affect the economy adversely, the effect of the former should be more pronounced. The theorem of Ricardian equivalence notwithstanding (Barro, 1974),[9] the act of borrowing defers tax liabilities into the future, allowing some individuals opportunistically to shift part of their share of the tax burden associated with the debt issue to others (Buchanan,

Table 3. Regression results (dependent variable: GROWTH)

	OLS	Panel estimates Comon intercept	Fixed effects	Random effects
Intercept	338.6973	393.5667	–	303.1664
GOVSIZE	–23.07866**	–18.44506**	–176.4118*	–11.00722*
	(9.253140)	(8.069855)	(36.31727)	(3.666538)
DEFPCT	–.021494	–.018196***	–.012662	–.015329***
	(.017251)	(.010883)	(.011588)	(.009116)
BURDEN	–.057010**	–.038894***	–.072455**	–.022694**
	(.022197)	(.020380)	(.033966)	(.009802)
TRA86	–1.313645*	–1.013868*	–.811828**	–1.402867*
	(.349521)	(.387955)	(.396806)	(.342683)
NORTHEAST	.561036**			
	(.275578)			
YEAR	–.165192*	–.193400*	–.222611*	–.148250*
	(.024324)	(.027305)	(.029846)	(.021826)
AR(1)		.131069*	.125094*	
		(.028581)	(.029346)	
R^2	.189	.209	.227	.159
D-W	1.792	2.025	2.026	1.731
F	49.20451*	53.44050*	68.56564*	–

Notes. Standard errors in parentheses. D-W is the Durbin-Watson *d*-statistic; AR(1) is the estimated first-order autocorrelation coefficient. N = 1,275.
* Significant at the one-percent level.
** Significant at the five-percent level.
*** Significant at the ten-percent level.

1976), and some to avoid it altogether.[10] Hence, while the estimated coefficients on BURDEN and DEFPCT are both expected to be negative insofar as any method of public finance siphons resources from the private economy, taxes are expected to have a larger adverse impact on growth than deficits.

3.2. *Empirical results*

Our empirical exploration of the growth consequences of government's fiscal stance begins with Table 3, which shows the results of estimating several versions of our basic regression equation using both ordinary least squares and panel data techniques.[11]

The results strongly support Friedman's reasons for preferring a small, unbalanced budget to a large, balanced one. There is a negative and statistically significant *ceteris paribus* relationship between the size of a state's public sector and the annual growth rate of state per capita income. (Using a two-tailed test, the estimated coefficient on GOVSIZE is significantly different from zero at the five-percent level in three of the specifications and at the one-percent level in the other.) At the data means, a ten percent increase in the ratio of total state direct general expenditures to total personal income leads to a reduction in income growth of between .2 percent and 3.7 percent per year. Moreover, while increases in both taxes and borrowing likewise result in lower growth rates, the estimated coefficients on the latter of these variables are different from zero at only the ten percent level of statistical significance in two of the panel estimates. A state's tax burden exerts a strongly negative impact on income growth, though: A ten percent increase in tax receipts as a share of total current revenues causes growth to decline by between 1.7 and 4.8 percent. As far as borrowing is concerned, a ten percent increase in the current deficit as a percent of current revenues causes the annual growth rate in per capita income to decline by about six-tenths of one percent.[12]

The remaining coefficient estimates are consistent with *a priori* expectations. By raising the effective after-federal-tax burden of state taxes, the Tax Reform Act of 1986 slowed economic growth by eight-tenths of one percentage point or more in the typical state over the sample period. Indeed, the 1986 law was the single largest cause of the slowdown in state economic growth that occurred between 1967 and 1992 – a downward trend that averaged around two-tenths of one percent per year. Moreover, the OLS estimates suggest that the per capita income growth of individuals living in the Northeastern United States were significantly above the national mean.

All told, the empirical results are consistent with Friedman's reasoning: Government spending and taxes appear to be the main cause of sluggish economic growth at the level of the states. Deficits likewise inhibit economic expansion, but their effects are of secondary importance.[13]

3.3. *Causality*

Our empirical model assumes – and our results support the conjecture – that government spending causes per capita income growth to decline, but that reductions in economic growth do not cause changes in the level of government spending. However, an element of circularity in this relationship cannot be ruled out *a priori*. The Keynesian model, of course, supposes that fiscal policy tools will be used countercyclicly, with government spending rising during economic downturns in order to help offset declines in aggregate demand. Although Keynesian policy prescriptions apply more directly to the federal government, it is possible that spending at the state level follows a similar countercyclical pattern, especially so because many of the programs comprising the federal government's "safety net" (food stamps, unemployment insurance, and so on) are in fact administered through state budgets.

In order to investigate this possibility, we ran Granger-causality tests for each of the 51 political jurisdictions in our sample. In each case, we regressed the first differences of GOVSIZE and GROWTH (labeled DGOVSIZE and DGROWTH, respectively) on two lags of itself and two lags of the other variable plus an intercept term. Our attention was focused on the estimated coefficients on DGROWTH in the DGOVSIZE equations in order to answer the following question: Do past values of income growth explain any of the variation in current government spending?

The results suggest that the answer to this question is no. Using an alpha level of .05, we were able to reject the null hypothesis that growth does not Granger-cause government spending in only six of the 51 cases. (The six states were New Jersey, Michigan, North Carolina, South Carolina, Wyoming, and Hawaii.) Unidirectional causality thus seems to characterize our data set. Just as importantly, the vast majority of the coefficient estimates provide further evidence of a negative – and causal – relationship between government spending and income growth.

3.4. *Fiscal discipline management tools*

Previous research suggests that constitutional (but not statutory) constraints requiring states to balance their budgets or limiting the amount of borrowing they may do are effective in limiting deficit spending at the margin (Rowley, Shughart, and Tollison, 1986). However, our results suggest that the attention hitherto devoted to constraining government's ability to engage in deficit finance has been misplaced. Indeed, we find that, at the level of the states, the difference between current revenues and current expenditures is the least worrisome aspect of public finance. At least insofar as the annual growth rate in per capita income is concerned, current government spending and current taxes have far larger negative impacts on economic welfare.

Hence, constraints on spending and taxes would seem to hold the greatest promise for limiting any of the public sector's harmful effects on growth in the private economy.[14] This conclusion is buttressed by evidence from a cross-section regression for 1992 suggesting that neither statutory nor constitutional provisions requiring the state legislature to pass – or the governor to sign – a balanced budget have statistically significant effects on the level of state spending.[15] These findings are consistent with prior empirical research on the line-item veto which finds that a governor's ability to strike individual spending items from the state budget has no detectable influence on total

Table 4. Effects of fiscal discipline management tools on spending, borrowing, and taxes, 1992[a]

Fiscal discipline tools	GENEXP	GOVSIZE (%)	DEFICIT	DEFPCT (%)	BURDEN (%)
No tools (N=2)	3,876.500	.026532	27.0000	.766685	57.00192
Item veto only (N=9)	4,295.444	.013621	−7.22222	−.186759	56.94024
Item veto and legislature must pass a balanced budget (C) (N=4)	3,523.500	.012383	−54.50000	−1.848300	56.48383
Item veto and legislature must pass (C) and Governor must sign a balanced budget (C) (N=13)	3,592.000	.009690	−10.23077	−.253878	52.67416
Item veto and legislature must pass (C or S) and Governor must sign a balanced budget (C or S) (N=29)	3,747.448	.010605	−40.75863	−.448562	52.75544
All tools[b] (N=3)	3,396.000	.003903	56.66667	1.546337	56.86308
All states (N=50)	3,838.120	.011552	−18.18000	−.227200	54.60506

Notes. C denotes a constitutional requirement, S a statutory one.
[a]Millions of dollars (except percent).
[b]Item veto authority plus both statutory and constitutional requirements that the legislature pass and the governor sign a balanced budget.

expenditures, in part because vitually all state executives enjoy such authority. The overall conclusion of this literature seems to be that by inserting the governor directly into the budgetary logrolling process, the line-item veto may affect the mix of spending, but little else (Carter and Schap, 1990).

The appendix shows three key state fiscal management tools in place as of 1992. Comparisons of the means of the fiscal variables in our data set based on the use of balanced budget requirements and line-item veto authority are shown in Table 4. Total direct general expenditures (GENEXP) in the two states without any fiscal discipline management tools at all were nearly the same as the overall average for all 50 states (the District of Columbia is excluded from these comparisons). These two states also had above-average tax burdens and they ran budget deficits in 1992, while the typical state ran a budget surplus of just over $18 million in that year. Line-item veto authority by itself is evidently of little consequence in controlling spending: The nine states in this category did post a budget surplus, but at the same their tax burdens were two percentage points above the national average.

There is some evidence that, when used in conjunction with constitutional or statutory balanced budget requirements, line-item veto authority helps curb total government spending, and, hence, limits government size. But the overall effects are mixed. When fiscal discipline management tools result in lower expenditures, this outcome is sometimes offset either by fairly substantial budget deficits, by higher average tax burdens, or both. This is particularly true for the three states having both constitutional and statutory requirements that the legislature pass and the governor sign a balanced budget. In general, states that have adopted balanced budget requirements of some sort tend to run budget surpluses, but as we have already seen, controlling the current deficit is the least helpful pro-growth policy.

4. Concluding remarks

This paper has presented theory and evidence supporting Milton Friedman's preference for a smaller, unbalanced budget over a larger, balanced one. Using a panel data set comprising the 50 states plus the District of Columbia for the years 1967 through 1982, our evidence indicates that growth rates in income per capita are higher in states with smaller public sectors. Moreover, we find that while both deficits and taxes reduce the rate of income growth in the typical state, the negative impact of taxes is considerably larger at the margin.

Our results suggest that controlling spending and moderating the tax burden are important to promoting economic growth. Neither one of these objectives is addressed effectively by constitutional or statutory requirements mandating a balanced government budget. In fact, by forcing government to rely more heavily on taxes and off-budget borrowing as methods of public finance, balanced budget requirements may in fact be counterproductive. A small public sector whose expenditures are financed in part by running a budget deficit appears to be the best way of fostering economic growth.

Notes

1. In particular, Friedman (1995: A12) argues that

> it cannot be emphasized too much that the real burden on the economy is what government spends (or mandates others to spend) rather than how much it receives in taxes. If total national income is, say, \$6 trillion, and federal spending is \$1.5 trillion, that leaves \$4.5 trillion for private individuals plus states and local governments to spend. If federal government spending is \$2 trillion, that leaves \$4 trillion for everybody else. And these statements are true regardless of how the government spending is financed, whether by taxes, borrowing or printing money. The method of finance is important, and affects the level of inflation, interest rates and other important phenomena, but it does not alter the basic real burden on the economy.

In my view our country would be far better off with a federal budget of $1 trillion and a deficit of $300 billion than with a fully balanced budget of $2 trillion. The deficit is a problem, but mainly because the possibility of running deficits tends to lead to higher spending than would otherwise occur.

2. Related models describing the behavior of a slack-maximizing bureaucrat can be found in Migué and Belanger (1974), Inman (1987), Wyckoff (1990) and Hayes et al. (1995).
3. We assume that production efficiency is consistently achieved in the provision of the public good. Indeed, the bureaucrat has an interest in seeing that least-cost input combinations are employed so that he or she can extract the maximum possible slack from the public budget.
4. Bohn (1992) reaches a similar conclusion.
5. The numerator of BURDEN includes revenues collected from all tax sources, including property, sales, individual income, and corporate income taxes.
6. The definition of this regional dummy variable follows that of the U.S. Bureau of the Census. Preliminary estimates indicated that only the northeastern states exhibited income growth rates significantly different from the rest of the country.
7. More specifically, the annual observations on state income per capita were taken from the following issues of the *Survey of Current Business*: 1967–68 (August 1982 issue), 1969–80 (August 1987), 1981–84 (August 1988), 1985 (April 1989), 1986 (April 1990), 1987–89 (April 1991), and 1990–92 (April 1994).
8. The alternative hypothesis that government responds to lower growth rates by increasing expenditures is explored more fully below.
9. See also Barro (1989) and the other contributions to the symposium on budget deficits in the Spring 1989 *Journal of Economic Perspectives*.
10. Individuals will prefer deficits to taxes if their planning horizons do not extend beyond their own lifetimes. Tobin (1980: 55–58) suggests that this would be the case for: (a) childless members of the generation living when government debt is issued; (b) parents who are indifferent to the welfare of their children; (c) parents who anticipate that, with compounding of any reasonable real rate of economic growth, their descendents will be richer than they are; and (d) households facing liquidity constraints that prevent them from transferring income intertemporarily. For evidence that Ricardian equivalence does not hold when the life expectancy of the population is taken into account, see Shughart and Tollison (1986).
11. All regressions were run on Econometric Views™ 2.0. The OLS estimates use White's (1980) heteroscedasticity-consistent standard errors and covariances.
12. To further assure ourselves that the estimates reported in Table 3 are not caused by mere trending in any of the continuous variables, we redefined the income growth and fiscal policy variables relative to their national averages. The results are reported below (standard errors in parentheses):

RELGROWTH = 133.14–

.132876RELSPEND	+.006023RELDEFICIT	−.217932RELBURDEN
(.060496)*	(.003773)	(.125609)**
−.000408TRA86	+7.310883NORTHEAST	+2.64E − 05YEAR
(4.631484)	(3.781743)**	(.284703)

(R^2 = .028; D-W = 2.004, F = 6.17*). Although the estimated coefficient on RELDEFICIT is positive in this specification, it is not different from zero at standard levels of statistical significance. What is more important is that the coefficient on spending remains negative and significant (p = .0282). In other words, states whose public sectors are above-average in size (measured by relative total direct general expenditures) exhibit below-average rates of per capita income growth. Income growth is likewise impaired significantly in states with relatively heavy tax burdens.

13. Chrystal and Dowd (1989: 1405) who, using data for the United Kingdom also find that "almost everywhere the impact of the deficit/GDP ratio is negative", suggest that results such as these "raise the serious possibility that the only positive impact of fiscal expansion may be upon the government sector itself".
14. But see Shadbegian (1996), who finds that tax and expenditure limits restrict government size and growth only in states with incomes below the national average.
15. These results are available on request.

References

Barro, R.J. (1974). Are government bonds net wealth? *Journal of Political Economy* 82: 1095–1117.

Barro, R.J. (1989). The Ricardian approach to budget deficits. *Journal of Economic Perspectives* 3: 37–54.

Bohn, H. (1992). Endogenous government spending and Ricardian equivalence. *Economic Journal* 102: 588–597.

Buchanan, J.M. (1976). Barro on the Ricardian equivalence theorem. *Journal of Political Economy* 84: 337–342.

Carter, J.R. and Schap, D. (1990). Line item veto: Where is thy sting? *Journal of Economic Perspectives* 4: 103–118.

Chrystal, K.A. and Dowd, K. (1989). Disaggregate supply: Evidence for the U.K. *Applied Economics* 21: 1397–1409.

Friedman, M. (1995). Balanced budget: Amendment must put limit on taxes. *Wall Street Journal* 4: A12.

Friedman, M. and Friedman, R. (1984). *Tyranny of the status quo*. San Diego: Harcourt Brace Jovanovich.

Hayes, K.J., Razzolini, L. and Ross, L.B. (1995). Bureaucratic choice and nonoptimal provision of public goods: Theory and evidence. Public Choice, forthcoming.

Inman, R.P. (1987). Markets, governments, and the "new" political economy. In A.J. Auerbach and M. Feldstein (Eds.), *Handbook of public economics*, Vol. II. Amsterdam: North Holland.

Migué, J.L. and Belanger, G. (1974). Toward a general theory of managerial discretion. *Public Choice* 17: 27–43.

National Association of State Budget Officers (1992). *Budget processes in the states 1992*.

Niskanen, W.A. (1971). *Bureaucracy and representative government*. Chicago: Aldine.

Rowley, C.K., Shughart, W.F. II and Tollison, R.D. (1986). Interest groups and deficits. In J.M. Buchanan, C.K. Rowley and R.D. Tollison (Eds.), *Deficits*. Oxford: Basil Blackwell.

Shadbegian, R.J. (1996). Do tax and expenditure limitations affect the size and growth of state government? *Contemporary Economic Policy* 14: 22–35.

Shughart, W.F. II and Tollison, R.D. (1986). The vote motive and the debt: A contingent liability approach. In J.M. Buchanan, C.K. Rowley and R.D. Tollison (Eds.), *Defitics*. Oxford: Basil Blackwell.

Tobin, J. (1980). *Asset accumulation and economic activity*. Chicago: University of Chicago Press.

U.S. Bureau of Economic Analysis. *Survey of current business*, various issues.

U.S. Bureau of the Census. *Government finances*, various issues.

White, H. (1980). A heteroscedasticity-consistent covariance matrix estimator and a direct test for heteroscedasticity. *Econometrica* 48: 817–838.

Wyckoff, P.G. (1990). Bureaucracy, inefficiency and time. *Public Choice* 67: 169–179.

Appendix 1. State fiscal discipline management tools, 1992

State	Legislature must pass a balanced budget (S)	Legislature must pass a balanced budget (C)	Governor must sign a balanced budget (S)	Governor must sign a balanced budget (C)	Line-item veto
Alabama	×				
Alaska	×		×		×
Arizona	×	×	×	×	×
Arkansas	×		×		×
California					×
Colorado		×		×	×
Connecticut					×
Delaware	×	×	×	×	×
Florida	×	×	×	×	×
Georgia		×		×	×
Hawaii			×	×	×
Idaho		×[a]			×
Illinois		×			×
Indiana		×			
Iowa					×
Kansas	×	×			×
Kentucky	×	×	×	×	×
Louisiana		×	×	×	×
Maine		×	×	×	
Maryland		×	–[b]	–[b]	
Mass.		×		×	×
Michigan		×	×	×	×
Minnesota	×				×
Mississippi	×				×
Missouri				×	×
Montana		×			×
Nebraska					×
Nevada		×		×	
New Hamp.					
New Jersey		×		×	×
New Mexico		×		×	×
New York					×
N. Carolina	×				
N. Dakota		×		×	×
Ohio		×		×	×
Oklahoma		×		×	×
Oregon		×		×	×
Pennsylvania				×	×
Rhode Island		×	×		
S. Carolina		×		×	×
S. Dakota		×		×	×
Tennessee		×		×	×
Texas	×	×			×

Appendix 1. Continued

State	Legislature must pass a balanced budget (S)	Legislature must pass a balanced budget (C)	Governor must sign a balanced budget (S)	Governor must sign a balanced budget (C)	Line-item veto
Utah	×	×	×		×
Vermont					
Virginia					×
Washington					×
W. Virginia		×		×	×
Wisconsin		×			×
Wyoming					×
TOTALS	12	31	13	26	41

Notes. C denotes a constitutional provision, S a statutory one.
Source: National Association of State Budget Officers (1992: 4, 6).
[a]Although the constitution requires the legislature to pass a balanced budget, there are no sanctions, and in recent years the legislature has over appropriated its general account revenue estimate for the coming year (National Association of State Budget Officers, 1992: 33).
[b]Budget becomes law immediately upon legislative enactment.

Public Choice **90**: 235–254, 1997.

© 1997 *Kluwer Academic Publishers.*

Public choice in a federal system*

JEAN-LUC MIGUÉ
University of Quebec, School of Public Administration, Quebec City, Canada G1V 3J9

Abstract. Except for the mobility constraints imposed on political decisions of lower-level governments, public choice analysts assume that the working of the political process under federalism remains the same at all levels of governments as under unitary state. This paper argues that one dimension of the political process in a federalist framework lends itself to specific economic analysis, namely the fact that, once constitutional limits break down and functions overlap, two or more levels of government compete for the same voters in the supply of services in a given territory. Viewing votes as inputs in the production of political outputs, the conventional analysis of allocation under common-property rule should shed light on the outcome of this process. The analysis shows that it is in the interest of both suppliers to seek to gain the votes in being first to implement programs. There are thus two forces operating in a typical federalist system, an expansionist one rooted in the political dynamics analysed here, and a restrictionist one based on the mobility of resources among decentralized entities. This may explain why the empirical record is rather mixed on the contribution of federalism to containing government growth. The consequences of this process are derived and possible avenues for improvement are explored.

1. Introduction

On the eve of the secession referendum in the Province of Quebec, a widespread opinion in Canada held that welfare and spending control was being put off by both levels of government as a result of their concern for the stability of the federation. In their desire to woo Quebec voters, the governing party at both levels refrein from taking any urgent redress action that would take away currently available privileges. It looks as if competition by two public goods suppliers for the support of the same pool of voters leads to an excessive supply of services. In the economic theory of federalism, this is not the way it is supposed to work. Federalism is expected to result in smaller budgets and less regulation. Partisans of devolution endlessly complain about the outrageous waste resulting from the duplication of functions in federal states. Do they have a theoretical case?

* The author has benefited from comments received from Brian Lee Crowley, Gérard Bélanger, William Niskanen, Michel Boucher, Barry Weingast, Richard Marceau, Charles Rowley and Pierre Simard.

2. Mainstream economics of federalism

In the Tiebout analytical tradition, mobility through decentralization offers a substitute to the political process as an instrument to discipline governments. The determining characteristic of a federalist structure is that most responsibilities are entrusted to decentralized authorities, who have no power to tax or regulate the whole area where movement of resources is free. Such arrangements enhance the ability of resource owners to move their goods, their capital or themselves away from detrimental tax and regulatory measures. Because inefficient government decisions cost more in a more open economy, the predicted outcome is less interventionism (Weingast, 1995; Migué, 1993).

Except for these mobility constraints on political decisions, public choice analysts assume that the working of the political process under federalism remains the same at all levels of government as under unitary state. While economic agents can choose the administrative location where to place their assets rather than seek to influence government directly, the fact remains that the exit mechanism is merely superimposed on politics as a constraint on decentralized authorities. Individuals act in their capacity as asset owners rather than as voters in their attempt to maximize value. In that respect, the voice process itself is not essentially changed. It can therefore be argued that there is no specific economic theory of federalist politics. Only indirectly is the analysis of federalism related to the public choice tradition. It happens however that one dimension of the political process in a federalist framework lends itself to specific economic analysis, namely the fact that, where functions overlap, two or more levels of government compete for the same voters in the supply of services in a given territory. This paper is an attempt to fill the gap in the federalist literature and to set out the analytics of politics under federalism.

3. Federalist politics, a virgin field

This writer knows of one earlier attempt to apply economic analysis to federalist politics (Breton, 1985). The starting point of Breton's discussion is the characterization of federalism as a competitive process. As applied to the Canadian context, ten political authorities in the provinces plus the central government compete for the support of residents distributed over the Canadian territory. As in the analysis of market structure, the working of competitive federalist politics is expected to improve welfare relative to the unitary state, inasmuch as more competition is better than less. And the more the responsibilities of both levels of government overlap, the more efficient the federal system is, as overlapping spurs competition. Democratic politics is improved under federalism to the extent that competition for votes is enhanced.

As described by Breton, the process of political competition is merely asserted rather than worked out however. No distinction is made between the forces of competition as they arise from federal-provincial rivalries and the forces of competition as they arise from interprovincial competition. Like the entry of a new firm into the private market, adding one competitor to the game is assumed to somehow increase competition, whether the added player is made up of politicians from the federal level or from lower-level administrations. To use Breton's terminology, vertical competition does not differ from horizontal competition in its impact on the performance of the political process. In a way, Breton's approach can be characterized as an arithmetic theory of competitive federalism. Eleven is greater than ten. Therefore when both the federal and provincial governments supply similar services through overlapping functions, competition is enhanced. The more overlapping, the better.

In addition, Breton is not clear on the process by which horizontal competition for votes between same-level governments operates, since politicians from one province or one municipality cannot directly compete for votes in a neighboring jurisdiction. Presumably the conventional process of resource mobility comes into play. Efficient policies by a regional government attracts resources while inefficient actions repel them. This seems implied by his opinion that equality between the provinces calls for equalization grants and regional policies, so that a province does not hold disproportionate power to attract firms and people from its neighbors. If this interpretation is correct, Breton's analysis falls outside the domain of politics proper. In relying on the exit process rather than the voice process, Breton's thesis adds little to our understanding of federalist politics. It cannot be viewed as a contribution to the specific analysis of politics under federalism. At the same time, in attributing the benefits of competitive federalism to inter-regional resource mobility rather than to competitive politics, the thesis verges on inconsistency inasmuch as the exit process cannot operate where interventions are made by the central government.

Can economic analysis do more than simply assume that the central supplier in a federal system is just another player in the political market? This paper attempts to show that indeed the distinguishing characteristic of federalist politics is that two levels of government *compete for the same votes in the same territory* for the supply of similar services. In conditions of horizontal competition, politicians from just one jurisdiction compete for the support of voters in their territory. When both levels of government supply overlapping services on the same territory, politicians of both levels find themselves competing for the same pool of votes. Viewing votes as inputs in the production of political outputs, we are then faced with a situation of two suppliers competing for a common pool of resources. Presumably the conventional analysis of allocation under common-property rule should shed light on the outcome of this process. I shall draw on the analysis of oil extraction to examine federalist politics as an application of the tragedy of the commons. Integration of the public-choice approach and the Tiebout approach to federalism follows as a by-product of the discussion.

4. Common property in private markets

Mainstream analysis of conditions where resources have common- pool properties holds that competitive market organization may lead to waste. Divergencies emerge between private and social costs and benefits. Considering for instance the case of a particular pool of oil, it sometimes proves difficult to identify and assert property rights over portions of the oil patch. Each owner has an incentive to exploit currently as much as he profitably can. He has no interest in calculating the effects of his actions on resource availability in the future, because he cannot expect to reap the future benefits. Oil in the ground belongs to whoever land owner pumps it first. Overoptimal rates of extraction are predicted. In the absence of clear property rights, competition leads to wasteful rent seeking. Either single ownership or collective agreements, such as unitization, is necessary for free market activity to yield efficient outcomes.

Every owner could be made better off by entering into an agreement with other co-owners, but technical difficulties or sheer numbers if there are more than two owners can prevent them from negotiating. Even after successful negociations, it may be costly to monitor each other's pumping, resulting in mutual cheating. The collective action paradox holds. Negotiating difficulties might explain why laws attempt to facilitate, or even impose, unitization. On the other hand, if it were inexpensive to mark each share of the oil pool, monitoring costs would be substantially reduced and the incentives to cheat reduced by easy detection. Pool-wide agreements could more easily be reached and incentives to oversupply reduced.

5. A common-property theory of federalist politics

In conditions where functions overlap between two levels of government in national federations, a similar common-pool problem arises. Let us assume for instance that both levels of governments have the power to offer aid to some group of voters. Let us further assume that such a policy of aid is

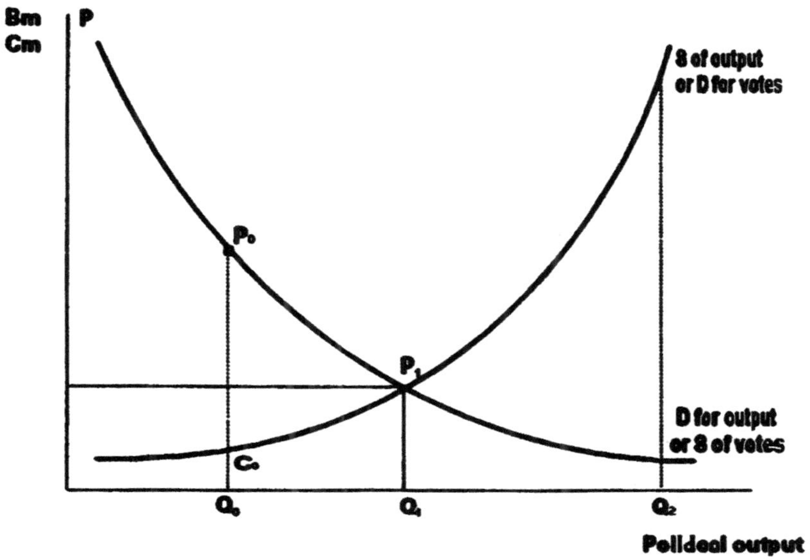

Figure 1.

politically profitable in that it attracts more votes than it repels. Under a single government system, a monopoly government would simply calculate the political benefits and costs of its actions to realize that there is political mileage to be made in adopting such a program. His calculus would lead him to supply the politically optimal level of aid. By contrast, in conditions of competition between two suppliers of the same services, it is in the interest of both suppliers to seek to gain the votes in implementing the program first. Should one of them abstain from supplying the political output, the potential gain of votes would be lost to him in favor of his competitor. Competition between two suppliers leads each one to attempt to realize the net political benefits for fear of losing them to its competitor. Yet to the extent that they are both equally adept at supplying political output, the political profit is dissipated *ex post* for both after the advent of the second player.

This process can be graphically represented in Figure 1. In substituting political output to oil on the horizontal axis, the outcome of competition for votes in a common- property setting can be graphically brought out. The nature of the political output supplied need not be specified. It may exclusively consist in transfers to interest groups with their attendant rent-seeking losses. The government may attempt to maximize revenue or surplus as in the Leviathan model, or in accordance with the tradition of normative economists, the government may be considered as an abstract benevolent despot only concerned with maximizing social welfare. We are thus faced with a negatively-sloped demand for political output D on the part of voters, who by the same token become suppliers of votes to politicians. As more and more favors or benefits are received by voters or a sub-group of them, their marginal value to them declines. Suppliers of votes demand a higher price for their support. Similarly governments or politicians can be viewed as suppliers of output or demanders of votes. The supply schedule S has to be upward-sloping in the relevant range, since the marginal cost of producing political output rises as supply increases. This is so because higher levels of output can only be attained by higher taxes or more severe regulation with their attendant increasingly depressing impact on economic activity and income. Furthermore to obtain more transfers, voters have to engage in additional rent-seeking activities, also subject to diminishing returns. Another way of viewing these various cost components would be in terms of vote loss to politicians. As the production of political output increases, the increasing marginal tax and rent-seeking costs imply that vote gains from beneficiaries of the policy are achieved at higher and higher sacrifices of votes from losers.

Assuming a single monopoly supplier of political output, as under unitary regimes, the politically optimal level of output is supplied, corresponding to the equilibrium point P_1 in Figure 1. This is the level that maximizes political profit or surplus. The *ex ante* output level sought by the monopoly supplier coincides with the *ex post* equilibrium level. This would be the level predicted by standard public choice analysis. To describe public choice under multi-level competition, let us now introduce a second level of government into the picture, competing for the same pool of voters in a specific portion of the federation.[1] Let us further assume that both levels of government are equally adept at producing any level of political output (an assumption to be relaxed below).

Then each of the two suppliers faces the same demand and supply conditions, D and S, that the single monopoly supplier originally faced. From the standpoint of each supplier, the whole pool of voters is up for grab. Each is led *ex ante* to consider only its own vote benefit and cost of supplying additional output and these are still defined by the D and S schedules in Figure 1. Assuming no particular strategic game on the part of any player, each will therefore be led to supply a level of political output equal to the level previously chosen by the monopoly supplier. At the limit the level of output should rise *ex post* to some multiple of what it was under single government, depending on the number of players and on specific elasticity conditions. The safer and more general conclusion is that relative to the situation under monopoly supply, the overall equilibrium supply of political output is higher. Such a condition can be represented by the political output level Q_2 in Figure 1.

To illustrate, assume that each level had initially elected to supply half the revenue-maximizing political output (Q_0, so that the overall level supplied would correspond to the amount that a monopoly would have chosen (Q_1. Then the amount of revenue or surplus that each could expect *ex ante* would be lower by the area $C_0P_0P_1$. The potential gain realisable from having each moved to P1 in the first place would be lost to each with no hope of ever capturing it. This is so because, once both suppliers are in the market, the price that the marginal voter would be prepared to pay for an additional unit of output or the price that he would demand for his vote would now be defined by the distance Q_1P_1. The collective-action paradox emerges. Phrased differently, the effective, overall unit cost of supplying additional output from the Q_0 level is now represented by Q_1P_1 from the standpoint of both suppliers. They could *ex ante* have done better, had they initially chosen level Q_1 and capture the whole political surplus. Should one of them choose the Q_0 level, he would leave the field open for the competitor to capture the remaining political profit. One conclusion emerges: each will attempt to be the first to grab the maximum voter support attainable at point P_1. Each player has an incentive to exploit currently as much of the market as he profitably can. He has no interest in calculating the effects of his actions on voter support availability in the future, because he cannot expect to reap those future benefits, once the vote pool is appropriated by his competitor. Like oil in the ground, votes belong to whoever captures them first.

All goes as if the overall supply curve S was shifted to the right, as if the political cost of supplying any level of output, *as seen by each of the two players*, was lower. Each level of government only calculates the potential *private* vote gain and loss to itself, to the exclusion of potential vote losses inflicted on the other level of government. And yet to the extent that they are both equally adept at supplying the additional output, the political profit is dissipated *ex post* for both after the advent of the second player. Even though the supply and demand schedules of each level are dependent on the actions of the other level, each supplier behaves as if they were independent. Any increase in the supply of output by one reduces the opportunities to gain votes by the other. Just as in the pumping of common-pool oil, each level of government seeks to outbid its competitor and attempts to pre-empt the political field in supplying its own output.

6. Implications of federalist politics

Some of the more significant implications of the theory are discussed in the next few lines.

6.1. *Oversupply*

In terms of social welfare, the outcome is guaranteed to be excessive supply, but the amount of waste depends on the assumptions retained for the public choice process. In the benevolent despot model assumed in normative neoclassical discourses, the politically optimal level of services coincides with the social optimal one. The logic of federalist competition therefore results in a wasteful expansion of the public sector. In the more realistic view of government offered by public choice analysts, a monopoly government already has an incentive to oversupply by virtue of its power to discriminate. Federalist politics then ends up in a doubly excessive supply of public services.

Here is an implication of public choice under federalism that runs counter to predictions derived from the more familiar Tiebout line of analysis. Our results show that there are two forces operating in a typical federalist system, an expansionist one rooted in the political dynamics analysed above, and a restrictionist one based on the mobility of resources among decentralized entities. This may explain why the empirical record is rather mixed on the contribution of federalism to containing government growth.[2] When one looks at the relative growth of government budgets in federal states as opposed to unitary regimes, it is hard to find strong support for the Tiebout process in holding back government inflation. By contrast, incorporating federalist politics into the picture implies that observed relationships between government structure (unitary or federal) and government growth cannot serve as a reliable test of the empirical validity of the economic theory of federalism, because of the contradictory forces in presence.

6.2. *Intrusion into lower-level functions by higher-level governments*

Another important consequence of the analysis is that, barring strict constitutional or technological constraints, all levels of government will have a tendency to enter every field of intervention. Whenever a domain or a sector offers the likelihood of political gains, all levels of government will bid to supply political output. The observed amount of overlapping should trend upward, a conclusion which could easily be empirically substantiated. Taking Canadian modern history as a case in point, Ottawa, along with the provinces, is active in all the following fields, which constitutionally are of the sole jurisdiction of the provinces: manpower training and apprenticeship, social services, culture, housing, tourism and sports and recreation. Furthermore, this listing fails to include the vast range of programs whereby Ottawa "bribes" provinces with federal money to influence decisions in provincial jurisdictions. All cost-sharing programs (medicare, higher education and welfare) and of course equalization programs, which by nature affect all provincial fields, must therefore be included in overlapping areas. Taken together, these fields account for the bulk of the modern expansion in public budgets.

One important lesson of the modern history of federations however is that the central government has the technological edge in this race. We have so far assumed that both levels of government are equally adept at supplying political output. Real-world conditions do not support this assumption. Because the ability of the central supplier to discriminate between citizens is greater due to its monopoly power over the whole national common market, the potential political "surplus" available to it from "invading" lower-level jurisdictions is higher than it is for lower-level governments to enter higher- level jurisdictions. This consequence is clearly confirmed by historical trends in all federations. In Canada, the bulk of the expansion in federal budgets and regulations over the past 50 years occurred in areas of provincial jurisdiction. In terms of Figure 1, the political cost schedule S of the central government is to the right of the cost schedule of its decentralized counterparts. This should not altered the basic argument of the thesis developed here, since by itself, the decentralized player will also seek to capture its potential vote harvest as if it were the sole supplier, even though less "surplus" is available to him. What it does however is to reinforce centralist tendencies of federal systems. The iron law of centralization holds with even greater force.

6.3. *Competition or collusion?*

This in turn means that in order to explain the lack of clear disparity between the rates of government growth in unitary and federal states, resort to the collusion hypothesis is not strictly necessary. Growing overlapping of functions and its attendant incentives to political competition are a sufficient condition for an oversupply outcome in federal systems. Taking Canada as an illustration, it is significant that the rate of growth in public expenditures over the last three decades is most pronounced in areas of provincial jurisdiction where the extent of intrusion by federal initiatives is most pronounced. Three areas of intervention have contributed most of the growth in provincial expenditures over this period: Education and training, medicare and welfare. It is significant that all three are characterized by the largest amount of overlapping. Note also that increases in budgets were the lowest at the municipal level (excluding public education), where the extent of overlapping and the level of monopoly power are minimal. This would mean that the restrictionist Tiebout effect was the strongest at the municipal level, while expansionist political competitive forces were limited. To complete the picture, the rate of growth of federal expenditures for own purpose (i.e., excluding grants) was intermediate. In the latter case, the Tiebout effect was inoperative, but so was the competitive effect in the absence of overlapping, the two opposite effects resulting in intermediate growth.

6.4. *Overexpansion of the Central Government*

A solid tradition offers an alternative interpretation for the growing involvement of central governments into the domains of lower-level administrations. In the federalist analytical tradition, coordination mechanisms are interpreted as collusive arrangements whereby component governments of a federation seek to form a cartel (Brennan and Buchanan, 1980: 181–183). The central government in those circumstances acts as the enforcer of the cartel agreement, in part in raising uniform taxes across the federation for the purpose of revenue sharing, i.e., of disbursing grants to lower-level jurisdictions. Freed from the resource mobility constraints, component governments need no longer cut their tax prices to attract resources from the rest of the federation.

The thesis developed here predicts that the overlapping of functions in federal systems would lead to explosive conditions, if left unchecked. It would be unstable in the long run. Both models therefore predict an enlarged role for the central government as the instrument to maximize political profit. In the collusion hypothesis, the incentive to collude derives from the concern of lower-level politicians to expand budgets and regulations. By contrast, vertical political competition as described in this paper leads to the dissipation of political profit through politically excessive supply. The role of the central government in those circumstances is to prevent budgets and regulations from reaching politically ruinous levels or to reduce them from such levels. The empirical problem raised is that both models predict an enlarged role for the central government and oversupply relative to the socially efficient level. In the one case governments collude to increase the level of political output and thereby overall government budgets and regulations. In the other, the role of the central authority is to reduce it from politically excessive levels. In terms of Figure 1, both approaches predict long-run efforts to move toward Point P_1, arrived at from the left in the collusion hypothesis, from the right in the multi-level competitive model. How to discriminate between the two forces remains a challenging, but promising empirical task?[3]

6.5. *Collusion or coercive takeover*

The theory of public choice in federal systems also predicts that lower-level governments would not be the most active and ardent party in pursuing harmonization and *de facto* centralization. Because of its higher monopoly power and larger profit potential, the central government has the most to loose from unrestrained political competition, if it were to engage in open, unrestricted rivalry with lower-level governments. Therefore it would more actively pursue coordination arrangements in order to avert the political disaster of unbridled expansion.

The truth is that federal-provincial agreements on a wide range of provincial-municipal services, arrived at as a result of institutionalized federal-provincial conferences, are in force in Canada for the purpose of injecting greater uniformity and standardization into the services provided by lower-level administrations. Federal mandates have played a similar role in the US system. While both revenue sharing and mandates can be viewed as incentives to expand for lower-level governments, they can alternatively be interpreted as offering the central government the opportunity to gain the political benefits of its interventions without the costs of politically destructive competitive programs. Centrally-planned programs with strings attached protect the central supplier from destructive competition from provinces and states. Standardisation and greater uniformity can be viewed as forced commitments by lower-level administrations not to compete with federal programs.

Actually, analysts and observers who are more inclined toward the descriptive method of examining intergovernmental relations are mostly left unmoved by the economic interpretation of the growing powers of central governments as actively pursued by the provinces or the states. Certainly in more recent times, the federal mandates in the United States can hardly be interpreted as resulting from pressures by the states to willingly form a national cartel. Historians, political scientists and journalists are almost unanimous in seeing expansive initiatives as originating from the federal government. In fact in both the United States and Canada, the history of the growing involvement of Washington and Ottawa in social and economic affairs, is one of unceasing resistance of component governments to infringements by the central government into their jurisdictions. In Canada as in the United States, traditionally provincial and state domains were transformed into "national" programs by decisions of the central government to invade those fields. Provinces and states have been coerced into embarking into so-called "national" programs by the centrally-devised financing arrangements. The expansion of provincial and state expenditures has occurred in reaction to the expansionist incentives incorporated into national programs, such as cost or revenue sharing by the federal government. Provinces and states who would not take part in the movement were financially penalized by being deprived of their allocated share of the revenue. Programs already in place at the lower level were transformed into "national" programs at the instigation of the central government with conditions attached. None could politically afford to abstain from embarking on the programs. In the long run, because of its technological edge in the race for political support, the central government would effectively supplant states and provinces.

To assume, as the collusion hypothesis implicitly does, that politicians from the central government gain little benefit from harmonizing initiatives raises doubts on the power of the collusion hypothesis. On the other hand, coordination arrangements make sense for the federal government as attempts to use its greater monopoly power to oubid its decentralised competitor, preempt the political field and realize the political benefits of supplying political output without costly outbidding by the lower-level administrations.

While it is true that service standardization among states or provinces implies gains to lower-level politicians in reduced resource mobility, it also carries large political costs to a great number. While grants to decentralized governments subsidize the local consumption of a service, say education or road services, in lagging areas through equalization grants or cost-sharing agreements, they act as regional trade barriers in favor of lagging regions. By virtue of the uniform tax regime implemented at the common-market level, productive resources in prosperous areas are penalized and have incentives to move away from jurisdictions burdened by their excess share of the common education or road programs. Variable handouts to investments and infrastructures in regions result in similar distortions detrimental to prosperous areas. By contrast, social and economic regulations by the central authority imply reduced investment and population in less prosperous regions. For instance, common environmental and labor standards are set by the demand of interest groups in the most developed and prosperous urbanized regions. The ability of lower-income, lagging areas to compete with the most productive ones are reduced in the same proportions. Poorer regions are denied the ability to compete with prosperous ones through lower wages, lower taxes or fewer environmental amenities. In all cases central handouts and regulations cause regional prices to be dissociated from regional costs. Central action becomes a dominant factor in balkanizing the economy.[4]

6.6. *Overexpansion more pronounced in Canada*

In a country such as Canada, with fewer component governments, physically wider provincial territories and in general less interprovincial mobility of resources than in the United States, the Tiebout effect would be less powerful, leaving more latitude for the provinces to realize political profit and a greater ability to engage in the political competitive game with the federal government in overlapping functions. Two empirical corollaries follow from this. The extent of overall public sector overexpansion would be greater, which is clearly confirmed empirically. Also implied is a second consequence. The political cost of engaging head-on into the competitive game with the provinces would be greater for the federal government, precisely because the risk of unrestrained expansion would also be greater. And so would be the political benefits of harmonization or *de facto* outright takeover of provincial responsibilities.

6.7. *Duplication of functions in political and journalistic language*

While an empirical determination remains to be done, it can be suggested that the federalist competition model does a better job of interpreting political and even economic discourses. Concern for avoiding the costly duplication of functions has constantly been alleged by politicians and normative economists as the basis for the movement toward increased involvement of the central authority in regional affairs. Harmonization has generally been viewed favorably in political and mainstream economic circles. While devolutionist have argued that growth in central powers have mostly served as excuses for suppressing horizontal tax and regulatory competition, it cannot be denied that the excesses of vertical political competition may have been held in check by the implicit cartel. That this mechanism could make a contribution to containing competitive waste in a common-property setting, albeit at the cost of destroying the federalist system itself, cannot be ruled out.

7. The absence of an exit outlet as a condition for the collective-action paradox

The full analogy with oil extraction can be carried further. Note how the source of waste is the common-property feature of the market for votes in conditions of overlapping government functions, not competition *per se*. Comparison with entry into a private market should make this point clear. It could indeed be objected that the advent of a new firm in a private market does cut into the share of a competitor and depress revenue of suppliers in place. Yet in its decision to enter the market, the new entrant only counts its own costs, to the exclusion of losses inflicted on others. It could therefore be argued that even in the absence of the common-property feature, competition implies waste through oversupply. The reply to this objection is that there is an essential difference between competition in a private market and competition in the political market. The distinction rests on the nature of the production process itself. Private firms supply private, divisible goods, which in general do not affect consumers who choose not to buy them. Consumers have an exit mechanism available to escape actions involving net cost to them. They cannot be coerced into buying goods with net negative value to them. They can be inexpensively separated and they can assign themselves to one or the other supplier. This is the basis of the general proposition that in typical market conditions, the advent of a new competitor is wealth creating to the extent that a newcomer succeeds only if it can add value for buyers. Competition between private firms for the favors of patrons do not give rise to the common-pool problem.

Governments' actions on the other hand impact on most citizens by the very fact of being taken. All government decisions take on characteristics of public, non-divisible goods. By virtue of its monopoly power, a government possesses the ability to perfectly discriminate in order to maximize its political revenue. For the purpose of the present demonstration, publicly-supplied services need not be indivisible in the polar Samuelsonian sense that governments engage only in activities that exhibit strong or extreme externalities. Even when governments produce or regulate pure private goods, like lotteries or energy, most people are affected by government decisions for better or for worse. Except in moving my assets or myself to another province or country, I cannot escape the tax and consumption consequences of actions by the ministry of education or welfare.

It could be argued that the instrument available to people as voters to escape the net excess cost of public decisions is the vote iself, i.e., the power to withdraw their support from governments that impose net costs on them, including the cost of oversupply in conditions of multi-level competition. This objection is not without value, but it is hard to avoid the fact that transaction costs in political markets are large, larger than those faced by buyers in private markets. Even the mobility exit of the Tiebout variety is far from costless, and in any case it is unavailable where interventions originate from the central government. By virtue of the Coase theorem, if the political market was perfect, then the common-property problem would vanish. Tiebout would be irrelevant and so would be federalism. The political process would possess its own exit mechanism. No distinction could be made between the political market and the pure and perfect private market. Institutions do not matter in a perfect world.

Given this "technological" property of public supply, this means that all political outputs have collective-good characteristics. They are public in nature. As for oil in the ground, there is no inexpensive method of assigning voters to each supplier under multi-level government supply. Voters cannot easily escape the consequences of political decisions at either level. Then both parties merely compete for a larger share of a given wealth represented by the fixed pool of voters. The process is merely redistributive. Yet as in all occurrences of rent seeking, resources are expended to acquire votes.

In a clear analogy with oil extraction, if a way were found of inexpensively marking each producer's share of the pool, then the common-property problem would be resolved. This could conceptually be realized by marking with a particular color or by clear apportioning to owners through some costless removal and storing of oil for future use.

It happens that a similar reasoning applies to the common-pool feature of federalist politics. What prevents voters in a given region of a federalist system from being "assigned" to a specific level of government is indeed the absence of an exit outlet from government action and the high transaction costs of political action. Even though marginal tax and rent- seeking costs are higher than marginal benefits at equilibrium, losing voters do not have the exit outlet as an instrument to move away from unfavorable legislation, since the central government is one of the two competitors in the market for votes. Individuals and groups bound by region A no longer have the option to escape its restrictions by emigrating to region B, or by moving their capital and assets elsewhere or by purchasing their supply from a neighboring territory. Furthermore, voters have no incentives to bribe governments into reducing their supply because of the high cost of political action.

8. Direct constitutional implications

A direct, if possibly naive, constitutional implication of the above analysis would be to radically decentralize federations by eliminating overlapping jurisdictions in favor of provinces and states.[5] The analysis developed above shows that the Tiebout theory of federalism was based on the assumption of firm constitutional limits on the powers of the federal government. Once these limits broke down, both levels of government began to exploit the common pool, with the expected consequences for the explosive growth of government.[6] Some of the desirable constitutional changes implied by this approach would provide that: Provinces and states have the sole jurisdiction in fields where overlapping presently is the rule; the federal spending power and its power to bribe lower- level jurisdictions be eliminated; a spending control provision prevent the federal government from amassing excessive debt; referendums, initiatives and recalls be required for all constitutional amendments, including regional majorities conferring veto powers to provinces/states; federal powers to disallow provincial laws or to legislate in areas of provincial jurisdiction be eliminated.

9. Parallel governments

As long as the central government retains the power to act in fields of lower-level government jurisdiction, it would appear that one can only jump from the frying pan of monopoly government in unitary states into the fire of government hypertrophy and harmonization in multi-level competitive systems. In point of fact, this is precisely what has been witnessed throughout the modern history of national federations. In the past, the constitutional division of powers has proved inadequate to contain unbridled government expansion in national federations. Federalism as experienced in the last 50 years contains the seeds of its own destruction. Coercive takeover is a necessary consequence of federalist competition.

Beyond constitutional reforms, conceptual and realistic remedies to this dilemma are suggested by modern-day conditions. Short of effective constitutional limits on the powers of the central government, if an inexpensive way of escaping the cost of federalist competition were available to citizens, voters experiencing a net burden from the combined central and regional government competition would readily seize the opportunity and move their assets outside the territory. There is a conceptually feasible arrangement capable of saveguarding the benefits of inter-governmental competition and at the same time allowing voters to escape the drawbacks of the common-property problem. It is called parallel federalism,[7] with some real-world representation visible on a small scale.

There is often no reason why governments should have geographic monopolies. Under present-day federalist arrangements, parallel governments are prevented from competing for the favors of voters outside their territory. A provincial or state government cannot compete for the supply of services on the territory of its neighbor and *vice versa*. Nor can the state of New York compete with Ontario for the supply, say, of a labor relations legal framework. Only higher, central authorities have the power to compete with lower-level authorities. The pitfalls resulting from these restrictions should now be obvious.

By contrast, parallel governments have jurisdiction of a non- geographic nature. All governments have equal, non exclusive jurisdiction over all territories provided they can obtain the consent of the governed. Members voluntarily enter the "association" or "club", which then has authority to tax the members. Arbitration to-day is available outside legal sources to resolve disputes. United States corporations may choose the state in which they are chartered, with adjudication under the law of this state, regardless of the state of the plaintiff. Extension of this legal framework to product liability laws has recently been advocated by analysts. The "choice in education" movement in Canada and the United States points to the kind of arrangements that can free voters from the shortcomings of monopoly governments. Parents in several jurisdictions can choose to "purchase" school services from a neighboring school board. Tax dollars follow pupils to the district that supplies the services, which implies that a school board implicitly has the power to tax resources outside its district. Exasperated by the lasting secessionist inclinations of some sections in the Quebec province, some Canadian observers are turning to the concept of parallel governments to brake the deadlock.[8] Canadians resident in Quebec and Quebeckers resident in Canada would choose the government by which they would be ruled. Those who self-identify as Canadian in Quebec would pay all their taxes to the Canadian government and would be guaranteed full civil and property rights by this government. The rule would be reciprocated for Quebeckers resident in Canada. Similarly, a proposal has been considered to constitute the numerous separated Aboriginal communities of Canada into a single province.

The relevant characteristic of this arrangement of our purpose is that it can both provide the benefits of government competition and at the same time protect voters-consumers against the common-pool risk of oversupply. This desirable result is accomplished as a result of voters having an escape mechanism available to them, whereby victims of net tax or regulatory burdens can move away from the excesses of hierarchical government competition. Parallel government competition would offer the equivalent of oil marking or apportioning in the exploitation of an oil well. Similarly, parallel government arrangements place every government in the position of individual firms in the private market. Indivisibilities inherent in public supply are removed by the availability of an escape from excess burdens. Then only wealth-creating entrants can hope to find a place in the market for votes.

10. Free trade as a substitute to parallel governments

Due to its limited applicability to real-world practices, the principle of parallel governments would appear to offer only a limited contribution to the solution of the common-pool problem of federalist politics. In reality, contemporary movement toward freer trade in goods and factors, and toward common-market arrangements throughout the world provides just such an opportunity to overcome the common-pool problem of multi-level government competition. Even though direct competition for votes is limited to hierarchically-structured governments of a federal nature, the incentive to oversupply is alleviated by free trade, viewed as a less expensive escape mechanism now available to losing voters.

The common-pool problem in traditional federations mainly originates from the central government having the power to legislate for the whole national area behind trade barriers. Now it seems that protectionism is no longer a viable alternative. Once protectionist obstacles to exit are removed, national governments find themselves in the approximate position of a province or a state or a canton vis-à-vis the national economy in a federal state. The Tiebout mechanism comes into play in any political structure where the power of political authorities extends to less than the size of the economy where trade is free. The competitive action of resource mobility can be at work within national economies between parallel governments in decentralized federal states or between countries associated in common-market arrangements with limited central powers. The determining characteristic of a federalist structure is that responsibilities are entrusted to authorities that have no power to tax or regulate the whole area where trade is free. In those conditions, the monopoly power of unitary government, as well as the common-pool problem of federalist politics, can be alleviated to the extent that free movement of resources allows resource owners to move away from excessive taxes and regulations.

This means that in countries of the European Union and of North America after NAFTA, residents can more easily escape the burden of monopoly or multi-level competition either by purchasing their supply outside the country or by moving their assets or their person to neighboring countries offering more favorable legislations. While strictly direct competition for votes by parallel governments remains ruled out, an equivalent state of affairs obtains, inasmuch as people can move themselves or their assets to jurisdictions of their own choosing. As under parallel federalism, asset owners voluntarily enter the "association" endowed with the power to rule over them. The end-result is essentially the same. Just like under private market competition, only a wealth- creating government stands some chance of entering the market for political output.

11. Conclusion

This paper argued that a distinguishing feature of public choice in a federal system is the fact that two or more levels of government compete for the same voters in the supply of similar services in a given territory. Viewing votes as inputs in the production of political outputs, the situation can be looked at as an arrangement where two suppliers compete for a common pool of resources. The conventional analysis of allocation under common-property rule could then be extended to these conditions. The endeavor was well rewarded in terms of the new light it can shed on the outcome of the political process under federalism. By analogy with oil extraction under common-pool property, it was shown that it is in the interest of both suppliers to seek to gain the votes in being first to implement public programs. Should one of them abstain from supplying the political output, the potential gain of votes would be lost to him in favor of his competitor. Yet to the extent that they are both equally adept at supplying the additional output, the political profit is dissipated *ex post* for both.

An important implication of the theory is that there are two forces operating in a typical federalist system, an expansionist one rooted in the political dynamics analysed above, and the more familiar, restrictionist one based on the mobility of resources among decentralized entities. This may explain why the empirical record is rather mixed on the contribution of federalism to containing government growth.

A second empirical implication is that resort to the collusion hypothesis is not strictly necessary to explain the growing involvement of the central government in society and the lack of clear disparity between the rates of government growth in unitary and federal states. Because of its higher monopoly power and larger political profit potential, the central government has the most to lose from unrestrained political competition. Standardisation and greater uniformity of service through "harmonization" can be viewed as forced commitments by lower-level administrations not to compete with federal programs. The historical truth is that provinces and states have been coerced into embarking into so-called "national" programs by the centrally-devised financing arrangements.

Contemporary movement toward freer trade in goods and factors across the world provides an opportunity to overcome the pitfalls of monopoly government as well as the common-pool problem of multi-level government competition. While direct competition for votes by parallel governments remains generally ruled out, an equivalent state of affairs obtains, inasmuch as people can more freely move themselves or their assets to jurisdictions of their own choosing.

Notes

1. Because traditionally and constitutionally governments have strictly geographic jurisdictions, direct competition for votes between "parallel" governments is seldom observed. Vertical competition occurs on the other hand, when a higher-level administration shares a field of intervention with a lower-level government.
2. For an overall view of the empirical record on this question, see Grossman and West (1994).
3. One recent attempt (Grossman and West: 1994) has been made to test the cartelization hypothesis, where collusion is measured by the share of federal grants in total provincial and local government receipts. The study shows not only that there is a positive correlation between total Canadian government size and grants-in-aid, but the federal government itself expands in terms of own purpose expenditures. This latter result is interpreted as inconsistent with the spillover and scale economies justifications for intergovernmental grants. This result is also consistent with the federalist public choice model described in this paper.
4. This balkanizing impact, as applied to Canadian conditions, is discussed more fully in Migué (1994).

5. Realistic or not, a proposal for a "constitutional assembly" has been advanced in recent years in Canada to better "consider the real costs involved in a federal system" (Breton and Scott, 1980: XVI). Such enlarged assembly would include government and opposition members from federal, provincial, and local levels of government, as well as a certain number of interested citizens from outside the political system.
6. I am grateful to William Niskanen for suggesting this historical coincidence between the *de facto* brake down of constitutional constraints in the 30's and after the War, and the massive expansion of government budgets and regulations.
7. Gordon Tullock (1994: Ch. 4), who has initiated analysis of this arrangement, designates it by various names, including "sociological", "non-geographic" federalism or simply "parallel" government, "clubs" or "associations".
8. For an explicit formulation of this arrangement, see Conrad Black (1995).

References

Black, C. (1995). Abandon the national effort to accommodate Quebec. *The Globe & Mail*, 7 November, A23.

Brennan, G. and Buchanan, J.M. (1980). *The power to tax: Analytical foundations of a fiscal constitution*. Cambridge: Cambridge University Press.

Breton, A. (1985). Comment *Report of the royal commission on the economic union and development prospects*, vol. 3, 486- -526. Ottawa: Department of Supply and Services.

Breton, A. and Scott, A. (1980). *The design of federations*. Montreal: The Institute for Research on Public Policy.

Grossman, P.J. and West. E.G. (1994). Federalism and the growth of government revisited. *Public Choice* 79: 19– 32.

Migué, J.-L. (1993). *Federalism and free trade*. Hobart Paper 122. London: The Institute of Economic Affairs. Migué, J.-L. (1994). The balkanization of the Canadian economy: A legacy of federal policies. In F. Palda (Ed.), *Provincial trade wars: Why the blockade must end*. Vancouver: The Fraser Institute.

Tullock, G. (1994). *The new federalist*. Vancouver: The Fraser Institute.

Weingast, Barry R. (1994). The economic role of political institutions: Market-preserving federalism and economic development. *Journal of Law, Economics, & Organization* 11: 1–31.

Public Choice **90**: 255–280, 1997.

© 1997 *Kluwer Academic Publishers.*

Federalism and the European Union: A constitutional perspective*

DENNIS C. MUELLER
Department of Economics, University of Vienna, BWZ-Brünner Str. 72, A-1210 Vienna, Austria

Abstract. Constitutional questions have resurfaced in the last few years with regard to the European Union. The Maastricht Treaty is a kind of constitutional reform. The rejection of this treaty by Denmark in its first referendum, and the subsequent debate of the treaty that has taken place, raise questions about both the nature of the European Union, and the process by which its rules (constitution) get revised and approved. Similar questions surround the entry of Austria and the three, additional Scandinavian countries into the Union. Perhaps, no event called the European Union's constitution, or lack thereof, into question more that way in which a new President of the Commission was chosen during the summer of 1994. This paper will reexamine the European Union's structure and procedures from a constitutional perspective. Drawing upon the author's recently completed book, *Constitutional Democracy*, the paper will review the purpose for the Union's existence, the implications of this purpose for the structure of the Union (federalism versus confederation), the rules for making collective decisions in the Union, citizenship, and in particular, the procedures by which the European Union's "Constitution" is written and revised. The constitutional perspective adopted is taken from public choice. The political institutions of the European Union are examined relative to those rational, self-interested individuals would choose to advance their interests.

1. Introduction

Denmark's first rejection of the Maastricht Treaty and the ensuing questions raised about the treaty in other countries have again brought to the fore the issue of whether a true European federalism can (should) be created. This is essentially a constitutional question, and the Maastricht Treaty, like its predecessors signed in Rome and Paris, is a form of constitution for Europe, although a rather unusual one written in a rather unusual manner. These features may help to explain the indecisive response to the treaty by citizens and governments across Europe.

Understandably, the post-Denmark debate within Europe focussed on the Maastricht Treaty's provisions and their likely impact on different countries

* The financial support for this research of the Ludwig Boltzmann Institut is gratefully acknowledged.

and groups in Europe. But the treaty implicitly raises, and answers, more basic issues about the desirability of a "United States of Europe", the structure it should have, and the process by which it should come into existence. These are old questions in Europe having been debated on and off since the Community's founding after World War II. They have assumed renewed importance, since the first vote of the Danes. This article's thesis is that the process by which European integration has moved forward has in effect dictated the form that integration takes, and that European citizens have not been allowed to decide whether or not they want a true federalist structure for the European Union.

The most basic question to be asked, of course, is whether such a European government should exist in the first place. This question is taken up in the next section. We then turn to the issue of the structure of government, and in particular whether a federalist structure as in North America and Switzerland, or a confederation, as has existed up until now in the European community, is more appropriate (Section 3). The answer to this question has important implications for the choice of representational structure (Section 4), and voting rules used (Section 5). It also impacts the criteria for citizenship (Section 6), and the process by which a European government should be created (Sections 7 and 8). Should Europe adopt a fully federalist structure, a key question for it would be how to maintain that structure given the pressures toward centralization that seem to exist in all federalist nations. This issue is addressed in Section 9. In Section 10 the admission of additional members is discussed. After taking up each of these issues in a general way, we return in the closing section to the Maastricht Treaty, and the constitutional questions it raises.

2. The purpose and role of government

We shall assume that the purpose of government is to advance the interests of the citizens. A citizen's interests include those things that advance her welfare narrowly defined, e.g., the pleasure she gets from owning a car, the pleasure she gets from driving her car on a road built and maintained by the government, etc. But they can also be construed to include preferences for outcomes that do not impact directly and narrowly on the citizen. The happiness she gets from, and thus interest in, food relief for starving citizens in another country, or more meanly the pleasure from knowing that a religious minority has been prevented from practicing its religion.

Many of these interests can be advanced without having to resort to governmental institutions. This is obvious for the pleasures one gets from consuming private goods, but it may even be true for the joint consumption of "public goods". All farmers in a valley may benefit from damming a stream to prevent flooding and aid in irrigation. Such a dam would be a public good for the community of farmers. But it might well be provided without the need for a government or government intervention, if the number of farmers is small. They might simply agree to build the dam with each voluntarily contributing time, effort and money to achieve the goal (Coase, 1960). Citizens across the world can enjoy the satisfaction from knowing that they have helped to relieve the pain from a disaster in a particular part of it by contributing to voluntary relief organizations like the Red Cross.

The farmers building the dam and the Red Cross may be thought of as voluntarily formed "clubs", ad hoc in the one case, permanent in the other, for providing particular public goods. They can accomplish this task efficiently so long as numbers are small, and free-riding is not significant. But if the valley and stream (river) are large with hundreds of thousands of inhabitants with different occupations, and differing benefits (some perhaps even negative) from the dam, the costs of finding out what each would be willing to contribute to build the dam, and of actually raising the money and building it may be large. Government, a form of "involuntary club" to which all members of the community belong and contribute, may be the lowest cost institution for determining what public goods and other collective actions should be undertaken and how to pay for them (Dahlman, 1979; Mueller, 1989: Ch. 2). Democratic government is an institution for revealing this information by voting.

Thus, each member of a community has an interest in seeing that institutions of government are created to provide public goods and other public policies that potentially can benefit all members of the community. Of course, each action of government will not make every member of the community better off. But we take it as axiomatic that the combined actions of government ought to make all citizens better off, and that the kinds of decisions that are peculiarly within government's domain of activity are those that could potentially make every citizen better off. Moreover, even these actions are undertaken by government only when other voluntary organizations, like private clubs and charities, cannot carry them out efficiently because of the high decisionmaking costs that accompany free-riding and other forms of opportunistic behavior in large communities.

We have here what is obviously a *normative* description of what government ought to do, not a positive description of what real governments actually do. Countless actions that governments undertake do not fulfill the requirement that they even *potentially* might increase the welfare of all members of the community. A tariff on shoes protects the wages and dividends of those who supply labor and capital to shoe manufacturers to the loss of all shoe buyers.

A small dam financed by the central government benefits a handful of farmers to the loss of all taxpayers.

That actual governments undertake actions that make some citizens better off at the expense of others can be easily understood once one recognizes that the individual interests that government advances are often quite narrowly focussed, and the democratic institutions that register those interests, like the simple majority rule, give those in government strong incentives to advance the interests of only *some* members of the community. But actual governments, of course, already exist. No community would agree to create a government just so that one part of the community could be made better off at the expense of the rest. Most purchasers of shoes would presumably oppose the creation of a government, if the only planned activity of that government was to impose a tariff on shoes.[1]

These arguments imply that, if no European-wide political institutions existed today, and the citizens of Europe were to contemplate creating a European-wide government, they would rationally do so only if they all expected to benefit from it. The citizens of France would not help found a European government, if all that this government would do is tax the French and subsidize the Germans. Thus, to determine whether or not a European government should exist, we must inquire whether there are European-wide public goods and other sorts of public policies which *would* benefit all Europeans, but would *not* be provided in the absence of such a government, because of the high decisionmaking costs from doing so. Both conditions are necessary. If there are no pan-European public goods, e.g., all environmental problems have no cross-national spillovers, no European government is needed. Even if individual environmental problems involve more than one country, a European-wide government is not required to solve them if the decisionmaking costs of solving these problems by say bilateral or multilateral negotiations among the affected countries are lower than the implicit costs of resolving them within the governmental structure of a European-wide government.

The European unification agenda has, of course, contained several items that would potentially meet the definition of a public good, e.g., a common currency.[2] I shall not pause here to discuss whether this or other items on the agenda would or would not in fact potentially benefit all Europeans. The point to be made is that such pan-European public goods must exist, *and* a European government must be the lowest cost way of obtaining them to justify its creation. Whether a European-wide government is the lowest cost method for Europeans to consume European-wide public goods jointly cannot be determined, however, without knowing more about the structure that should underlie this government. We turn to that question now.

3. A federation or a confederation of Europe?

We can conceptualize three distinct governmental structures:[3]

(1) *Unitary government.* A single level of government exists in which all citizens participate directly or are represented directly by a person or party which they elected. All collective decisions affecting the citizen are made by this level of government.

(2) *Federalist government.* Two or more levels of government exist, each of which has primary if not sole responsibility for particular collective decisions. An individual is a citizen of the federal state and of each of the lower levels of government in which she resides. She participates directly or elects representatives to the legislative assemblies for each level.

(3) *A confederation of governments.* Separate autonomous governments are represented in an assembly to make collective decisions. Individuals are citizens in the constituent governmental units, but are represented only indirectly through their elected governments in the confederation's assembly.

The city states of ancient Greece or Renaissance Italy are examples of unitary states. Switzerland and the United States are prototype federalisms. NATO is a typical confederation of governments.

Which of these three governmental structures is best for making the collective decisions a community faces depends on its size, location and degree of heterogeneity. A community living on a small island may be able to make all of its collective decisions with a single governmental unit. A community living on a big island, like Australia, may find it optimal to subdivide its decision process in the form of a federalist structure. The invasion of any part of Australia by a foreign army puts all Australians at risk, thus all Australians have a common interest in defense against foreign invasion. But Australians who live in Melbourne are not affected by burglaries and fires in Perth. Optimal levels of fire and police protection and the taxes to finance them are better decided at a local level of government in a country the size of Australia. Federalism is the obvious form of government to employ.[4]

Under an ideal federalism the citizens at a given level of government consume the same government good or service, e.g., defense at the national level, police protection at the local level. Citizens may have different views as to the optimal quantity and characteristics of a public good provided at a particular level, but these views are not determined by the geographic location of the citizens. Hawks on defense are just as likely to be found in Sidney as in Perth. The task of democratic procedures is to aggregate these differing views and determine the optimal policy for the entire community.

It can happen, however, that the views on a particular government action are to a large extent defined by the location of their holders. For example, one's hawkishness on defense may depend in part on one's distance from the likely point of an initial attack. When this is the case, and when the views of all citizens in a given area are already represented in a government, their views on more macro collective action can be adequately represented by the governments to which they already belong. If the views of Americans about common defense policies with Europeans were fundamentally the same, and the same was true for members of each European country, then the NATO confederation can be claimed to be an optimal governmental structure. The issue facing Europe is whether the common issues that it faces, and the attitudes of its citizens to these issues, are such as to make a federation or a confederation the optimal governmental structure.

Consider the following two environmental issues. The thinning of the ozone layer, let us assume, affects all Europeans equally. Some Europeans spend more time outdoors than others, some are genetically more vulnerable to skin cancer, some are more risk averse. But these characteristics vary uniformly across all of Europe. A Frenchman is no more likely to feel strongly about protecting the ozone layer than a Dane. For this type of issue, the optimal representational structure would weigh the preferences of each Dane for environmental protection identically to those of each Frenchman. If all collective choice issues that extend beyond national borders in Europe were of this type, then the optimal governmental structure for Europe would be a federalism. Environmental issues like the thinning of the ozone layer and global warming would be decided at the highest level of government in a European parliament in which Europeans were represented on the basis of their preferences with respect to these pan-European issues, not their place of residence. Given the importance of cultural and language differences, regional governments corresponding to the present nation states would most certainly exist with public issues like education assigned to them. Still other lower levels of government to handle police and fire protection and other local issues might also be present.

Now consider a second type of transnational environmental issue. A river's source is in country *A*, its mouth is in *C*, and in between it flows through *B*. The preferences of the citizens of each country for clean water, economic development, etc., are similar. Local communities and businesses along the banks of the river all contaminate it to an equal degree. The citizens of *A* suffer the least from the river's pollution, however, since the river starts off unpolluted and obtains only a modest level of pollution while flowing through its borders. Citizens of *C* suffer the most from the river's degradation, since it contains not only the pollutants its residents put into it, but also those remaining from *B* and *A*. The antipollution policies advocated for protecting the river advocated by citizens in *A* can be expected to be somewhat similar and quite different from those advocated by citizens from *B* or *C*. For this kind of collective decision all citizens of *A* may be adequately represented by a delegate from their government, as is true for *B* and *C*. If the only transnational issues to be decided in Europe were of this type, a confederation would suffice.

Thus, the question of whether a federalist or a confederalist structure of government is appropriate for Europe can be seen to depend on the nature of collective decisions Europeans have to make. If they are pan-European in the sense that they potentially affect all Europeans equally, a federalist structure is most appropriate. If they are transnational but not pan-European, i.e., they affect the citizens of more than one country, but not necessarily all Europeans, and certainly not all Europeans in the same way and to the same degree, then a confederation is more appropriate. We shall not venture an opinion on whether collective issues in Europe are more of one form or the other. We turn instead to the issues of optimal representation in each case.

4. The representation of citizen preferences

Many types of representation systems exist, but they can be broadly grouped into two categories – two-party and multiparty systems. The rationale behind the two is quite different. The objective under a two-party system is to "choose a government", i.e., to choose that party or party leader who a majority of citizens believe will best run the government until the next election (Bagehot, 1872; Mueller, 1996: Chs. 9, 10). The logic underlying a multiparty form of government is to have all the different views and preferences toward government action represented in the parliament, which in turn will decide government policy based on these preferences. A case can be made for each form of government. I shall not make that case here.[5] With the exceptions of the United Kingdom and sometimes France, all European countries have opted for some form of multimember-district representation which generally produces multiparty systems. I shall assume, therefore, that a European parliament would have its membership chosen by a proportional representation (PR) formula.

Within the PR systems one can again distinguish two broad categories: those which require that a citizen vote for a party, and those which allow her to designate her choice of person within the party. If the former were employed, its logical structure would have all parties listed on the ballots each voter marks regardless of the voter's country of residence. The voter would select the party she most preferred to have represent her views in the European parliament and seats in the parliament would be allocated in proportion to the number of votes each party received.

Most countries use a variant on the above system in which the electorate is divided into geographic districts within which the procedure is followed to elect a subset of the total number of seats in the parliament. This procedure is also used to elect representatives to the European Parliament in Strasbourg. The disadvantage of this variant is that it prevents those in a district who favor a minority party from being proportionally represented. If there are ten parties running, and there are ten seats, say, to be filled from a district, the major parties will fill a majority of them and the smallest parties will fill none.

The goal of having representatives from different countries taking seats in the parliament can and would be achieved under a party list system that treated all of Europe as a single electoral district, if each party chose members from the several countries to occupy positions on its list. Alternatively, a single-transferable-vote (STV) system could be used in which the voters designated not only the party they preferred, but their ranking of candidates within the party. If European citizens favored candidates of their own nationality, they could indicate that by ranking them higher. An STV system could lead to both proportional representation of parties and of nationalities of representatives. But it would also allow voters to disregard such provincialism if they chose, and simply vote for the persons from their favored parties whom they most preferred, regardless of their nationality.[6]

In a purely confederate form of government, all citizens within a country are presumed to have the same or at least very similar preferences with respect to the issues to be decided by the confederation. Thus, one delegation from the country, indeed one person, could adequately represent all of the citizens' views. Having a single parliament in which all citizens are represented, but the representatives are selected by country, as occurs in the European Parliament, is, therefore, a kind of halfway house between a fully proportional parliament in which Europeans are represented qua-preferences and regardless of where they reside, and a fully confederate assembly in which Europeans are represented exclusively according to where they reside.

5. The voting rule

If the role of government is to provide those goods that can potentially benefit all citizens, then the obvious choice for the voting rule is the unanimity rule. The main objections to its use are that it can take too long to find a formulation of a proposal that benefits all even when all participants vote sincerely, and that it encourages the strategic misrepresentation of preferences by individuals who "hold out" for a greater share of the gains from collective action (Black, 1958: 146–147; Buchanan and Tullock, 1962: Ch. 6; Barry, 1965: 242–250;

Samuelson, 1969). For these reasons the optimal voting rule is generally thought to be some qualified majority less that unanimity.

Under any qualified majority rule less than full unanimity, some individuals can be made worse off by a collective action. Under a federalist governmental structure, these individuals can be expected to be spread throughout the entire community. For example, assume a federalist structure existed in Europe with a European Parliament with the authority to take certain actions on behalf of all citizens. Defense would be an obvious policy to assign to the highest governmental level. A Pacifist Party might come into existence, but it would probably win only a small fraction of seats in the European Parliament. Under any reasonable choice for a qualified majority voting rule, the Pacifist Party would not have enough votes to prevent the European Parliament from passing defense appropriations and authorizing other defense related actions. Supporters of the Pacifist Party would be net losers on defense issues.

Thus, under a federalist system where each party represents citizens from across all of Europe, the winners and the losers on any issue would tend to be spread throughout the community. In contrast, if a qualified majority voting rule were used in a confederate assembly, the losers on any vote would be the representatives from specific countries. If the kinds of issues voted on in a confederation are those that favor its creation, i.e., issues with benefits and costs which vary by country, then the losers on any vote in a confederation under a qualified majority rule would be the citizens – in principle all of the citizens – of one or more specific countries. Both gains and losses would be geographically concentrated.

Any individual or group which is a net loser over the set of *all* collective actions of the community has a strong incentive to exit the community, of course. For an individual, exit is often very costly, however. It is also costly for a group, if it is widely dispersed across the community. In a confederation, on the other hand, the losers are geographically concentrated. Moreover, they are already organized into a political unit. Exit is easy. Accordingly, the threat of exiting is more effective, and the assembly of confederate delegates must take more care to ensure that every member, i.e., each constituent country, is a net gainer from its actions. In practice, this can be expected to result in greater constraints upon the kinds of issues that can come to a vote in a confederate assembly, and a higher required majority to pass proposals with unanimity being the likely choice for important issues.[7]

6. Citizenship

The constituents in a federalist state are the citizens of that state. The constituents in a confederation are the autonomous states conjoined. These differences have important implications for the criteria by which citizenship is established.

If a federalist structure is optimal, the nature of the issues decided at each level of government is such that a person living anywhere within a given governmental jurisdiction can be presumed to have *potentially* the same preferences for government action as the person at any other location. Pacifists and hawks are equally likely to be found anywhere. Logically, individuals should have the same rights and obligations as citizens of a particular governmental unit regardless of where they reside within that jurisdiction. If Europe were constituted as a federalist state with defense assigned to the highest level of government, and its federal parliament decided to introduce the draft, all citizens of Europe regardless of where they resided, should be equally obligated to serve in the military. In addition to considerations of fairness, this form of equality would be necessary to discourage individuals from migrating from one part of Europe to another to avoid military service. Both the taxes and benefits from collective action should be uniform across a given governmental jurisdiction for equity and efficiency reasons.

This logic also suggests that a single set of criteria should exist to define citizenship in a particular governmental jurisdiction. If a Federation of Europe existed, the same minimum residency requirement should apply before an immigrant is eligible for European citizenship regardless of whether the immigrant lives in England or Italy. Were this not the case, migrants seeking citizenship in Europe might tend to concentrate on the countries with the most lax citizenship qualifications.

There is no reason, however, to require identical qualifications for citizenship in any lower level of government across the different governmental units. In a federalist Europe, the present nations would most certainly exist as rather powerful "regional" governments. If citizenship in a Federation of Europe required a minimum of five years residence, say, there is no reason why Italy could not require two years or ten years residency before an immigrant could apply for citizenship and participate in Italian politics. Each regional government (i.e., current nation state) would be free to define the criteria for citizenship in its polity as it so chose. The same could, in principle, hold for smaller regional governments and cities and towns.

In a confederation, definitions of citizenship are logically the prerogative of each autonomous state. If the confederate structure is optimal, then the costs and benefits from collective action at the cross-national level must be presumed to be unequal. The assembly of national delegates to the confederate assembly might choose to require equal contributions on a particular occasion, say for a military action, but it need not do so. Given the asymmetry of benefits and costs of collective action that makes the confederation the optimal structure, it most certainly would not choose equal contributions on all occasions. Since the benefits and costs of participation in the European confederation are presumed to differ across states, there is no reason to assume that a common set of criteria for citizenship should exist across states. Each state could define its own set of rights and obligations according to its perception of its needs.

7. The European Union as a constitutional democracy

A constitution can be thought of as the set of rules that define a community's political institutions. By this definition all communities, even dictatorships, have a constitution.

In many cases history delineates the boundaries of the community and writes the provisions in its constitution. Great Britain is a collection of disparate peoples formed into a political community by a history of wars both amongst themselves and against common enemies. Its constitution, like the political community it defines, has evolved through a series of steps large and small over the course of centuries.

In contrast the United States, originally, was a far less diverse collection of people forged into a political community by the necessity of fighting a war against Great Britain. Having been suddenly apprised of their political identity, they were forced to choose consciously the political institutions that would govern them. The United States is the archetype of a constitutional government created by design and with purpose.

Europe, like Great Britain, is a collection of disparate peoples, whose history is characterized more by the wars fought among them than by their cooperative efforts to achieve common ends. But World War II, like the Revolutionary War in North America, made many Europeans like Jean Monnet (1978) suddenly aware that they too had common interests that were far more important than their differences, namely the interest in preventing future wars in Europe. Thus, the Europeans began the process of consciously crafting a constitution for Europe. But they did not choose to do so like their North American predecessors two centuries ago, in one fell swoop at a single convention. Rather they have chosen to proceed by small steps much more reminiscent of the evolutionary process by which Great Britain's constitution has been formed. This choice has important consequences to which we shall return. But first let us consider the various options, which Europe might have chosen and still could choose, if it wished to draft a constitution in a single step.

8. Founding a European government

Before one could call a constitutional convention one would have to decide what sort of union of European states one wished to create, a federation or a confederation. If one wished to create the latter, the obvious procedure for selecting delegates would be for each potential member state to send a delegation.[8] Although in principle the constitutional assembly could employ any voting rule it pleased, *de facto* a convention to create a confederation must employ the unanimity rule with each state effectively receiving one vote. Should any state not approve the agreement creating the confederation, it is free to remain apart from it. It is an autonomous state to begin with and can remain so, if it does not expect to be a net winner from joining the confederation. A confederation of n states can be formed only if all n think they will benefit from its creation.

Where a confederacy's constitution is necessarily an agreement, a contract, among its member states, a unified or federalist state's constitution is *ideally* a contract among its individual citizens. The purpose of the state is to advance the interests of all citizens, and it is most likely to achieve this goal if all citizens participate in its creation. Some method for representing the views of all citizens at the constitutional convention is required. Consider the following four options.

(1) Members of an existing government. By far the most common method by which nation states draft new constitutions is for a part of an existing government to draft the rules by which the future governments will function. If the existing government is a parliamentary democracy, its current parliament, or a subcommittee thereof, might write the constitution. Dictators often appoint commissions to draft new constitutions. The new constitutions in several post-communist European countries have been written in this way.

(2) Representatives from existing states. When a suprastate is to be formed out of several existing states, each state may send delegations to the convention in much the same way as they would if a confederation was to be formed. These delegations might be from either the parliaments of the individual states or from their executive branches. This format is essentially the same as that for creating a confederation.

(3) A specially elected assembly. Delegates from across the community could be elected for the sole purpose of drafting the constitution. Costa Rica's first constitution was drafted in this manner in 1812 (Seligson, 1990: 460), as was its present constitution, drafted in 1948 (Ameringer, 1982: 37). The Philadelphia convention of 1787 was made up of specially chosen delegates, albeit delegates chosen as under (2) by the several states that were to be conjoined.

(4) A randomly chosen cross-section of the citizens, selected in much the same way as one would select a jury.

Each of these alternatives differs with respect to the competencies of the delegates to carry out their task, and the incentives they have to do so in a way which is optimal for the future citizenry. Members of an existing parliament will, of course, have considerable expertise regarding the processes of government. But they may also think of themselves as representatives of particular interests and not of the interests of all future citizens. Members of the Labor Party may press worker interests to the exclusion of all others, members of the Green Party environmental interests. So long as *all* interests are adequately represented this partisanship may not be harmful, although it could stand in the way of achieving the kinds of compromises that are inevitably needed to reach agreement on constitutional questions.

A more serious form of partisanship arises with respect to the delegates own personal stakes in the outcomes of the constitutional process. In deciding what structure of government will be best for the future, a member of an existing parliament, or a prospective member of a future parliament, may find it difficult to abstract from the consequences of the various alternatives for her own political future and that of her party. Members of large parties will favor first-past-the-post systems and large minimum cut-offs for party representation under a PR system. Small parties will favor elections from large, multi-member districts and low cut-offs. If the current chief executive has a hand in the constitution writing process, she will favor provisions that produce a strong executive office. What best serves the citizens' interests gets adopted only by chance.

This point is well illustrated by European experience in constitution writing at the nation state level. For example, Italy's current constitution was drafted shortly after World War II by members of the parties that existed prior to Mussolini's takeover. They drafted a constitution designed to protect incumbent parties not to advance citizens' interests. It has achieved the former goal admirably, with the major parties (except for the Communists) playing dominant roles in the myriad governments that have come and gone since the end of World War II. How well the Italian constitution has served Italy's citizens is a more debatable issue (Spotts and Wieser, 1986). Several attempts have been made to improve the situation by reforming the constitution, but these too have been blocked by the parties in parliament fearful of the consequences of reform for their future.[9] Resentment against the major parties has reached new highs in recent years and some changes in the constitution now seem likely.

Olaf Ruin (1988: 329–331) has made the following observations concerning the revision of Sweden's constitution in 1974 by the Swedish Parliament. "...

the agreement ... hammered out [did not] rest on any version of the right constitutional framework for an advanced welfare society of the Swedish type. Rather, the agreement was characterized by calculations from different quarters of what maximally favored or disfavored their own political party. The Swedish version of constitutional politics appeared as the interest politics of political parties *par excellence*."

The same type of partisanship appears under the second method of selecting delegates to a convention, except in this case the partisan interests have a significant geographic flavor. If a federalist state is to be created out of autonomous smaller states, having each of these represented can help to ensure that the central level of government does not engulf the smaller levels, since the latter will wish to preserve as much authority as possible. On the other hand, if voters are represented at a constitutional convention only through existing, geographically defined governments, the latter's interests in preserving their autonomy may well stand in the way of creating the kind of central government that will best serve all citizen interests.

Although the United States' Constitution was not written by members of an existing Parliament, nor were many delegates likely to have expected to serve in the national assembly in the future, they were selected by state, and many saw themselves as representatives of the states that sent them and of their various economic interests.[10] Thus, the Philadelphia convention was a cross between a convention to create a confederation and one to create a federation. The results of this confusion of purposes are most blatantly apparent in the compromise that resulted in the overrepresentation of the small states in the Senate.[11] The ambiguity as to the United State's governmental structure created by the constitutional process also contributed in no small way to the belief of the Southern states in 1860 that they retained the right to secede from the Union. Canada's recent tribulations in trying to write a federal constitution through assemblies of representatives of each provincial government is a further illustration. Not surprisingly, given this mode of representation, one of the proposals surfacing in Canada during this process has been to convert its upper house into the kind of anachronistic, gerrymandered institution that the U.S. Senate is. The British Government's threat in the summer of 1994 to veto the entry of new members into the EU, because of the implication of their entry on the power of Great Britain to block initiatives in Brussels, is yet another illustration of geographically based representatives viewing an essentially constitutional choice, that affects the whole community (i.e., Europe), only in terms of its impact on the narrow, geographic interests directly represented.[12]

These considerations underline the importance of selecting delegates to a constitutional convention to write a *federalist* constitution, who are representatives of all citizens regardless of location of residence, and are chosen for the sole purpose of writing this constitution. If they are elected as under the third of the four procedures enumerated above, the delegates should be chosen from common lists of candidates that are presented to all voters. Ideally, the delegates should be chosen on the basis of their expected skills in writing a constitution that takes into account and advances the interests of future generations of citizens. To further ensure the impartiality of the delegates to the constitutional convention, provisions might be adopted to bar them from serving in any capacity in the federal government designed by the convention for a fixed number of years after the convention. More generally, impartiality could be fostered by having the entire constitution not go into effect for several years after the convention.[13]

The goal of impartiality might best be achieved by having the delegates to the constitutional convention selected, like members of a jury, by a random draw from the entire population. To my knowledge no constitution has ever been written by such an assembly, and if one were to be constituted it would obviously be somewhat lacking in expertise. But the latter objection can and has been levied against the use of the jury system, and yet it is believed by many in the Anglo-Saxon countries that use it to function well. A constitutional convention, like a jury, could call upon the advice of experts to assist it in its work.

John Rawls (1971) placed considerable stress on the role of impartiality in the selection of the provisions of the social contract to the subsequent willingness of individuals to comply with the terms of that contract. James Buchanan and Gordon Tullock (1962) placed similar emphasis on impartiality in the choice of a constitution (see also Buchanan, 1975). Citizens are more likely to identify with a constitution's provisions and attempt to comply with them, if they believe their interests were fairly represented at the convention that created it. Either of the latter two methods for selecting delegates is likely to be superior to the first two by this criterion.

The issue of compliance is also relevant for the choice of a voting rule to be used at the convention. While only a unanimous agreement among the participant states at a convention will lead to the founding of a confederacy, unanimity among the delegates is not necessary for a unitary or federal government to come into existence. The difficulty in exiting from a community may force some individuals to remain in a polity, even if they oppose the rules adopted at its creation. But such opposition bodes ill for the future success and stability of the polity. Thus, the heavy emphasis on unanimity at the constitutional stage to foster future compliance with the constitutional contract in most contractarian writings (Buchanan and Tullock, 1962; Rawls, 1971; Buchanan, 1975).

9. Maintaining a federalist structure

The optimality of federalist governmental structure stems from the geographic characteristics of the kinds of goods government should provide. Some of these public goods, like defense, are ideally provided to large numbers of people across great expanses of land. Others, like fire protection, can be optimally supplied to small communities. The ideal federalism consists of several levels of government, each responsible for those public goods whose geographic impact most closely corresponds to it. In the European context this idea has been referred to as the "subsidiarity principle" in recent discussions.

There appears to be a tendency in all federalist systems for responsibility for government services to shift upward in the federalist hierarchy (Aranson, 1992a). The highest level of government serves as a kind of magnet drawing ever more government activities away from the regional and local governments that are under it. This process of centralization is perceived to result in a federal government which is too large and unresponsive to the local and regionally defined needs of the citizens. A challenge facing those who would design a federalist system is to construct effective safeguards against the overcentralization of government activities that seems inevitably to transpire. Five possible safeguards are as follows:[14]

(1) Perhaps the simplest and most effective safeguard against overcentralization is to avoid having lower level *geographic* interests represented at each level of government. Every representative, who seeks reelection, has an incentive to bring before the parliament in which she sits issues of concern to those who elected her. If the Green Party of Belgium elects a delegate to a European parliament, it is the environmental issues of most concern to Belgians that she will press upon the parliament. Some of these may concern mainly or exclusively Belgians, and could better be resolved by the Belgian Parliament than by a European one. But this is of no concern to the delegate, who seeks only to please her constituents in every way that she can so as to retain their favor and thereby her seat. An important step toward preserving the integrity of a federalist system is to have the delegates to the legislative bodies at each level elected from common lists available to all voters across the areas covered by the respective governmental units.

(2) When a federalist structure is formed as a constitutional democracy, the framers may attempt to forestall the future concentration of government activity at the higher levels by explicitly assigning in the constitution specific governmental functions to each level of government. The U.S. Constitution did this for the federal level of government, and the federal government by and large stayed within its proscribed set of activities *until* the 1930s. The activist New Deal government sought the permission of the Supreme Court to expand the scope of federal government *greatly*, and was given it.[15] Although

the device of assigning each governmental unit specific functions ultimately (after 150 years) failed in the United States, it is not obvious that this must inevitably be so.

(3) The constitution framers could not anticipate all types of collective decisions that a federalist state will have to make in the future, and assign each to a level of government. Therefore, they will need to devise a general principle for assigning new issues. One possibility, which would seek to preserve the federalist structure, would be a provision in the constitution that prohibited any issue from coming before the parliament that did not promise substantial benefits for the citizens in at least 50 percent, say, of the constituent states. Thus, in a federalism composed of 15 states, a proposal to construct a dam would have to have anticipated benefits for the citizens in at least 8 of the 15 states. Such a provision would prevent purely local issues (a small dam) from being funded at higher levels of government than necessary.

(4) To protect federalist institutions, constitutional provisions must not only be written, they must also be enforced. Given the likely importance of this issue in Europe, the best way to ensure effective enforcement might well be to create a special federalist court charged with the responsibility for preserving European federalism and settling jurisdictional disputes among the member states. If a proposal came before the parliament of a federalist Europe that materially affected the citizens of only one or two states, any member of parliament could challenge the bill under the aforementioned provision. The constitutional court would then decide whether it was appropriate to consider the proposal in the parliament before a vote was taken.

(5) Yet another device for preserving federalism's strength is the referendum (Schneider, 1992; Frey, 1993). Of all federalist states, Switzerland has been without doubt the most successful at maintaining its decentralized federalist structure, and it has done so in large part by a liberal use of the referendum. Rather than challenging a proposal of merely local or regional interest in court, when it comes before the national parliament, the Swiss can petition for a referendum on it. If it would benefit only those in a small area of Switzerland, it is likely to be defeated in a national referendum. Those seeking funding for public goods of limited scope must do so at the level of government that corresponds most closely to the beneficiaries of the action, i.e., to those who are most likely to support it. The example of Switzerland illustrates that federalism need not give way to a giant, oversized government. The principle of subsidiarity can be withheld, if institutions for doing so are set into place.

10. The admittance of additional member states

Expanding an existing confederate or federalist state does not raise any fundamentally new issues. All parties should anticipate being made better off by such a move. A unanimous agreement among the delegates from the existing members of the confederation is obviously needed, and correspondingly the citizens of a federalist state should unanimously approve the entry of a new subunit into their system. Once again full unanimity cannot practically be required, but a large supramajority of either the representative assembly of the federalist state, or of its citizens directly in a referendum could be. Similarly, the new entrant needs to poll its citizens regarding the desirability of the move.

Indirectly, the expansion of a federalist state raises another potentialy important issue, however. The choice between a federalist and a confederalist structure should rest on the nature of the collective decisions to be made. The federalist structure is to be preferred if the benefits and costs from the collective decisions are likely to be spread uniformly across the polity. The confederalist structure is more appropriate when the costs and benefits are spread unevenly, and the asymmetries tend to be related to existing state boundaries. The benefits and costs of a collective action, say regulations to curb air pollution, are more likely to be uniform across a polity, the smaller its size. Thus, as a federalist state grows by adding new territory of once autonomous other states, the number of collective decisions it makes *at its highest level of government*, which satisfy the uniformity-of-benefits-and-costs condition that favors a federalist structure, can be expected to decline. If it retains its federalist structure as it expands, it will eventually find it optimal to add new sublevels which better match the distribution of benefits and costs of the collective decisions that need to be made. As it expands, the collective decisions a federation makes may begin to resemble more and more the kinds of decisions that favor a confederate governmental structure.

It is perhaps because of this that enthusiasm for an integrated, federalist-type structure for the EC has been strongest among the original six members. The United Kingdom and Greece, which are situated more on the periphery of the community, along with Denmark, have exhibited the most lukewarm attitude to further integration and appear more to favor the confederate over the federalist structure (Holland, 1992: 149–150).

11. Implications for the Maastricht Treaty and further European integration

11.1. *The European Community's confederate past*

Jean Monnet's original vision for Europe was for it to become a "federation of the West" (Holland, 1992: 5–6). The steps by which it has progressed toward this goal have been a series of treaties and more informal agreements among representatives of the several governments. Thus, the decisionmaking process by which integration has advanced has taken the confederate form. Not surprisingly, therefore, it has moved forward only when consensus has been reached. Not surprisingly, consensus has often come at the cost of compromise between alternative views of what the community should be, and in particular alternative views regarding federalism and confederation. Given that the process of integration has been governed by a confederate structure, it is not surprising that the end product resembles much more closely the confederation model than it does the federalist one. The bulk of political power lies with the Council of Ministers in Brussels, not with the European Parliament in Strasbourg. Jean Monnet's vision of a European federalism remains unfulfilled.

There are several, perhaps unintended, consequences of the Community's continued reliance on a confederate decisionmaking structure. Not only is a confederate structure better suited to resolving issues in which the gains and losses differ across countries, it tends to focus the Community's attention on such policies. No better example exists than European Farm Policy.

Subsidies to farmers have been for a generation and remain the Community's biggest budget item. But the "gains" and costs of this policy differ greatly across the member countries. If a true federalist structure existed with parties elected to a European Parliament using a European-wide party list system, a Farm Party might come into existence and win some, but undoubtedly not many, seats. It might be able to find enough support among the other parties for some general protection and subsidies for farmers. But it is inconceivable that it could induce a broadly representative parliament to institute the kind and scale of protection for farmers that now exists.

Farmers' demands for assistance within each country are more concentrated and specific than they are across Europe. In one country it is the dairy interests which are most powerful, in another wheat growers, in a third soybean farmers. These specific interests can put relatively more pressure on the governments of their respective countries than they would be able to muster under proportional representation in a European parliament. Moreover, the effectiveness of protests which disrupt traffic and the lives of ordinary citizens is much greater under the present confederate structure than it would be under a federalist system. The protests of French farmers affect mostly other Frenchmen and can put great pressure on the French Government to give in to the farmers' demands. But demonstrations by French farmers would put far less pressure upon a European parliament to act. No single party, other than a Farm Party if one existed, would feel the necessity to take up the French farmers' cause. Each party would gather its support from across all Europe, not just from France, and would feel less pressure to give into the French farmers to spare the rest of the French the inconveniencies caused by the protests. The unwillingness to give in to the demands of protesters would be strengthened by the losses imposed on other Europeans from giving in to the French farmers. Of course, simultaneous protests by all European farmers would put considerable pressure on a European parliament, but protests on such a scale are far more unlikely to occur because of the differences in farm interests that exist across Europe, and because of the sheer transaction costs of organizing effective protests on that scale.

Not only does the confederate structure of collective decisionmaking in the community tend to focus its attention on issues with disparate benefits and costs across the members, but it blocks taking up the kinds of pan-European issues that would be a federalist Europe's *raison d'être*. If one pan-European issue exists, it is most certainly defense. All Europeans benefit from a peaceful and secure Europe and do so, presumably to an equal degree. Yet the community has failed to come up with an effective security force and policy under its confederate organizational structure (Nugent, 1991: 39–40; Holland, 1992: Ch. 5). Again the problem undoubtedly stems from each government's ministers viewing European defense policy from the perspective of its own *marginal* benefits and costs from participation.[16]

With the exception of the United Kingdom, and from time to time France, all European countries have adopted some form of multimember district representation. Incongruously, the system of representation that is used to decide European community policy resembles much more closely that employed in the United States and the United Kingdom than that used throughout Continental Europe and Scandinavia. Just as a citizen from the south side of Chicago is represented in the lower House of Congress by the person who got the most votes in her district, regardless of whether she voted for that person or shares his ideology, a German citizen is represented in Brussels by the party or coalition which got the most votes in the last German parliamentary elections, regardless of whether she voted for that party or shares its ideology. All German citizens can be adequately represented in this manner on only those issues that affect all Germans in the same way. The European Community continues to function largely as a confederation of independent states with its political agenda constrained to those kinds of issues that a confederation can resolve.

Are there other issues of a pan-European nature like defense or some environmental problems that are best suited to a federalist decisionmaking structure that are not being dealt with optimally, or perhaps not at all, due to Europe's political organization as a confederation? This was the key question Europeans needed to answer when the idea of a European political community was first broached. It remains the single most important question to be answered before further changes in Europe's political structure take place. It is a question for all Europeans to ponder and answer.

11.2. *The European Community's federalist future?*

The European Community's "constitution" is based on three treaties: two signed in Rome, one in Paris. Thus, from its inception it has been a confederalist structure (Nugent, 1991: 42). Its institutions have been created through negotiations between the representatives of the member governments, and these institutions have lodged authority in an assembly of representatives from these same governments. The basic elements of the Maastricht Treaty, the most ambitious step toward European political and economic integration to date, were conceived in Brussels and, not surprisingly, retain most political authority in Brussels. So long as the institutions of European government are designed by the ministers of its constituent governments, it will always retain a largely confederate structure.

This is the lesson, as noted above, to be learned from the experience individual countries have had when writing their constitutions. If the constitution is written by members of the parties who expect to hold seats in future parliaments, then the constitution will be designed to favor their interests. Nowhere is this lesson more apparent than in Great Britain's actions with respect to representation in the European Parliament. All members of the EU elect members to the European Parliament in Strasbourg using some variant of a PR formula except for Great Britain, which uses the same form of single-member-per-district representation as it uses in its domestic elections. Single-member-per-district-representation overrepresents the larger parties in the Parliament relative to a strictly proportional system (Rae, 1971; Lijphart, 1986, 1990). The usual defense made for this type of system is that it is more likely to award a majority of seats to the largest party and thus produce strong and effective government. When applied throughout the polity, this argument has merit. But the use of single-member-per-district representation by the UK, while all other EU countries use PR formulas, is not going to result in a single party having a majority of seats in the Strasbourg parliament. It does, generally, result in the largest parties in the British Parliament being overrepresented in Strasbourg (Jacobs and Corbett, 1990: 16–17), and this of course explains why the British Parliament opts for this mode of representation. (An exception to this general tendency occurred in the 1994 elections to the European Parliament, however, when British voters revealed their displeasure with the Conservative Government's handling of domestic issues by sending a disproportionately *small* number of Conservatives to Strasbourg. Perhaps, no single event better illustrates the inadequacies of the present rules for electing a European Parliament, then that voters in one country should use an election to the European Parliament to express their preferences *not on panEuropean* policies, but on policies of purely domestic concern.)

European political unification has gone the furthest, perhaps, in creating a common set of rights for Europeans (Magiera, 1991; Holland, 1992: Ch. 6). If there is such a thing as a European citizen, with common civil and political rights and obligations, which are identical regardless of where he resides in Europe, then there must exist a European citizen with interests in government which he shares in common with other Europeans regardless of where each lives. If the institutions of government are to advance the common interests of all European citizens, then they should have a hand in their creation and ratification.

To date the European citizen's role in the creation of the EU's political institutions has been indirect and reactive. His most direct participation has come through the occasional *national* referenda that have been held regarding entry into the EU or approval of the Maastricht Treaty. But such participation has always been after the fact. Does the Briton want to join the EU as it exists in 1973? Does the Dane want to adopt the treaty of Maastricht? A more participatory role for European citizens would have them involved in the drafting of the treaties, as say through a constitutional convention.

If a government of Europe is to advance the interests of all Europeans, then the constitution which creates this government should reflect the interests and ideas of all Europeans. The surest way to accomplish this goal is to hold a constitutional convention with delegates selected from across Europe. The delegates should not be members of existing national governments or parliaments for they will have difficulty divorcing their own political futures and interests under the constitution from those of the citizens on whose behalf they must act. Rather a special convention with delegates chosen solely for the purpose of drafting the constitution is required. If the delegates were elected, the best procedure would have them elected from across all of Europe, as ideally would be the case for a European parliament. Although most Europeans might be expected to vote for delegates from their own country, a widely respected European statesman might well win votes from many countries. Most importantly, the delegates to the convention should not think of themselves as representing the interests of any specific group or country, but rather of all Europeans. To help accomplish this goal one might bar individuals, who hold elective office in any country from running as candidates to be delegates to the European Constitutional convention.[17] The ideal candidates would be, like the octogenarian Benjamin Franklin at the Philadelphia convention, senior statesmen and stateswomen capable of looking beyond their own personal interests in the outcome of the convention, or even that of their country of birth, to the interests of all Europeans.

Given that the areas that would form a European federalism are currently autonomous states, no federalist constitution drafted by a convention, however constituted, could take effect if a majority of the citizens of any country opposed. Thus, the delegates to a constitutional convention would have to consider its impact on each country and be confident that it benefited all, but again this can be accomplished without having delegates selected to *represent* each country. As a further check on the convention, a European wide referendum to ratify it would be appropriate, so that citizens would be forced to weigh the likely benefits and costs of the constitution on themselves, and express their opinion on them.

The United States' Constitution was written by delegates from the individual states who kept in mind the interests of their constituents. Thus, it suffers from some of the same maladies upon which I have laid stress. Yet, this constitution is generally given credit for this country's maintaining its democratic institutions for more than two centuries, and is widely respected by its own citizens. There are several reasons for this. First, although the citizens played little role in the selection of delegates to the convention in Philadelphia, and were kept in the dark regarding its deliberations, they were informed of its content and treated to an active debate on its merits by the Federalists and the Antifederalists during the interval between the convention and the Constitution's ratification by the individual states. Second, the participants in the convention included men like Washington, Madison and Franklin, whose intellect and character added lustre to the outcome. Most Americans today probably identify with the Constitution not because they took part in its creation, but because they cannot imagine that they would have done any better than the men who did, if they had.

In contrast, the Maastricht Treaty was neither widely debated nor understood by Europeans before the first Danish vote. Whatever the talents of the people who drafted it are, they were not selected by Europeans for this task, and are not widely regarded as statesmen and intellectual leaders. Although the actual content of the Treaty has much merit, there is nothing in the process by which it was drafted or the personages who drafted it to make Europeans identify with it as *their constitution*, and the same is largely true of the Treaties of Rome and Paris that preceded it. To bring about such an identification, a different process would be required.

The participants at the constitutional convention in Philadelphia recognized that they were at an important juncture in world history, and that they were engaging in an experiment with possibly profound consequences for future generations both in the United States and elsewhere. The events in Europe commencing in 1989 make the present another historic juncture in world history. Democratic experiments are taking place today, as they did in North America 200 years ago, that might define the character of European life for centuries to come. Even if it wanted to, the European Union could not stand by and ignore what happens to its east, since events like those in Bosnia will inevitably impinge upon it. But given its location and its resources, it is obviously in a position to be able to do much more. But before it can it must decide what it is, and what its interests are. Is it mainly a cartel for regulating agricultural prices, steel production, airline landing rights and the like? Is it mainly a customs union for encouraging free trade within its borders? Is it mainly a confederation of nation states capable of making only those collective decisions that are perceived to benefit all countries by the governments which hold majorities in each? Or is it a full-fledged democratic community, composed of individuals with common interests, and governed through political institutions that allow its citizens to express and advance these common interests?

Notes

1. There are some special cases, like infant industries, in which all members of a community might benefit from a tariff, but these are far rarer than the number of tariffs one observes. Nor can one argue persuasively that all members of the community might benefit from a set of many tariffs that protected most/all wage earners and capital suppliers. A central tenet of economics since its inception has been that the entire community is better off with no tariffs than with many. The initial "public good" the European Community consumed was, of course, the benefits from free trade within the "common market" created by the Treaty of Rome.
2. For a discussion of monetary union and other issues of European integration from a constitutional perspective, see Kirchgässner (1994).
3. For a distinction between federation and confederation in the European context similar to that made here, see Forsyth (1981).
4. Oates (1972) and Tullock (1969) provide classic discussions of the allocation issue, Inman and Rubinfeld (1996) and Tullock (1991) provide more recent discussions.
5. See my discussion in (1996, Chs. 8–10), however.
6. The voting system used in Luxembourg also allows voters to express their preferences for the *persons*, whom they want to see represent them as well as the parties.
7. Several alternatives to simple qualified majority rules have been developed, which have superior properties, but we shall not take the space to discuss them here. See descriptions in Mueller (1989: Ch. 8; 1996, Ch. 11).

8. States may send delegations of several individuals, and voting at the convention could be by delegate or by state. The convention could also agree to adopt a qualified majority rule to pass on each proposal for inclusion in the constitutional contract. But the final vote approving the constitution must *de facto* be a unanimous vote of the *delegations*, although not necessarily of the delegates. Even if balloting on this final vote were by delegate using a qualified majority rule, if a majority of one state's delegation opposed the constitution it could simply withdraw leaving the remaining delegations to form a confederation without it.
9. See Hine's (1988: 218–223) discussion of the fate of the Bozzi Commission's proposals for reform.
10. For further discussion of the roles of self- and constituent interests of the delegates at the convention in Philadelphia, see McDonald (1958), Roche (1961), Jillson (1988), and McGuire (1988).
11. For further examples of jockeying by party representatives at constitutional conventions see Merkl (1963: 90–103) on the Federal Republic of Germany's Constitution and Bonime-Blanc (1987: 77) on Spain's.
12. Worse still the British delegation in Brussels appeared not even to be weighing the impact of entry and the choice of voting rule on the welfare of *all* British citizens, but rather to be most concerned with placating the anti-Europe faction of the Conservative Party.
13. For further discussion of these options, see Mueller (1996, Ch. 21).
14. Several authors have wrestled with this and other questions of institutional structure and protections in the EU, for example, Bernholz (1993), Frey (1993), and Schneider (1992).
15. See Ackerman (1991), Aranson (1992a, b), and Niskanen (1992).
16. Burgess (1989: 95) stresses that politics at the European level continues to be dominated by the member states, despite the progress toward federalism that has been made.
17. Gordon Tullock suggested this to me.

References

Ackerman, B.A. (1991). *We the people*. Cambridge: Belknap Press.

Ameringer, C.D. (1982). *Democracy in Costa Rica*. New York: Praeger.

Aranson, P.H. (1992a). Federalism at founding. Mimeo. Emory University.

Aranson, P.H. (1992b). Federalism: Doctrine against balance. Mimeo. Emory University.

Bagehot, W. (1872/1961). *The English Constitution*, 2nd ed. Garden City: Doubleday, 1961 (reprint of 1872, ed.).

Barry, B. (1965). *Political argument*. London: Routledge and Kegal Paul.

Bernholz, P. (1993). Constitutional aspects of the European integration. In S. Borner and H. Grubel (Eds.), *The European Community after 1992*. London: Macmillan.

Black, D. (1958). *The theory of committees and elections*. Cambridge: Cambridge University Press.

Bonime-Blanc, A. (1987). *Spain's transition to democracy*. Boulder: Westview Press.

Buchanan, J.M. (1975). *The limits of liberty: Between anarchy and Leviathan*. Chicago: University of Chicago Press.

Buchanan, J.M. and Tullock, G. (1962). *The calculus of consent*. Ann Arbor: The University of Michigan Press.

Burgess, M. (1989). *Federalism and European Union*. London: Routledge.

Coase, R.H. (1960). The problem of social cost. *Journal of Law and Economics* 3 (October): 1–44.

Dahlman, C.J. (1979). The problem of externality. *Journal of Law and Economics* 22 (April): 141–162.

Forsyth, M. (1981). *Unions of states: The theory and practice of confederation.* Leichester: Leichester University Press.
Frey, B. (1993). The role of direct referenda in institutional reform. Paper presented at a conference at Universita degli Studi 'La Sapienza', Rome.
Hine, D. (1988). Italy (1948): Condemned by its constitution? In V. Bogdanor, *The people and the party system,* 206–228. Cambridge: Cambridge University Press.
Holland, M. (1992). *European Community integration.* New York: St. Martin's Press.
Inman, R.P. and Rubinfeld, D.L. (1996). The political economy of federalism. In D.C. Mueller (Ed.), *Perspectives on public choice.* Cambridge: Cambridge University Press.
Jacobs, F. and Corbett, P. (1990). *The European Parliament.* Boulder: Westview Press.
Jillson, C.C. (1988). *Constitution making: Conflict and consensus in the Federal Constitution of 1787.* New York: Agathon Press.
Kirchgässner, G. (1994). Constitutional economics and its relevance for the evolution of rules. *Kyklos* 47: 321–339.
Lijphart, A. (1986). Degrees of proportionality of proportional representation formulas. In B. Grofman and A. Lijphart (Eds.), *Electoral laws and their political consequences,* New York: Agathon Press.
Lijphart, A. (1990). The political consequences of electoral laws, 1945–85. *American Political Science Review* 84 (June): 481–496.
Magiera, S. (1991). A citizen's European personal, political and cultural rights. In L. Hurwitz and C. Lequesne (Eds.), *The state of the European Community,* 153–164. Essex: Longman.
McDonald, F. (1958). *We the people.* Chicago: University of Chicago Press.
McGuire, R.A. (1988). Constitution making: A rational choice model of the federal convention of 1787. *American Journal of Political Science* 32 (May): 483–522.
Merkl, P.H. (1963). *The origin of the West German Republic.* New York: Oxford University Press.
Monnet, J. (1978). *Memoirs.* Trans. R. Mayne. New York: Doubleday.
Mueller, D.C. (1989). *Public choice II.* Cambridge: Cambridge University Press.
Mueller, D.C. (1996). *Constitutional democracy.* Oxford: Oxford University Press.
Niskanen, W.A. (1992). The case for a new fiscal constitution. *The Journal of Economic Perspectives.* 6 (Spring): 13–24.
Niskanen, W.A. (1992). Autocratic, democratic and optimal government. Mimeo. Cato Institute.
Nugent, N. (1991). *The government and politics of the European Community.* Durham: Duke University Press.
Oates, W.E. (1972). *Fiscal federalism.* London: Harcourt Brace.
Rae, D.W. (1971). *The political consequences of electoral laws,* revised edition. New Haven: Yale University Press.
Rawls, J.A. (1971). *A theory of justice.* Cambridge: The Belknap Press of Harvard University Press.
Roche, J.P. (1961). The Founding Fathers: A reform caucus in action. *American Political Science Review* 5: 799–816.
Ruin, O. (1988). The New Constitution (1974) and the tradition of consensual politics. In V. Bogdanor (Ed.), *The people and the party system,* 309–327. Cambridge: Cambridge University Press.
Samuelson, P.A. (1969). Pure theory of public expenditures and taxation. In J. Margolis and H. Guitton (Eds.), *Public Economics,* 98–123. New York: St. Martin's Press.
Schneider, F. (1992). The federal and fiscal structures of representatives and direct democracies as models for a European Federal Union. Mimeo. Linz.
Seligson, M.A. (1990). Costa Rica. In H.J. Wiarda and H.F. Kline (Eds.), *Latin American politics and development,* 3rd ed., 455–466. Boulder: West View Press.
Spotts, F. and Weiser, T. (1986). *Italy: A difficult democracy.* Cambridge: Cambridge University Press.
Tullock, G. (1969). Federalism: Problems of scale. *Public Choice* 6 (Spring): 19–30.
Tullock, G. (1991). *The new federalism.* Mimeo. Tucson, AZ.

Public Choice **90**: 281–310, 1997.

© 1997 *Kluwer Academic Publishers.*

Subsidiarity and ecologically based taxation: A European constitutional perspective

JÜRGEN G. BACKHAUS
Department of Economics, University of Limburg, 6200 MD Maastricht, The Netherlands

Abstract. The principle of subsidiarity through its re-affirmation in the Treaty of Maastricht became an integral and central part of European constitutional law. Its relationship to ecological issues, however, has so far not been explored. Subsidiarity is a general principle of organization. It can apply to all areas of policy: financial, agricultural, technological, education, defense, economic development and, e.g. environmental policy. The principle of subsidiarity is silent about the specific purpose, direction or content of a particular policy.

Whatever be the purpose of any such policy, the principle of subsidiarity requires that it be carried out within that context which is the smallest viable one in which the objective can successfully be attained. When a task is too complicated for a small unit such as an office or a firm to be successfully performed, that unit has to be augmanted to the point where the task can be effectively performed. Likewise, if an organization is too large to successfully handle particular problems as its procedure may be too cumbersome or as it lacks sufficient detailed information or experience repeated recurrences of problems it has tried to settle, then a different organizational form must be found, preferably an existing one, which is closer to the problem at hand and able to carry out the policy. With the shift in responsibility will also travel the access to resources with which to carry out the task.

Since ecological units rarely co-incide with political units, the principle of subsidiarity poses a specific challenge to politicians and administrators who have to decide on assignments of tasks and responsibilities as well as funding within the different echelons and among the different Member States of the European Union.

This essay explores those tasks and, in particular, advances the notion of establishing ecological tax units.

1. Introduction

The principle of subsidiarity, since it became part of the treaty of Maastricht and thereby of European constitutional law, has received a lot of attention. Its relationship to ecological issues, however, has to my knowledge rarely been explored. Subsidiarity is a perfectly generalizable principle of organization. It can apply to all areas of policy, financial, agricultural, technological, education, defense, economic development and, of course, environmental policy. The principle of subsidiarity is an organizing principle. Taken as such, it is silent about the specific purpose, direction or content of a particular policy. Whatever be the purpose of the policy, the principle of subsidiarity requires that it be carried out within that context which is the smallest viable one in which the objective can successfully be attained. When a task is too complicated for a small unit such as an office or a firm to be successfully performed, that unit has to be augmented to the point where the task can be effectively performed. Likewise, if an organization is too large to successfully handle particular problems as its procedures may be too combersome, as it lacks sufficient detailed information or experiences repeated recurrence of problems it once has tried to settle, then a different organizational form must be found, preferably an existing one, which is closer to the problem at hand and able to carry out the policy at hand. It goes without saying that with the shift in responsibility will also travel the access to resources with which to carry out the task.

2. Aspirations and policy goals: Enforced and selfenforcing rules and policies

In constitutional and environmental economics, we can distinguish between different types of approaches, notably those that need to be enforced and those that are designed to be selfenforcing. Given the difficulties enforcement agencies have in enforcing rules laid down and sometimes agreed to beforehand, there is always a preference for selfenforcing rules. These are, as we have seen before, the domain of constitutional environmental economics.

Rules have a better chance of being self-enforcing if there is a close match between the functions of a particular unit and the means and responsibilities to serve this function, where the rules have the purpose to ensure a proper use of the means and responsibilities with a view to performing the functions in question. The crucial issue then is to define that unit which is most appropriate for fulfilling a particular function. Very often in constitutional public choice, this question is not addressed head on. Typically, we start from the assumption that there be a state or a commonwealth, without exploring the question of which domain this commonwealth or state should actually occupy, and in relation to what other public bodies. Therefore, the first section of Part B is devoted to an indepth discussion of the subsidiarity principle. It is shown, in particular, that the principle has a strong history in European thought, and that it therefore deserves to be systematically relied upon in constitutional and environmental economics.

The following two sections deal in turn with five different approaches to environmental taxation. Most of these, notably Pigouvian taxation and fees as well as user charges are largely in need of being enforced, where rates need to be set and the objects of taxation, the environmental effects in this case, need to be correctly identified. When taxes are to be assessed and charges to be levied, the procedure must be challengable in court. Since tax courts tend not to be equipped to deal with issues of environmental taxation, this requirement can turn out to be a very important one and a very difficult one for legislators to meet. Some environmentally relevant approaches to taxation are more in line with traditional models of taxation than others. In this case, the probability of the tax invoice to survive in court is higher, which is why these approaches deserve to be explored in more detail.

3. Subsidiarity

The principle of subsidiarity has earned a solid position in European intellectual history. Since due to its incorporation into the Maastricht treaty it has become international law, it is worth briefly retracing its intellectual history.

3.1. *Historical context and theory*

This short section tries to clarify the meaning of the principle of subsidiarity – which is far from unambigious – and to explain some of its implications in the context of European unification and the accompanying legal discourse.

Perhaps one of the earliest formulations of the principle of subsidiarity, which is at the same time one of the first formulations of a full scale state welfare program, can be found in Christian Wolff's *Principles of Natural Law*, published in 1754. There, in §1022, he states the following:

> Das Leben gehörig hinzubringen, wird auch erfordert, dass man vor die Dürftige und Bettler besorge, was zur Nothdurft des Lebens nöthig ist, und, damit die Unterthanen nicht gar zu sehr mit Allmosengeben beschwehret werden, ist in sorfältige Betrachtung zu ziehen, was das Naturgesetz von den Allmosen feste setzt (§488.sequ.). Daher sind Zuchthäuser aufzubauen, worinn diejenigen zur Arbeit angehalten werden müssen, welche, ob sie gleich Arbeiten könnten, doch lieber betteln wollen; ingleichen Armenhäuser, worinn man die dürftigen ernähret, die sich durch Arbeiten das nicht zu erwerben im Stande sind, was sie zur Lebensnothdurft gebrauchen, und keine Anverwandten oder Freunde haben, welche sich ihrer Bedürfnisse annehmen könnten; noch ferner Kranckenhäuser, worinn krancke Arme theils ernähret, teils geheilet werden; So auch Waysenhäuser, worinn man arme Waysen erziehet; endlich Armenschulen, in welchen man die Kinder armer Eltern umsonst in demjenigen unterrichtet, was ihnen zu wissen nöthig und nützlich ist. (Wolff, 1754)

Several elements of this exposition are particularly noteworthy. This is first of all the scope of the program of the welfare state, including measures in order to alleviate the consequences of sickness, unemployment, poor health, orphanage and more generally poverty, in which case access to public schools is guaranteed. Yet the rationale for this government welfare program, as Wolff explicitly states, is to keep the burden of the welfare taxes to be borne by citizens at a minimum. The welfare state intervenes if and because this is the least expensive way to alleviate the problem. Equally noteworthy is the precise circumscription of the instance under which the welfare state has to intervene, e.g., if the person in need has no "relatives or friends who can take on the satisfaction of his needs." The welfare state, therefore, is only subsidiary to the traditional bonds of family and friendship. Yet it would be wrong to think of the principle of subsidiarity as conceived by Christian Wolff as one built around individualism. It is not the individual which is considered the smallest unit of support (of others), since that would not have been a realistic description of the political economy of his time. Rather, Wolff puts forth a different economic constitution of his welfare state, with the big households comprehending the extended family as the nuclear entity of which the larger economy is composed:

> §972. Wir erkennen sehr leicht, dass eintzele Häuser sich selbst dasjenige nicht hinreichend verschaffen können, was zur Nothdurft, Bequemlichkeit und dem Vergnügen, ja zur Glückseligkeit erfordert wird, noch auch ihre Rechte ruhig geniessen, und was sie von andern zu fordern haben, sicher erhalten, noch auch sich und das ihrige wider anderer Gewaltthätigkeit schützen können. Es ist also nötig, dasjenige durch gemeinschaftliche Kräfte zu erhalten, was eintzele Häuser vor sich nicht erhalten könen. Und zu dem Ende müssen Gesellschaften errichtet werden (§836). (Wolff, 1754)

We realize then, that in Wolff's conception the principle supporting the unit of the welfare state was the house, i.e., the classical household or micro-economy; only if it failed, a larger politico-economic unit had no intervene.

The interesting question then is what form this intervention was supposed to take. The answer is already implicit in Wolff, but a more explicit statement can be found in the writings of another authority on political thought in continental Europe writing about a hundred years after Wolff.

> Natürlich folgt aus dieser Notwendigkeit des Besitzes genügender Lebensbedürfnisse noch keineswegs, dass sie gerade der Staat zu liefern habe. Im Gegenteil wird er sich zu diesem Bedüfnis wie zu jedem anderen Verlangen seiner Bürger verhalten. Er hat also namentlich polizeiliche Hilfe nur dann zu gewähren, wenn bei der grösseren Allgemeinheit

> eines Bedürfnisses auch die Unmöglichkeit vorliegt, dasselbe mittels Privatanstrengung zu befriedigen. Und in der Regel wird Lezteres nicht der Fall sein, wenn die allgemeinen Massregeln zur Erwerbung von Vermögen gehörig getroffen sind und benützt werden. (Mohl, 1844)

In brief, Mohl suggest that the mere existence of needs of its citizens are an insufficient reason for the state to directly satisfy those needs. In general, the state, rather than satisfying needs of its citizens directly has the task to create the conditions under which the citizens can accumulate sufficient wealth in order to satisfy their needs themselves. Note that this application of the principle is twofold, and twice correct. On the one hand, Mohl correctly identifies the state as the better provider of the (mostly legal) infrastructure which allows its citizens to prosper and accumulate wealth in order to satisfy the needs of themselves and their dependants. He correctly assumes that the provision by the state will detract from this objective, since the provision by the individual households will be more cost effective than the provision by the state which would, by necessity, have to be financed through taxes to be borne by the tax paying households. Consequently, the state is responsible for providing the infrastructure in which the individual households can prosper. Since, on the other hand, provision of welfare services and the satisfaction of needs can be better targeted and more effectively rendered by the (larger) households, it is to them that the task also falls, relieving them of the otherwise necessary tax burden. In applying the principle of subsidiarity, it is of pivotal importance to continuously consider both sides of the coin, the expenditure side and the revenue side. The determination of the primary and the subsidiary service entity can only be accomplished if both expenditure and revenue factors have been properly and completely taken into account.

A more recent and perhaps the most widely read formulation of the principle of subsidiarity is contained in a Papal letter (encycle) named after the two beginning Latin words *Quadrogesimo anno* in Section 79 of the encycle of 1931. The text reads:

> Wie dasjenige, was der Einzelmensch aus eigener Initiative und in seinen eigenen Kräften leisten kann, ihm nicht entzogen und der Gesellschaftstätigkeit zugewiesen werden darf, so verstösst es gegen die Gerechtigkeit, das, was die kleineren und untergeordneten Gemeinwesen leisten und zum guten Ende führen können, für die weitere und übergeordnete Gemeinschaft in Anspruch zu nehmen; zugleich ist es überaus nachteilig und verwirrt die ganze Gesellschaftsordnung. Jedwede Gesellschaftstätigkeit ist ja ihrem Wesen und Begriff nach subsidiär; sie soll die Glieder des Sozialkörpers unterstützen, darf sie aber niemals zerschlagen oder aufsagen. (Cited after Herzog, 1963)

In this formulation, the subsidiarity principle appears rather matter of factly as a restatement of an old principle in political theory and also church doctrine. Secondly, it receives an organiz twist which blurs its sound economic interpretation. If a community can reasonably discharge its duties, a larger community (of which it is conceivably a part) should not take over these duties as a matter of (ethical) principle. In this formulation, no mention is made of the costs and benefits to the larger and the smaller community respectively, nor to the costs and benefits facing other smaller communities being part of the larger whole. It is not surprising that the formulation from the encycle, rather than the traditional formulation, has given rise to much controversy and contradictory applications.

Yet the economic core of the principle is readily crystallized. In order to optimize the performance of the larger political entity, primary liability for the solution of problems lies with the smallest functional unit. This need not be the lowest functional unit in a hierarchial sense. This smallest functional unit can be a single unit or a group of such units as shown in the quote from Wolff, these units can be linked by friendship, neighbourhood, a common religion, history or some other such link. The concept of joining several small units may be referred to as lateral subsidiarity.

In the clear case of insufficiency of a particular level, the nearest functional one needs to be found. The search can go either up or down, depending on where one starts. If a particular province, e.g., cannot adequately solve an environmental problem, it might look at a cooperation with:

a) another province (lateral subsidiarity), or
b) the nation state or the European Community (upwards subsidiarity), or
c) the local communities inside the province, where the problem is most urgent (downwards). The situation might arise where the provincial government takes care of the environmental problem for the smaller communities, whereas the larger communities or those where the environmental problem is most urgent take the matter into their own hands.

It should be emphasized that this principle provides a pattern of thought in order to delineate public responsibilities. The historical survey shows the principle of subsidiarity to be a long standing constitutional principle which actually dates back to the very beginnings of constitution writing based on natural law systems. The natural law source also makes the principle an integral part of church teachings. In its original formulation, the principle of subsidiarity is a constitutional principle determining the definition and delineation of rights and responsibilities of private bodies on the one hand and public bodies on the other. This is, e.g., still the case for the role of the principle in the German Basic Law (article two). In the Maastricht Treaty, the principle primarily (but not exclusively) is used to define the relative responsibilities of the European Communities on the one hand and member states or parts of member states (in the German and Belgian case federal states or "gewesten") on the other. In the tug of war between the community and the member states, where the community tries to expand its programs while these attempts are sometimes met with resistance on the part of at least some of the member states or parts thereof, the principle has assumed a substantial importance. It is enforcable and regularly enforced.[1]

In brief we can interpret the principle of subsidiarity as an economic principle of functional organization. First, the function needs to be clearly defined: in our cases, the function was always the efficient management for sustainable use of an ecological unit. Secondly, that organizational unit needs to be defined in terms of a constitutional environmental economic analysis determining which unit can best fulfill this function. A third step will necessarily consist in finding a legal counterpart to the organizational unit defined in this way.

3.2. *Lateral subsidiarity*

Perhaps the most difficult concept in this context is the notion of lateral subsidiarity. All minds are trained to think in terms of analogies and parallels, and it is difficult to conceive of putting bodies of different legal and political status together into one common cooperation. Yet, in the environmental context where historical and political developments transcend geographical and ecological reasons, such cooperations with a binding legal form are perfectly normal. By way of example, the Lake of Constance flows into a condomenium through the river Rhine, of one republic (Austria), two federal German states (Bavaria and Baden-Württemberg), and the Swiss canton of Thurgau. In cooperations between highly centralized countries such as France or the Netherlands and highly decentralized countries such as Belgium and Germany, many lateral forms of subsidiarity can develop.

4. Typical problems – Ecological units

The branch of environmental economics to which this essay is a contribution is best described as constitutional environmental economics. The questions addressed in this essay refer not to a specific environmental policy problem, such as SO_2 reduction in general, but rather to an entire set of inter-related environmental problems experienced by a specific ecological unit. The reduction of SO_2 may be one such problem to be addressed by the ecological unit, but pursuit of this objective will have to be weighed against the pursuit of other objectives with respect to the means available. Constitutional environmental economics deals with "the constitution" of viable ecological units which satisfy these two criteria:

1. The organizational unit is built around an ecological unit with a minimum of overlap.
2. The organizational unit is also a decision unit, able to weigh policy options in the light of available resources, all related to the ecological unit in question.

The distinction between two separate analytical tasks, the analysis of processes and the analysis and design of structures in which these processes take place lies at the heart of modern political economy. In public choice, the discipline which deals with non-market decisions, the distinction is between constitutional political economy and public choice.[2] Public choice deals with the analysis of decisions and their outcomes within well determined structures on which the decisional outcome will be based. The analysis can lead to the suggestion of a change in these structures. On the other hand, constitutional political economy deals with the question of how a particular problem can be dealt with by the appropriate choice of a structure which then determines the constraints under which decisions can be taken. This is the question at hand. Ecological units rarely go in step with political units. Ecological units pose specific problems which are tied to each other and to the ecological unit. To retain our example, an SO_2 reduction can be an important policy goal, but its relative importance depends on other aspects as well. In a particular ecological unit, an SO_2 reduction may not be a problem at all: pursuing that goal anyway would conceivably leave other more important ecological problems unattended and waste resources as the available means are not systematically put to their most effective use. From the point of view of constitutional political economy, the (constitutional) principle of subsidiarity requires a search for an ecological unit around which an organizational structure can be built so as to allow responsible decisions in the light of both current (and future) ecological problems and the resources available to meet these and conceivable other challenges. In order to illustrate these general principles, let us look at five different fields of applications.

4.1. *River basins*

By way of example, one such ecological unit is a river. A river such as the river Rhine that extends through Europe, is clearly an ecological unit, but it is not an organizational unit.[3] That the river Rhine is an ecological unit is a rather unalterable geographically and biologically given fact. That, on the other hand, no organizational unit corresponds to this ecological unit is a historical fact which, from the point of view of constitutional environmental economics, can be changed. As an ecological unit, the river serves as a connecting link between the Alpine mountain range and the North Sea ensuring the water circulation between the ocean and the mountain range and through the tributary rivers the land mass in between. This is a complex ecological function, and it needs to be preserved in the interest of ecological stability. On its course, the Rhine traverses an entire ecological system by itself, the Lake of Constance, which is dependent for its own survival upon the in- and outflow of the river.

Next to his ecological function, the Rhine is a waterway, an area for recreational use, a source of drinking water and the receptical of waste water. All these functions clearly compete one with the other, each has to be eased out at the expense of the other, and all four cannot be indefinitely extended without damaging the river's ability to fulfill its ecological function. As the different functions of the river compete one with the other, choices have to be made as to how much of each activity should be carried out, where and at which time, possibly depending on either simultaneous or successive activities, the seasons, the tide etc. Today, such a large ecological entity as the river Rhine, as it is not simultaneously an organizational entity through which decisions about the use of this scarce recourse could be taken, is subject to abuse and overuse next to underutilization. Since the three seem to be mutually contradictory, a short word of explanation is in order.

In its current very minimal organizational form, the river Rhine is organized as a common pool. Due to international treaties, the river is freely accessable for navigation, and the amount of both drinking water taken out and the amount and quality of waste water added are largely subject to international cooperation. Not all the States which have riparian rights are members of the European Union, and the outcome of international consultations on such issues as water quality is not independent of the position – either upstream or downstream – of the negotiation entity. When resource use of a common pool is to be decided upon, we can basically distinguish between an open use arrangement and a regulated use arrangement. Next to the use itself, the identity of the users needs to be subject to decision. We thereby arrive at a matrix of four fields.

	Access	
Use	restricted	unrestricted
open	restricted access and open use 1	unrestricted access and open use 3
regulated	restricted acces and regulated use 2	unrestricted access and regulated use 4

The simplest form of common pool resource use is form number 1, when the number of users is restricted but their use is in principle open. This is an arrangement of property rights which is not stable if the uses by the different users are mutually rivalrous, i.e., they compete with each other. Since the marginal benefit can be appropriated by the individual user, while the marginal costs are distributed over the total number of users who are granted access, each user will use too much and, since this is true for each and every one of them, the common pool will soon be exhausted if appropriate action is not taken 2. The most common form of common pool resource use is the regulated use by a restricted number of users. The regulation can take the form of prices but also rules, and prices can be levied on both the option of use, i.e., the access and the actual use according to quantity, quality of use, time of use etc.

Case 3 involving open use by an unrestricted number is even less stable than case one, since the costs are even spread over a larger number of users and therefore the discrepancy between marginal benefits from use and the marginal costs of the use are still larger. Finally, an unrestricted but regulated use partly contains the diversions between individual benefits and social costs, and it depends on the form the regulation takes how well the use can be optimized.

As we return to the river Rhine, we notice that the number of users is typically restricted as far as water intake and discharge are concerned. It is unrestricted but highly regulated as far as shipping and recreational use are concerned. However, no one social entity can optimize the different uses of the river as an ecological resource entity. This is not an unavoidable outcome. Even granted free navigation of commercial shipping on the Rhine, which probably has to be interpreted as meaning that access charges cannot be levied yet service charges can, it is conceivable that all the entities enjoying riparian rights to the water resource can join in a large independent body, irrespective of their country of origin and irrespective of their special legal status: they may be provinces, cities, water districts, water recycling installations and corporate entities with licenses of different water use: they may be port authorities, canal authorities, etc., depending on the differences in public law in the various countries who have legally protected interests in using the river Rhine. The number of such entities is in principle fixed and can be clearly determined, which would make the river a restricted common resource. The main task of this body would be to optimize the different uses of the common resource, and since the resource is a valuable one, the new body, lets call it the Rhine Authority, needs no separate source of revenue other than those sources directly related to making decisions on the resource use. Charges can be levied for water intake and discharge, both depending on quantity and timing, the latter also depending on location and quality. Since the further downstream water intake has to be effected, the more expensive it is to maintain water quality, water intake probably would also have to be priced according to quality. In addition charges can be levied for water purification, traffic surveillance, commercial and recreational shipping, ferries and the like.

Why should any upstream city such as the city of Basel with its chemical industries be interested in joining such an associative body? Would it not have to expect to be restricted in its use of the river, as that use is heavily competing with the downstream use of the river as a water reservoir? And why should a downstream city be interested in cooperating, as it can now discharge waste water almost at will, and might all of a sudden face an authority imposing strong regulatory tariffs or standards and stiff water effluent charges? The answer is that both entities form the extremes of a continuum, each having an interest in one particular aspect of the river use, and all the other riparian interests lying in between. The upstream city needs the river for commercial navigation, and it faces liabillity charges from downstream communities if common standards on waste water emission cannot be agreed upon. The downstream city wishes to increase the quality of the water it receives even as it may be disregardful of the quality it releases. Finally, the downstream city, just as the upstream one, is strongly interested in maintaining commercial navigation on the river, certainly if its harbor belongs to its most important assets.

There is then a constellation of interests conceivable which makes it possible to design economic organizations for ecological use management which, in their own interest, may ensure an optimal resource use in a sustainable way. This principle can be generalized.

4.2. *Mountain ranges*

Mountain ranges pose problems very similar to river basins, although less obvious ones. Many different uses of mountain ranges compete with each other. Agriculture, tourism, water ased electricity generation etc. Typically, national parks are part of the picture, too. Forestry and dairy farming can be important parts of agriculture, and forestry in particular is affected by high levels of air pollution which may be stemming from far away. The higher the mountain range, the more susceptible it is to air pollution and the less sustainable continuous and increasing pollution levels are. There is a clear common interest binding the mountain range and its inhabitants together, but the mountain range as an ecological unit typically does not have a corresponding organizational unit which can effectively balance and represent these various interests. Most mountain ranges are part of different countries, some countries may be completely part of the mountain range (e.g.

Liechtenstein), but for most countries the mountain range is only a part, and the interests of the mountain may be easily traded off against the interests of metropolitan areas, as in the case of tourism or electricity generation.

The subsidiarity principle can guide the appropriate collection of all those partly heterogenous entities into an effective functional organisational unit that can balance the interests of the mountain range in a long run and sustainable way. Since the entities here joining together are part of different political organizations, they will in all likelihood only be allowed to integrate the most minimal package of responsibilities and resources into the mountain range organization. As, on the other hand, the other members of the organization are likely only to accept a fully competent partner on equal terms, even highly centralized countries will find it in their best interest to endow the smaller functional units representing the mountain range with sufficient own prerogatives and resources so as not to lose the influence on policy making in the ecological unit.

4.3. *Water reservoirs*

Water reservoirs can be above grounds, but often times they can be found deep below the ground. As they are invisible from above in these cases, it would be pure chance if their boundaries were drawn in order to reflect these ecological subsurface units. Since these water reservoirs can, however, be located so deep below the ground, it is very difficult to monitor their use. Hence, this common pool resource can only be regulated with great difficulty. In the sense, we get a common pool resource of the unregulated kind with open use, where the number of users may be either unrestricted or (as a consequence of the geographical location of the common pool resource and the political demarcations on the surface) restricted to the number of users who happen to be within the relevant geo-political demarcations. The users will be those who dig deep wells, but irrigation, river regulating and the buildong of dams and dikes can affect the underground water reservoir as well. So sometimes can the use of the surface land (as in the case of fertilization) and the release of waste water into the surface and ground water.

Under these circumstances, it is unavoidable that the surface use is actually carried out by a potentially large number of entities where different legal states prevail: private individuals, corporations, cooperatives (in particular water commons), water districts, industrial users, regional public or private entities etc. It is extremely unlikely that there will be any one existing public authority that can effectively manage the subsurface water reservoir given the informational requirements posed by such a large number of diverse users. However, an association of these different users, on the basis of the common interest of exploiting the common pool subsurface water reservoir in a sustainable way could, conceivably, provide a solution for this problem, if it is in the interest of the overwhelming majority of users to maintain access to the common resource in a sustainable way.

Even if, however, this interest does not exist at the helm of each and every one of these users, a sufficiently large group of them will be bound together by their wish to ensure their continued ability to provide co-operating members with sustainable access to the common pool resource. Again, application of the principle of subsidiarity will ensure the composition of a viable entity that can effectively police water use with a long run perspective.

4.4. *Climate units*

In may respects, climate units are ecological units that can be much more easily dealt with than those mentioned before. Typically, they are much better contained than for instance a river basin or a mountain range: sometimes they are very small, but almost always they are continent. The climate is well known and has been observed by the population for a long time. The knowledge about the climate is rather dependable, and citizens are not easily misled about causes and effects of quality changes. This means that changes in climate quality and the likely causes of such changes stand a good chance to be introduced into the political arena, and when the climate zone is regionally contained, there is likely to be a regional body which can serve as the arena for political dispute and finally conflict resolution. Yet, again, a complete match between the climate zone on the one hand and an appropriate politcial or a social unit that can effectively take decisions on the issues involved is rarely found. Even if the climate zone consists of only one valley, city interests may be pitted against village interests, such as when village interests consist mainly in agricultural (e.g. wine growing) and residential use, and city interests consist in industrial use which is conducive to the formation of mist. In this case, a better solution to the problem of an optimal and sustainable use and management of the environmental resource "climate" might be the formation of a valley authority, which can be either publicly or privately constructed and which, in turn, should have a revenue source the fertility of which is closely and positively related to the sustainable use of the environment.[4]

4.5. *Cultural ensembles*

One of the most overlooked aspects of environmental economics is the preservation of the cultural heritage to the extent that it has become embodied in the environment. It is a common misunderstanding to think of the environment as some pristine state of nature. It is hard to find a single aspect of the environment as we know it today which has not somehow been shaped by human forces and often beyond recognition.[5] Very often, the cultural heritage appears in traditional agricultural patterns, dairy farming and forestry, in the maintenance of ponds, lakes, creeks and small tributary rivers, the maintenance of wild life in forests and on the water, an active water life, a sustainable fish population etc.: but also as it is reflected in cultural architectural ensembles such as parks, farm and village ensembles, not to speak of historical cities with traditional architectural features, larger monuments such as palaces and cathedrals, but also the heritage that is embodied in these composites and which to preserve but also to keep alife is often difficult in the face of environmental effects which can prove humful to this cultural heritage in many ways. Sustainable use in this context refers to the ability of the users, and this is probably above all the population to whoes cultural heritage the piece or ensemble in question belongs, to keep using the ensemble while preserving its essence and allowing it to adapt to changes both cultural and technological as they occur over time.

It should seem that this case should be easiest in terms of finding a social unit that is able to manage the inherited cultural ensemble for sustainable use. Yet again difficulties loom large.

Consider a city with a historical core of buildings dating from different periods, located in its historical setting where the basic layouts of streets (and perhaps waterways) is still intact. At the city's outskirts, several new developments of industrial sites, traffic centres including railroads and a harbor are located, and in order to reduce the substantial residential and industrial waste produced in both parts of the city, the city has also built an incinerator which during part of the year emits effluent into the air which is detrimental to the stock of historical buildings.

If both parts of the city remain locked into the same organizational structure, it will be difficult to ensure the sustainable use of the historically developed ensemble that has been inherited from previous generations and is supposed to being available to future generations. The basic difficulty lies in the diverging interests of owners of parts of historical ensembles and other citizens who would incur higher taxes or charges or miss opportunities for work or business if they had to tolerate higher standards (in this case for air pollution, inner city traffic etc.) in order to preserve the historical ensemble. Yet the owners of the historical ensemble, among them public institutions and the church, also incur real losses as their structures need to be maintained more frequently and at high expense. In this case, we face a common pool problem of a very special kind. Although private property rights are defined in the elements of the historical ensemble, these property rights are not sufficient to internalize the externalities caused by the environmental abuse. This is the case not only for externalities reaching the historical ensemble from outside. In the case of innercity traffic, the inhabitants of the historical ensembles face a true common pool resource problem, as the externalities generated by car use are being spread over the entire group of owners, while the benefit remains concentrated by the user of the car. If owners of the historical ensemble can jointly agree on traffic regulations reigning in their part of town, one aspect of environmental abuse could be readily internalized. Environmental damages caused from the exterior could, on the other hand, only be internalized if ownership rights were defined in the historical ensemble in such a way that they provided for standing and ability to sue for damages. This is, in principle, possible in both forms of public and private law.

The last paragraph illustrates the possibility that while a large body, the comprehensive city, is unable to address a particular environmenal problem, a smaller one may very well be able to do so in an effective manner. This is a strong case for applying the principle of subsidiarity.

5. Ecologically based taxation

5.1. *The Pigouvian tax*

The Pigouvian tax, named after Arthur Cecil Pigou (1877–1959) is the most basic and generally discussed of environmental taxes. Its rationale is simple, as it is shown in the accompagnying Figure 1.

A product is supplied at a certain cost that meets with the respective demand. However, the product has a negative environmental effect, which is proportional to the cost of production. Hence, by taxing this environmental externality, the equilibrium quantity is reduced from q to q* as the price has been raised by way of taxation from p to p*. The most important feature of this approach is the resulting tax revenue. This revenue is depicted by the area ABPP*. The basic idea of Pigouvian taxation lies in the notion that negative externalities should be taxed and positive externalities be subsidized. If information is costless to the taxing authority, if the costs of taxation are zero and if there are no excess burdens of taxation, and if positive and negative externalities weigh up against each other, then this is an interesting policy instrument.

It appears that none of these conditions can be met. Information about negative externalities may be less available to a taxing authority than information about positive externalities. The producer of positive externalities will have an incentive to claim the tax benefit or subsidy, whereas the producer of a negative externality does not. Accordingly, there is an informational asymmetry between the producers of externalities and the taxing authority. Secondly, an excess burden will be present as long as either supply or demand are less than

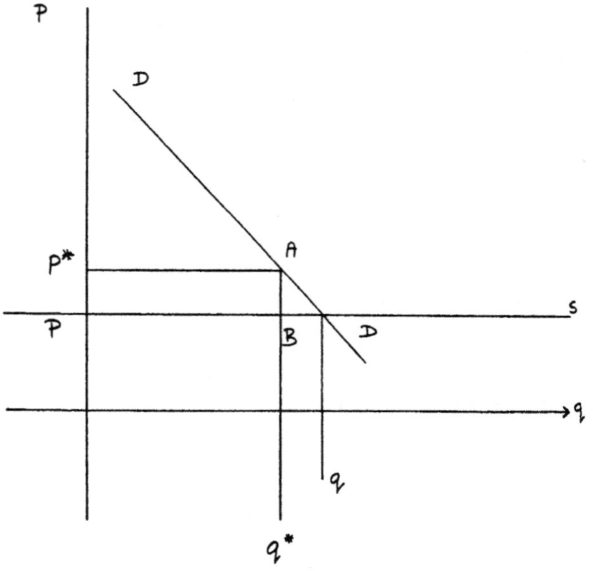

Figure 1.

perfectly elastic. This condition is only met in very rare cases. Thirdly, to the extent that positive and negative externalities, at least as they are presented to the taxing authority, do not wash out one against the other, there remains need for event further taxation with further accompanying excess burdens. Finally, nothing in the logic of the economic analysis of market failure suggests that in environmental affairs, positive and negative externalities should be the same in absolute value terms.

From the point of view of public choice, however, Pigouvian taxes have the disadvantage that they create a tax source by essentially socializing negative externalities. The taxing authority becomes a silent partner in the production of negative externalities, as it is interested in reaping the tax yield from the Pigouvian tax. This feature of the Pigouvian tax will become the more powerful, the bigger is the taxing entity and the farther it is removed from the technology choices taken by individuals, households and firms. In this context, it is no surprise that the ecological tax to be levied by the European Union is such a Pigouvian tax serving purely revenue interests and socializing the costs of externalities not reigned in over the entire community, i.e., the largest possible political entity. Applying the principle of subsidiarity with respect to well defined ecological problems would lead to a completely different choice of taxing units and tax instruments.

The problem can be substantially solved even within the context of the Pigouvian analysis if instead of taxing externalities unit by unit as they are

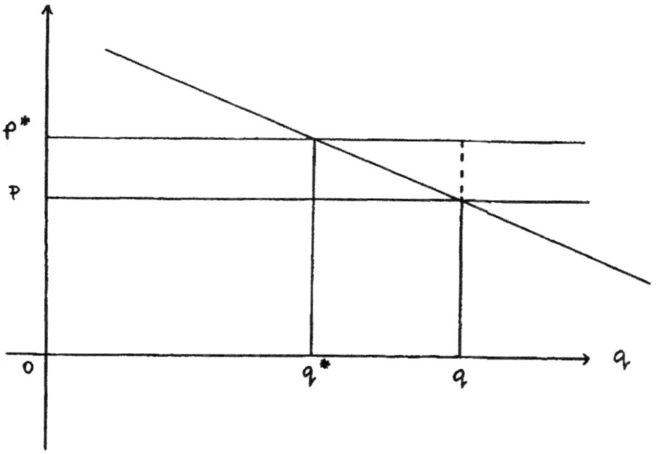

Figure 2.

being produced one taxes the ability of producing negative externalities in terms of assessing different technologies of production differently in terms of their ability to produce negative externalities. If the good q can be produced by either using the production function A1 or the production function A2, and if producing by using A2 requires a higher initial investment in order to have a clean technology, the Pigouvian tax may actually produce more environmental damage than the alternative, a quasi Pigouvian tax on the dirty technology. This is because the clean technology, with respect to the taxed dirty technology will experience increasing returns to scale. When the Pigouvian tax reduces pollution but leaves the inframarginal pollution intact (but taxed), the quasi Pigouvian tax on technology instead of volume will not only marginally but absolutely reduce pollution. This is shown in Figure 2.

The simple output oriented version of Pigouvian taxes can therefore be seen as not achieving the desired result. Environmental damages are certainly reduced, but not to an optimal level. A Pigouvian optimality analysis is partial and rests on the assumption that there is no choice involving the different technologies used. If, on the other hand, we focus our attention on the choice of technologies, taxes can be an important instrument for reducing environmental damages. These Pigouvian taxes do not yield any revenue, if they are successful. Therefore, the revenue generated in any particular situation can be seen as a negative indicator of success or else a positive indicator of failure.

In order to be successful, Pigouvian taxes aimed at influencing technology choice have to be accompanied by supporting measures, e.g., in order to inform citizens and firms about different technological options, conceivably changes in building codes and safety regulations may be necessary in order to accomodate the introduction of new technologies.

5.2. *Fees and user charges*

Fees and user charges can be employed by a community in order to arrive at an efficient and sustainable use of its natural resource or resources. It is well known that citizens and accordingly their communities value environmental benefits differently, depending on their economic position (Vaubel, in press and 1993). Generally speaking, the wealthier a community is, the more environmentally conscious it is at the same time. On the other hand, when communities are depressed and unemployment is high, it is not unusual that a trade off is perceived between environmental quality and economic prosperity as it typically comes through employment. On the basis of this reasoning, there is often a laxness in enforcing environmental standards during depressions, and generally speaking depressed communities are more likely to tolerate environmental spill overs generated by their local industries then are prosperous communities. There is even in the European community a north-south difference in environmental awareness and willingness to act.

Laxity in enforcing standards against local producers is, however, an inefficient way of using the environmental endowment to the end of furthering employment. If environmental and employment considerations are weighed differently in different communities when obviously the policy choices have to be made according to those differences, and they cannot be jointly made for both types of communities alike, the subsidiarity principle requires moving the policy choices into governing bodies that represent fairly homogenous views on these trade-offs. This will typically require endowing lower levels of government, perhaps even local levels of government with these choices to the extent that a contained ecological unit can be defined consistent with the policy to be carried out. It is conceivable to employ an explicit procedure, which does not prefer existing over new industries and which therefore also would have a chance to survive in court when challenged. Let me sketch such a licencing procedure (see also Backhaus, 1988): consider a community that has two explicit goals next to preserving its stock of environmental resources in a sustainable way. The community wants to further employment[6] and is willing to sacrifice its environmental resources, to an extent, for this purpose. The treasurer of each community that pursues employment policies is fully aware of how much this community is willing to sacrifice in money terms. This sacrifice can take the form of tax amenities, cheap land, reduction of charges for public infrastructure investments, direct subsidies or credit facilities. In the United States, these subsidies often amount to more than two hundred thousand dollars per job created.

The community wishing to pursue this policy then has to decide on the extent of the environmental sacrifice it wants to allow. This is probably done in terms of quantities of emission of various substances, for the sake of convenience we can assume the substance to be SO_2 and the allowable amount to be $\overline{x}$. The community now anonounces a tender offer, inviting bids for emission permits of SO_2 to be granted in terms of either jobs guaranteed or tax revenue guaranteed. As we assumed earlier, jobs translate into tax revenues in the treasurer's mind. Let one job (J) be worth two hundred currency units (CU). The allocation of emission rights is then simple enough. Jobs are being translated into currency units, and the bid with the highest ratio of currency untis in terms of pollution units receives the first share. Once that allotment has been exhausted, the next best bid will receive the next share until all the shares $(x_1, x_2, \dots x_n)$ in the bid have exhausted the predetermined amount $\overline{x}$. The last share x_n may come to less than the amount they asked for.

In order not to create any competitive disadvantages for newcomers and in order to encourage technological change, the bids and the licences granted have to be fully publicized and they also have to be temporary, for a period of perhaps five or ten years. During the period while the licenses are valid, if a more environmentally efficient (in terms of the ratio $CU/\overline{x}$) is found by a potential bidder, current licence holders have to be served notice that during the next bidding procedure, a more environmentally efficient bid is to be expected. This will allow them to either engage in efforts to employ more environmentally friendly technologies, or to apply for a transfer of their licence to the new bidder, if they decide that their technology is no longer competitive in the bidding procedure and that the best way to retreat from this business is to sell the existing licence. Such a sale should be subject to approval by the local authority and the approval should rest on only formal criteria in order to ensure that the licence transfer as well as the entire bidding procedure cannot be successfully challenged in a court of justice.

In order to prevent default by the licence, the granting authority should seek sufficient collateral such as a bank garantee covering the amount of jobs or tax revenues to the extent of which the licence has been granted. This procedure ensures that local communities can effectively pursue radically different economic policies reflecting their different evaluations of benefits stemming from the enjoyment of environmental goods on the one hand and other important streams of benefits such as employment on the other. Applying the principle of subsidiarity allows for such diverse policy choices.

5.3. *Radical environmental tax approaches: The case of Henry George*

Henry George (1839–97) was a self-taught American economist and political writer whose name is commonly associated with the notion of a Single Tax on land. George had worked as a sailor, printer and newspaperman when he became fascinated with the rapid and uneven development of California and began to probe the economic causes determining the price of land. This investigation he undertook in order to solve "the great enigma of our times", which he held to be "the association of poverty with progress" (1979: 10). His insights he systematically developed in his *Progress and Poverty*, first published in 1879.[7] The book began to receive wider attention in Britain in connection with the Irish question and later made George famous in his own country, too. He spent the last part of his life as a public speaker at home and abroad, and it was George himself who made the Single Tax proposal a political issue in his (unsuccessful) bids for the mayoralty of New York first in 1886 and again in 1897.

His place in the history of economic analysis is aptly sketched by Joseph Alois Schumpeter (1954: 865) who writes:

> The points about him that are relevant for a history of analysis are these. He was a self-taught economist, but he was an economist. He acquired most of the knowledge and of the ability to handle an economic argument that he could have acquired by academic training as it then was. In that he differed to his advantage from most men who proffered panaceas. Barring his panacea (the Single Tax) and the phraseology connected with it, he was a very orthodox economist and extremely conservative as to methods. They were those of the English 'classics', A. Smith being his particular favorite. [...] Even the panacea – nationalization not of land but of the rent of land by a confiscatory tax – benefitted by his competence as an economist, for he was careful to frame his 'remedy' in such a manner as to cause the minimum injury to the efficiency of the private-enterprise economy. [...] The proposal itself [...] is not *economically* unsound, except in that it involves an unwarranted optimism concerning the yield of such a tax. In any case, it should not be put down as nonsense. If Ricardo's vision of economic development had been correct, it would even have been obvious wisdom.

Schumpeter was correct in characterizing George's economic methods as conventional. Yet *Progress and Poverty* is not mainly a work of economic analysis, but a decidedly unorthodox and non-conservative social reformer's treatise. The book was written in order to provide the answer to a practical question of economic policy: How can we design an institutional order in which economic progress goes hand in hand with a reduction of poverty? Schumpeter, like many other critics of George, probably was incorrect in casually dismissing George's assertion about the practical possibilities of George's tax constitution from the standpoint of revenue yield. George may very well have been justified in his optimistic estimate of the yield of his Single Tax. This tax is a far cry from the real estate taxes a superficial reader may associate with the term "tax on land". Rather, as I try to explain on the following pages, George presents us with a comprehensive package of an environmental tax reform which, politically, has teeth. The program is, in fact, a tax constitution so comprehensive and far-reaching that no attribute could be more misleading than the term "conservative".

As this author reads *Progress and Poverty*, George comes across as a scholar in the best tradition of political economy. His analysis is motivated by a clearly defined social policy problem. George analyzes a problem in order to solve it. He succeeded in designing a solution – his "remedy" – which relies on an institutional reform, i.e., George understood the interdependence between economic processes and the institutional order in which they take place. Finally, George went about his analysis in what today would be described as an inter-disciplinary approach, i.e., the questions he would consider were forced upon him by the subject matter under consideration and not by some disciplinary boundaries as they might have developed over time. When, e.g., he looks at the effects of his "remedy", he takes them up in this order: effects on (1) production, (2) distribution, (3) individuals and classes, and (4) social organization and social life (1979: IX).

The shortest book in *Progress and Poverty*, and at the same time the most important, is book VI in which George spells out his program. The central chapter, entitled "The True Remedy" barely covers two printed pages, and the solution itself is stated in just one sentence: "We must make land common property" (1979: 328).

The explosive potential of his program is wrapped into this rather innocuous sentence. The true extent of the proposal can be discerned by looking at the implementation rule and his concept of land. The implementation rule is stated in equally concise terms: "It is not necessary to confiscate land, it is only necessary to confiscate rent" (1979: 405). Finally, there is an underlying principle also worth reporting: "What is necessary for the use of land is not its private ownership, but the security of improvements" (1979: 398). This quote also points to Henry George's differentiation between improved and unimproved natural resources and the idea of the unearned improvement. The unearned improvement today turns out to be a hindrance to improvements tomorrow, since the possibility of gaining unearned improvements diverts energies from the very process of improving upon natural resources. In contemporary language, one might say that George tried to prevent wasteful rent-seeking activities by insisting on the principle that the benefits from improvements should accrue to whoever made the improvements, whereas unclaimable externalities belong to the common domain.

The purpose of the entire reform program, according to this principle, is to encourage the use of land by designing a structure of property rights which allows individuals to reap the benefits of their labor, viz. the 'improvements' without barring the use of common property resources by others. His definition of 'land', as spelled out in a chapter appropriately entitled "The Meaning of the Terms" (1979: I 2) is not confined to the surface of the earth. His is an analytical definition based on the concept of factors of production. There are in George's model two original factors of production, called 'labor' and 'land'. 'Capital' is a secondary or derived factor of production, comprising only things "which have resulted from the union of these two original factors of production" (1979: 39). Since 'labor' is defined in a more standard way as "all human exertion", including, by the way, 'human capital', because "human powers, whether natural or acquired can never be classed as capital" (1979: 39); this leaves land as the all encompassing category of those original means of production which are not labor. In short, 'land' stands for the endowment of natural resources.

Characteristically, George defines land both analytically and by giving a sequence of examples illustrating the basic, comprehensive concept:

> The term land necessarily includes, not merely the surface of the earth as distinguished from the water and the air, but the whole material universe outside of man himself, for it is only by having access to land, from which his very body is drawn, that man can come in contact with or use nature. The term land embraces, in short, all natural materials, forces, and opportunities, and, therefore, nothing that is freely supplied by nature can be properly classed as capital. A fertile field, a rich vein of ore, a falling stream which supplies power, may give to the possessor advantages equivalent to the possession of capital, but to class such things as capital would be to put an end to the distinction between land and capital, and, so far as they relate to each other, to make the two terms meaningless. (1979: 38).

It is obvious that, commensurate with technical progress, the window of opportunities granted by nature is pushed ever more open, and in this way the Georgian term 'land' assumes an ever more encompassing meaning. Simultaneously, the tax base of the State entrusted with the power of the Single Tax on the rent of natural resources is also broadening in pace with technical progress. While George defines 'land' in exactly the same way as we define natural resources today, George differs from most present-day proponents of environmental tax reform by wishing to encourage the prudent use of natural resources, whereas the standard approach today is to design schemes seeking restriction of such use.

Henry George's definition of land clearly includes also natural resources beyond land and certainly also energy resources. The application of the term goes ever beyond this, however, in that it can also include collectively used natural resources, such as the oceans, the air, even the climate. This aspect points to a wider applicability of George's approach than is usually suggested. It is here where the potential for applying George's approach to the issue of ecological taxes comes in.

The twin objective to open access to the use of all opportunities provided by the natural environment while, at the same time, granting full security of all improvements made upon the resource as found in the state of nature requires a partitioning of property rights along this distinction. This partitioning[8] must have struck many of George's contemporaries as unusual or artificial. But, as he tries to show in his long survey of "Property in Land Historically Considered" (1979: VII 4), the partitioning should not be considered that unusual after all. You don't saw a ship in half if it is owned by two men, is his common sense comment.[9]

The partitioning of property rights is effected through the instruments provided by the modern tax state. Owners retain their property titles, but these titles are re-interpreted as designating the accumulated improvements, while the entire land rent remains in the common property of the state. The tax state, in this way, becomes a partner in the development of the land (country), a residual claimant of all the *external benefits* not appropriated by the individual owners. Since this point is very important for understanding the dynamics of the Georgian scheme, let us look at his own statement:

> Every productive enterprise, besides its returns to those who undertake it, yields collateral advantages to others. If a man plant[s] a fruit tree, his gain is that he gathers the fruit in its time and season. But in addition to his gain, there is a gain to the whole community. Others than the owner are benefitted by the increased supply of fruit; the birds which it shelters by far and wide; the rain which it helps to attract falls not alone on his field; and, even to the eye which rests upon it from a distance, it brings a sense of beauty. (1979: 435).

Assigning the unappropriable positive externalities of production to the State implies that George's concept of common property in natural resources actually goes even beyond the original state of nature. It likewise includes the accumulated externalities or, put in more accessible terms, the cultural heritage of a country, its vegetation, climate, architecture and landscape, etc. And, by virtue of the tax scheme, this cultural heritage also forms the tax base which the state is expected to foster.

"Nature laughs at a miser" (1979: 436), Henry George tells us in characteristic prose, and he certainly laughs at too parsimonious a use of the natural endowment. Not only is the tax scheme designed to minimize disincentives (1979: IX 1); stronger still, it co-erces people into either making productive use of the resources they possess or else relinquishing them: "If land were taxed to anything near its rental value, no one could afford to hold land that he was not using" (1979: 413). As Von Weizsäcker and Jesinghaus suggested, the purpose of making the most productive use of an environmentally based energy source is completely consistant with Henry George's approach. However, productivity in George's terms is measured in such a way that the economist can make use of its. As a consequence of the tax levied on natural resources, irrespective of whether they are used or not, the user has to make the most productive use of the natural resource made available to her, and this use has to be made in such a way that the source is not being depleted.

This growth oriented fiscal constitution, however, has a clever check on public sector growth built into it. It is here where the seemingly ideological and often misunderstood insistence on the *Single* Tax assumes importance. This feature of the Georgian proposal has always bewildered so many commentators, including the public finance expert[10] Schumpeter. The explanation lies in the systematic unity of George's proposal. George suggested a tax constitution which defines incentives faced by the tax collecting authorities. George wanted to foster progress by using the power to tax in a very specific way, but he was also suspicious of government bureaucracies (1979: VIII 3). By designating a broad tax base but limiting the power to tax to just one tax, the tax of up to 100% on the rent of natural resources, he hoped to find the proper balance. On the one hand, the Georgian tax constitution creates incentives for those in public office to support equitable economic development, which flushes ever increasing tax revenues into public coffers. The State can grow unimpeded by any pre-conceived restrictions, as long as this public sector growth is financed from the increasing rental value of natural resources. On the other hand, as soon as the value of these rents stagnates or even declines, the state has to curtail its own expenditures. By virtue of the Single Tax constitution,[11] the State is harnessed into prudent, long term natural resource use, just as the private sector is coerced into attaining the production possibility frontier. Built into George's reform is a 'tax constitution for Leviathan', to use Buchanan's term, a public choice approach *avant-la-lettre*. In one respect, however, George's tax constitution is different from the typical Leviathan tax constitutions which we owe to the modern public choice school. The limits on the size of the state budget are not predetermined, but determined according to the tasks the state may face. For instance, as natural resource use creates negative externalities, to the same extent it increases the claim of the state on financial resources to mitigate these effects. On the other hand, if nature is left in a pristine state, the state's claim on financial resources is very limited indeed; but so are the state's tasks in such an economy.

Even more surprisingly, this growth-oriented tax constitution clearly deserves the label "environmental" due to its built-in dynamic structure. By an "environmental" or "ecological" tax scheme one understands a fiscal constitution which induces economic agents to make optimal use of the environmental resources, neither squandering nor oversparing them. This is precisely what the Georgian system is designed to accomplish. The clue to the conservational feature of the Georgian tax constitution, again, lies in the partitioning of property into (internalizable) improvements (private ownership) and the rent of the resource as such (public ownership). The size of this rent is a positive function of the state of economic development of the surrounding economy and a negative function of the exhaustion of the natural resource. Obviously[12], the rent on resource use is paid exclusively for the use of the natural endowment and not for its abuse. Depletion of a natural resource requires an additional compensation owed to the community which, in the Georgian model, is represented by the Tax State. The State is thereby entitled to two streams of revenues, viz. the rent collected from the use of its natural resources and, more generally, the environment; and the compensations for the abuse of those resources. Clearly, George was not a strict conservationist in the sense of sparing nature from any form of depletion. He wanted the ore to be mined and not to be left in the ground (1979: 38). Yet, at the same time, he wanted the community to extract a fair compensation for this impairment. While the guarantee of improvements is the core of the State guarantee of private property rights, impairments of common property resources require a compensation. The State thereby can plan the inter-temporal use of the natural resource endowment in the interest of overall fiscal concerns.

The operational coherence and conclusivity of the abuse correction mechanism, of course, needs to be spelled out in institutional detail. Much will depend on the particular tax administration a country has set up. Such an administration would have to be backed by a system of tax courts in such matters as when judgement is required as to when an action constitutes an abuse or not.[13]

This inter-temporal dimension embedded into Henry George's tax constitution assumes additional importance when we consider the change or reversal of uses environmental resources may be put to. Keeping the door of change and, notably, changes in resource use wide open is vital for preventing the rise and persistence of monopolies. The Georgian scheme, of course, requires that every resource be put to its most productive use. Again, the dynamic adjustment process is carefully conceived. The most productive use determines the rent of the resource, irrespective of whether the owner operates at the production possibility frontier or not. The automatic adjustment of rents, as a consequence of technical progress, constantly pushes economic agents to make the most judicious use of environmental resources. This implies that the Georgian system actually encourages the reversal and change of production methods involving natural resources. Unlike the present system of private property in land (1979: VII 5), the scheme does not favor the first user at all, since a more valuable use makes it too expensive to continue the first use. The opportunity costs of natural resource use, by virtue of the land rent tax, enter into the present user's cost function.

Reversal of use can be more vexing a problem if natural resources are irretrievably devoted to some production (or consumption) process. The safeguard provided by the Georgian system is not a perfect one, since George opposed the conservation of natural resources for their own sake. Yet, George provided for two checks. The irreversible use of an environmental resource is checked on the one hand by the compensation payment required for abuse. The amount of this payment, in turn, will increase with the introduction of competing, more valuable uses as a consequence of technical progress. The second check lies in the communal nature of environmental resources. Since the environment is in the common property, i.e., State domain, a political decision can override private commercial concerns. The political decision will be informed, above all, by the revenue consequences for the Single Tax State, a State which George has placed in the position of guardian of the environment in order to ensure its own fiscal survival.

In looking at Henry George's proposal, one has to keep in mind that it is one of several environmentally relevant options that can be combined one with the other. Its strength lies in its actually providing for a tax constitution that is built on the principle of making the most effective long-term and sustainable use of the environment, wasting environmental resources is being punished through the one hundred percent tax on impairments, underutilization of natural resources is punished through the tax on the land rent. For instance, there is no incentive to employ dirty technologies, as the damage imposed needs to be re-imbursed through the 100% taxation of impairments. Again, the subsidiarity principle has to play a substantial role in defining the appropriate unit that can effectively serve as the taxing authority. Since George builds his entire concept around the notion of natural resources (all subsumed under the terms of "land"), it is conceivable that around different natural resources different taxing authorities can develop, as it is not unusual to have different taxing authorities even in the same municipality, as US school districts have their own taxing authority.

The definition of these authorities, again, is a matter of constitutional choice, but constitutional choice driven by the principle of subsidiarity and therefore taken in the smallest viable public body.

5.4. *Revenues and yields?*

The options so far surveyed differ substantially in terms of their revenue potential. The static Pigouvian tax generates substantial revenues, but its environmental impact is limited. The dynamic Pigouvian tax, on the other hand, generates no revenue at all if it successful. But its environmental impact can be drastic. Generally, user fees can generate substantial revenues, but it is questionable whether the desired environmental impact can be attained by relying on this instrument. The employment oriented licencing procedure on the other hand, which has been sketched in Section 5.2, generates no direct revenue, although by generating either jobs or tax revenues it is very attractive from the treasurer's point of view. The procedure is also attractive from the point of view of the environmentally conscious. This is the case because the procedure ensures that the use of the environment becomes more and more efficient. The same can be said for the scheme in the tradition of Henry George. It can generate substantial revenues, and it can be a core element of any environmental policy, the more so, the more revenues it is able to generate.

5.5. *Pitfalls and options: Summary*

Of the three options, the employment oriented licencing procedure is probably the most realistic. It can be implemented at a local level, and it has been designed with a view to legal feasibility. In a European context, yet it is not optimal from an economic point of view. The dynamic Pigouvian tax, on the other hand, is by no means unrealistic. Typically, it takes the form of a tax credit when a clean technology is introduced. The tax credit can cover either the total investment or the difference in the costs in investing in either the clean or the traditional technology. The Georgian proposal, on the other hand, entails an entire tax constitution. So far, it has only been introduced at the local level[14] apparently with substantial success whenever it has been tried. The modifications this tax constitutions requires for local tax administrations should not be underestimated, nor should they be overestimated, since successful attempts can be documented.

6. Conclusion: Subsidiarity and ecological units

In this essay the principle of subsidiarity has been developed as an organization principle to be used in constitutional environmental economics. Constitutional environmental economics is that part of environmental economics in which we try to set out the structures in which decision making processes with respect to ecological units can take place. As applied to river basins, mountain ranges, water reservoirs, climate units but also cultural ensembles, the principle of subsidiarity has been shown to help in defining ecologically relevant organizational units in which political decision making can take place in order to ensure an efficient and sustainable management of ecological units.

It is by no means unusual that the central government may have to cooperate with a state government (such as between the Netherlands and the state of North Rhine WestPhalia, were such cooperations are common between The Hague and Düsseldorf), a district or even a county or city. In Switzerland and Belgium, many tasks which are normally reserved for the central government fall to the canton (Switzerland) or de gewest (Belgium). Germany has a traditional system, since the reforms by Stein and Hardenberg in the first decade of the 19th century, emphasizing local independence and responsibility, even the residual right of taxation. It is true that central governments are often reluctant to enter into consultations with foreign governments at lower levels. But this is what the principle of subsidiarity requires. Logically the subsidiarity principle requires the cooperation of the smallest viable units, and if a country does not provide for local authority, that authority has to be found at which ever is the lowest level. In highly centralized countries such as France and the Netherlands, the principle of subsidiarity will therefore point towards the center, when in highly decentralized countries such as Belgium, Germany and Switzerland it points to local bodies.

Notes

1. I am, however, not aware of any rulings on the part of the European court of justice. There is extensive jurisdiction by the German constitutional court in Karlsruhe.
2. Both are titles of leading journals in this field.
3. There is a contractual agreement governing the river, the "Rhine Navigation Act of 1868"(Mannheim Act) which also provides for a dispute resolution procedure.
4. The American Tennessee Valley Authority comes to mind: although its prime purpose was regional development by means of electrification, using the water of the Tennessee river, and a secondary purpose was combatting poverty and unemployment through economic development. Still, the environmental goal can clearly be incorporated into the mission of such an authority, and it would let decisions, for instance to operate nuclear power plans appear in a different light.
5. This is the main point in Zirnstein (1994).

6. I am not arguing here that an explicit employment policy by a local community is a commendable policy as such. It may lead to an inefficient capital-labor mix. However, many communities wish to pursue these policies, and I am assuming such a policy therefore for reasons of realism. Any other policy goal that sacrifices the environment can be substituted for employment.
7. *Progress and Poverty* was first published by D. Appleton & Co. in New York in January, 1880. However, in his preface, George refers to the November 1890 edition already as the fourth. His account of the editorial history as follows: "This work was written between August, 1877, and March, 1879, and the plates finished by September of that year. Since that time, new illustrations have been given of the correctness of the views herein indicated [. . .]. But there has been nothing in the criticisms they have received to induce the change or modification of these views – in fact, I have yet to see an objection not answered in advance in the book itself. And except that some verbal errors have been corrected and a preface added, this edition is the same as previous ones." (1979: xxx).
   A twenty-fifth anniversary edition with a preface by Henry George jr. was published in 1905. The son explains that the publisher had insisted on George bearing the cost of making the plates, which George did in the shop of a friend in San Francisco. There, "an 'Author's Proof Edition' of five hundred copies was struck off" (1979: xxiii). A centenary edition prefaced by his grandaughter, Agnes George de Mille, appeared in 1979 in New York, published by the Robert Schalkenbach Foundation. This 1979 edition contains the aforementioned prefaces as well as an extensive index and a glossary of terms.
   In conclusion, the first edition was San Francisco 1879, the first published edition New York 1880, and the final authorized edition with any changes New York 1890 (4).
8. For a modern statement see Furubotn (1979).
9. An anonymous referee has pointed to the difficulty of measuring what part of the "unearned" increment is due to nature, what part due to society, and what part due to entrepreneurship or effort. Dr. Krabbe and I have dealt with this issue elsewhere and at length. (See Backhaus and Krabbe, 1991/1992).
10. The welfare theoretic aspects of the Single Tax have been dealt with in a separate paper, see Backhaus (1991).
11. This modern language should not lead the reader to suspect that the single tax might be without problems. It is conceivable that the single tax might not be Pareto optimal, notably because of effects on the timing of development. But one should keep in mind that George was making a contribution to economic policy, and not to the theory of optimal taxation. Even in the case of suboptimality just mentioned, one has to keep in mind that these cases require resort to second best analysis, and that it is by no means inconceivable that the lest distorting tax regime in the world of second best remains the single tax.
12. The following paragraphs are not literally grounded in Henry George's *Progress and Poverty*; they follow directly from his definition of land as including all natural resources and his definition of improvements. But he did not himself spell out these implications, nor did he spell out details of the requisite implementation rule.
13. For the United States, one can start thinking about such procedures by looking at the reclamation of land used for surface strip mining. See US Surface Mining Control and Reclamation Act of 1977, (P.L. 95–87). This law calls for bonding and specifies landscape contours, vegetation, etc. For Germany, an actionable procedure has been described in Jürgen Backhaus (1988).
14. One interesting case is in Fairhope, Alabama USA.

References

Backhaus, J. (1988). Justitiabele Bedarfsprüfung im Genehmigungsverfahren: Ein Lüneburger Vorschlag. In J. Finsinger und J. Simon (Eds.) *Recht und Risiko*, 96–112. München: VVF.

Backhaus, J. (1991). "Henry George and the Environment", *Journal of the History of Economics Thought*, Spring 13(1): 90–98.
Backhaus, J. and Krabbe, J.J. (1991). Henry George's contribution to modern environmental policy: Part One: Theoretical postulates. *American Journal of Economics and Sociology* 50(4): 485–501.
Backhaus, J. and Krabbe, J.J. (1992). Henry George's contribution to modern environmental policy: Part Two: An application to industrial siting. *The American Journal of Economics and Sociology* 51(1): 115–127
Furubotn, E. (1979). Property in land historically considered. 4 July.
George, H. (1880). *Progress and poverty*. New York: D. Appleton $ Co. January.
Herzog, R. (1963). Subsidiaritätsprinzip und Staatsverfassung. *Der Staat*, 3: 339–423. 400 pp.
Mohl, R. von (1844)[2], *Die Polizeiwissenschaft nach dem Grundsätzen des Rechtsstates*, 265–266. Tübingen: Publisher.
Vaubel, R. (1993). *Das Sozialpolitische Abkommen von Maastricht widerspricht dem Subsidiaritätsprinzip*. Universität Mannheim, 23, and 24 April.
Vaubel, R. (in press). A public-choice view of the Delors Report. In R. Vaubel and T.D. Willet (Eds.), *The political economy of international organizations: A public choice approach*, 306–310. Boulder, CO: Westview Press.
Wolff, Chr. (1754). *Grundsätze des Natur- und Völckerrechts*, III, 2.1. Halle: Renger.
Zirnstein, G. (1994). *Ecology and the environment in history* (Ökologie und Umwelt in der Geschichte). Marburg: Metropolis.

Public Choice **90:** 311–324, 1997.
© 1997 *Kluwer Academic Publishers.*

Rule and policy spaces and economic progress: Lessons for Third World countries

GERALD W. SCULLY*
School of Management, University of Texas at Dallas, Box 830688, Richardson, TX 75083-0688, U.S.A.

Abstract. Despite greater rates of capital accumulation, per capita growth rates among Third World nations (particularly, Africa) are much lower than among the advanced, capitalist nations. In this paper I examine the critical roles of the rule space and policy on economic growth. Empirically, nations with poor institutions and policies grow at about a fifth of the rate of nations with good institutions and policies.

1. Introduction

For twelve centuries after the fall of Rome there was no growth of per capita output in the West (Maddison, 1982: 6). In the last half of the eighteenth century two meta-events occurred: the Industrial Revolution and the rise and spread of democratic capitalism (free markets, private property, rule of law, and representative government). From 1820 to 1980 real per capita growth was about 1.6 percent per annum (Maddison, 1982: 6). As such, the living standard increased thirteen-fold.

Economic growth has remained high in the mature capitalist nations in this half of the twentieth century. For Europe/North America it has averaged 3.2 percent per year, over the period 1951–92 (see Table 1).[1] Aside from some Asian nations, with export-led growth policies, economic growth in the Third World has been low. This is so despite roughly comparable rates of capital formation per head. Why do so many Third World nations, particularly in Africa, have such poor rates of economic growth?

Capital formation (including human capital in modern treatments) and technical change are recognized as the main engines of economic growth. But, all nations are not equally adept at transforming increases in capital and technology into increases in output. Plainly, some are just economically

* This paper was written while visiting the Centro Internazionale di Ricerche Economiche, Turin, Italy

Table 1. Means of the variables

Area	(1)	(2)	(3)	(4)	(5)	(6)
World	$4246	62.8	2.08	4.64	2.07	3.40
Advanced	12776	76.3	2.83	3.38	1.01	2.39
Third World	2705	60.3	1.94	4.86	2.26	3.61
Europe/N. Amer	11076	75.9	3.20	3.89	1.06	2.43
Oceania	7482	67.9	1.62	2.32	1.06	5.00
Asia	3937	65.2	3.66	6.83	2.18	3.05
Latin/Caribbean	3843	67.3	1.78	3.43	1.89	3.27
Africa	1328	53.1	1.08	4.81	2.64	4.09

Key:

(1) Real gross domestic product per capita, 1985
(2) Life expectancy
(3) g_y = Average rate of growth of real per capita GDP
(4) g_k = Average rate of growth of real gross per capita investment
(5) Institutional framework measure
(6) Policy measure

inefficient. In this paper I analyze the crucial roles of the rule space and policy as the main filters that affect economic efficiency.

Measures of the institutional framework and policy are presented in Table 1. Both measures will be discussed in more detail later. Briefly, the measure of the rule space is an average of four subindices: the type of political system, the degree of political and civil liberty, the type of economic system, and the degree of economic freedom. The scale is bound between 1.0 (most free) and 3.25 (least free). The policy measure is an average of three policy subindices: money growth and inflation, trade policy, and freedom of capital markets. It is scaled from 1.0 (best) to 5.0 (worst). As is seen in the table, Europe/North America and Oceania have the freest institutions; Africa the least free. Asia and Latin America/Caribbean are in between. Europe/North America has the best set of policies and Africa and Oceania the worst. Again, Asia and Latin America/Caribbean are in between.

2. The rule space and economic growth

There are two legal ways of obtaining income. People employ their resources productively and earn a return. Or, they withdraw resources from productive pursuits and employ them in the political market to redistribute income from someone else to themselves. Resources employed in rent-seeking activities have an opportunity cost equal to their return in productive activity in the private sector.

In a previous paper (Porter and Scully, 1995) a general taxonomy of institutions or rules on Pareto-criteria was identified. Rules arise from many sources: custom, religious precept, law, constitutions, and so on. A large subset of these rules have wealth effects. Some rules are efficient (wealth-promoting) and some are inefficient (wealth-reducing). A rule (or a change in a rule) is said to be efficient if someone's wealth rises and no one's falls (Pareto-efficient) or, less restrictively, if the total wealth gain to society is greater than the total wealth loss (Hicks-Kaldor-efficient). A rule is said to be inefficient if the total wealth gain is less than the total wealth loss (Hicks-Kaldor-inefficient). Government policy can be treated to the same taxonomy.

Define the rule space of a society as Ω. Let Ω_t be the sum of all separate rules, ω_i, that have been adopted and exist at time t:$\Omega_t = \sum_i \omega_i$. Let each rule have a private wealth effect, θ_i, which is positive for an efficient rule and negative for an inefficient one: $\theta_i = g(\omega_i)$.[2] The monetary value of the rule space at time t, which is a measure of the efficiency of the rule space, then, is $\Theta_t = \sum_i \theta_i = \sum_i g(\omega_i)$. Θ_t may be treated as an index and normalized: $0 < \Theta_t \leq 1$.

The rule space is not time invariant, although it tends to change slowly, except during periods of revolution or crisis. Let the rule space grow according to $\Theta_t = \Theta_0 e^{rt}$, where Θ_0 is some initial value and r is the growth rate of the rule space. The change in the rule space (efficiency) is:

$$d\Theta = \Theta_o e^{rt}(dr\, t + r\, dt). \tag{1}$$

Thus, the change in the efficiency of the rule space is determined by time and by the change in the rate of growth of the rule space. The rate of growth of the rule space may be positive, zero, or negative. For dr = 0, the rule space becomes more efficient, is constant, or becomes less efficient over time depending on the sign of the growth rate, r. If the change in the rate of growth or the rule is positive (negative), the efficiency of the rule accelerates (decelerates) over time for $r > 0$. For $r < 0$, the inefficiency of the rule space accelerates for $dr < 0$ and decelerates for $dr > 0$.

Let national output be produced by a Cobb-Douglas production function in intensive form: $y_t = k^{\beta}{}_t$, with y = Y/L and k = K/L. The simplest way of incorporating the rule space into the production function is as a scaler. Suppressing the time subscript this is:

$$y = \Theta_0 e^{rt} k^{\beta}. \tag{2}$$

Then, the effect of a change in capital per head on the change in output per head is the partial differential:

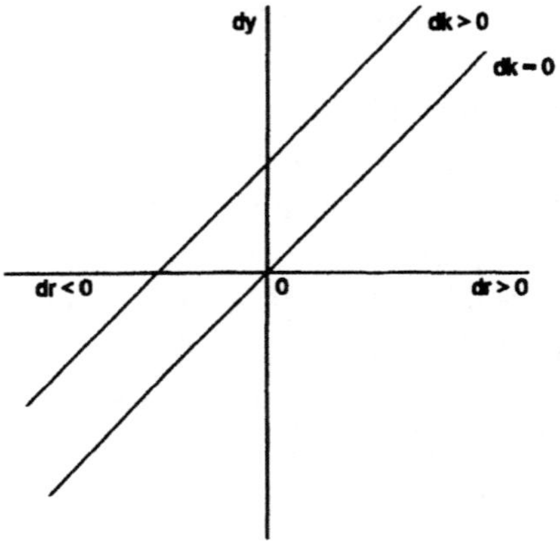

Figure 1. The effect of rule change on economic growth.

$$d_k y = (\Theta_0 e^{rt} \beta k^{\beta-1}) dk. \tag{3}$$

The effect of time on the change in output per head is:

$$d_t y = (\Theta_0 e^{rt} r\, k^{\beta}) dt. \tag{4}$$

And, the effect of a change in the rate of evolution of the rule space on the change in output per head is:

$$d_r y = (\Theta_0 e^{rt} t\, k^{\beta}) dr. \tag{5}$$

The change in per capita output is the total differential:

$$\begin{aligned} dy &= \Theta_0 e^{rt}[t\, k^{\beta}\, dr + r\, k^{\beta} dt + \beta k^{\beta-1} dk] \\ &= \Theta_0 e^{rt}[(t\, dr + r\, dt) k^{\beta} + \beta k^{\beta-1} dk] \end{aligned} \tag{6}$$

The result can be illustrated. For simplicity, in Figure 1, let the growth rate of the rule space be some initial value, let the rate of capital accumulation per head be constant at two rates (i.e., $dk = 0$ and $dk > 0$), and let there be various values for dr. For values of $dr > 0$, the rule space is becoming more efficient over time and the rate of economic growth is positively affected despite a constant rate of capital formation. Where there is no increase in capital per head (not uncommon in parts of the Third World) and the rule space is becoming less efficient over time ($dr < 0$), the rate of economic growth is negative. Even if there is positive growth in capital formation per capita, at some value of $dr < 0$ the rate of economic growth can turn negative.

3. Measures of the rule space and policy

Data are insufficient to comprehensively measure the rule space. But, important elements of the rule space can be crudely measured with information on the political institution, political and civil freedoms, the economic system, and the degree of economic freedom.

Political regimes are classified as authoritarian or representative. Within that broad division some regimes are more constrained than others. Thus, I classify four types of political regimes that are coded as follows: freely democratic = 1, limited democracy = 2, limited autocracy = 3, and authoritarian = 4.

Freely democratic regimes are those with elected government, universal (extensive) suffrage, credible political party competition, a credible legislative function, an independent judiciary, and extensive protection of political and civil liberties. Limited democracies have elections, but they may have dominant parties and other limitations on the electoral process, and they also have less protection of civil liberties. I have relied on the evidence of Freedom House's (1994) and Bank's (1993) comparative political surveys in making these classifications. Where ambiguity existed, I read up on the post-World War II histories of the nations for further evidence.

Many authoritarian governments are dictatorships or dominant one-party states with a powerful executive. It is transparent to make the classification. But, there are a number of nations with significant limitations on autocratic rule. As such, they were classified as limited autocracies.

Political regimes were classified over the period 1950–90. Some nations have been continuously democratic or authoritarian throughout the period. Others have had short bouts of one form of government, but long periods of another form. Where this is the case the classification is the modal form.

Africa has the highest incidence of dictatorship with 90 percent of the 50 nations in the sample classified as fully authoritarian. Only three African nations were classified as limited democracies. Asia had the next highest incidence of authoritarian rule. Of the 26 nations in the sample, 9 were fully authoritarian and 7 were limited autocracies. Three Asian nations were democratic and three were limited democracies. Among the 26 Latin and Caribbean nations roughly half were authoritarian and half democratic, with about an equal division between full and limited. Europe/North America (22 countries) and Oceania (four nations) are democratic.

The political and civil freedom measure is based on data from Freedom House. It is coded as free = 1, partly free = 2, and not free = 3.

The measure of political rights basically is one of the degree to which citizens may choose their political leaders and get rid of them, if they do not care for the way they are running things. Obviously, in democratic systems there are elections, while in dictatorships the polity has no say. In democratic systems elections may be fair or not, political opposition may be strong or weak, the military may be under civilian control or not, power may be centralized or decentralized, and minorities may be included or excluded from the political process. In autocratic systems, dictatorships may be totalitarian or less malevolent. In some autocracies there may be some political freedom at the regional or local level.

The measure of civil liberty is based on considerations such as the degree of press freedom, the degrees of freedom of speech, assembly, and association, the degree of freedom from search and seizure of property, the degree of independence of the judiciary and the protection of the individual under the law, and so on.

The politcal and civil freedoms are combined into a single rating and are the modal values for the countries over the period 1973, when the Freedom House survey began, to 1990.

The highest incidence of a lack of political and civil freedom is in Africa. Some 29 nations were not free, 19 were partly free, and only two were free. In Asia six nations were not free, twelve were partly free, and four were free. In Latin America/Caribbean one nation was unfree, fifteen were partly free, and ten were free. Europe/North America and Oceania are overwhelmingly free.

Economies are classified as market-capitalist = 1, restricted market-capitalist = 2, and statist = 3, largely based on Freedom House's classifications. Among the African nations, 19 are market-capitalist, 13 are restricted market-capitalist, and 18 are statist. Africa has the highest incidence of statist economies. In Asia, seven nations are market-capitalist, thirteen are restricted market-capitalist, and two are statist. In Latin America/Caribbean, five countries are market-capitalist, twenty are restricted market-capitalist, and one is statist. Europe/North America and Oceania are overwhelming market-capitalist.

The degree of economic freedom is coded as free = 1, partly free = 2, and not free = 3 and is based on the rank of economic freedom constructed from fifteen attributes of economic liberty (Scully, 1992).

Africa is mainly economically not free (15 nations) or partly free (30 nations). Only five African countries are economically free. In contrast Asia is economically free (6 countries) or partly free (13 nations), with only three countries not free. The situation is similar in Latin America/Caribbean, where ten countries are free, thirteen are partly free, and three are not free.

In summary, Africa tends to be nearly uniformly authoritarian with restricted economic freedom. Asia and Latin America/Caribbean nations tend to have had fairly restricted political environments, but have a greater degree of economic liberty than does Africa. Obviously, Europe/North America and Oceania are mainly politically and economically free.

Measures of various aspects of the institutional framework tend to be rather highly intercorrelated (Scully, 1988). This is true, also, for this set of measures.[3] As such, not a great deal of information is lost by combining them into one measure of the institutional framework. This was done by averaging them.

Apart from the rule space, governments make policy choices. Some measures of policy are available. Gwartney, Block, and Lawson (1993) have constructed measures on monetary growth and inflation, freedom of international trade, and freedom of capital markets for a large number of nations over the period 1970–90.

The measure of monetary growth and inflation is based on three components: the growth of the money supply less the real rate of economic growth, the standard deviation of the annual inflation rate, and restrictions on foreign currency holdings. The index is scaled from 0 (worst) to 10 (best) and is available for four five-year subperiods. I have averaged them to construct a long-term policy measure.

The second policy index is a measure of trade openness and is based on three subindices: trade taxes as a share of imports plus exports, exchange rate controls, and a measure of the size of the trade sector. The data are available for 1975, 1980, 1985, and 1990 and I averaged them.

The capital market index is composed of two subindices: the difference between the domestic and world real interest rate and direct foreign investment as a share of GNP. I dropped the 1975 observations, because of a paucity of observations, and averaged the 1980, 1985, and 1990 values.

Like the attributes of the institutional framework, the quality of policy is intercorrelated. The simple correlation of monetary policy with trade policy is .66 and of monetary and capital market policy is .67. Hence, I averaged the three measures into an overall measure. The grade scaling is A = 1, B = 2, C = 3, D = 4, and F = 5.[4]

Africa has very poor policy with 30 of the 35 nations scoring a D or F and no nation scoring A. In Latin America/Caribbean fourteen nations had a grade of B or C and eight had a grade of D or F. In Asia the nations were about evenly divided over the five grade intervals. In Europe/North America the modal grade was C (seven nations), but eleven countries had a grade of A or B and only three had a grade of D or F. Oceania had uniformly bad policy.

4. Empirical results

4.1. *Economic growth*

Estimation is by two methods: linear OLS and nonlinear least squares (NLLS). The later approach is justified on the basis of the theoretical existence of diminishing returns in the neoclassical growth model. The specific functional form for the NLLS estimation is:

$$g_y = [\alpha/(\beta + \delta e^{-\alpha g(k)})]e^{\gamma INST + \rho POLICY)}. \tag{7}$$

The derivatives of g_y with respect to g_k are consistent with neoclassical growth theory.[5] The limits of the nonlinear functions are:

$$\lim_{g_k \to 0} g_y = [\alpha/(\beta + \delta)]e^{\gamma INST + \rho POLICY)} \tag{8}$$

and

$$\lim_{g_k \to \infty} g_y = (\alpha/\beta)e^{\gamma INST + \rho POLICY)}. \tag{9}$$

Table 2 presents the linear OLS estimates for the world sample. The coefficient of the growth rate of real capital formation per head (g_k) evidences only small variation as the institutional framework variable (INST) and policy variable (POLICY) are added as regressors. The institutional variable has a large coefficient value (–1.08). Multiplying the g_k coefficient times the mean value of g_k and adding it to the constant term and, then, subtracting –1.08 yields the mean growth rate of per capita RGDP of 3.24 percent for nations with a free institutional rule space. At the other extreme, a representative nation with the least free constitutional environment (INST = 3.25) has a mean growth rate of 0.80 percent for the same growth rate of real capital formation per head.

The policy variable is statistically significant when added as a regressor. The representative nation with the best policy (POLICY = 1) has a growth rate of 3.31 percent, while the representative nation with the worst policy (POLICY = 5) has a growth rate of 1.30 percent.

When both INST and POLICY are entered as covariates, the coefficient of POLICY on g_y is reduced in size by half, but remains significant. The representative nation with the best rule and policy space has a growth rate of 3.64 percent, while the representative nation with the worst institutions and policies has a growth rate of .57 percent. Also, note that there is a trade-off to be had between policy and institutional reform. Changing policy from a grade of F to B+ has the same effect on the growth rate as reforming the institutional framework one point (e.g., from 3.0 to 2.0). Partly, this may help

Table 2. OLS estimates of economic growth rate

Variable	Dependent variable, g_y (1)	(2)	(3)	(4)
Constant	1.4652	3.7416	3.2166	4.2390
	(7.44)	(9.64)	(7.39)	(9.46)
g_k	.1317	.1258	.1289	.1234
	(4.65)	(5.14)	(4.67)	(4.94)
INST		−1.0862		−.9135
		(6.53)		(4.80)
POLICY			−.5039	−.2541
			(4.40)	(2.19)
$\bar{R}^2$	.1434	.3611	.2817	.4112
N	124	124	103	103

Note: t-values in parentheses.

Table 3. NLLS estimates of economic growth rate

Parameter	Dependent variable, g_y (1)	(2)	(3)	(4)
α	.5533	.4151	.4547	.4128
	(2.55)	(3.67)	(2.63)	(3.84)
β	.1706	.0368	.0663	.0295
	(2.11)	(2.55)	(2.00)	(2.50)
δ	.7651	.1962	.3033	.1758
	(0.96)	(1.58)	(1.13)	(1.64)
γ		−.5420		−.4882
		(6.98)		(5.84)
ρ			−.2001	−.0863
			(4.57)	(2.26)
$\bar{R}^2$	.2368	.4850	.4071	.5645
N	124	124	103	103

explain the above average growth rates of some nations with rather poor rule spaces. Higher growth is being achieved through better policy.

The NLLS estimates in Table 3 are superior to the OLS estimates. Since $\beta > 0$, the function is concave, which is consistent with neoclassical assumptions.

Utilizing equation (4) in Table 3, again one can compare the growth rate of the representative nation with the freest institutions and best policy with that of the representative nation with the least free institutions and worst policy. For the mean growth rate of investment per head $\alpha/(\beta+\delta e^{-\alpha g(k)}) = 7.45$ percent. For the free nation $e^{(\gamma \mathrm{INST}+\rho \mathrm{POLICY})} = .563$. Thus, the growth

Table 4. OLS estimates of economic growth rate for advanced and third world nations

Variable	Advanced	Third World			
	(1)	(2)	(3)	(4)	(5)
Constant	.9590	1.2869	4.1430	3.3030	4.9192
	(3.19)	(5.87)	(7.58)	(5.69)	(7.61)
g_k	.5524	.1343	.1162	.1263	.1125
	(6.78)	(4.52)	(4.42)	(4.31)	(4.20)
INST			−1.2238		−1.0382
			(5.58)		(4.31)
POLICY				−.5480	−.3351
				(3.73)	(2.35)
$\bar{R}^2$	.7142	.1576	.3483	.2783	.4057
N	19	105	105	85	85

rate is 4.2 percent. For the least free/worst policy nation $e^{(\bullet)} = .271$. Thus, the growth rate is 2 percent.

Another use of the parameters in equation (4) in Table 3 is to answer the question of what gain in economic growth arises from increases in capital formation, improvement in the rule space, and amelioration of policy and how is the gain distributed? The answer is obtained by taking the total differential of equation (6), which is $dg_y = w_{g(k)}\, dg_k + w_{INST}\, dINST + w_{POLICY}\, dPOLICY$, where the weights (w) are the partial derivatives of the variables with respect to the growth rate.[6] Assume that there is a ten percent improvement in each of the independent variables around the mean. Then, using the parameters from equation (4) in Table 3, we have $dg_y = .45 = .39(.46) - .99(-.21) - .175(-.34)$. A ten percent improvement in each factor (g_k from 4.64 to 5.1, INST from 2.07 to 1.863, and POLICY from 3.40 to 3.06) raises the rate of economic growth by .45 percent. Approximately, forty percent of the change in growth is due to the change in capital formation, 47 percent from improved institutional technology, and the remaining 13 percent from better policy.

In Table 4 the sample is subdivided into the advanced nations (n = 19) and the Third World (N = 105). Noteworthy is that the coefficient of g_k on g_y is four times as large in the advanced nations as in the Third World and this difference is more or less stable as the institutional and policy variables are added as regressors. The statistical results for the Third World are quite similar to those of the all nations sample. This is satisfying, since it means that the statistical results in Tables 2 and 3 do not arise from lumping the advanced nations with the less advanced ones.

Table 5. NLLS estimates of economic growth rate for advanced and third world nations

Parameter	Advanced	Third World			
	(1)	(2)	(3)	(4)	(5)
α	.2500	.5469	.4340	.5142	.4277
	(1.62)	(2.43)	(3.05)	(2.48)	(3.09)
β	.0250	.1683	.0386	.0774	.0276
	(0.67)	(1.97)	(2.15)	(1.90)	(2.00)
δ	.1511	1.0656	.2192	.5349	.1686
	(1.26)	(0.89)	(1.19)	(0.90)	(1.15)
γ			−.5443		−.5032
			(5.90)		(4.92)
ρ				−.1968	−.1141
				(3.71)	(2.40)
$\bar{R}^2$	.6984	.2571	.4550	.4125	.5428
N	19	105	105	85	85

Table 5 contains the NLLS estimates. For facility of comparison I calculated the path of g_y with respect to g_k for two representative nations: (1) less advanced with free institutions and good policy and (2) less advanced with unfree institutions and poor policy. The predicted growth rate at the mean growth rate of capital accumulation is 4.74 percent and the asymptotic growth rate $((\alpha/\beta)e^{(\bullet)})$ is 8.36 percent for the less advanced nation with free institutions and good policy. For the nation with unfree institutions and poor policy the predicted mean growth rate is 1.53 percent and the asymptotic growth rate is 1.71 percent. While the less advanced nations with free institutions and good policy do not grow at quite the rate as do the advanced nations for similar rates of capital formation, the performance differential is modest. The really poorly performing nations are those whose institutions are not free and who engage in poor policy.

4.2. *Life expectancy*

Economic growth is not the only welfare standard by which nations can be compared. Justifiably, life expectancy is an alternative standard on the argument that a longer life is preferred to a shorter one. Life expectancy is highly correlated with the living standard, and the relationship is nonlinear (the symbol y is used for the 1985 value of RGDP in the equation below). The question raised here is that given the living standard, does institutional freedom independently promote a longer life? The nonlinear function to be estimated parallels that in equation (6) and takes the form:

Table 6. NLLS estimates of life expectancy

Parameter	All countries		Third World	
	(1)	(2)	(3)	(4)
$\alpha^* 10^3$	.5065	.5852	.5791	.6244
	(9.09)	(7.39)	(6.05)	(5.46)
$\beta^* 10^5$	.6687	.7385	.7834	.7986
	(8.44)	(7.24)	(5.41)	(5.04)
$\delta^* 10^5$	.4626	.4358	.5332	.4724
	(6.21)	(5.18)	(4.52)	(3.93)
γ		–.0418		–.0398
		(3.02)		(2.59)
$\overline{R}^2$	.8022	.8147	.7234	.7384
N	121	121	102	102

$$\text{LE} = [\alpha/(\beta + \delta e^{-\alpha y})]e^{\gamma \text{INST})}. \tag{10}$$

The NLLS estimates for all countries and for the Third World countries appear in Table 6. The fitted function for all nations appears in Figure 2. The coefficient for the institutional framework is highly significant.

Focusing on the results for the Third World, consider two pairings of representative nations. One pair has a per capita RGDP of $1,000, the other pair has $5,000. One of each pair is free (INST = 1.0), the other is unfree (INST = 3.25). The predicted life expectancies in the poor pair of nations are 57.1 and 52.2 years, respectively. The difference in life expectancies is 4.9 years. The predicted life expectancies in the moderate per capita income pair are 73.2 and 67 years, respectively.

5. Conclusions

I think it is now fairly well established that rules or the institutional framework matter a great deal for economic growth and, hence, for the achievable living standard. This paper contributes to the measurement of the size of the effect of rules and policy on economic growth. The poor economic performance of many Third World nations has less to do with capital accumulation and technology transfer, although they do matter, than with economic, legal, and political institutions and with policy that are anathema to economic transformation. One is tempted to conclude that a modern standard of living is quite impossible to achieve without free institutions.

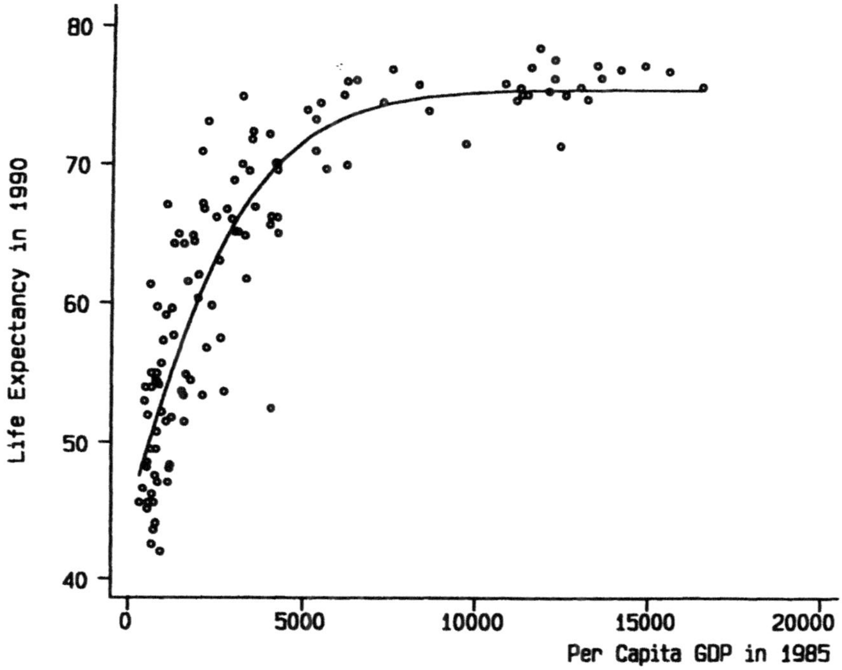

Figure 2. Life expectancy and per capita income.

Further insight into the importance of the rule space for economic growth will require finer measures of the attributes of the institutional framework. While the crude measures that have been utilized here capture the main differences across a wide sample of very heterogeneous nations, they are insufficient for distinguishing outcomes among more homogeneous blocks of nations (e.g., Africa, Latin America).

Notes

1. The data are the growth rates of real per capita GDP from Summers and Heston (1991). The sample used throughout the paper is all nations with at least ten years of data less the communist countries and the Middle East oil-exporting nations.
2. The addition of a rule may make other rules more (less) efficient. For this reason one should think of the wealth effect of a new rule or a rule change as net of changes in other rules.
3. The correlation between the type of political system and the political/civil liberty measure, the type of economic system, and the degree of economic freedom is .87, .46, and .72, respectively. Other correlations among the variables are similarly high.
4. I followed the grading scheme in Gwartney et al. (1993: 22): 7.0 or greater = A, 6.0–6.9 = B, 5.0–5.9 = C, 4.0–4.9 = D, and less than 4.0 = F.

5. The first derivative of the first part of the expression is:

$$\partial g_y/\partial g_k = \alpha^2 \delta e^{-\alpha g(k)} \ln(e)/(\beta + \delta e^{-\alpha g(k)})^2.$$

The second derivative is:

$$\partial^2 g_y/\partial g_k^2 = -\alpha^3 \delta \ln(e)^2 (-e^{\alpha g(k)})\delta + e^{2\alpha g(k)}\beta / (\beta e^{\alpha g(k)} + \delta)^3.$$

6.

$$\begin{aligned} dg_y &= ((\alpha^2 e^{\gamma INST + \rho POLICY} \delta e^{-\alpha g(k)} \ln(e))/(\beta + \delta e^{-\alpha g(k)})^2) dg_k + \\ &\quad ((\alpha e^{\gamma INST + \rho POLICY} \gamma \ln(e))/(\beta + \delta e^{-\alpha g(k)})) dINST + \\ &\quad ((\alpha e^{\gamma INST + \rho POLICY} \rho \ln(e))/(\beta + \delta e^{-\alpha g(k)})) dPOLICY \\ &= w_{g(k)} dg_k + w_{INST} dINST + w_{POLICY} dPOLICY. \end{aligned}$$

References

Banks, A.S. (Ed.). (1993). *Political handbook of the world 1993*. Binghampton, NY: CSA Publications.

Gwartney, J.D., Block, W.E. and Lawson, R.A. (1993). Rating the economic freedom of 100 countries: 1975–1990. Rating Economic Freedom VI, Sonoma, CA: Liberty Fund/Fraser Institute.

Karatnycky, A. (1994). *Freedom in the world: The annual survey of political rights and civil liberties 1993–1994*. New York: Freedom House.

Maddison, A. (1982). *Phases of capitalist development*. Oxford: Oxford University Press.

Porter, P.K. and Scully, G.W. (1995). Institutional technology and economic growth. *Public Choice* 85: 17–36.

Scully, G.W. (1988). The institutional framework and economic development. *Journal of Political Economy* 96(June): 652–662.

Scully, G.W. (1992). *Constitutional environments and economic growth*. Princeton: Princeton University Press.

Summers, R. and Heston, A. (1991). The penn world table (mark 5): An expanded set of international comparisons 1950–88. *Quarterly Journal of Economics* 106(2)(May): 327–368.

GPSR Compliance

The European Union's (EU) General Product Safety Regulation (GPSR) is a set of rules that requires consumer products to be safe and our obligations to ensure this.

If you have any concerns about our products, you can contact us on ProductSafety@springernature.com

In case Publisher is established outside the EU, the EU authorized representative is:

Springer Nature Customer Service Center GmbH
Europaplatz 3
69115 Heidelberg, Germany

Batch number: 10755284

Printed by Printforce, the Netherlands